William Golding

William Golding
The Unmoved Target
By
Virginia Tiger

MARION BOYARS
NEW YORK · LONDON

Published in the United States and Great Britain in 2003 by
MARION BOYARS PUBLISHERS LTD
24 Lacy Road, London SW15 1NL

www.marionboyars.co.uk

Distributed in Australia and New Zealand by Peribo Pty Ltd, 58 Beaumont
Road, Kuring-gai, NSW 2080

Some of this material first appeared in a different form in 1974 as *William
Golding: The Dark Fields of Discovery* published by Calder & Boyars Ltd, London.
Reprinted by 1976 by Marion Boyars Publishers Ltd, London.

Printed in 2003
10 9 8 7 6 5 4 3 2 1

A CIP catalog record for this book is available from the Library of Congress.
A CIP catalogue record for this book is available from the British Library.

ISBN 0-7145-3082-4 Paperback

Typeset in Bembo 10/13.
Printed in England by Creative Print and Design (Wales), Ebbw Vale.

Contents

To the memory
of
Mark Papineau Conner
1970–1988

Acknowledgements

Any critical book has perhaps more elaborate need than others to contain its author's statement of intellectual debts owed and personal ones unrepayable. As in the past, I record again my gratitude to the late Sir William Golding for his generous commitment to the ambience of literature that stimulated a private man to discuss his works in conversations and letters. Sir William, despite his passionate avowal of the hermetic nature of imaginative work, had suspended this principle to respond to my earlier study: *William Golding: The Dark Fields of Discovery*. Here it is important to reiterate that only the words attributed to him in quotations were his own. And for her irreplaceable help in responding to my dozens of queries it is a serious statement to thank J. D. Carver, herself engaged in governing and guarding her father's published and unpublished work.

Libraries have become part of the bloodstream of literary critics; and for their unfailingly congenial transfusions I am grateful to the Reading Room of the British Library, its Newspaper Library at Colindale, the New York Public Library at 42nd Street and Dana library at Rutgers University, Newark, with its especially generous and accomplished director, Lynn Mullins. I should here also thank my research assistant, Patricia Leyden, for her indefatigable search and discovery tracings of copyright holdings.

I wish also to thank the following for permission to quote from William Golding's works.

Reprinted by permission of Faber and Faber Ltd: excerpts from *The Double Tongue* by William Golding © 1995. Excerpts from *Free Fall* by William Golding © 1959. Excerpts from *The Hot Gates* by William Golding © 1965. Excerpts from *Lord of the Flies* by William Golding © 1954. Excerpts from *The Pyramid* by William Golding © 1967. Excerpts from *Rites of Passage* by William Golding © 1980. Excerpts from *The Spire* by William Golding © 1964. Excerpts from *To the Ends of the Earth: A Sea Trilogy* by William Golding © 1995.

Reprinted by permission of Farrar Straus & Giroux Inc: excerpts

Reprinted with permission from the *New York Review of Books*: excerpt from 'The Good Ship Britannia' by Robert Towers *New York Review of Books* (December 18, 1980) ©1989 NYREV, Inc.

Personal debts may be the most preposterous to try to acknowledge in formal terms since they are themselves, by definition, so outside formality. Generous ingredients to this book's life have been richly provided by my colleagues and friends: Steven Aronson, Patricia Bruckmann, Veronica Calderhead, Nelson Canton, Ana Daniel, Barbara Foley, Nan and Lewis Griefer, my editors Ken Hollings and Julia Silk, Elizabeth Hopkins, my publisher Catheryn Kilgarriff, Roger Kirkpatrick, Helen McNeil, Sebastian Tiger and the late Marion Boyars, publisher *extraordinaire*.

Virginia Tiger
New York City

Introduction: Prologue From The Pyramid

And it could be, in this great grim universe I portray, that a tiny, little, rather fat man with a beard, in the middle of it laughing, is more like the universe than a gaunt man struggling up a rock.

William Golding[1]

Campus cult figure of the 1960s and the finest English writer of the late twentieth century, not all readers (or critics) were to value William Golding's work as highly as his reputation would seem to have warranted. Regarded by some as old fashioned, a white male misogynist, essentialist in intellectual tendencies, fabular in practice and *echt*-English by way of his literary persona, Golding's achievements came to be not so much debated as descried, even denied. Authorial performances like his – both in fiction and in comments about fiction – seemed to resist the currents of change, represented by such post-modern critical maxims as polyvalency, indeterminability of textual meanings, the creator as inferred encoder or the death of the author. Consider, for example, the following where the authorial stance uncomfortably combines diffidence with self-regard, as though he were playing to the reading public's expectations about an author famously famous from Brisbane to Berlin, Toronto to Turin, New Orleans to Nice[2]: 'Ladies and gentlemen, you see before you a man, I will not say more sinned against than sinning; but a man more analyzed than analyzing.'[3] '[F]or better or worse,' observes the essay 'A Moving Target', 'I am the raw material of an academic light industry [...] The books that have been written about my books have made a statue of me, fixed in one not very decorative gesticulation, a po-faced image too earnest to live with.'[4] Later a mischievous fiction, *The Paper Men*, would show an alcoholic novelist pursued by his natural enemy, the critic-biographer, as though Roland Barthes had never signalled the death of the author nor Jacques Derrida abolished the conceptual boundary between creative and critical discourse. And yet Golding's early and later fictions – if not post-modern, if not post-colonial, if not post-feminist – were fundamentally about the post-war age and presages of an age of new war.[5]

For readers like me there have continued to be moments of exhilaration where the ice imprint of the uncanny and the frightful mark the reading experience. Speculations once brought to the early works, however, have been readjusted by those to follow. Certainly summary statements such as the one I once made that all the fiction played with the puzzle of *Proverbs* XXXIII – 'Where there is no vision the people perish' – benefited from being revised in the light of the later works. When it became possible to view Golding's achievement from the terminus of his death rather than through the continual progress of a living author, it also became possible to see that the several enterprises of a Golding fiction could seldom be exhausted by a single critical approach. For the author, once so summarily read as absent from his grim allegorical fables, rewards by being reread through various autobiographical enactments present in the novels with their mixture of moral seriousness, sensitivity to the semiotics of social class, eruptive humor, aggressive wit, parodic slyness and (sometimes) surprising cheer.

The chapters in this book treating Golding's fiction from *Darkness Visible* through *The Double Tongue* have been shaped by this view. While the chapters on *Lord of the Flies*, *The Inheritors*, *Pincher Martin*, *Free Fall* and *The Spire* collected here appeared in *The Dark Fields of Discovery*, I have taken the opportunity to revise substantially or expand the original text. But in both the revised and new chapters of *William Golding: The Unmoved Target* [6] I have been guided by the conviction that – however unfashionable such a stance may be construed – the fiction demands close reading, grounding my interpretive criticism of the novels in their forms. Golding's art/artfulness consists so very often in subverting expectations, playing with readers' anticipations by way of veiled clue, partial revelation, manipulation of narrative knowledge and the narrative habit of what I call the 'ideographic structure', whereby readers are made to move outside one world of sensation and into another. Badgered by baffling puzzles and lacunae, unbalanced by each text's defamiliarizing techniques, the reader is necessarily put in the very center of narrative production. It is to this end that a Golding narrative is directed. Alliteration, emblem, metaphor, symbol, refrain, rising and descending tempi: all the formal elements of narrative are employed to allow that reader's eye, ear, mind to make connections – conscious or unconscious. [7] As Golding once described that narrative intention: 'I don't simply describe something. I lead the reader round to discovering it anew.' [8]

2

II

Thanks to art, instead of seeing one world, our own, we see it multiplied and we have at our disposal as many worlds as there are original artists, worlds that differ more widely from each other than those which revolve in infinite space.

Proust, *Time Regained*

Occupying 'a kind of no man's land between the first group of novels and the late novels, beginning with *Darkness Visible*,'[9] William Golding's *The Pyramid* seems an informing site from which to glance forward, for it appeared to have announced a new direction, surprising its first readers with what it had rejected. Rather than remote world and monolithic allegory, this not unconventional *bildungsroman*, which described growing up in middle-class rural England in the first third of the twentieth century, addressed the tensions of what was at the time the most provincial of worlds. In its kinship with a more commonplace tradition of English fiction, it appeared to be − in Anna Wulf's dismissive phrase about English fiction from *The Golden Notebook* − 'one of those small circumscribed novels, preferably about the neuroses of class or social behaviour.' Indeed, upon its 1967 publication, Golding remarked to me that he had toyed with the idea of subtitling the book *The Pyramid, Or As You Like It* as an ironic poke at reader and critic alike, claiming that it was designed in part as a *jeu* to demonstrate he could write − as he put it − something 'limpidly' simple. Unquestionably, the rich resources of language had been pared away, the book's preoccupations with social class and spiritual entombment implied by its title requiring sometimes a prose as enervated as the place it would depict: the aptly named town of Stilbourne. Adopting the techniques of nineteenth-century classic realism, everything in this novel was scaled down to the immediately observable. Its subject matter was deliberately ordinary, the narrator made deliberately imperceptive and the social norms hugely conventional so that readers would − when certain ambiguities arose − come to question the viability of a world so stillborn.

Oliver, the unreliable narrator, is the reader's focalizing perspective in this retrospective reminiscence. Critical hindsight confirms that the wryly observed, very English provincial town − with its warped respectability and genteel proprieties − was Marlborough, the Wiltshire market town where Golding himself grew up. 'Totally conditioned by the pyramidical structure of society identical to that of Golding's childhood,'[10] the fictional exercise in reminiscence amounted to his first autobiographical work. As such, it gains by being linked to Golding's other narrative acts of memoir and memory: 'Billy the Kid', 'Egypt from My Inside', 'The Ladder and the Tree', and the posthumously published 'Scenes from A Life'.

Plagued by what would remain a lifelong question, 'How can one record and not invent?', both 'Billy the Kid' and 'Egypt from My Inside' depict a small child, word-besotted, self-involved, and terrorized by his own histrionic imaginings, rushing past the familiar streets of Marlborough to the safety of home. 'Past the Aylesbury Arms, across the London Road, through Oxford Street by the Wesleyan Chapel, turn left for the last climb in the Green' ('Billy the Kid'[11]). A seminal essay about his adolescence, 'The Ladder and the Tree' also describes that place, childhood, boyhood, and young adulthood spent in a house abutting a churchyard on the town green. This home is literally at the opposite – and so inferior – end of the High Street from the rather famous public school still metonymically registering for many the meaning of Marlborough. His father, explosively brilliant science master and polymath though he was, could never have taught there. Instead he was employed at Marlborough Grammar School for forty years, 'teaching the rudiments of science to the rather stolid children of local tradesmen and farmers'.[12] 'The Ladder and the Tree' was to re-invoke the family's precise place in that stratified society:

> [...] we were all the poorer for our respectability. In the dreadful English scheme of things at that time, a scheme which so accepted social snobbery as to elevate it to an instinct, we had our subtle place. Those unbelievable gradations ensured that though my parents could not afford to send my brother and me to a public school, we should nevertheless go to a grammar school [...] In fact, like everybody except the very high and the very low in those days, we walked a social tightrope, could not mix with the riotous children who made such a noise and played such wonderful games on the Green.[13]

If the society of Golding's Marlborough childhood fuelled the fictional community of *The Pyramid*'s Stilbourne with its contaminating social divisions and precisely graded social pyramid, the narrative method of this midpoint book was – to borrow an observation from Brocklebank, the inebriate painter in *Rites of Passage*

– as much about concealing and obscuring reality as it was about revealing it. In that much later work another unreliable first-person narrator, the journal-writing Talbot, represents an exchange where he has been warned by the painter that he has been 'confusing art with actuality'. At the center, of course, is the storyteller's dilemma, where clarity of recall jostles with imaginative construction: a dilemma especially disorienting when the story told is one's own.

A more compelling effort to claim actuality as unvarnished memory, rather than as product of the imagination, would seem to have propelled a third autobiographical enactment. 'Scenes from a Life' is a text transparent in its picture of what one can now recognize as the biographical beds in which the novels were rooted and from which they grew. Posthumously published, the extracts – written evidently in Golding's eighty-first year – seem an attempt 'to record memories honestly without the process he call[ed] "retouching",' as J.D. Carver put it in her preface to her father's unfinished manuscript, which she also edited.[14] Preternaturally alerted to how the very act of recording could falsify experience, 'Scenes from a Life' was to describe – in depicting some nine very early memories – the child's-eye view as it was itself perceived some seven (perhaps even eight) decades earlier. Marlborough is again a prominent source for the memory of 'being pushed down the north pavement of Marlborough [High Street] by Lily in a push chair' ('Scenes from a Life')[15] at the age of three. Even earlier, perhaps even younger than eighteen months, 'in 29 The Green before I was old enough to fear and hate the place' (p. 26) – with its nearby graveyard and cellar infected by every sort of apprehension – he remembers himself remembering himself lying in a cot and seeing a strutting small cockerel, emanating friendliness. Had he been able to determine whether that sighting was 'the exercise of clairvoyance before growing up into a rationalist world stifled it' or '"only" a dream', the diarist in advanced old age concluded: 'I would have settled many more life-long preoccupations than the question of a single incident.' (p. 27)

The same question as to whether the child's indulging eye sees what the wearied reductive eye of adulthood no longer can was raised by the memory of a second, similarly searing, encounter. A mile from the Marlborough home lies ancient Savernake Forest through whose frond-fortified glades deer traversed at that time. It was here that Golding vividly recalled a terrifying encounter – indeed a confrontation that surely provided the biographical mulch for *The Inheritors*' rutting-stag ritual seen from the vantage point of a species unable to reason beyond sense data and that novel's vision of indifferent malignancy. Having been momentarily separated from his parents one late winter afternoon during what should have been a typical Sunday walk, the boy saw a stag's dark head staring straight at him – or through him – over the bramble brake in the darkening forest. Screaming down the path and running towards his parents, the child – and the man writing the memory of the child – remembered the dark stag head's quality of 'stillness and terrible indifference' (p. 34). The figure (as perceived by those two pairs of eyes) is a polar opposite of the strutting white cockerel with its 'friendliness like a whole atmosphere of natural love'(p. 27), an opposition we may now construe as one of evil to innocence.

Innocence and evil, friendliness and indifference, such contrasts – embedded so very early in the unadulterated awareness of an infant's perception – would become traceable as guiding patterns that Golding's novels would both employ and explore. There would, for example, be the pervasive play in *Darkness Visible* with doublings, pairings, and binary oppositions, where fire is both purgative and destructive while water is both cleansing and cloacal. The oppositions orchestrated in *Close Quarters*, in particular, are played out in the persons of two ship's officers: the level-headed, equable Summers and inventive Lieutenant Benét: poet, lover, and seaman *extraordinaire*.[16] And, of course, *Lord of the Flies'* fierce vision had as its bedrock 'innocence' and 'the darkness of man's heart', coral growths from those early antipodean opposites rendered in 'Scenes from a Life': the strutting cockerel emanating friendliness and the dark indifferent stag's head.

III

Song before speech
Verse before prose
Flute before blowpipe
Lyre before bow
William Golding, 'Clonk Clonk'

Rereading *The Pyramid* in the context of the narrative habit of biographical reshapings – one of the least explored themes in Golding criticism[17] – can allow one to see how underestimated the work had been. 'Much more complex than most of its early reviewers and critics […] found it to be,'[18] *The Pyramid*'s narration has been put in the hands of a character reviewing his past from the vantage point of middle age. In fact, the novel's focalization is very accomplished, with reminiscence by the older – ironic – narrator of his younger self shifting between the 'I' as reporter and the 'I/eye' of the interior monologue and indirect interior monologue. Well-ordered sequential reminiscence gives way to sheaves of memory 'snapshots' from infancy and boyhood. The novel's interruptions of the chronological, its discontinuous time schemes, its flashbacks and flash-forwards depict the reminiscing mind and owe much to the memory scaffolding modeled in *Free Fall*, heralding the memoryscape technique in 'Scenes from a Life'. As is the case in *Rites of Passage* and *Close Quarters*, the facetious, adroitly mannered, and mocking surface of the text disguises a darker substratum. Slapstick jostles a rather more bitter irony as the narrative progresses, the mode adopted being not that of the *bildungsroman* – as several critics have argued,[19] but rather the world of tragicomedy.[20] That mixed mode was hardly new to Golding's practice. The grotesque and pathetic had already been fused in one short story's portrait of a ghastly religious spinster, Miss Pulkinhorn, as they would be in the figure of Reverend Colley in *Rites of Passage*. But unlike Colley, and like *The Pyramid*'s Bounce Dawlish as well as *Free Fall*'s Rowena Pringle, Pulkinhorn is depicted as suffering the miseries of frustrated virginity. This particularly gender-specific English brand of loveless snobbery and the grim egotism of the time eat acidly into the soul until they erupt to infect others outside. Any tracing, however, of the continuity of this mixed mode insists that such fictions be reconsidered in the light of hitherto neglected authorial biography: that of a storyteller whose own story had so sounded with the crystal caws of pyramidal social class.

So when *The Pyramid* adopted a materialist principle, the one enjoined in 'The Ladder and the Tree' when the young man accepts his father's conviction that 'Cosmology was driving away the shadows of our ignorance…the march of science was irresistible […] and I should be part of that organization marching irresistibly to a place which I was assured was worth finding' (p. 173), it was retelling Golding's own capitulation to his father's kindly admonition that he come down from mystery's figurative tree, learn his Latin, go up to Oxford, study science and so succeed. 'Physics and Chemistry were the real, the serious thing,' *The Pyramid*'s narrator is made to opine. 'The world, my parents implied, was my oyster by way of Chemistry and Physics' (p. 193). Just as Trollope's Barchester series ignored the real matter of religion, so *The Pyramid*, with its several Trollopian place names, pictured a place where religious possibilities are deliberately blocked out, a place conspicuously devoid of religious ambiguity, mystery, spirituality and their attendant terrors. The world's spiritual dimension becomes simply 'the sky over Stilbourne' (p. 196). 'Church fetes are no longer religious feasts that inspire particular devotions but rather are dull and class-ridden social events frequently ruined by angry cloudbursts'.[21] The four hundred-foot spire of Barchester Cathedral may still be seen from Stilbourne's Old Bridge, but, no longer beckoning prayer in stone, it merely roofs over that socially signifying place where an upscale Stilbourne wedding can take place. A conspicuously named character, Evie, recalling Eve from Genesis, may wear a gold cross inscribed with Chaucer's Prioress' signature *Amor Vincit Omnia*. However, the adolescent narrator only eroticizes it in describing how it nestles between 'two smooth segments of spheres with […] pink tips,' (p. 72) then translates the motto as 'Love Beats Everything', a particularly telling rendering in a place whose subterranean life has adults, either psychologically or physically, beat children into compliance.[22] Another conspicuously named character, the town's music teacher may share the name of the patron saint of music and musicians – reputed in life to be so close to heaven that she could hear the singing of angels – but no Saint Cecilia is she. Heavenly music hardly fires her soul, as she slips into sleep beside her charges. Besides, Stilbourne knows her as 'Bounce' on account of her ungainly pace, her massive bosom and thickening haunches. And although the air may be singing with the strains of Bach, Brahms, Chopin, Handel, Holst, Stravinsky, Wagner, and the artistry of Casals, Corot, Myra Hess, Kreisler, Moisewitch, Paderewski, and Solomon, music is no food of love. Music no more touches Stilbourne's inner ear than it does that of Shakespeare's calculating Cassius, who 'hears no music'. Nor is Stilbourne an idyllic English landscape. The whole literary tradition of the English rural world is subverted with the punning place names – Cockers, Bumstead Episcopi, Phillicock, Leg-O'-Mutton Pond, Omnia – puncturing that false image as surely as *Lord of the Flies* perforated *The Coral Island*'s easy optimism.

But if 'Love, in Stilbourne society, like music, machinery and science is ambivalent […] both harmony and torture, understanding and power,'[23] the day-to-day life depicted represents no small achievement in the novel's evocation of a parochial provincial town in the early part of the twentieth century. Along its sleepy High Street lie an ironmongers, a Needlework Shop, a sweet shop, the Tobacconist, the Saddlers, the Antique Shoppe, the Jolly Tea Rooms (where gossiping college wives eat buns and sip endless cups of coffee), a former Corn Exchange converted to a cinema and covered with Douglas Fairbanks posters, the Crown with its Axminster-carpeted saloon bar, the Running Horse where stable boys guzzle beer, the Town Hall in which is resurrected triennially that year's production of the Stilbourne Operatic Society (SOS). Below the Green rests the town's square with its hiccuping gas lamps, through which marches the Town Crier with his hand-bell, 'wearing his Town Crier's dress – buckled shoes, white cotton stockings, red knee breeches, red waistcoat, cotton ruffle, blue frock coat and blue, three-cornered hat' (p. 25). And close to the humpbacked Old Bridge squats Chandler's Close, the slum with its tumbledown cottages and barefooted boys wearing the 'uniform of a Poor Boy; father's trousers cut down, his cast-off shirt protruding from the seat' (p. 53), for Stilbourne's very topography declares its suffocatingly gradated social pyramid.

Placed at first in the 1920s and extending through the 1960s, the plot consists of a first-person narration of three interconnected but distinct stories whose time sequence is complex and overlapping. 'Whereas the third part [set in 1963] is a long flashback to early childhood reaching the age of three…with another flashback to the fifties when Oliver, a married man with children, had paid a visit to his former town,'[24] the first part follows a chronological order with one flashback and one time gap while the second part is a sequential narrative taking place in the late 1930s. Golding regarded the structure as the literary equivalent of the sonata form in music, where the dual themes of social class and deficient love – and their variants 'public exhibition and private exposure'[25] – are successively set forth, developed, and restated. The *scherzo* or comic interlude, where appropriately enough the deadly serious antics of an amateur musical society are spoofed, treats farcically the motif of musical – and by extension sexual, emotional, and imaginative – entombment while the first and third parts treat it more seriously.

In the first part, eighteen-year-old Oliver, the town dispenser's son, avidly and ineptly is initiated into the prerogatives of his class position when, with considerable social guilt, he manages to seduce Stilbourne's 'local phenomenon', the sexy Evie Babbacombe. Both because she is the daughter of the Town Crier, someone much his social inferior, and because it appears to the mortified Oliver that she has already been possessed by Dr Ewan's son, his rival and social superior, Oliver drags Evie off to a clump of woods, convinced that the eighteen-year-old beauty is promiscuous and available. 'She was no part of high fantasy and worship and hopeless jealousy. She was the accessible thing' (p. 89). They meet a few times – on one occasion Oliver happens to flick up Evie's skirt and finds her body covered with welts, a shocking discovery whose emotional import he cannot at all grasp. He imagines – since it is the only kind of perception he possesses – a socially inferior culprit: 'staring at her and not seeing her but only the revelation, the pieces fell into place with a kind of natural inevitability' (p. 89). He immediately decides a Great War wreck, Captain Wilmot, was responsible since Wilmot lives opposite the Babbacombes in the squalor of Chandler's Close. But before anything is actually said, the frightened Evie mutters, 'I was sorry for 'im.' A few minutes later she says 'it' (meaning the sex? the blows?) started when she was fifteen.

What follows from this cryptic exchange amounts to a modified use of what I have called the 'confrontation scene', where we watch two worlds in collision. This narrative habit is consistently used from *Lord of the Flies*, with Simon before the pig's head on a stick, to Talbot's encounter with the iceberg in *Fire Down Below*. Face to face – with his eyes upon hers – Oliver can only laugh in sheer embarrassment; he then turns away in loathing and refuses to encounter her timid efforts to explain: 'You never loved me, nobody never loved me. I wanted to be loved, I wanted somebody to be kind to me' (p. 89), she weeps. Instead, rather in the manner in which the New People are represented in *The Inheritors*, Oliver constructs out of his own imagined sadistic explanation for the beating a devilish world of fallen bestiality with Evie as its central 'object':

> I looked away from her, down at the town made brighter by the shade under the alders, it was full of colour, and placid [...] and there below were my parents, standing side by side [...] All at once, I had a tremendous feeling of thereness and hereness, of separate worlds, they [...] clean in that coloured picture; here, this object, on an earth that smelt of decay, with picked bones and natural cruelty – life's lavatory (p. 91).

On their next meeting, Evie contrives to have Oliver perform – such is his lubricity – on an exposed escarpment in full view of

Stilbourne as well as his father's binoculars, since the latter has been alerted by Evie's comments to him that 'All men are beasts'. Presumably in response to his reply that no, not all men are beasts – 'I said our Olly here...had his faults, of course, lots of them; but he wasn't a beast' (p. 95) – Evie had promised as evidence the public exhibition of his son's bestiality. But another reason for this public display becomes clear in the concluding coda of the first part, where the pair happen to meet each other after two years' absence. Oliver, having abandoned the dream of becoming a pianist, has gone up to Oxford to study chemistry. Meanwhile, Eve has gone down to London, having been banished from paradisiacal Stilbourne because – and this makes the crystal of the social pyramid tinkle – a tiny smear of lipstick was spied on the face of Dr Jones, the young partner of lofty Dr Ewan, for whom Evie had been secretary.

As they sit in the Crown's saloon bar, the two reminisce almost affectionately, although Evie feels stifled by the drab weight of the town. Warming to the brown ale and Evie's new sexual briskness, Oliver refers – he thinks with sophistication – to Captain Wilmot. He then coarsely toasts her health: 'Bottoms up'. The callous insult is too much for Evie and she loudly declares to the pub's respectable gathering that Oliver had raped her, in the clump, when she was fifteen. Of course, Oliver is convulsed with shame and astonishment and beats a hasty escape to the High Street. In a sudden explosion of frustration with the abject meanness of the town, its innate snobbery, and obscene voyeurism, Evie cries out that she no longer cares if Oliver goes on laughing snidely and telling about 'me 'n' Dad' (p. 110). We leave Oliver brooding on 'this undiscovered person and her curious slip of the tongue' (p. 111).

The apparent and obscuring contradiction in the coda to *The Pyramid*'s first part follows the habitual ideographic technique whereby readers have to reconsider a preceding narrative in the light of new information, a technique most boldly at work in the startling information provided by the coda to *Pincher Martin*. What we discover in this mid-point novel is that adolescent Oliver's musky obsession with sex and social caste determines his first notion of Evie's lower-class promiscuity. Just as he has been misinformed about her age – a crucial mistake since her admission in the earlier confrontation scene that 'it' began when she was fifteen made us assume she had already had three years of perverse sexual experimentation – so he was probably mistaken

11

about her intimacy with Bobby Ewan. As the older Evie remarks, Bobby was simply her 'first sweetheart', an allusion more girlish in tone than her knowing reference to her London boss and Dr Jones: 'now there's a man.'

My understanding of the coda is that readers were being expected to reconstruct – free of the unreliable narrator's limited and egotistical point of view – Oliver's moral culpability in shaping Evie's future. He may see Evie in a new light so that 'this object of frustration and desire had suddenly acquired the attributes of a person rather than a thing,' but we register how small this degree of expansiveness is, particularly when we recall Dr Jones' flirtation with Evie, following Oliver's seduction. It is quite possible to see that Evie would have to suffer another loveless manipulation. And no matter how ruthlessly the religious dimension had been rooted out in *The Pyramid*, an expletive's eruption – reiterated fully five times – could mean more than mere blasphemy, particularly when its speaker is an Eve wearing a Catholic cross whose inscription reads not just *Amor Vincit Omnia* but also I. H. S:

> That's all you want, just my damned body, not me. Nobody wants me, just my damned body. And I'm damned and you're damned with your cock and your cleverness and your chemistry – just my damned body… (p. 88).[26]

The crucial question concerns the beating, however, and how the coda throws new light on this episode. The obtuse Oliver's interpretation may be inaccurate, made histrionically out of his own sadistic fantasies as well as a kind of atavistic loathing for the misshapenness of a cripple. Several clues are planted throughout the narrative to make us associate brutality with Sergeant Babbacombe. Very early on Evie sports a black eye, presumably inflicted by her father when she returns late from an escapade. In a much more important scene, later in the story, Evie hears her father's bray, in the town below, and inexplicably her desire quickens. Passionately she urges Oliver to take her and 'hurt' her. Perhaps the concluding remark about 'me 'n' Dad' is meant to indicate this depraved relationship. The welts on her body could, then, be the ugly marks of incestuous congress.

We knew from *The Spire* how ambiguity in a Golding narrative is always instructive and designed to demonstrate the complexities inherent in any human situation. By such strategies of ambiguous indirection, the novels test the moral imagination of their readers, leaving it open to one's private set of priorities which solution to the riddle one would choose to adopt. In *The Pyramid* I believe there is another explanation for Evie's demonstrable masochism. Quite possibly she has been punished physically for her disobedience so often that she needs love to be expressed in some sadistic manner. From this perspective, her father has not sexually molested her, but certainly he has warped her capacity for tender love. The ghastly welts could, in this view, be another example of paternal tyranny, which recalls Bounce Dawlish's father as he strikes his daughter's fingers while instructing: 'Heaven is Music'.

Conceivably, Evie's 'slip of the tongue' at the conclusion of the episode could represent no more than a lament that the more securely situated Olivers of the world, with their bathrooms and Oxford-promised futures, find the socially inferior, with their poverty and cockroaches, contemptible, ridiculous, and worthy of hilarious gossip. Like the puzzle that closed *Free Fall* and the mystery surrounding *Close Quarters'* all-knowing Wheeler, Evie's riddle about 'me 'n' Dad' is not so much explanation as a means by which readers are forced to inspect their own values. And we can conclude that, in a real way, the title of the book could well have been *The Pyramid, Or As You Like It*.

I shall not treat the novel's two other parts in such detail, except to underscore how pivotal a work *The Pyramid* is. The adroitly timed slapstick of its *scherzo* is a prelude to *The Paper Men's* play with farce, particularly in its very first scene where guns accidentally fire, pajama trousers drop, and kitchen doors open on cue. Low comedy of this kind is much in evidence in *The Pyramid's* second part. Oliver has returned from a first term at Oxford several months after the previous summer's baptismal fire. His mother bullies him into performing in a banal light opera, which brings about a second initiation. In a long, besotted conversation at the Crown with the foppish director down from London, Evelyn De Tracy – forerunner to *The Paper Men's* Johnny St John John – Oliver dimly comprehends Stilbourne's sterility. In a torment of words, he cries out:

> Everything's – wrong. Everything. There's no truth and there's no honesty. My God! Life can't – I mean just out there, you have only to look up at the sky – but Stilbourne accepts it as a roof. As a – and the way we hide our bodies and the things we don't say, and things we

daren't mention, the people we don't meet – and that stuff they call music…(p. 147)

Provoked by the youth's demand for honesty, Evelyn presents a set of photographs of himself dressed as a ballerina. But the class-bound, respectable, and untutored Oliver is again inadequate to the moment's revelation and he can only roar with laughter – as with Evie earlier – at this public display of frustrated love. Far apart in social rank though the two Evelyns may be, these two outsiders meet one another on equal footing in their capacity to expose the hidden inadequacies and stifling proprieties of Stilbourne.

Of *The Pyramid*'s three parts the third is most silted by biographical details. It includes portraits of the young Golding's violin teacher[27] and that woman's (on-the-rise) chauffeur as well as a 'snapshot' memory from age three that matches the memory of being pushed up the High Street in a pushchair that would be re-invoked much later in 'Scenes from a Life'. Indeed, *The Pyramid* describes the 'child's retina' as 'a perfect recording machine' (p. 165) by way of its 'primary ignorant perception', the very validation that 'Scenes from a Life' would later give. And if the third part is the most biographical, it is also the most elaborately structured. Here we watch an adult Oliver returning to Stilbourne. In an extended reverie he explores moments in his past and his slow, mean metamorphosis under the twin gods of class prejudice and longed-for prosperity. Brooding upon the grave of his eccentric music teacher, Bounce Dawlish, he relives his gradual abandonment of music, an imaginative repudiation once associated with Bounce's frustrated pitiful love for Henry Williams, now Stilbourne's most prosperous garageman. Lettering stretching up the High Street in the mid-sixties now reads Williams' Garage, Williams' Showrooms, Williams' Farm Machinery and no longer Wertwhistle, Wertwhistle, Wertwhistle, Solicitors, or Feathers, the Blacksmith. Change in Stilbourne over the years has been subtly documented by the introduction and growing significance of the car, and it is not irrelevant that Henry Williams, as Bounce's chauffeur, should show his inadequate affection for her by polishing and attending to her car. The commercial success of his garage (and the means by which he climbs the slippery pyramid) comes to alter the face of Stilbourne, 'the small huddle of houses by a minimal river – a place surprised by the motor road' (p. 157), in ways completely irrevocable.

In an agony of remembering Oliver recalls one day when Bounce in a grotesque bid for Henry's attention stepped into the town square decorously dressed in hat, gloves, shoes, and 'nothing else whatsoever' (p. 207), a public display linked to, but more wretched than, those of the two Evelyns. The relived memory of her massive, ungainly nakedness pitches Oliver back to the present. Suddenly he knows that, although Stilbourne prevented him from admitting this to himself, he had loathed the pathetic woman.

> I caught myself up, appalled at my wanton laughter in that place [...] For it was here, close and real...that pathetic, horrible, unused body [...] This was a kind of psychic ear-test before which nothing survived but revulsion and horror, childishness and atavism, as if unnameable things were rising around me and blackening the sun. I heard my own voice – as if it could make its own bid for honesty – crying aloud, 'I never liked you! Never!' (p. 213)

Again we have Golding's narrative practice of the confrontation scene, where a protagonist faces darkness, unnameable things blackening the sun, as surely here as when *The Inheritors'* Lok saw the old woman drowned and drifting, like a log, towards him in the fearful water. What marks a departure from the earlier efforts, however, is that for the first time in the fiction we are watching a protagonist developing through time and frustration, change and professional success. The two outsiders, Evie and Evelyn De Tracy, try to help Oliver transcend the limitations imposed by the town. The lesson imparted by the epigraph from the *Instructions of Ptah-Hotep* instructs: 'If thou be among people, make for thyself love the beginning and end of the heart.' As the two codas indicate, Oliver partially learns to unharden his heart and observe the pain in others, which we have seen grow infinitesimally as the years pass.

The method of narration is, in my judgement, particularly accomplished in the Bounce section, where Golding employs, but transforms, the elements of the ideographic structure so rigidly in place in his earlier fiction. For there are three perspectives to which readers have access throughout the developing story. Oliver sees events first with the immediate eyes of childhood, 'primary, ignorant perceptions', a way of seeing that 'Scenes from a Life' would later call 'the absolute worth, absolute primacy, and importance of the experiencing ego' (p. 35). As adolescence sharpens class prejudices, he sees events with the eyes of 'gradual sophistication' (p. 165), defined by 'Scenes from a Life' as 'the same ego…aware of its own inheritance as a child of worthlessness and evil from whom only wrong-doing was to be expected' (p. 35). And finally, in what 'Scenes from a Life' would call 'average, reductive awareness' (p. 35), he sees in retrospect with the weary eyes of middle age. Thus the third part opens with the successful Oliver, armored by his car of 'superior description' (p. 159), returning to the Old Bridge, 'gliding down the spur to all those years of my life' (p. 158). It closes with his driving back over the Old Bridge towards the motorway and 'concentrating resolutely on my driving' (p. 217). In contrast to *Free Fall*, where the revelation of character in retrospect is a depiction of character not as process but as state of being, and heralding what would be the tracing of a maturing growth in understanding in *The Sea Trilogy*, *The Pyramid*'s fusion of the developing point of view with the developed point of view is accomplished in the narrative through the device of recollection and meditation. As Oliver looks Henry 'in the eye' and '[sees his] own face' (p. 217) (another re-orchestration of the confrontation scene), readers discover simultaneously with Oliver that he has paid the same price of love for success as has Henry. And such an insight is an appropriate concluding lesson to draw from the stillborn world of *The Pyramid*.

IV

I've given you a story… Besides – what was it – gaps? Unmotivated actions? Implausibilities? Don't you see? That's life.
Golding, 'Caveat Emptor'

In the following chapters I shall work closely with the novels, exploring the narrative strategies adopted, all in the service of bringing about the reader's experience and construction of meaning. I shall view such consistent textual practices as the unorthodox structure – what I have called the ideographic structure – the presence, absence, or trans-formation of the coda, dyadic and triadic patternings, the confrontation scene and the thematics of the darkness trope, the scapegoat and the saint. I will inspect other formal practices: partial concealment, delayed disclosure, embedded riddle, oblique clue, signifying gap, baffling crux.

As a narrative habit, each of these devices is intended to position the reader to follow innuendo, actively ferret out significance, and so become implicated as participant rather than absented observer. Intertextual allusions will be treated as well as the mimetic subversion of literary models and – since the fiction was much concerned with history and pre-history – a particular novel's relevant historical epoch will be surveyed.

I have had the fortune to be guided, informed – and frequently enlightened – by critical works which, over the years, the novels have stimulated, together with the immediate reception delivered at the time of their publication; my indebtedness is indicated in individual chapters as well as in the bibliography. I have tried here to build on these critical works by exploring some of the central points of tension between the author's conception of his work and those of his critics. Towards this analysis Golding's extratextual writing about his novels – especially from *The Hot Gates* and *A Moving Target* – and material from countless interviews (as well as from my personal exchanges with him) have been assembled in the context of the critical material and employed in a relatively detailed probing of each of the novels. Where relevant minor and occasional pieces like *Miss Pulkinhorn*, *An Egyptian Journal* or *The Scorpion God* have been absorbed into general arguments, these frequently function as prefaces to individual sections in the chapters that follow.

Endnotes

1 Jack Biles, *Talk: Conversations with William Golding*, New York, Harcourt, Brace & Jovanovich, 1970, p. 53.

2 'After he won the Nobel Prize, Golding's admirers became a serious oppression, some of them stood at his garden gate in Wiltshire staring […] He fled down to Cornwall where he was born and where his mother came from. The house he bought, which was secluded[had a] drive [which] opened on to a road too busy for anyone to stand and stare.' (Stephen Medcalf, 'William Golding', *Independent*, June 21, 1993).

3 William Golding, 'Utopias and Antiutopias', *A Moving Target*, New York, Farrar, Straus & Giroux, 1982, p. 171.

4   William Golding, 'A Moving Target', *A Moving Target*, New York, Farrar, Straus & Giroux, 1982, p. 169.

5   On the very day I was revising and updating my early chapter on *The Spire*, with Jocelin's anxious questions at its conclusion as to whether the stone hammer of his complex egoism still stood, in my own city the Twin Towers fell, immolated with over 3000 severed lives. Evidence again of the human nature Golding's fiction consistently, if unevenly, struggles to comprehend. That September 11 I could not help but recall how *Darkness Visible* began concretely in the inferno of London's wartime Blitz, where a fireman wonders whether the flickering furnace he sees before him is the Apocalypse. 'Nothing could be more apocalyptic than a world so ferociously consumed,' he decides. If, for Golding, the years of wordless brooding that went into *Lord of the Flies* were a period blanketed by grief, 'like lamenting the lost childhood of the world' ('A Moving Target', p. 163), so too would I – with others – lament anew that lost childhood.

6   A subtitle chosen to both play against and pay homage to the author, who declared himself 'a moving target'.

7   In 'Light and Darkness Visible', *Times Literary Supplement* (September 16, 1994), p.13, describing the kind of effect that Golding wanted his novels to have, John Bayley summarized: 'He would like his books to work on his readers,' and quoted him as saying: 'First a questioning, even a rejection and then an uncovenanted fact of being carried away regardless.'

8   Owen Webster, 'Living with Chaos', *Books and Art* (March 1958), p. 16.

9   S. H. Boyd, *The Novels of William Golding*, New York, St Martin's Press, 1988, p. 106.

10 Lawrence S. Friedman, *William Golding*, New York, Continuum, 1993, p. 108.

11 William Golding, 'Billy The Kid', *The Hot Gates*, London, Faber and Faber, 1965, p. 163.

12 Peter Moss, 'Alec Albert Golding, 1876–1957' in John Carey (ed.), *William Golding, The Man and His Books: A Tribute on his 75th Birthday*, New York, Farrar, Straus & Giroux, 1986, p. 16.

13 William Golding, 'The Ladder and the Tree' *The Hot Gates*, London, Faber and Faber, 1965, p. 168.

14 Judith Carver, 'Editor's Preface', *Areté* 1, Spring/Summer 2000, p. 23. To my knowledge, my inclusion and discussion here of the posthumous fragment represent the first to date.

15 William Golding, 'Scenes from a Life', *Areté* 1, Spring/Summer, 2000, p. 26.

16 Even such slight works as 'The Scorpion God' and 'Clonk Clonk' would be shaped by the habit of contrasting doubles. In the latter work, for example, the volatile, narcissistic, and fantasy-ridden virility of the male warriors is juxtaposed with the wisdom of women who, like Palm, the tribe's Head Woman, are matter-of-fact, cautious, devious in hiding their deceits, and outrageously skilled in their flattery of male vanity. At the time, it seemed deeply, even comically, characteristic of the novelist's imagination that he should have explored our contemporary preoccupation with gender differences by casting a fabular eye upon the possibilities and probabilities of sexual dimorphism in a remote Stone Age community.

17 A notable exception were Crompton and Briggs: 'Oliver and his mother and father [...] resemble Golding's own family [...] Like their counterparts in *The Pyramid*, his parents were both skilled amateur musicians [...] both were lovingly concerned with their son's welfare while finding it difficult to understand him or answer his deepest needs' (Donald Crompton, *A View from the Spire: William Golding's Later Novels*, edited and completed by Julia Briggs, Oxford, Blackwell, 1985, p. 54).

18 Arnold Johnston, *Of Earth and Darkness: The Novels of William Golding*, Columbia and London, University of Missouri Press, 1980, p. 92.

19   See Crompton and Briggs, op. cit.; Friedman, op. cit. and Johnston, ibid.

20   See Leighton Hodson, *William Golding*, Edinburg, Oliver and Boyd, 1969; Rebecca Kelly, 'The Tragicomic Mode: William Golding's *The Pyramid*', *Perspectives on Contemporary Literature* 7 (1981) pp. 110–16; Johnston, op. cit.; and Marc Maufort, 'Golding's Stilbourne: Symbolic Space in *The Pyramid*' in Jeanne Delbaere (ed.), *William Golding: The Sound of Silence*, Liège, English Department of the University of Liège, 1991, pp. 125–32.

21   Boyd, op. cit., p. 110.

22   Among the novel's several running motifs is that of the abusive manipulation of emotional attachment and the power of parent over child. A Great War wreck, Captain Wilmot, in his electric invalid chair, flagellates a young girl's bottom. A thwarted musician cracks his daughter's knuckles when fugues are incorrect, jabs her ribs with his violin bow and bops her head with a roll of music, all the while droning 'Heaven is Music'. Another father wallops his adolescent daughter, so that she perambulates down the High Street with a swollen eye exposed to all. Even the narrator's mother blithely manipulates her son into performing as a gypsy violinist in the Operatic Society's production of *The King of Hearts*. Loving though she is, even she is not exempt from using her child for her own ends.

23   A. S. Byatt, '*The Pyramid*', *New Statesman* (June 2, 1967), p. 761.

24   Jacques Leclaire, 'William Golding: *The Pyramid* as a Study in Mediocrity' *De William Shakespeare à William Golding*, Rouen, Publications de L'Université de Rouen, 1984, p. 146.

25   Avril Henry, '*The Pyramid*,' *Southern Review* 3 (1968), p. 9. Like the opposing doubles detected in 'Scenes from a Life', the habit of the contrasted pair is much in evidence in *The Pyramid*. Not only is there the opposition between concealment and publicity but also 'the relation between the mechanical and natural, between discipline and spontaneity [...] the exploitation of the weaker by the stronger [and] the gap between ideal and fact'.

26 A similar reading of Oliver's exasperated expostulation to Evie outside the pub – 'Oh – go to hell!' – may be made, particularly as Evie is then described as nodding 'solemnly' and saying: 'Ah. That. Yes. Well – ' (p. 110). Twice, Oliver is made to pass by the Catholic Church Evie attends, a buried clue all the more significant for its apparent evanescence; that Oliver associates that church only with its geographical position – in the 'dark jaws of Chandler's Close' – need not influence the reader in this way.

27 Of relevance to my view that *The Pyramid* is embedded in Golding's biography is the fact that Bounce Dawlish was based on his first music teacher; one can in fact see what was once her home across the road from the Marlborough house where the Golding family lived.

Lord of the Flies

I would like to make a point about the writing of *Flies* and its position in the world of scholarship. I said to Ann [Golding] in about 1953, 'Wouldn't it be a good idea to write a book about real boys on an island, showing what a mess they'd make?' She said, 'That is a good idea!' So I sat down and wrote it. You see, neither I nor she nor anyone else could dream of the sheer critical firepower that was going to be levelled at this mass of words scribbled in a school notebook. Then, carried away by the reverence of exegetes, I made the great mistake of defending the thing [...] It's astonishing that any of the book still stands up at all. It has become painfully and wryly amusing to me when people throw things like the Summa at my poor little boys. Of course, that trick works. How not? Dialectic has always clobbered rhetoric, from Socrates down. But – remembering the words scribbled in the school notebook – is the journey really necessary? Isn't it cracking an opusculum with a critical sledgehammer?

Golding, Letter, 1970

Lord of the Flies, the *Robinson Crusoe* of our time, still enjoys – like the earlier island story of shipwreck and survival – a pre-eminent place in the cultural climate of the West. Both cultural document and modern classic, the novel continues to provoke critical attention at the same time as it continues to prompt great general interest; over the past fifty years it has sold countless millions of copies. An obdurate and uncompromising story about how boys – very 1950s British boys – become beasts when the constraints of authority are withdrawn from their closed world, *Lord of the Flies* has proved to be a sustained literary and popular success.

Two feature films of the book have been produced, as well as a theatrical adaptation by the actor Nigel Williams – with performances in schools in England tied to an education programme which included interactive resource packs on the Internet – and ongoing productions in such venues as Canada's Stratford Festival in Ontario. Surf the Internet and one comes upon several sites referencing as well as simplistically analyzing the novel, including one that posts a (wholly concocted, unauthoritative, and unascribed) visual image of the novel's unnamed South Sea island. Regularly, and more painfully, the novel's title has been used to ponder the seeming rise in the United States and

Great Britain of killings of children by children, from two-year-old James Bulger's murder in 1993 by two ten-year-old boys in Liverpool to the mass maiming and murder of children at Columbine High School in Utah by two teenage boys in April 1999.[1]

The book itself may well be one of the most internationally taught of twentieth-century novels. 'It's a great pleasure to meet you, Mr Golding,' remarked King Carl Gustaf XVI of Sweden on presenting the esteemed literary award in the 1983 Nobel ceremonies. 'I had to do *Lord of the Flies* at school.'[2] It has also, like its author, been 'endlessly discussed, analyzed, dissected, over-praised and over-faulted, victim of the characteristic twentieth-century mania for treating living artists as if they were dead,' as the novelist John Fowles once observed.[3] In fact, Golding's first novel is not nearly as long as the critical commentary it has spawned, with Golding himself contributing in no small degree to the phenomenon he once laconically described himself as having become: 'the raw material of an academic light industry'; 'the books that have been written about my books have made a statue of me.'[4]

Packets of pamphlets and articles on source, genre, meaning, archetype, symbolism, and casebooks and master guides for secondary school children have appeared over the years.[5] Unquestionably, the novel's teachability has fostered — as well as sustained — its reputation. Some would argue that this pedagogic feature, 'rather than any clearly established merit,' was 'responsible for the general acclaim with which it has been received'.[6] Others would more generously judge that the novel has 'an artfulness, even an air of demonstrating fictional possibilities, which make it eminently suitable for teaching and which must owe a lot to the well-trained critical habits of the author'.[7] Such is the critical position of a book-length volume, *Lord of the Flies: Fathers and Sons*, devoted to solving the riddle of how the novel could be both 'a tract for the times…[and] a fable of timeless import, transcending its immediate occasion'.[8] Then there are the many doctoral dissertations taking as their point of departure *Time* magazine's 1962 quip that the novel was 'Lord of the Campus' in order to argue either the existence of a Golding vogue or the decline in popularity of a once generationally 'relevant fable', all of which can be put beside the many testimonials to the impact of the work on the untutored adolescent. Reading the novel when he was a thirteen-year-old, the novelist Ian McEwan apprehended immediately its applicability: 'As far as I was concerned, Golding's island was a thinly disguised boarding school.'

And years later: 'When I came to write a novel myself, I could not resist the momentum of my childhood fantasies nor the power of Golding's model, for I found myself wanting to describe a closed world of children removed from the constraints of authority [in *The Cement Garden*, an urban *Lord of the Flies*...] Without realizing it at the time I named my main character after one of Golding's.'[9]

If the book can be situated in that tradition of narrative where the young reader is rewarded along with the individual whom Virginia Woolf called 'the common reader', *Lord of the Flies* is also expressive of, at the same time as located in, contemporary sensibility and historical context. Appearing in the years of drab austerity immediately following World War II, where, despite Britain's lost imperial power and the partial break-up of the class system, there was still a mixture of smug superiority and complacent Philistinism among the ruling establishment, the novel was written under the indirect presence of such great traumas as Belsen, Dachau, Hiroshima, Nagasaki, and the direct presence of the Cold War. Addressing more than the disillusioned pessimism of the 1950s, the work germinated from 'years of brooding that brought me not so much to an opinion as a stance. It was like lamenting the lost childhood of the world.'[10] Yet, as was the case with Doris Lessing's early fiction, readers seemed compelled to account for their initial astonishment and appalled recognition that a novelist was confirming what had previously only been privately understood about human behavior. For just as Lessing's *The Golden Notebook* in 1962 made public the private tone of female grievance, so Golding's *Lord of the Flies* tugged at private hunches that males – even small boys – enjoyed aggression, group hierarchies, and the savor of blood. So its appearance in 1954 and subsequent popularity in the 1960s did not so much coincide with as mirror emerging ethological/socio-biological investigations into male bonding, innate behavioral aggression, *Homo sapiens* as a hunting animal, and the evolutionary substratum of the male child's behavior.[11] Golding was 'typical of modern novelists in seeing his child characters as belonging to their own order of being,'[12] a practice continued by Lessing in *The Fifth Child* as well as *Memoirs of a Survivor* and Marianne Wiggins in her declared female *Lord of the Flies*, *John Dollar*, in which a group of island-bound and unattended girls cannibalize a corpse. This conflation of 'savagery' and the brutality of children in the popular imagination was further fuelled by a kind of scopophilia: the noble savage negated.

II

> There are novelists who never make a mistake — a mistake, I mean, of fact. To them fact is sacrosanct, partly, it may be, because they suppose themselves capable of distinguishing between fact and fiction [...] The rest of us — sessile versions of the rogues and vagabonds who grace the stage — radiate from this central position to a circumference where it is fiction that is rock hard and history that is a dream or nightmare.
>
> Golding, *Foreword* 1994

The story itself is by now familiar. A group of schoolboys, educated by British public schools in a system still designed to control an empire, are dropped on an Edenic island in the Pacific Ocean. There they confront the task of survival. First the boys proceed to set up a pragmatic system based on a 'grown-up' model: government, laws, shelters, plumbing facilities, and food supplies. Quickly, however, the society disintegrates under the dual pressures of aggression and superstition. Signal fire becomes defensive hearth, then ritualistic spit: the darkness of night becomes a monstrous 'beast' to be propitiated by totemic pig heads. Hunting becomes killing as Jack's hunters break loose from Ralph's fire-keepers to form a tribal society with gods, rituals, and territory at the island's end. When two boys from the original group invade this territory they are killed, Simon ritually as a totemic beast and Piggy politically as an enemy. Finally a scapegoat, Ralph, is hunted down so as to offer his head to the Lord of the Flies. Then the adult world intervenes in the person of a naval officer, who has observed the dense clouds of smoke from the flaming fire: the scorched-earth strategy that Jack orders to ferret out the fleeing Ralph. The novel concludes with the pathetic image of the survivor, Ralph, crying for 'the end of innocence, the darkness of man's heart, and the fall through the air of the true, wise friend called Piggy'.

And yet, 'How romantically it starts,' wrote E. M. Forster in his 1962 introduction to *Lord of the Flies*, an essay that was influential in establishing Golding's early reputation as an unfashionable allegorist, writing from deep religious convictions about mankind's essential depravity. He 'believes in the Fall of Man [...] his attitude approach[ing] the Christian; we are all born in sin, or will all lapse into it.'[13]

Powerful thematic conceptions such as these seem to govern early readings of the narrative. As many of us now realize, the book's resonance comes only in part from its strong structural shape. While terms such as 'allegory', 'parable', 'fable', 'science fiction', 'romance', and 'speculative fiction' have been variously suggested to describe what was then felt to be the novel's chief characteristic, its element of arbitrary design, its form eluded easy categorization. Nevertheless, a consequence of such programmatic readings of the text was to fault the novel with reductive simplifications, rather than faulting its commentators. And Golding's complicity in this context must also be considered, for his lecture 'Fable' encouraged early on such interpretative methods. At the time, Golding's own preference was the term 'fable', which he once defined for me as 'allegory that has achieved passion'. This gnomic clue I took to imply the peculiar conjunction of contrived pattern and fictional freedom, which seemed a characteristic feature of not only *Lord of the Flies*, but *The Inheritors* and *Pincher Martin* alike. Gregor and Kinkead-Weekes put the matter rather cleanly in their 1962 introduction to Faber and Faber's school edition when they described *Lord of the Flies* as 'fable and fiction simultaneously'.

Another early and persistent classification was based on the book's intellectual schema – its affinity to neither romance nor realism, its definition as neither parable nor fable, but its relation to the Christian apologia. For just as the mid-century's New Criticism's allegiance to Christian belief shaped its approach to texts as containing authentic, stable meanings, so its method of close discussion of systems and structures facilitated the discussion of books like Golding's, which appeared to have levels of meanings entirely accessible to the authoritative interpreter. Frederick Karl's 1962 discussion in *A Reader's Guide to the Contemporary English Novel* was one of the first – but by no means the last[14] – to insist that Golding wrote 'religious allegories' whose conceptual machinery undermined the 'felt life' of the tale: 'the idea [...] invariably is superior to the performance itself.'[15] The notion that *Lord of the Flies* was somehow intellectually or philosophically contrived was to become the major critical assumption about the rest of his work. Ignoring the fictional landscape altogether, many early commentators constructed explications of 'meaning' more relevant to social, cultural, political, psychological, or anthropological history than the nature of the narrative itself. Later critics have adopted a comparable approach, although the terms of their critique have switched to colonialism and imperialism. Setting the work within the history of decolonization (in particular the 1952 liberation movement in Kenya where the Kikuyu people were balefully misrepresented by the colonial regime as savage 'Mau Mau' engaged in atavistic rituals), one critic has charged that *Lord of the Flies* amounts to 'a defence of colonialism', one which reinscribes 'the old Empire misrepresentation of white enlightenment and black savagery'.[16] If later skirmishes have charged the book with incipient racism, false essentialism, and immoderate misogyny, their denunciations are not unlike the teacup controversies that early on raged in religious journals such as *Commonweal* and *America*. A passage from one of these critics neatly sums up all the pertinent critical attitudes of this type in one sentence. I quote it at length to underscore the not insignificant fact that Golding's reputation was established on the basis of *Lord of the Flies*. Against these hardened assumptions, judgements of the other books – even the often ebullient *Rites of Passage*, the 1980 novel that brought about a resurgence of interest in Golding's fiction – all too frequently adopt the first novel as the single prototype for excellence or failure. That 1964 summary assessment reads:

> [*Lord of the Flies*] is, in fact, a cannily constructed – perhaps contrived – allegory for a twentieth-century doctrine of original sin and its social and political dynamics and it conforms essentially to a quite orthodox tradition not really more pessimistic than the Christian view of man.[17]

III

Original Sin. I've been rather lumbered with Original Sin.

Golding to Carey

That the text itself bears no such single or stable meaning is a matter made evident by its susceptibility to a range of critical interpretations: religious, philosophical, sociological, psychological, political, deconstructionist, post-colonial, and the evidence that any literary text is mediated by way of its readers' diverse subjectivities.[18] As moral fable, it can be construed as examining individual (male) disintegration where the inadequacy, not the necessary depravity, of human nature is emphasized; a legitimate abstraction from this is that people are governable inasmuch as they can be the responsible authors of their own actions. Simon is a 'saint' – Golding's extra-literary term for the boy – because he tries to know comprehensively and inclusively. He possesses a quality of imagination that forces an 'ancient inescapable recognition' (p. 171). Before the obscene pig's head on the spike, Simon comes to acknowledge the existence of his own capacity for evil and his own capacity to act on behalf of others – thus his freeing of the tangled dead parachutist. In contrast, Ralph, in what might be read as a failure of moral imagination, exhibits only a 'fatal unreasoning *knowledge*' (p. 226, my italics) of his approaching death, which is directed towards his own survival, not that of the community. Read as a defensive imperialist fable, the novel's reiterative coding of hunters as 'savages' – Piggy's climactic charge before Jack's tribe at Castle Rock: 'Which is better – to be a pack of painted niggers like you are, or to be sensible like Ralph is' (p. 221) – the novel could be valorized as a Eurocentric racist text. On the other hand, juxtaposing *Lord of the Flies* with one of its intertextual influences, *The Coral Island*, one could just as easily conclude that 'Golding's distinct post-colonial inflection is to attribute savagery, in principle, to the British ruling elite.'[19] Taken as a political fable, the text could be seen to explore social regression, where it is not so much the capabilities of the boys as their depravity, and by fabular extension humankind's inability to control aggression, within a workable social or political order.[20] While Piggy and Ralph do exercise good will and judgement, nevertheless they are inadequate politically, ultimately participating in the *Bacchae*-like murder of Simon, a murder effected by the tribal society that Jack leads.

From the perspective of mythic fable, the book could be viewed as offering an account of postlapsarian loss. As Adam unparadised, the boys cradle within themselves the beast of evil, 'Beelzebub' (the Hebraic original of the English translation, 'lord of the flies' [*Kings* 1.2]; 'the chief of the devils' in *Luke* 11.15). They turn the Edenic island into a fiery hell, although one must remember that on their arrival the island has been smeared by human intent, technology, and weaponry: the scar of the plane's discharged tail cutting across coconut trees and verdant jungle growth. Other readings have seemed equally pertinent. Using the lens of Freud's *Three Essays on Human Sexuality* or *Totem and Taboo* would open *Lord of the Flies* to a reading where the boys become representatives of various instincts or amoral forces. In anthropological terms the boys' society could be seen to mirror the societies of prehistoric man: theirs seems a genuinely primitive culture with its own gods, demons, myths, rituals, taboos. Seen from the vantage point of ethology, where, according to Lorenz's *On Aggression*, natural aggression which once enhanced survival has, with the advent of technological weaponry, come to threaten that survival, the novel enacts on a small scale 'the pathological nature of contemporary aggression'.[21] One here recalls the nuclear warfare that initially occasioned the schoolchildren's evacuation and their ejection on to the island. Then again, viewed from the position developed by Hannah Arendt's *The Banality of Evil*, *Lord of the Flies* comes into focus as a dystopia, showing how 'intelligence (Piggy) and common sense (Ralph) will always be overthrown in society by sadism (Roger) and the lure of totalitarianism (Jack)'.[22]

Whatever the intellectual taxonomy in the wide range of explanations suggested, yet not wholly endorsed, by *Lord of the Flies'* rhetorical density, each could carry with it the critical error of magnifying into men what remain young boys. And English boys at that, stamped through with Britishness like seaside rock, educated by public schools in a system designed to rule an empire, stained, rung after pyramidal rung, by the class prejudices of a stratified society towards which Golding had a lifelong bitter antagonism. As he remarked to a *Guardian* interviewer, a quarter of a century after the writing of *Lord of the Flies*:

> I think that the pyramidal structure of English society is present, and my awareness of it is indelibly imprinted in me, in my psyche, not merely in my intellect but very much in my emotional, almost my physical being. I am enraged by it and I am unable to escape it entirely [...] It dissolves but it doesn't disappear; it's fossilized in me.[23]

As one of the multiple chords playing through *Lord of the Flies*, social class contributes to the narrative's outcome as surely as does any other critique of conventional, civilized values. And the point is well made in one commentator's posing of the question as to how far the island group is a collection of boys (thus representative of human nature in a reductive state) or 'a collection of *English* boys'. Are they 'very much English boys responding to the island situation in an English way, so that what's true of them mightn't be true of a company of American, Chinese or Indian boys?'[24] Such is the position taken by Harold Bloom in a jaunty 1996 lambasting of a novel that he (presumably) thought highly enough of as 'a great literary work' to include in his study guide series on just such great works, when he asks: 'Do the boys [...] represent the human condition or do they reflect the traditions of British schools with their restrictive structures, sometimes brutal discipline, and not always benign visions of human nature?'[25] So another informative way to view the island-world would be to see it as a microcosm of *middle-class* wartime 1940s English society.[26] Thus, lower-middle-class Piggy – with his auntie's sweet shop as signifying the then despised tradesman class, as do the dropped aitches in the lad's speech – is derided because he's a social inferior. The fat boy with the short-sightedness of the caricature bookworm, Piggy's wounds – his asthma, his matronly body and his balding head – disqualify him as surely as his social class from any kind of resistance to the inbred insolence of a Jack Merridew. Instinctively sighting an inferior, Jack commands him to be quiet, and the boy obliges, instinctively knowing his place in the English class system: 'He was intimidated by this uniformed superiority and the offhand authority in Merridew's voice. He shrank to the other side of Ralph and busied himself with his glasses' (p. 32).

Middle-class Ralph, with his boy scout skills, fair complexion, and sense of fair play, is the son of a naval officer, thus is he closely linked to Britain's past magisterial powers on the seas. A demonstrable type of British schoolboy, his tolerant reasonableness is as much a product of breeding as schooling, but he is no match for the arrogance of the 'born leader', Jack Merridew. An elected leader only, Ralph cannot maintain the seat of power. 'We're English; and the English are best at everything,' declares Jack (p. 72), his complacent imperialism the love-child of a union between upper-middle-class chauvinism and an educational system designed to emphasize leadership, tradition, and the ingrained sense of superiority: indeed, all the requirements needed to reinforce social, racial, and colonial bigotry and maintain an empire – at any cost. Head boy at a cathedral school – 'the most highly organized, civilized, disciplined group of children it's possible to find anywhere,' as Golding once observed[27] – Jack inhabits the upper-middle-class rung. From his first appearance on the island, Merridew (for so he announces himself, with that implicit social class signal) is in command, barking orders at the snake-line of black-cloaked choristers, their Canterbury caps topped by – what will all too soon become ironic– silver crosses.[28] If the semiotic of the choirboys' dress distinguishes them from the middle-class boys in their grammar school uniforms, the supercilious jingoism of Jack is the idiom of imperial rule. We will hear it balefully reiterated at the novel's conclusion in the naval officer's dismissive comment: 'You're all British aren't you?' (p. 248). In a story all the more striking because wonderfully real children are depicted – children who yank up socks, stamp feet, and quarrel over sandcastles – it is fitting that Jack's choir should march across the brilliant beach in tight military formation. It is also appropriate that, on being ordered to stand to attention, its most pacific chorister, Simon, should faint, the sun and the heavy costume overwhelming him. Perhaps one of the several reasons why Simon seems insufficiently drawn for many critics, a figure more symbolic than substantial, is because he is least connected to the web of social class and all that this is meant to imply in the novel's critique of 'the very roots of English society [...] how we have lived and how we ought to live'.[29] Unlike the other schoolboys, he never quite sheds the conceptual label assigned to his figure in the workings of the plot and his generalized significance. Epileptic, thus diseased by that strain which the ancients called sacred, he is the author's mouthpiece, given voice from the outside – as Virginia Woolf said of Brontë's *Jane Eyre* when its heroine declared a feminist manifesto – not giving voice from the inside. Piggy, by contrast, may well function as a kind of Augustan man of reason, easily able to prick illusion. His representativeness, however, diminishes to the human scale as the novel progresses: Piggy is no more and no less then a frightened boy, as he stands at the neck of Castle Rock, sightless, the beloved conch clutched in his hands. To appreciate the disparity in the depiction of these two characters is to see how literary a construction Simon is: garmented less in the chorister's signifying gown than the literary trappings of the holy fool, whose vatic insight, mystic unity with 'great creating nature', epilepsy, and illnesses are all traditional signs for holiness.

IV

I knew about *Lord of the Flies*. I planned that out very carefully.
William Golding to John Carey, 1986

Simon's symbolic function in the novel as the agent who provides the text's fabular message – that 'mankind is both heroic and sick' – has provoked the greatest negative criticism over the years, underscoring the charge that *Lord of the Flies* was thesis-ridden, facile in its didactic intent, an over-schematic allegory whose rhetorical effects were too rigidly patterned. 'Whether the psychological representations of *Lord of the Flies* remain altogether convincing seems to me rather questionable; the saintly Simon strains credibility as a naturalistic portrait. In many ways the book is remarkably tendentious, and too clearly has a program to urge upon us,' goes a late twentieth-century judgement.[30] Such an *idée reçue* can now be given the lie, informed as one is by the editorial revelations which appeared in 'Strangers from Within', Charles Monteith's page-turning account of the publisher's transformation of what Faber and Faber's first reader described as:

> An absurd and uninteresting fantasy about the explosion of an atomic bomb on the colonies and a group of children who land in jungle country near New Guinea. Rubbish and dull. Pointless.[31]

A sales director concurred, saying the manuscript (alternately titled *A Cry of Children*, *Nightmare Island*, *To Find an Island*) was 'unpublishable'. Monteith stuck with the novel despite this response; then there was an advance of £60, and the novel was published a full year to the day after first being submitted, its new title, *Lord of the Flies*. The now redolent and sumptuously evocative title was suggested by an editor, Alan Pringle, and, as Monteith observes: 'It has turned out to be the most memorable title given to any book since the end of the Second World War.'[32]

Those 365 days from September 17, 1953 to September 17, 1954 witnessed an editorial excision of the original novel's structure, with Golding being advised to abandon the tripart division of Prologue, Interlude, and Epilogue, all of which, evidently, described an atomic war being waged. Ralph's hair came to be cut; Simon was not permitted to lead 'Good Dances' on the lagoon side while the painted hunters began their sanguineous circling, high above on Castle Rock. As for what has appeared to his detractors to be further evidence of Golding as schematic fabulist, the chapter headings that, like 'Beast from Water' or 'Cry of the Hunters', pinpoint the symbolic momentum of their respective sections were proposed as absolutely necessary by the firm's production and design department.

That the manuscript's major flaw was a structural one in my judgement casts a new light on what one had assumed to be Golding's practice. The austerity of structure was not so much a Pallas Athene born from the head of an inspired Zeus as the work of very good, very mortal, editors. It also calls into question the veracity of several of Golding's comments on the writing of the novel. Alternately he has claimed that he thought of the last sentence first. That the draft of the novel, from first page to last, took from three to four months to complete, having been planned from the beginning to the end before the writing began.[33] That he had 'two pictures in his mind: one of a small boy waggling his feet in the air on an empty beach in sheer exuberance; the other, of the same boy crawling bloodstained through the undergrowth, being hunted to death.'[34] As with the contradictory explanations he has given for the origins of *Lord of the Flies*, the suggestion is that he no longer knew, or cared to know, how the story had evolved; the act of writing itself having been forged in the smithy of necessity at 'a time of great world grief'[35]

V

A cluster of conventions determines the medium of a literary generation – the repertoire of possibilities that a writer has in common with his living rivals. Traditions involve the competition of writers with their ancestors. These collective co-ordinates do not merely permit or regulate the writing of a work. They enter the reading experience and affect its meaning.

Claudio Guillen

Conceptual accounts of origins and enhancements like the ones I have assembled above obscure – sometimes destroy – the primary strength of a novel. For *Lord of the Flies* is first and foremost a gripping story: 'It falls well within the mainstream of several English literary traditions. It is a "boys'" book, as are *Treasure Island*, *The Wind in the Willows*, *High Wind in Jamaica* and other books primarily about juvenile characters which transcend juvenile appeal.'[36] In its dialogic relation to pre-existing literary patterns, it necessarily involves the reader as a party in that dialogue, the reader's response to the work being shaped by knowledge of previous literary conventions. Thus, in the intertextual relation of writings to other writings, survival narratives form a background to *Lord of the Flies*: *Robinson Crusoe*, *The Swiss Family Robinson*, and literature's pre-eminent island tale, *The Tempest*, with its repeated treacheries, knaves, fools, and insurrectionists, debates on the noble savage, and Gonzalo's fond conception of the ideal commonwealth.[37] The reader's expectations, arising from those associated with the pre-existing genre of shipwreck on tropical islands, are radically debunked in *Lord of the Flies*' transformation of that pattern in the context of its historical circumstances. For example, *Robinson Crusoe*'s reinforcement of eighteenth-century ideals of individualism, progress, and imperialist rule are subverted and in their place are the mid twentieth-century inversions of those conceptions: aggression, disorder, the child as predator. Indeed, the Augustan man of reason here is the child Piggy, who suffers from asthma, diarrhoea, laziness, and abominable grammar.

Texts generate other texts, of course. Milton had his debt to Virgil, while Virgil and Joyce had theirs to Homer, just as Austen's *Northanger Abbey* parodically displaced Ann Radcliffe's *The Mysteries of Udolpho*. That *Lord of the Flies*, so explicit about its own forms, is patently dependent for its point on that of another novel links the work to this long-standing practice of intertextual mimesis. Readers are now more than familiar with the novel's ironic – indeed, subversive – recasting of R. M. Ballantyne's *The Coral Island* (1857), a Victorian boy's adventure that Golding admitted had 'a pretty big connection'.[38] *Lord of the Flies*' main characters are, like *The Coral Island*'s, named Ralph and Jack – although Ballantyne's third character, Peterkin, is split into two boys: Peter and Simon. Shipwrecked on an uninhabited island, Ballantyne's boys lead prosperous lives, whereas Golding's boys progressively deteriorate. Explicit references to Ballantyne's title occur twice in the text: the intertextual allusion being more than ironic in the second instance when, at the end – surveying the hideous children before him – a naval officer remarks: 'I should have thought that a pack of British boys – you're all British aren't you? – would have able to put up a better show than that – I mean […] Like *The Coral Island*' (p. 248).

As embedded narrative, *The Coral Island* amounts to a revisionist strategy that recasts the nineteenth-century tale from a post-World War II perspective; the twentieth-century island is inhabited by English boys just as smug about their decency, just as complacent, and – except for Simon – just as ignorant. While Ballantyne showed unshakeable faith in the superiority of the white race – 'White men always [rise to the top of affairs] in savage countries,' remarks a *Coral Island* empire-builder – Golding questions not just English chauvinism, but English civility itself. If in *The Coral Island* the natives' faces 'besides being tattooed were besmeared with red paint and streaked with white,' in *Lord of the Flies* it is the estimable choirboys who color their faces so their aggressive selves can be released from shame: 'Jack began to dance and his laughter became a bloodthirsty snarling […] the mask was a thing of its own, behind which Jack hid, liberated from shame and self-consciousness' (p. 80). To debunk pastoral evocations of life on a tropical island where everything at first seems glamorous, *Lord of the Flies* stresses such physical realities as the diarrhoea of the 'littluns', who 'suffer untold terrors in the dark and huddle together for comfort' (p. 74); the densely hot and damp scratching heat of a real jungle; the remote and 'brute obtuseness of the ocean' (p. 137), which condemns the boys to the island; the filthy flies which drink at the pig's head; and the hair grown lank: 'With a convulsion of the mind, Ralph discovered dirt and decay; understood how much he disliked perpetually flicking the tangled hair out of his eyes' (p. 96). And in a book that intended to tell a story 'about real *boys* on an island, showing what a mess they'd make',[39] that the boys grow frightened of the unknown demonstrates fictional realism as well as psychological verisimilitude. In fact, it is just this fear of the beast – and its ambiguous existence on the island – which forms the dramatic core of the novel.

VI

Ralph found himself understanding the wearisomeness of this life, where every oath was an improvisation and a considerable part of one's waking life was spent watching one's feet. He stopped […] and remembering that first enthusiastic exploration as though it were part of a brighter childhood, he smiled jeeringly.

Lord of the Flies (p. 95)

Had *The Coral Island*'s morality simply been recast, *Lord of the Flies* might well have become a derivative fable along the lines of Richard Hughes' *High Wind in Jamaica*, demonstrating a mid-twentieth century belief that, without the discipline of adults, children will deteriorate into savages. No such single account emerges, it seems to me; rather than finding one stable meaning residing in the text, I note its encouragement to create meanings. A structural reversal has been added to the initial source reversal and its revisionist strategy, making the text interrogate its own grounds by way of an ingenious coda, one that elevates *Lord of the Flies* above mere diagrammatic prescription. The text implies a correspondence between the schoolboys' island world and that of the adult: it is the operation of the text's structure – what I call its ideographic structure – that permits the reader to conclude that the children's experiment on the island has had a constant counterpart in the world outside. Hints are given – although never fully disclosed – in the children's comments about their aerial voyage from an apparent war zone; we come haltingly to surmise that the occasion of the boys' landing, like the mysterious arrival of a dead parachutist, may be unbenevolent gifts from the adult world. As the narrative progresses, the reader is lulled into the unguarded hope that adults may save the situation, while simultaneously decoding certain ironic clues, which the coda will confirm. Take the reiteration of motifs – for example, the schoolboy phrase 'Let's have fun', which Ralph as elected leader introduces and which the pig's head on a stick seems to throw obscenely back at Simon; finally, the phrase sits alarmingly easily on the tongue of the rescuing adult. The reader becomes entangled with these motifs, forcing a reconsideration of what seemed innocuous before. The heaving of logs by the twins Samneric, the rolling of larger and larger stones, the several donations to the sea, the several pig hunts, the two desperate races by Ralph: these sequences of repeated actions, placed at intervals during the story, intensify the ambiguous threat and give the illusion of a vastly speeded-up denouement. The cumulative effect for the reader is to suffer from a vague yet familiar threat, a sense of doom that cannot be adequately located in the narrative's thrust until its confirmation in the coda.

The coda, with its reversed point of view on events contradicting initially established expectations, is a narrative feature of some subtlety, and not a 'gimmick'.[40] In *Lord of the Flies* the ideographic structure consists of two movements; in the first, the events are seen from the point of view of the childish protagonist, Ralph, as he gradually grows more and more aware of the island's disintegration, although his perspective is supplemented by austere narratorial commentary. In the second movement, the coda which concludes the text, the reader encounters events from a new point of view, that of the adult officer, who is completely unaware of and largely indifferent to the suffering. The coda, in conjunction with the parachutist, reveal that adulthood – what the boys have thought of as the 'majesty of adult life' – is also inadequate to prevent destruction: behind the epauletted officer a 'trim cruiser' floats, metonym for barbarism in ancient and contemporary civilizations alike.

And although Golding once observed (extratextually) that the entangled, decaying corpse represents history, [41] textually it does haunt the boys, a haunting appropriately represented by its uncanny position and repetitive motion: 'the figure sat on the mountain-top and bowed and sank and bowed again' (p. 119). When the figure is released by Simon, this other metonym for the killing fields becomes the air combatant it once was as it 'trod with ungainly feet the tops of the high trees' and up, past the demented children, themselves engaged in Bacchae-like excess.

The children then should be read as behaving like the grown-ups, whose world Piggy and Ralph mistakenly believe can help theirs. But the child's world on the island is a painful microcosm of the adult world, and the ruin they bring upon themselves is widespread – recall again that it is atomic warfare in the air that brings about their initial descent to the island. The cruel irony of this matter is made all the stronger by the sudden switch in perspective. Here the officer's dismal failure to comprehend the 'semicircle of little boys, their bodies streaked with coloured clay, sharp sticks in their hands' (p. 246) is testimony to what the narrative voice describes as 'the infinite cynicism of adult life' (p. 170) and silent witness to the Lord of the Dung's general sway. It is as though the naval officer has sailed straight from the pages of *The Coral Island*, moments after we have suffered the consequences of that novel's banal optimism.

In fact, the story's riveting power comes precisely because the characters are children, children who belly-flop from trees, suck thumbs, suffer inestimable fears as the darkness falls, bully weaklings and grunt in then schoolboy slang: 'Wacko… Wizard… Smashing… Golly'.[42] 'I'm not going to play any longer. Not with you,' (p. 132), a mutinous Jack mutters, the puerility of his words in incongruous contrast to his all too adult deeds. The arrival of the officer, with its sudden shift from Ralph's agonized eyes to the benign view of the adult, throws the story back into grotesque miniature. The children are dwarfed to children again. Here is how the officer sees Jack:

> A little boy who wore the remains of an extraordinary black cap on his red hair and who carried the remains of a pair of spectacles at his waist, started forward at the question [Who's boss?] then changed his mind and stood still. (pp. 247–48)

Throughout the narrative's first movement – and with appalling momentum – the children appear to be adults, dealing with adult problems. Now they are whining little boys, held in control by the presence of the adult. Yet the reader cannot forget the cruelty of what has gone before. For the conch of order has been smashed, the spectacles of reason and rescue have been used to destroy the island. An unnamed child with a mulberry mark has burned to death. Two individuals have been murdered. An aggressive tribal society has been hunting down another. Nor can the reader forget that Ralph's piteous weeping at the end transcends the smug cynicism of the rescuer, for Ralph attains awareness of the real nature of the 'pack of British boys' (p. 248).

Ralph is saved because the adult world has intervened, yet his rescuer is on the point of returning to an 'adult' war, which in numerical terms is infinitely more extravagant in its potential for disaster. Given the barbaric chaos the boys have been reduced to, the officer appears to them (to us) as order. It is only on a delayed decoding of the earlier clues that the reader comprehends that the officer is involved in a nuclear war and yet still represents 'order'.[43]

The resonances of *Lord of the Flies* are not allegorically simple but ideographically suggestive. 'Everything is twofold, every perspective provokes a competing alternative';[44] it is the reader's work to hold this sea-changing duality. The task undertaken by the reader, by way of the work's ideographic structure, is to make the apparent discordance of the two clashing patterns connect, to cross the child's educated view of things with the adult's uneducated view and by joining the two perspectives probe the rhetorical question: 'Who will rescue the adult and his cruiser?'

I write that *Lord of the Flies* is not allegorically simple, although readers have conferred social, political, moral, spiritual, and mythic universalities upon it, addressing readers' historical need for a universal text about aggression. Perhaps a useful elaboration on what I am suggesting about a contrast between an ideographic strategy and an allegorical one would be to examine one allegorical feature of the work upon which no doubt can be cast. In Golding's view, the innocence of the child is a crude fallacy. If 'there is a simplicity about human goodness, then it is just as true that there is a corresponding complexity about human evil,' Golding observed, some forty years after *Lord of the Flies*', in an essay on the murder of two-year-old James Bulger by two ten-year-old boys.[45] By nature – and given certain conditions, to whose recipe fear must be added – *Homo sapiens*, Golding argued, has a terrible potentiality for evil. And this potentiality cannot be eradicated by a humane political system, no matter how respectable. Thus in 'Beast from Water', one of the work's most contrived chapters, the fundamental inadequacy of parliamentary systems to deal with atavistic superstition is portrayed. In this episode, the scene's physical and psychological atmosphere is as schematically constructed as the major characters' different pronouncements on the 'beast'.

A parliamentary assembly begins at eventide; consequently, the chief, Ralph, is merely 'a darkish figure' (p. 96) to his group. Light is, at first, level. Only Ralph stares into the island's darkness; his assembly before him faces the lagoon's bright promise. But the light gradually vanishes, accompanied by increasing superstition and fear. The place of assembly on the beach is narratorially described as 'roughly a triangle; but irregular and sketchy, like everything they made'. The assembly's shape can be likened to that of a receding boat, a kind of mirror image of the island-boat. Ralph remarks at the outset that the island is 'roughly boat-shaped'; because of the tide's configuration, he feels that 'the boat was moving steadily astern' (p. 38).

Since Ralph sits on 'a dead tree' (p. 96) that forms the triangle's base, no captain occupies the boat's rightful apex, where 'the grass was thick again because no one sat there' (p. 97). Like the island that appears to move backward, the assembly-boat is pointed to the darkness of the jungle, not the brightness of the navigable lagoon behind. Hunters sit like hawks on the right of Ralph; to the left are placed the doves, mostly littluns who giggle whenever their assembly seat, 'an ill-balanced twister', capsizes. And Piggy stands outside the triangle, showing his moralizing ineffectuality. 'This indicated that he wished to listen but would not speak; and Piggy intended it as a gesture of disapproval,' as summarized by the narrative voice. The conch in his hands, a littlun says he's seen a snake thing, a beastie. Both Piggy and Jack emphatically deny its existence, but – to Ralph's astonishment – Simon agrees that it does exist, but that 'maybe it's only us'. Ludicrously, ineptly, damagingly, Ralph determines that a vote on its existence should be taken. Darkness descends on the shattered assembly and, for the first of many times, the 'beastie' is ritually appeased. Island boat, assembly boat, and what should be the ship of civilization itself, rational government, all drift bleakly into darkness. The wail of Percival Wemys Madison of the Vicarage, Harcourt St Anthony, turns into an inarticulate gibber, the 'dense black mass' (p. 115) of mock hunters swirls, and the 'three blind mice' (p. 116), Ralph,

Piggy, and Simon, sit 'in the darkness, striving unsuccessfully to convey the majesty of adult life' (p. 117).

If theme in this episode is schematically stable, Golding's 'symbols are not in fact clear, or wholly articulate, they are always the incarnation of more than can be extracted or translated from them.'[46] Consider, for example, Simon's secret sanctuary with its perfumed candle-buds. Rendered in terms of the island/ship metaphor, Simon's canopied bower is likened to a captain's 'little cabin' (p. 72); its 'creepers dropped their ropes like the rigging of foundered ships' (p. 71), and its centre is occupied by a 'patch of rock' (p. 71) on which a foundering ship could strike. On this rock a demonology, not a church, will be built, one recalls; Jack has instructed his braves to '"ram one end of the stick in the earth. Oh – it's rock. Jam it in the crack"'(p. 169). The reverberations of this imagistic cluster are intensified when, with the advance of evening, Simon's cabin is submerged by the sea: 'Darkness poured out, submerging the ways between the trees till they were dim and strange as the bottom of the *sea*' (p. 72, my italics).

Consider as well the initial figuring of the island as a ship at sea; or is it not also a civilization threatened with submergence, a tooth in a sucking mouth, a body dissociated from nature, consciousness divorced from the brute passivity of the subconscious? On it, the boys are certainly islanded by the ineluctable sea to which they turn in awe and distaste. The trope is woven into the narrative texture at various places and, by a technique of clustering, suggestion engenders suggestion. By gathering to itself other metaphors, the island trope evolves a logic of association, the organizing principle being recurrence with variation. Thus Ralph's final isolation at the tail end of the island – 'he was surrounded on all sides by chasms of empty air. There was nowhere to hide, even if one did not have to go on' (p. 130) – is the isolation of the despairing hero. And when a now blind Piggy is described as 'islanded in a sea of meaningless colour' (p. 91) while he embraces the rock with 'ludicrous care above the sucking sea' (p. 217), the microcosmic/ macrocosmic resonances are rich. Since the dual clusters are associative rather than syntactical or logical, meaning hovers over several referents so that the reader experiences the text as dynamic, with shifting shapes like cells under a microscope or stars at the end of a telescope.

VII

What was that enemy? I cannot tell. He came with the darkness and he reduced me to a shuddering terror that was incurable because it was indescribable. In daylight I thought of the Roman remains that had been dug up under the church as the oldest things near, sane things from sane people like myself. But at night, the Norman door and pillar, even the flint wall of our cellar, were older, far older, were rooted in the darkness under the earth.

William Golding, 'The Ladder and the Tree'

In the passage above, drawn from an early essay about his childhood home in Marlborough, Golding describes the autobiographical origins for an atavistic quest through darkness that came to preoccupy much of his fiction. Pondering over the church graveyard at the foot of his garden, the child Billy grew terrified of some enemy he imagined was lurking there to harm him. A comparable mythopoeia of a beast is interleaved through *Lord of the Flies*, although its dimensions/implications are by no means as fully realized as they come to be in *Pincher Martin*, *Darkness Visible*, or even *The Paper Men*. Nevertheless, the hallucinatory process is depicted in crucial confrontation scenes where two apparently irreconcilable views of one situation are brought slap up against each other. Such scenes are a narrative feature characteristic of Golding's subsequent fictional practice as well, the confrontation scene bringing about a single crystallization of a work's total structure, bringing together contradictory, yet complementary, concepts.

And what is this enemy, this creature that haunts the children's imaginations and which Jack hunts and tries to propitiate with a totemic beast? In extratextual conversation, Golding may have called it 'one of the conditions of existence, this awful thing', but how exactly does the novel prompt the reader to create such a meaning? Through the presence, actions, and transformational death of the strange visionary child, Simon? A stubborn conception in the Golding mythopoeia is the figure of the holy fool; forerunner to *Pincher Martin*'s Nat, *Darkness Visible*'s Matty, or *Rites of Passage*'s Parson Colley, unsimple Simon comes to be wise. Sitting before the Lord of the Flies, a stinking, fly-ridden pig's head on a stick, Simon is made to recognize the human nature of the real beast: that he himself has the capacity for evil as well as for good. 'Whenever Simon thought of the beast,' intones the narrative voice,

41

'there arose before his inward sight the pictures of a human at once heroic and sick' (p. 128). Motivated by the mythopoeic requirements of the tale, Simon intuitively identifies the beast, which allows what is a narratorial puppet to solve the problem terrifying all the other creatures in this imagined world. Acting with the sheer simplicity of any agent of good, Simon ventures arduously and alone to the mountain-top where he releases what he discovers is a harmless but horrifying corpse; then he tries to tell the boys below about 'mankind's essential illness' (p. 111).

At the heart of the developing mythopoeia in *Lord of the Flies* is the trope of the severed head of the pig, to which Simon turns in distaste and awe, and from which he at first tries to escape. Grinning cynically, its mouth gaping and its eyes half closed, the head has been placed on a rock in a sea-like clearing around Simon's secret sanctuary. As a trope, the Head also can be likened to an island surrounded by the sea, thus operating macrocosmically and microcosmically. A larger macrocosm, the Castle Rock at the island's end is like a severed head as well: another variant on the pig's head. Described as a 'rock, almost detached' (p. 38), this smaller landmass is separated − a point which the text makes repeatedly − from the island's main body by 'a narrow *neck*' (p. 130, my italics). 'Soon, in a matter of centuries' (p. 130) this head will be severed too, although the impersonal narratorial distancing invokes a nature as indifferent to the boys' rescue as geological time is to man's 'little life'. At the tale's conclusion, giggling black and green savages will swarm around and over the head of Castle Rock as the black and green flies swarmed around the Lord of the Dung's head.

As readers know, Piggy's death occurs at this rock head; Roger's releasing of the boulder re-enacts the slaughter of a pig, for Piggy is swiftly decapitated by 'a glancing blow from *chin* to knee' (p. 222, my italics). Traveling through the air, with a grunt he lands on the square red rock in the sea, a kind of grotesque refectory table. And the monster-sea sucks his body, which 'twitched like a pig's after it has been killed' (p. 223), the emblematic nature of the character's name being reasserted from objective narratorial distance, even narratorial indifference. Piggy's head has been smashed and Ralph, running along the rocky neck, jumps just in time to avoid the 'headless body of the [sacrificial] sow' (p. 223) the hunters are planning to roast. The preparation is clear; another head is needed.

A traditional reading would have the head − the centre of reason − destroyed at Piggy's death with the island society's regression cutting 'the bridge' (p. 134) between rationality and irrationality. But in the developing mythopoeia of *Lord of the Flies* rationality is a suspect concept just like the common sense of Piggy, who 'goes on believing in the power of reason to tame the beast'.[47] Nor is the severed head of the pig Beelzebub; it does not represent an evil external to the individual, but rather the corrupt and corrupting consciousness, that very human malaise – in Golding's construction – that objectifies evil rather than recognizing its subjectivity: the kind of moral distancing we understand to be committed by both the officer and Piggy alike, the latter believing that Jack alone is the cause for 'things break[ing] up'. Such is the intellectual complication that the severed head represents to Simon; it prospers on the island's head, Castle Rock. Three confrontation scenes formulate the mythopoeia: Simon before the head, Ralph before the skull of the pig, Ralph before a 'savage'.

It is Simon alone who is made to recognize the real beast and – like a Moses with tablets of law – bring the truth from the mountain: a truth he understands as he broods before the totemic sow's head, having witnessed its anal rape and decapitation. Then, in the only idiom a child of Simon's age could give to a hallucinatory authority, the pig's head begins to deliver 'something very much like a sermon to the boy', and this in the 'voice of a schoolmaster' (p. 178). It insists that the island is corrupt and all is lost: 'This is ridiculous,' the head, now named the Lord of the Flies, expostulates. 'You know perfectly well you'll only meet me down there – so don't try to escape!' Shifting by way of the ironic motif of 'fun' into schoolboy patois, the head assures: '*we* are going to have fun on this island' (p. 178, my italics), even though 'everything' is a 'bad business' (p. 170). Such counselling of the acceptance of evil amounts to 'the infinite cynicism of adult life': the cynicism of the conscious mind, the cynicism that can ignore even 'the indignity of being spiked on a stick', the cynicism that 'grins' – as does the pig's head – at the obscenities that even make the butterflies desert their beloved bower. For the reading of the encounter involves also the recollection that during the anal mistreatment of the sow and its bloody killing, the butterflies continued to 'dance preoccupied in the centre of the clearing' (p. 178). That they now leave suggests the head must represent something a great deal more obscene than blood savor or rape. Counselling acceptance amounts to the kind of cynicism and easy optimism of the naval officer – in all his meanings – who '*grinned* cheerfully at the obscene savages while muttering "fun and games"'(p. 247, my italics).[48]

43

The meaning that the reader is prompted to create in this confrontation scene is twofold. Not only does this pig's head 'weld together other aspects of the beast. It is the beast, the head of the beast, the offering to the beast, left by the boys whose bestiality is marked by the head on the stick,'[49] but also, and importantly, this Lord of the Dung *is* Simon. The Lord of the Flies that counsels acceptance is his own strategic consciousness. Myopically viewing the head as an objectification of evil, independent of consciousness, would be to repeat the same error as Jack makes in externalizing and objectifying his own evil. The identification of Simon and the head is worked out very carefully indeed. Consider the following similarities: speaking in schoolboy patois, the Lord's head has 'half-shut eyes' (p. 170), while Simon is described as keeping 'his eyes shut, then shelter[ing] them with his hand' (p. 171) so that vision is partial; he sees things 'without definition and illusively' (p. 171) behind a 'luminous veil'. Simon comprehends his own savagery: he 'licks his dry lips' and feels the weight of his hair. Later, after his epileptic fit, blood 'dries around his mouth and chin' (p. 180) in the manner of the 'blood-blackened' (p. 170) grinning mouth of the head. Detecting the shared identity, the flies – although sated – leave the pig guts 'alight by Simon's runnels of sweat' (p. 171) and drink at the boy's head. By a profound effort of will, Simon forces himself to penetrate his own loathing and break through his own consciousness: 'At last Simon gave up and looked back; saw the white teeth and dim eyes, the blood – and his gaze as held by that ancient, inescapable recognition' (p. 171).

Of course, the orchestration of this recognition is conducted through the narratorial voice, which positions the *two heads* opposite each other. It is Simon himself he is looking at. His double, the head, grins at the flies of corruption and Simon acknowledges it as himself. Like the boy before the Egyptian mummy in Golding's essay 'Egypt from My Inside', Simon prepares 'to penetrate mysteries' and 'go down and through in darkness'. Looking into a vast mouth, Simon submits to the terror of his own being. 'Simon found he was looking into a vast mouth. There was blackness within, a blackness that spread [...] He fell down and lost consciousness' (p. 178). Having penetrated here his own capacity for evil, he returns from non-being to awaken next to 'the dark earth close by his cheek' (p. 179) and to know that he must 'do something'. All alone he does what no other boy could dare to do: encounter the beast on the hill. There Simon discovers that 'this parody' (ringed as well by green flies) is nothing more 'harmless and horrible' (p. 181) than was the head. In releasing the figure 'from the rocks and […] the wind's indignity' (p. 181), Simon demonstrates the heroism that has been posited as one side of humankind's dual nature.

Twice Ralph is confronted with just such a primal confrontation: face to face, eye to eye. Earlier we saw that he could not connect with the primal. For example, standing at the island's rock shore 'on a level with the sea' (p. 136), Ralph follows the waves' 'ceaseless, bulging passage' and feels 'clamped down', 'helpless', and 'condemned' (p. 137) by a 'leviathan' (p. 131) monster with 'arms of surf' and 'fingers of spray' (p. 137). Nor can he accept Simon's intuitive faith when the latter whispers 'you'll get back all right' (p. 137), that 'the brute obtuseness' (p. 137) of nature can be escaped from.

Much later, after the deaths of Simon and Piggy, Ralph stands in the clearing, confronted by the same offensive head, looking steadily at the skull that 'seemed to jeer at him cynically' (p. 227). The skull's 'empty sockets seemed to hold his gaze masterfully and without effort' (p. 228), as the narrative voice observes in its re-orchestration of Simon's earlier encounter. But, unlike Simon, Ralph turns away from acknowledging the identification to externalize the monstrous.

> A sick *fear* and *rage* swept him. Fiercely he hit out at the filthy thing in front of him that bobbed like a toy and came back, still grinning into his face, so that he lashed and cried out in loathing (p. 228)

Although he keeps 'his face to the skull that lay grinning at the sky', Ralph can no more recognize his own face than Jack can recognize his own image behind the 'awesome stranger' (p. 80) with his mask of war paint when he looks into the water-filled coconut.

But Ralph cannot penetrate this 'parody thing', which in its motion amalgamates the parachutist's bowing and the 'breathing' of the sea, whose movements are those of an ancient primal rhythm that does not so much 'progress' as endure 'a momentous rise and fall' (p. 137). Such a 'minute-long fall and rise and fall' (p. 131) is the rhythm that engulfs the parachutist's body on its way to sea: 'On the mountain-top the parachute filled and moved; the figure slid, rose to its feet, falling, still falling, it sank towards the beach' (p. 189), the rhythm that imparts to Piggy some serenity: the water became 'luminous round the rock forty feet below, where Piggy had fallen' (p. 234). It is especially this rhythm that transfigures Simon in death. I quote at length, so foregrounded in this benedictory requiem is the steadfast movement:

> Somewhere over the darkened curve of the world the sun and moon were pulling; and the film of water on the earth planet was held, bulging slightly on one side while the solid core turned. The great wave of the tide moved further along the island and the water lifted. Softly, surrounded by a fringe of inquisitive bright creatures, itself a silver shape beneath the steadfast constellations, Simon's dead body moved out towards the open sea. (p. 190)

Yet for Ralph it is a terrifying rhythm, 'the age-long nightmares of falling and death' (p. 235) that occur in darkness, intimating the 'horrors of death' (p. 228).

Ralph is given a second experience of this atavistic rhythm. In his last desperate race (depicted in the penultimate scene where many of the earlier motifs are recapitulated) Ralph hides himself in Simon's cell, which notably is now described as 'the darkest hole' (p. 242) on the island. Like Simon before him, Ralph connects in terror with the primal: 'He laid his cheek against the chocolate-coloured earth, licked his dry lips and closed his eyes' and feels the ancient rhythm: 'Under the thicket, the earth was vibrating very slightly' (p. 243). Jerking his head from the earth, he peers into the 'dulled light' and sees a body slowly approaching: waist, knee, two knees, two hands, a spear sharpened at both ends.

A head. Ralph and someone called a 'savage' peer through the obscurity at each other, repeating in their action Simon's scrutiny before the head. Just at the moment his eyes connect with those of the 'savage', Ralph repeats Simon's early admonition, 'you'll get back' (p. 245), and with this partial acknowledgement of his own darkness he breaks through the cell. Expecting nothing he strikes out, screaming: 'He forgot his wounds, his hunger and thirst, and became fear; hopeless fear on flying feet, rushing through the forest towards the open beach' (p. 245).

Rushing, screaming through the fire that is described as undulating 'forward like a tide' (p. 245), screaming and rushing and *trying to cry for mercy* (p. 246, my italics), he trips and – fallen on the ground – sees, before him, the officer. In a manner of speaking Ralph is saved; in a manner of speaking Ralph is given mercy.

VIII

For I have shifted somewhat from the position I held when I wrote the
book. I no longer believe that the author has a sort of *patriae potestas* over
his brain-children [...] Once they are printed [...] the author has no more
authority over them [...] perhaps knows less about them that the critic.

Golding, 'Fable'

As Fredric Jameson remarked in *The Political Unconscious*, "Genres are
essentially literary [...] or social contracts between a writer and a
specific public whose function it is to specify the proper use of a
particular cultural artefact."[50] And *Lord of the Flies* is no exception to the
ways in which reading practices make meanings. From my perspective,
a germinal eschatology of the scapegoat/sacrificial victim can be seen
emerging here. Simon's recognition of humankind's complicity
occasions his ritual death with him meeting the fate of those who
remind society of its guilt: we prefer to destroy the objectification of
our fears rather than recognize the dark terrors in ourselves. In 'Fable'
Golding (extratextually) declared this strategy as a 'failure of human
sympathy', one that amounts to 'the objectivizing of our own
inadequacies so as to make a *scapegoat*.'[51] Of course the ritual enacts the
confinement and destruction of the boys' own terrors. They kill Simon
as a beast, a point underscored by the perspective employed so that the
frenzied crowd first sees 'a thing [...] crawling out of the forest', which
immediately becomes 'the beast [that] stumbled into the [empty]
horseshoe'. Then that crowd itself becomes the ravenous beast: 'the
mouth of the new circle crunched and screamed' as its 'teeth and claws
tore flesh' (p. 188). No scapegoat, Piggy is killed because he is alien, a
pseudo-species, his death marking the inadequacy of any rational,
logical world, for the conch is smashed as a blind Piggy falls into the
sea. But the mild and ordinary Ralph operates only within the
community's pattern; such a figure could never exorcise its fears. With
no way to release fully the fear in himself, he can only weep, as the
mezza voce of the narrative voice directs, 'for the end of innocence, the
darkness of man's heart' (p. 248).

Implicit as this eschatology is in the narrative texture of *Lord of the
Flies*, little is explicit in the plot itself. True, Simon's encounter with the
airman brings about his death, while unravelling the mystery of the
bobbing figure. Likewise, Ralph's foray with the 'savage' does release

the dénouement; the fire sweeps through the island thus signalling the naval ship — a not implausible arrival given the earlier ship — and the ultimate, ironic rescue. So are charges of 'gimmickry', manipulation, and allegorizing ill considered? Do such tonally weighted episodes as those before the head contribute to, or detract from, the narrative's authenticity? And does *Lord of the Flies* present a really rather simple dictum: mankind's evil?

My sense is that, experienced at the level of reader response, these confrontation episodes reverberate beyond the allegorizing mandate. By way of their density and ambiguity, and yet familiarity, these confrontation scenes draw the reader into the imaginative act the characters themselves are depicted as making. Which is to say that the confrontation scenes construct a parallel between the focusing of individual characters' vision and the focusing of the reader's vision. Point of view, having been so skilfully handled when Simon is made to recognize that he must affirm his face, puts the reader into just such a position of recognition. As with confrontation scene so with ideographic structure, the text's total structure bringing about a similar fusion in the readers' focusing of events. By means of this ideographic structure, *Lord of the Flies* permits the reader to create textual thematics that are generated again and again, depending on the context in which it is read.

Endnotes

1   In the short article Golding published on James Bulger's murder, he insisted that 'There is nothing the slightest bit simple about what happened to the two-year-old [...] after he was led out of a Liverpool area shopping centre by two older boys,' suggesting, however, that 'there are certain things about cruelty — and especially the cruelty of boys — which may be true and from which we can learn' in 'Why Boys Become Vicious' (*San Francisco Examiner*, February 28, 1992, B-1). No recent phenomenon, the killing of children by children has a concentrated horror. In 1983, a two-year-old pushed from a roof by a seven-year-old in an argument over a toy car; in 1989, a seven-year-old shot by a nine-year-old in an argument over a Nintendo game; in 1994, a fourteen-year-old shot by an eleven-year-old boy, himself shot by gang members worried

he would tell authorities about the aborted plan to kill rivals; in 1994, a five-year-old thrown from a window by ten- and eleven-year-old boys; in 1994, a five-year-old beaten to death allegedly by two children, one of them nine; in 1994, an eleven-year-old girl raped and murdered by seven- and eight-year-old boys; in 1998, fellow students (five killed and ten wounded) shot by twelve- and fourteen-year-old boys outside Jonestown, Arkansas; in 2001, a Columbine copycat fatal shooting of schoolmates at Santana High School in California, the killers provoked by perceived mistreatment and ridicule by other students.

2   Charles Monteith, 'Strangers from Within' in John Carey (ed.), *William Golding, The Man and his Books: A Tribute on his 75th Birthday*, New York, Farrar, Straus & Giroux, 1986, p. 63.

3   John Fowles, 'Golding and "Golding"' in John Carey (ed.), *William Golding, The Man and his Books: A Tribute on his 75th Birthday*, ibid., p. 149.

4   Golding, *A Moving Target*, New York, Farrar, Straus & Giroux, 1982, p. 169. Bibliographic articles like Maurice McCullen's early 1978 survey of the critical reception since *Lord of the Flies*' first publication in 1954, '*Lord of the Flies*: The Critical Quest' from *William Golding: Some Critical Considerations*, Jack Bills and Robert O. Evans (eds.), Kentucky, The University Press of Kentucky 1975, pp. 203-236, Patrick Reilly's *Lord of the Flies: Fathers and Sons*, New York, Twayne Publishers, 1992, pp.41-42, Virginia Tiger's *William Golding: The Dark Fields of Discovery*, London: Calder & Boyars, 1974, pp. 41-46, or the chapter in James Gindin's *William Golding*, New York, St Martin's Press, 1988, pp. 20-30, reviewing the popular and critical reception – indeed, a 1994 full-length book, *William Golding: A Bibliography 1934-1993* by R.A. Gekoski and P.A. Grogan, London, André Deutsch, 1994 – all give witness to 'the sheer critical firepower' that Golding charged had been levelled at the novel, now over five decades of sometimes repetitive exegeses

5   See here, for example, Harold Bloom, *William Golding's Lord of the Flies*, Broomall, PA, Chelsea House Publishers, 1996; Gillian Hanscombe, *William Golding: Lord of the Flies*, Penguin Passport,

1986; Raymond Wilson, *Macmillan Master Guides: Lord of the Flies by William Golding*, London, Macmillan, 1986; Brian Spring, *Lord of the Flies: Helicon Study Guide*, Dublin, Helicon, 1976, Clarice Swisher (ed.) *Readings on Lord of the Flies*, San Diego, Greenhaven Press, 1997; as well as the Pamphlet entry in the bibliography of Tiger's study, covering items from 1963–1977. That *Lord of the Flies* was eminently teachable in a period following 1945 where English literature came to dominate the curricula in universities and schools in Britain, North America, India, and Pakistan (indeed, the Anglophone world, at large) was never lost on the publishing industry.

6   A.C. Capey, 'Questioning the Literary Merit of *Lord of the Flies*' in Clarice Swisher (ed.), *Readings on Lord of the Flies*, ibid., p. 146.

7   Neil McEwan, 'Golding's *Lord of the Flies*, Ballantyne's *Coral Island* and the Critics', *The Survival of the Novel: British Fiction in the Later Twentieth Century*, London, Macmillan Press, 1981, p. 148.

8   Reilly, op. cit., p. 6.

9   Ian McEwan, 'Schoolboys' in John Carey (ed.), *William Golding The Man and His Books: A Tribute on his 75th Birthday*, ibid., p. 159.

10   William Golding, *A Moving Target*, New York, Farrar, Straus & Giroux, 1982, p. 163.

11   Such preoccupations were seen in the work of Konrad Lorenz, Lionel Tiger and Edward O. Wilson, who themselves built upon Freud's earlier discoveries about infant sexualities

12   Ian McEwan, op. cit., p. 157.

13   E.M. Forster, 'Introduction', *Lord of the Flies*, New York, Coward McCann, 1962, p. x.

14   See L.L. Dickson's *The Modern Allegories of William Golding*, Gainsville, University of South Florida Press, 1990 and Lawrence S. Friedman's *William Golding*, New York, Continuum, 1993, the

publication dates of which would seem to suggest the authors might have taken into account developments in literary theory, particularly the interrogation of textual symptoms of doubt and duplicity.

15 Frederick Karl, 'The Novel as Moral Allegory: The Fiction of William Golding', *A Reader's Guide to the Contemporary English Novel*, New York, Noonday Press, 1962, p. 247.

16 Stefan Hawlin, 'The Savages in the Forest: Decolonizing William Golding', *Critical Survey* 7 (1995), p. 126.

17 George Herndl, 'Golding and Salinger, A Clear Choice', *Wiseman Review* (1964–1965), p. 310.

18 In this context see the concerns of late twentieth-century readers in Caitlin Quinn-Lang, 'Jets, Ships and Atom Bombs in Golding's *Lord of the Flies*' in Will Wright & Steven Kaplan (eds), *The Image of Technology in Literature, the Media and Society*, University of Southern Colorado Society for Interdisciplinary Study, Pueblo & Co, 1994, pp. 78–83, and Steven Connor, 'Rewriting Wrong: On the Ethics of Literary Reversion' in Theo D'haen (ed.), *Liminal Postmodernisms: The Post Modern, the (Post) Colonial and the Post Feminist*, Amsterdam-Atlanta, GA: Rodopi: B.V., 1994, pp. 79–97. One should be reminded, however, that in the fifty years of exegesis, never once has the question been asked as to what would have happened had girls been dropped on the island.

19 Alan Sinfield, *Literature, Politics and Culture in Postwar Britain*, Oxford, Blackwell, 1989, p. 141.

20 Quite diverse interpretations have emerged, even when there was the agreement that the novel should be read as a political fable. 'A population of interpretations', generated by some two hundred undergraduate students' responses to the novel, was the result of an experiment undertaken in a political theory course where such idiosyncratic views as the following appeared: 'The novel has Marxist overtones of the connections between economic conditions and social structure.' (Quoted in Steven Brown's 'Political Literature and the Response of the Reader: Experimental Studies of Interpretation,

Imagery, and Criticism' *The American Political Science Review* 72, 1977, p. 569). Golding was at pains to make 'economic conditions' on the island so embracing that, literally and metaphorically, fruit was for the plucking; with physical hardship banished, the experiment in living could be tested on its own grounds.

21   Kathleen Woodward, 'On Aggression: William Golding's *Lord of the Flies*' in Martin H. Greenberg and Joseph D. Olander (eds), *No Place Else: Explorations in Utopian and Dystopian Fiction*, Southern Illinois University Press, 1983, p. 216.

22   C.B. Cox, '*Lord of the Flies*', *Critical Quarterly* 2 (1960), p. 112.

23   Golding to Webb, 'Interview with William Golding', W. L. Webb, *Guardian* (October 11, 1980), p. 12.

24   Bergonzi, Berhard & John Whitley, *The English Novel: Questions in Literature*, London, Sussex Books, 1976, p. 176. The second film adaptation of the novel (Harry Hook, Director; Castle Rock Entertainment with Nelson Entertainment, 1990) changed the children from English preparatory school boys to American Naval cadets, thus damaging the movie's narrative specificity, for me at any rate.

25   Bloom, op. cit., p. 6.

26   That Golding chose 'a homogeneous group of middle-class white children, all of whom are boys' is not so much an omission which prevented the emergence of 'racial tension [...] sexual tension... [and] the tension of cultural difference' (Woodward, op. cit., p. 208) as one which included class acrimony, an abiding British malignancy and one which English authors, from Austen onwards, have castigated.

27   Adding that the choice of the cathedral school was deliberate, Golding explained that the intent was to intensify the narrative's peripatetic reversal of fortune: 'It's only because of that civilized height that the fall is a tragedy' (Golding in Douglas M. Davis, 'A Conversation with William Golding' *New Republic*, May 4, 1963, p. 29).

28   Many commentators have remarked upon Golding's unsentimental

assessment of the culture of schoolboy society, with its bullying, and correctly ascribed that familiarity to his years as a master at Bishop Wordsworth School in Salisbury. However, to my knowledge, it has yet to be pointed out that (unlike his father before him, who taught at a grammar school in Marlborough, the town itself being dominated by Marlborough College, attended by the sons of the upper echelons of British society since 1843) Golding taught in a public school, adjacent to Salisbury Cathedral, with its choristers. The class disparity would not have gone unnoticed. The former lay vicar and adult singer in the choir of Salisbury Cathedral, Richard Shepard, observed that the cathedral's choristers corresponded quite closely to Jack's in terms of their clothes. 'The boys used to march crocodile fashion across from the school to the cathedral [...] The head chorister would shout the words "Stand erect, by the left, quick march" and the procession would march off across the green into the cloisters and on into the cathedral. The shouted commands "LEFT! RIGHT!" were, for the sake of decency and decorum, silenced once the boys were inside the cathedral.' 'Programme Commentary', Nigel Williams, *Pilot Theatre Company Production of* Lord of the Flies, Lyric Theatre Hammersmith, July 1998.

29 Golding to Williams, ibid., p. 4.

30 Bloom, op. cit., p. 5.

31 Monteith, op. cit., p. 57.

32 Monteith, op. cit., p. 62.

33 Jack Biles, *Talk: Conversations with William Golding*, New York, Harcourt, Brace & Jovanovich, 1970, p. 53.

34 Ian Gregor, '"He Wondered": The Religious Imagination of William Golding' in John Carey (ed.), *William Golding The Man and his Books: A Tribute on his 75th Birthday*, New York: Farrar, Straus & Giroux, 1986, p. 99.

35 'Interview with William Golding', Henry David Rosso, *Ann Arbor News* (December 1985) p. 5.

36   Bernard S. Oldsey and Stanley Weintraub, *The Art of William Golding*, New York, Harcourt, Brace and World, 1965, p. 16.

37   Indeed, '[t]]here are echoes of *The Tempest* throughout *Lord of the Flies*: a shipwreck, transactions with evil, a final ambiguous rescue' (Reilly, op. cit., p. 119).

38   Kermode's analysis of the parodic features of the two books ('The Meaning of It All', *Books and Bookmen*, August 1959, pp. 10–16) was amplified by Carl Niemeyer in '*The Coral Island* Revisited' *College English* (1961), pp. 241–45, still a useful essay, although one that maximizes this dependence into a limitation. As a corrective, McEwan's 'Golding's *Lord of the Flies*, Ballantyne's *Coral Island* and the Critics' (op. cit.) makes the point that the academic community of the 1960s, 'eager to explain the "contemporary sensibility" [of *Lord of the Flies*]' rested its case 'on a mid-Victorian book for boys' (p. 151).

39   Golding to Kermode, op. cit., p. 12.

40   The term was James Gindin's in a 1960 essay, 'Gimmick and Metaphor in the Novels of William Golding' *Modern English Studies* 6 (1960), pp. 145–52, one which provided arms for attacks on the author's allegedly contrived and manipulative ('cheating') endings. This acrimonious, if influential, criticism, seems odd when one considers the following: Joyce's narrative shift was not seen as a gimmick when in *Ulysses* we move from Leopold Bloom to Molly; Euripides is nowhere described as cheating when a *deus ex machina* concludes the *Ion*. Golding has gone on record more than once in ascribing his own structures to the influence of the Greek dramatists; see Golding in conversation with Davis (op. cit.) and in conversation with Carey (op. cit.).

41   Problematic as authorial explications are, since they impose extra-literary 'meaning', in 'Fable' Golding wrote: 'What the grownups send them is a sign [...] [T]hat arbitrary sign stands for off-campus history, the thing which threatens every child everywhere, the history of blood and intolerance, of ignorance and prejudice, the thing which is dead and won't lie down [...] it falls on the very place where the children are making their one constructive attempt

to get themselves helped. It dominates the mountaintop and so prevents them keeping a fire alight there as a signal' (pp. 95–96).

42   Waves of expletives roll from the schoolboy tongues in the 1990 American movie adaptation, presumably in an effort to update schoolboy slang. Is the mimetic change successful?

43   Golding's explication of the book's thematics is once again problematic, since authorial commentary tends to immobilize the play of meanings in a text, creating another potential text. As he explained: 'The whole book is symbolic in nature except the rescue in the end where adult life appears, dignified and capable, but in reality enmeshed in the same evil as the symbolic life of the children on the island. The officer, having interrupted a manhunt, prepares to take the children off the island in a cruiser, which will presently be hunting its enemy in the same implacable way. And who will rescue the adult and his cruiser?' (Golding to Epstein, E.L. Epstein, 'Notes on *Lord of the Flies*', *Lord of the Flies*, New York, Capricorn Books, 1959, pp. 191–92)

44   Patrick Reilly, op. cit. p. 102. Amplifying this doubleness, Reilly examines what he felicitously describes as the novel's 'competing narratologies': 'the two parallel texts, the first in a "low" style of schoolboy slang evocative of the world of Greyfriars and Billy Bunter, the other in the "high" style of the narrator's gloss and commentary, his reinterpretation of the action to reveal its underlying import' (p. 100). Reilly's point, that without the narratorial commentary the reader would be limited to the incomprehensible perceptions of the children, is well taken.

45   Golding, 'Why Boys Become Vicious', op. cit.

46   Ian Gregor and Mark Kinkead-Weekes, *William Golding*, London, Faber and Faber, 1967, p. 19.

47   Reilly, op. cit., p. 111.

48   In an essay entitled 'Digging for Pictures' there is a re-orchestration of these motifs; excavating for ruins in the chalk hills

of Wiltshire, the Golding-persona discovers a victim of prehistoric murder in a 'dark quiet pit'; its 'jaws were wide open, *grinning* perhaps with *cynicism*' (p. 60, my italics).

49   John S. Whitley, *Golding: Lord of the Flies*, London, Edward Arnold, 1970, p. 48.

50   Fredric Jameson, *The Political Unconscious*, Ithaca, Cornell University Press, 1981, p. 106.

51   Golding, 'Fable', p. 94 (my italics). In the many years that he had been compelled to 'explain' *Lord of the Flies*, this was the only occasion where he publicly uses this term.

The Inheritors

I

We stand, then, on the shore, not as our Victorian fathers stood, lassoing phenomena with Latin names, listing, docketing and systematizing. Belsen and Hiroshima have gone some way towards teaching us humility [...] It is not the complete specimen [...] that excites us. It is the fragment, the hint [...] We stand where any upright food-gatherer has stood, on the edge of our own unconscious, and hope, perhaps, for the terror and excitement of the print of a single foot.

Golding, 'In My Ark'

Much more explicitly than *Lord of the Flies*, *The Inheritors* endorses its author's view that the proper end of literature is imaginative discovery; it is not the level of knowledge that literature can raise, but the level of knowing. Here Golding explores the possible origins of human guilt and violence in the evolutionary appearance of *Homo sapiens*. But the text, mythic in impulse, consciously tries to construct a mythopoeia relevant to the contemporary context by using anthropological conventions in the same way as *Lord of the Flies* uses the literary convention of the desert island narrative, and *Rites of Passage* the traditional sea voyage of discovery. 'What Golding does in *The Inheritors* is essentially to fuse Darwin and Genesis.'[1] This text presents its version of the loss of the Edenic not by a full and rich creation of life, but by the opposite strategy: there is a tight funnelling of character, episode, metaphor, and motif. Repetitive pattern – 'the backbone of the novel'[2] – combines with startling techniques of defamiliarization to yield what, for the reader, is the mimetic equivalent of 'delayed comprehension'.[3] Furthermore, an ideographic structure, with its contradictory perspectives, illustrates imaginative truths which are complex, mysterious, even incomplete.

As would be the case with *Pincher Martin*, what we initially experience in reading *The Inheritors* is a severe formalism of structure where the superfluous has been erased. Both novels are rigorously restrictive in mood, tone, and setting. Golding's imagination tends to work away at a single focus – an island, a droning fall – yet it discovers, as its spirit shapes and scrapes and polishes the mystery of that single focus, how that focus has to be translated from coherence to incoherence. Glancing back from the vantage point of all the novels, so many of which have one kind of enigmatic crankiness or another, what becomes apparent is how much *The Inheritors*, like its companion *Pincher Martin*, constructs 'an uncountry', a landscape only remotely connected to the overt world. Indeed, each seems to be a discrete independent universe with laws provided by the author alone and by the verbal resonances of language itself.[4] Looking in *The Inheritors* at the origins of humanity and in *Pincher Martin* at its end, the two texts reveal, in my judgement, important fragments of Golding's mythopoeia, one that he had intended to be relevant to the contemporary context.

In *The Inheritors*, as well as in *Pincher Martin*, an initial narrative pattern is imposed and, by an abrupt conjunction with the coda's other pattern, it is released, reformulated, and in its reinterpretation transcended. We, the readers, build the bridge between the two views, experiencing mimetically two modes of consciousness: thus we are the inheritors of the new conjunction. It is the reader who shares the expanding consciousness of both the character Lok and his opposing double Tuami. It is the reader who sees in the confrontation of the 'prelapsarian' People and the 'post adamite' (Golding's extratextual phrase) New People the inadequacies as well as the strengths of both species of consciousness. It is chiefly through the point of view adopted that the reader constructs this wider view. We come to know both tribes; within the protagonist Lok's mind we gradually lose our innocence, but throughout the loss we experience, almost as an afterimage, the abstractions of guilt of the antagonist Tuami. We knit together the two perspectives, seeing from the inside and the outside simultaneously, until they merge in the wider perspective of what Golding would have called myth. In *The Inheritors* – especially in its objective, bracketed section separating Lok's focalization from that of Tuami, where the reader alone engages in synthetic comprehension – mythic reconciliation involves the integration of such opposites as fire and water, light and dark, forest and plain, inclusion and exclusion, even alienation and unity. The bridge that the ideographic structure directs us to build is between innocence and guilt, love and fear, creation and destruction: making a place for each. The ability to focus opposites in this way is the vision Lok – the clown and storyteller[5] – achieves when he discovers 'like' as an imaginative tool, and which his double, Tuami – the artist and shaman – captures intimations of as he starts to sculpt the death-weapon into a new shape at the story's close. It is also discovered by the reader as we take hold of the complexity of the total experience and understand that the downward path of the innocent and the upward path of the guilty are essentially related.

II

> We know very little of the appearance of the Neanderthal man, but this […] seems to suggest an extreme hairiness, an ugliness, or a repulsive strangeness in his appearance over and above his low forehead, his beetle brows, his ape neck, and his inferior stature […] the dim gorilla-like monsters, with cunning brains, shambling gait, hairy bodies, strong teeth, and possibly cannibalistic tendencies may be the germ of the ogre in folklore.
>
> H.G. Wells, *The Outline of History*

Prefixed to *The Inheritors* – a fact now repeatedly commented upon – is the passage above from Wells' *The Outline of History*. As Golding first remarked to a BBC commentator in 1955 on the publication of his novel, the epigraph was an initial springboard for his own account about the encounter between *Neanderthalis* and what was then thought to be its immediate Cro-Magnon descendant. The anthropological terms, however, are never present in *The Inheritors*; nor is there any encoding of the intertextual reference, as was the case with *The Coral Island* in *Lord of the Flies*. *The Outline* seems to have been one source of information and narrative detail: when the glaciers of early modern Eurasia retreated leaving lakes and rivers, a new type of human appeared on the waters to migrate into the Neanderthal realm, there ultimately to replace its shambling predecessor. The geographical setting of *The Inheritors* as well as the physical characteristics of the two species – with some modifications – would appear to have derived from Wells' account.[6] As in *Lord of the Flies*, Golding intended another ironic rebuff to nineteenth-century smugness and explained to Frank Kermode the ironic inversion at length:

> Wells' *The Outline of History* is the rationalist gospel *in excelsis* […] too neat and too slick. And when I reread it as an adult I came across his picture of Neanderthal man […] as being these gross brutal creatures

who were possibly the basis of the mythological [...] ogre. I thought [...] [w]hat we're doing is externalizing our own inside.[7]

Another novel born of an historical context that included Nazi atrocities, the siege of Leningrad, the bombing of Dresden, Nagasaki, and Hiroshima, the Gulag Purges, and the Japanese invasion of Manchuria, what was being questioned here was easy faith in 'nineteenth-century meliorist interpretations of history and liberal assumptions of progress.'[8] Rejecting Wells' 'furtive optimism'[9] that the 'fact' of evolution presumed a similar ethical evolution, *The Inheritors* suggests instead that the necessary coming of *Homo sapiens* represented a falling away from a state of comparative innocence. Palaeontological and archaeological evidence now indicates that contrary to Wells' hypothesis, *Neanderthalis* may well have had a culture demonstrating some gentleness. Petrified flowers, for example, were discovered in Iraq beside skeletal fragments in a mid twentieth-century excavated Neanderthal grave. Skulls placed in a cup-like position seemed to indicate a libation ritual with a concomitant concern for the individual and life after death. Flutes and other artefacts have been discovered elsewhere, including a polished mammoth tooth, bones and rocks with scratches, as well as a pendant made from reindeer phalange and fox teeth.

In Golding's view, humanity's biological and evolutionary superiority in consciousness was an incalculable asset gained at an enormous price. Guilt and human consciousness – as Frank Kermode and Gabriel Josipovici commented early on in their discussions of *The Inheritors* – go hand in hand, a position some linguistics schools share; two have used Golding's novel to substantiate how developing cognitive and linguistic abilities are connected to intellectual instrumentalism.[10] Added to this is the ethologists' proposal that a critical factor in the enlargement of the human brain was a development of higher-brain inhibitions of lower-brain patterns. This 'development of tameness is the suggested basis upon which co-operative social life can emerge in hunting communities.'[11] Such an inhibiting pattern has been termed guilt. And consciousness' true test is in the ability to lie, as Julian Jaynes observed in his 1976 study, *The Origin of Consciousness in the Breakdown of the Bicameral Mind*. Like others then, Golding saw guilt as the result of technological, linguistic, and intellectual power.

With intertextual allusions as diverse as the King of the Wood in Frazer's *The Golden Bough*, the oak tree in the Scandinavian myth of

Balder,[12] biblical parallels to, and inversions of, *Genesis'* flood and *Revelation's* apocalyptic fire, *Beowulf* [13], and Tennyson's *Idylls of the King*, *The Inheritors* also made use of Wells' semi-documentary adventure story, *The Grisly Folk*, by re-exploring the encounter between the two species of gatherers and hunters. In doing so it reversed the moral values of *The Grisly Folk* in a strategy akin to that of the *Aeneid*, for example, where Virgil recast the Homeric adventure with the Cyclops by deepening the pathos of the one-eyed giant and coarsening Odysseus' craftiness. In Golding's reworking, the moral natures of the two species are exchanged; Wells portrays the Neanderthals as monsters easily conquered by a clever species. Golding's People become a gentle and harmonious tribe unable – for a very long time – to conceive of the New People's violence, rapaciousness, and corruption.

Akin to the range of its own intertextualities, critical views on the novel have been singularly diverse. Noting its 'erratic critical history', one essayist concludes: 'It provides both curiosity and disappointment.'[14] Some have insisted – like B.R. Johnson – that questions, rather than allegorical prescriptions, are pursued: 'Golding's novels are much more than *tour de force* renderings of unusual points of view, certainly much more than dramatized portraits of dualism.'[15] Point of view techniques have been the major focus of discussion over the years, some charging obscurantism for its own sake.[16] Others, however, have argued that 'The novel is extraordinary in many ways, but the point of view and the effects that it and its stylistic consequences have on the reader are especially noteworthy.'[17] Interestingly, stylistic and linguistic scholars came to work with the technical patterns of grammar in the text.[18] By way of close analysis, they have demonstrated how the specific use of 'concept metaphors', 'syntactic structure',[19] 'underlexicalization [the use of restricted vocabulary]',[20] 'transitivity' (where inanimate objects are the subjects of transitive verbs), and limited, causative 'agency'[21] create the world-view of an essentially passive, animistic Neanderthal.

Early criticism, in contrast, tended to see the novel as fairly exciting prehistory, as pseudo science fiction or as bad anthropology. No doubt the several anthropologists with whom I have had conversations over the years would find fault with one conclusion that the novel is 'a complete picture of the Neanderthal's life on earth'.[22] Reluctantly, anthropologists have dismissed the book because modern palaeon-tology does not support Golding's picture of Neanderthal man's relation to Cro-Magnon man. Evidently, there is no evidence that the second species exterminated the first, it being more likely that *Neanderthalis* was over-evolved and over-specialized for the peculiar conditions of the late Pleistocene. Beside such criticisms, one must put Golding's 1970 comment to *Talk* that he had then read everything there was to read on Neanderthal man; contradictions which have since emerged may well be the result of new evidence, new conjecture.

Certainly, the first and final preoccupation of *The Inheritors* was with the nature of evolution. In this sense, it shares the wide mythic sweep of *The Spire* and *The Double Tongue*. Each explores not simply the loss of one way of life, the fall of one kind of perception, but the loss-and-gain, the fall-and-rise as one form of culture takes over from another, willy-nilly, despite itself and just because that is the nature of the cosmos: to change. This is not to say that Golding was restating the smug myth of progress; neither was he endorsing the rival myth of unregenerate evil. Somewhere, in the ideal world of the imagination – that golden land Golding called myth – the whole truth of the two partial views would be accessible and discoverable. What resides then in *The Inheritors*, *The Spire*, and *The Double Tongue* is not in competition with historical or scientific truths; each novel derives from them and is supplementary to them. To this end, it seems to me unimportant that *The Inheritors*' picture of Neanderthal and Cro-Magnon may be technically inaccurate. It does matter that the work gives a translucent image of that possible time.

The novel itself exhibits what I have described as an ideographic structure; it is built in two unequal sections: Chapters One to Ten and Eleven to Twelve. Like *Darkness Visible*, however, it has a third section that brackets parts I and II, a slim corridor that functions much in the way the baleful 'Time Passes' section of Woolf's *To the Lighthouse* links the first and third blocks of that novel. *The Inheritors*' first part makes up most of the novel's action while the slighter final coda section is, in part, a meditation upon the preceding drama. In the first part, events are viewed from the limited perspective of the Neanderthal Lok's mind, a mind that, at first, cannot reason beyond sense data. We participate as readers in a world in which ideas and communications are a series of images, not a function of speech and causality. Thus, *The Inheritors* differs dramatically from *Lord of the Flies*, where the island is viewed at first through the comparatively broad scope of Ralph's reasoning mind, and then seen from a more and more restricted angle as the 'curtain' of memory drops and Ralph fumbles for reason. In *The*

Inheritors understanding expands rather than shrinks: gradually and simultaneously with the protagonist the reader is made aware of New People occupying the People's territory. In fact, narrative interest derives solely from this gradual intrusion. There is a scent, then an obscurely familiar sound which Lok cannot place, 'from the foot of the fall, a noise that the thunder robbed of echo and resonance' (p. 43), then a horrifying shape moves up a tree, and finally white-boned figures with tufted heads appear. In these figures we gradually recognize ourselves.

Towards the conclusion of Chapter Ten, a shift occurs from Neanderthal Lok's point of view to that of Cro-Magnon Tuami. This remarkable transition is brought about by tonal alterations as the style modulates into the rhetoric of the scientific and the objective. Third person singular is abandoned at exactly the moment when Fa, the last Oa-priestess, drops over the fall, caught in a dead tree. The authorial voice[23] seems to retreat away from the person of Lok, who becomes, in the distance, simply an impersonal creature. 'The red creature stood on the edge of the terrace and did nothing [...] Water was cascading down the rocks beyond the terrace from the melting ice in the mountains [...] It was a strange creature, smallish, and bowed. The legs and thighs were bent and there was a whole thatch of curls on the outside of the legs and the arms' (pp. 216–19). It is the first time we have seen Lok as an animal; the description recalls – indeed, repositions – Wells' epigraph. But divesting Lok of his humanity paradoxically deepens his pathos. 'He' becomes 'it', a tiny bent creature, loping aimlessly, its nose lowered and searching, its forepaw digging from some ashes a worn, contoured root and a small white bone. We readers know, without authorial intervention or the mediation of third person point of view, that this creature has connected root to bone and arrived at a knowledge that we have already acquired. And Lok becomes a tiny bent creature overwhelmed by the immensity of loss and the immensity of gloom, cold moonlight, and the long curved fall of water that heralds the Ice Age's end and the end of his species. Understatement is superbly used in the whole transition section and is coupled with extraordinary visual stillness and linguistic precision; one passage, for example, describes the physical business of weeping, but not by denoting that the red creature is crying. The reader becomes simply the observer of a natural occurrence – until the point in the rhythmic repetition where the reader imparts meaning, and thus grief, to the action:

The lights increased, acquired definition, brightened, lay each sparkling at the lower edge of a cavern. Suddenly, noiselessly, the lights became thin crescents, went out, and streaks glistened on each cheek. The lights appeared again, caught among the silvered curls of the beard. They hung, elongated, dropped from curl to curl [...] one drop detached itself and fell in a silver flash, striking a withered leaf with a sharp pat (p. 220).

The passage is characteristic of the best of Golding's style – one thinks of the poetic description of Simon in death here – where things assume anthropomorphic properties, while that to which one normally imparts humanity is figured in non-human naturalized terms. As I will argue, *Pincher Martin* makes especially successful use of this technique of defamiliarization.

In *The Inheritors'* final chapter a coda brings about a dramatic reversal. James Gindin, once again the devil's advocate in these matters, thought the reversal broke the fable's unity without adding a relevant perspective.[24] But quite the contrary is the case; the reversal is vital both to the dramatic outcome of the narrative and to the larger mythopoeia that *The Inheritors* constructs. Suddenly we are placed in the pragmatic minds of the New People, the opposing Cro-Magnon tribe, and the tone shifts from the People's emotive lyricism to nautical gruffness: 'A fair wind, steerage-way, and plenty of water all round – what more could a man want [...] Forrard there under the sail was what looked like lower land, plains perhaps where men could hunt in the open, not stumble among dark trees or on hard [...] rocks' (p. 224), Tuami mutters to himself as he broods on the 'devils' that have hindered the passage of his people from island and fall to the lake's upper regions. The subtle effect is to make us now revise our unsympathetic assumption about the wholly malevolent nature of the New People and, by an act of imaginative extension, to understand their part in the week's furore.

III

I'd say I'm passionately interested in *description*, the exact description of a phenomenon. When I know what a wave looks like or a flame or a tree, I hug that to me or carry the thought agreeably as a man might carry a flower round with him.

Golding, Personal Letter

Onyx marsh water, hard haunted rock, the shock head of a dead tree, a droning fall, the murmuring of wood pigeons, the prolonged harsh bellow of a rutting stag, the sea white bitter smell of salt: the world of *The Inheritors* is anchored, like its restoration to vital meaning of the emptied metaphor of the *fall* of man, in the substantial world. Its inception resulted, Golding told me once, from a vision of such a fact: 'When I discovered Lok running in I was able to introduce the rest of the characters and the thing wrote itself – in a month.' The novel begins and ends in utterly solid surfaces and sensuous shapes, smells, sounds, and sights. Partly because it is so delimited, its landscape – the physical patch of land itself with a beech tree, an overhang, a terrace, logs, two paths, sheer cliffs from a terrace, an island, a river, and two falls – becomes intimately known. The reader seems to lie with the character Lok against the face of real things, confusedly caught in these things, stationary with these things:

> By his face there had grown a twig: a twig that smelt of other, and of goose, and of the bitter berries that Lok's stomach told him he must not eat. The twig had a white bone at the end. There were hooks in the bone and sticky brown stuff hung in the crooks. His nose examined this stuff and did not like it. He smelled along the shaft of the twig. The leaves on the twig were red feathers and reminded him of goose. He was lost in generalized astonishment and excitement (p. 106).

Though the point of view here is technically omniscient, sustaining for three-quarters of the tale primitivistic, anthropomorphic descriptions and perspective, the formal mode constitutes something very different, a technical feat that has been hailed as wholly original. For we see most events, the activities of *Homo sapiens*, over the shoulder of a pre-rational mind. In *Lord of the Flies*, *Pincher Martin*, *The Spire*, *Free Fall*, even *The Paper Men* we enter rational minds which gradually grow obscured and irrational – there to be upset by the coda's reversal; here the reader shares Lok's perspective, inhabiting a creature whose sensory equipment perceives but does not understand. In the other works, the protagonists 'understand', as it were, but they do not 'perceive'; this is especially true of *The Spire*, where Jocelin must learn, with a new clarity of eye: 'What's this called? And this?' (p. 147). But in *The Inheritors* there is an interesting variation, for '[p]erception is itself, no more; not what we normally expect it to be, a stepping stone to an idea rapidly transferred from the eye to the mind.'[25]

In the extended passage above, everything – the part by part shape of what *we* deduce to be an arrow sunk in the tree beside Lok's face – is rendered through physical sensations, about which he is wholly unconscious. As he is bombarded by arrows, smells, associating in his first fall the smell from the island with the fire that the People's old woman carries, Lok attends scrupulously to the concrete. He can no more abstract from a twig to an arrow than impart hostility to the New People shooting an arrow at him: 'Suddenly Lok understood that the man was holding the stick out to him but neither he nor Lok could reach across the river. He would have laughed if it were not for the echo of screaming in his head' (p. 106). Lok's senses merely report a series of inexplicable events: at the novel's opening an ominously missing log, the old woman's bundle of fire that mysteriously moves to the island yet remains, as he discovers when he falls at the terrace, in her hands beside him, a smell without a 'picture' which brings him 'blank amazement' (p. 62). Lok's senses convey a dislocation of self that not only tears him from the People but also fragments him between an inside-Lok with a 'tidal feeling' and an outside-Lok that grows tight fear like another skin, then finally, gruesomely, a New People with bone faces, log bodies, bird-fluttering language, who 'walked upright [...] as though something that Lok could not see were supporting them, holding up their heads, thrusting them slowly and irresistibly forward' (p. 144).

The plot, a dramatic account of the extermination of one species by another, is simple. We follow the migration of a small band of People from their winter quarters by the sea to their summer quarters in coastal forests at the edge of a river, an island with two waterfalls. For a long time – if we choose to construct meaning by way of the epigraph from Wells – *The Outline* offers the only clue to the story's actors. The band of eight (Lok, Fa, Ha, Nil, the old woman, Mal, Liku, and the new one) is the only Neanderthal group to have survived a Great Fire, biblical in its rapaciousness. Coming to a marshy stretch of water, they discover a log-bridge is missing – an ominous fact since in the past it has always been there and should remain. 'Today is like yesterday and tomorrow' (p. 46), they console themselves. But this faith is to be bitterly shattered. The leader of the band, Mal, the old man with all the memories of sweeter times, falls into the dreaded water. The tribe tortuously climbs up a cliff, forced to make a new passage to their ancient overhang. They set about finding food, but it gradually becomes clear that for some inexplicable reason Mal has miscalculated the seasons, and they have arrived at their summer quarters too early. Then Ha falls victim to some unknown calamity – in swift succession Mal dies of overexposure, Nil and the old woman are killed, perhaps by some creature, the two children, Liku and the new one, are kidnapped. Only Lok and Fa remain, frantically trying to rescue the children, whose kidnapping Fa gradually comes to understand; indeed, she devises a plan to exchange hostages, the new one for the New People's Tanakil.

The narrative has by now turned to the activities of the New People, the starving tribe having been gradually introduced: the artist Tuami; the four braves, Pine-tree, Chestnut-head, Bush, and Tuft; Twal and her daughter, Tanakil; the magician Marlan; and the beautiful Vivani. The last couple have their literary origin in Tennyson's *Idylls*, which is inventively adapted. Marlan, the witchdoctor of the totemic cult of the stag, recalls the twelfth-century Arthurian enchanter Merlin.[26] *The Inheritors'* enchanter is forced to make a perilous journey to a devil-infested forest, Tuami tells us at the end, because he is fleeing the wrath of another tribe from whom he kidnapped Vivani. Like the wily Vivien in the *Idylls*, who wins magic from the ageing enchanter Merlin and uses the charm to leave him spell-bound in a tangled tree, Vivani accompanies Marlan to the island. Against his better judgement – for by now Marlan is losing credence among the starved tribe – he is beguiled by Vivani into capturing two forest devils: Liku and the new one. Recasting Tennyson's Merlin in the tangled tree, Golding places a now smaller and much weaker Marlan at *The Inheritors'* close in the hollow hull of an *oak* canoe.

But before Tuami's meditation on his tribe's flight, we watch through Lok's eyes, from the summit of the dead tree, the mysterious gestures of this tribe, their mimetic rituals, their rapacious orgies, their terrified brutal efforts to escape from some unknown danger. A last crucial episode occurs; the New People are confusedly trying to accomplish the portage of their canoes past the waterfall: 'There was an hysterical speed in the efforts of Tuami and in the screaming voice of the old man. They were retreating up the slope as though cats with their evil teeth were after them,' as though 'the river itself were flowing uphill' (p. 209). (A variation of this paradoxical oxymoron of falling upward closes *The Spire*, when Jocelin glimpses the tower he has had constructed as an 'upward waterfall'.)

Lok and Fa make one last desperate effort to rescue the children, Fa distracting attention so that Lok can rush for the new one. In contrast to the inventive New People with their canoes, paddles, arrows, knives, sails, levers, and rollers, the People seem simple. However, they too come to have skills, and the appearance of these marks how duress breeds change. Gender reversal is the first and most notable mutation, with Fa leading (yesterday is *not* like today and tomorrow). Developing a logical capacity, Fa (not Lok) invents transport, leverage, agriculture, and retaliation, the building of bridges and hostage exchange. The rescue attempt fails, however. Several of the New People fall over the fall while Tuami draws a savage totemic figure, which is seen by Lok as: 'some kind of man. Its arms and legs were contracted [...] There was hair standing out on all sides of the head as the hair of the old man had stood out when he was enraged or frightened' (p. 215). Bewildered Lok may be, but we readers deduce the totemic demonology here being enacted: the drawing is the totemic image of the Neanderthals as *Homo sapiens* sees them. Lok does not recognize himself in the fierce red figure; it is merely 'some kind of man'. In a later passage, the novel's real ogre is portrayed. With the point of view having switched to that of the New People, Tuami stares fixedly at Marlan, who lies sprawled 'asleep in the canoe. The sun was blazing on the red sail and Marlan was red. His arms and legs were contracted, his hair stood out and his beard, his teeth were wolf's teeth and his eyes like blind stones' (p. 229). The red figure here is the mirror image of the totemic beast Tuami had drawn: a doubling strategy intended to prod the reader into making connections. When Tuami attributed devilish qualities to the Neanderthals he is really, like the boys' creation of the 'beast' in *Lord of the Flies*, commenting on his own evasion.

A confused scuffle ensues – in part because Lok ignores Fa's instructions and keeps on asking where his daughter Liku is – whereupon Fa is chased to a log. The log spills over the cascading waters of the fall and she is carried, as the other People were, to her death by water. The objective transition is placed at just this point. From a great distance we watch a red creature, imparting to it the dumb pain we know Lok is suffering as he scurries back and forth looking for Liku, discovering a bone with a scent he knows intimately. Finally he unearths her Oa-doll and, with these two talismans, folds himself into a foetal position at the ancient grave in the overhang. At the novel's close one solitary canoe is seen carrying the tormented New People towards some new camp. Tuami broods on the change and his bedevilled irrational grief 'as though the portage of the boats [...] from the forest to the top of the fall had taken them all onto a new level not only of land but of experience and emotions' (p. 225). As he studies the tribe before him, their history is swiftly reviewed. They too have been overcome by water; Tuami thinks: 'I am like a pool […] some tide has filled me, the sand is swirling, the waters are obscured and strange' (p. 227). And *The Inheritors* ends with Tuami staring out at an ambiguous 'line of darkness' (p. 233).[27]

IV

Some of [my memory from childhood] is quite extraordinarily early. Some is approaching the threshold of average reductive awareness. I am not agreeing that we come trailing clouds of glory […] I would claim rather that raw sense impressions in early childhood which have no assumptions or custom smeared over them can be blinding. It is as if there were a sun everywhere.

Golding, 'Scenes from a Life'

To achieve in *The Inheritors* the linguistic counterpart of what Golding describes above as the earliest sense impressions of childhood, formulations or deductions of events are deliberately limited by means of Lok's focalization and the omniscient authorial voice. Familiar inanimate things are defamiliarized, anthropomorphized, animated. The cliff leans out 'looking for its own feet in the water'; the island 'rearing' against the fall is a 'seated giant' whose 'thigh that should have supported a body like a mountain lay in the sliding water of the gap'; the river 'sleeps' and 'fell over on both sides of the island' (p. 23). The reader becomes, through these kinds of animated agents, immersed in reality, with the trick of abstraction blanked out.

The first four chapters, where we follow the People in their movement upstream from their winter quarters to their summer quarters in the overhang directly adjacent to the fall, are static, propelled not by action but through description, a mode fundamental to the growth of the narrative. From what is encountered, indeed discovered, by the reader in these chapters – the tree by the clearing where Lok swings Liku, the ice cavern beyond the waterfall where 'the drone of the fall diminished to a sigh' (p. 81), the fall itself with logs slowly descending – physical phenomena assume a dramatic, then a symbolic, role as the tale proceeds. They are at first points in the actual narrative scene which, by introduction and reintroduction, begin to assume a symbolic import, much as I argued the island and the head do in *Lord of the Flies*. Furthermore, they absorb verbal echoes as they grow out of the fabric of each event. The use of trees is an example of this: not only do falling trees, falling over the fall, result – at each point – in disaster, the New People are made to resemble, in the People's view, their awful nature. Lok thinks that they are trees and calls one Chestnut-head and another Pine-tree. Of course, humans can in no way be identified with trees. If, however, they share the food of the Dead Tree, send the old woman over the fall like a log, or utilize trees to get beyond what for them is the terror of the dark forest and the ringing fall, then they can be said to participate in the nature of the Fallen Tree.

Basically, our sense of the People – their code of ethics, their solicitous community, their common emotions, their deep reverence for, and awe of, life – is a matter of accumulated physical sensation. Moreover, the nature of the narrative's first movement becomes our mimetic immersion in their substantial world and through it, in a very real sense unique to this novel, we may be said to enact the return of the characters with them. An ingenious and integral unit in this context is 'the picture', for it allows the text to move away from the immediate and constant present and Lok's point of view. The People communicate by 'sharing pictures' or imagining simultaneously images of events. Through these pictures, the reader has access to the People's past and tradition. Mal has a memory, what he calls a 'picture' of a time of perpetual summer 'and the flowers and fruit hung on the same branch' (p. 35), their Edenic myth that was destroyed by a 'Great Fire', a nightmare of which begins to recur in Lok's mind when he hears the droning of the fall and its hated water. Lok's only picture, 'a picture of finding the little Oa' (p. 33), introduces the People's female-centred religion, a concept of the numinous, the power dwelling in the caverns of the glacier – the loins of the ice woman – and in the blackened woman-shaped root cuddled by the child Liku:

> There was the great Oa. She brought forth the earth from her belly. She gave suck. The earth brought forth woman and the woman brought forth the first man out of her belly (p. 35).

Likewise we learn of the old woman's dreadful but unfearful sanctity. Oa's earthly representative, she carries the fire, breathing into the clay like her Greek counterpart, and 'awakening' the flame – the ruddy sunset and those points of fire-love in the People's eyes. To Lok, her own eyes are those of the visionary; she wraps things in understanding, compassion, and remote stillness. 'He remembered the old woman, so close to Oa, knowing so indescribably much, the door-keeper to whom all secrets were open. He felt awed and happy and witless again' (p. 61).

Together the People share emotions, perhaps even sexual partners; they either share a picture spontaneously or exert themselves to get another to share a picture. This becomes the major device for Lok's characterization, and it is a mark of the tragedy that Lok – the witless clown – as the last surviving adult male has many words but few pictures, whereas Fa develops what hitherto only men were thought to possess. However, words – and this is central to the book's exploration of our linguistic inheritance – are indefinite; some members occasionally emit them more or less at random to express excitement, joy or terror. But before the old woman's hearth, they sink into a kind of undifferentiated darkness, a communal whole without speech, without identity, without thought. This slow bonding is wonderfully visualized in both microcosmic and macrocosmic terms. As the flame wavers, nursed by a creature of 'mixed fire and moonlight' (p. 72), their skins grow ruddy and 'the deep caverns beneath their brows' are inhabited 'by replicas of the fire and all their fires danced together' (p. 33).[28]

The 'pictures are visualizations not conceptualizations, telepathic snapshots not of an idea but of an entire event.'[29] Significance mysteriously resides in them inasmuch as they represent some rounded aspect of a whole truth, unfragmented and unabstracted, like the raw childhood impression Golding explores autobiographically in 'Scenes from a Life' and which, at the opening of his last fiction, *The Double Tongue*, he gives to that novel's protagonist: 'No words, no time, not even I, ego, since [...] the warmth and blazing light was experience itself' (p. 3). For Lok even a smell is accompanied by a picture, 'a sort of living but qualified presence' (p. 74); alternatively he can, at great expense of energy, evolve a new picture 'not by reasoned deduction but because in every place the scent told him – do this!' (p. 77). Such intuition amounts to a comprehensive understanding of a new – that is unexperienced – phenomenon. Unlike deduction from a thing to its essential nature, this mode of consciousness makes the knower, in knowing, become that which is known, as one observes when Lok follows the New People's scent:

[T]he scent turned Lok into the thing that had gone before him. He was beginning to know the other without understanding how it was that he knew. Lok-other crouched at the lip of the cliff and stared across the rocks of the mountain [...] He threw himself into the shadow of a rock, snarling and waiting (p. 77).[30]

Technically the 'picture' is a fine instrument for revealing the People's incapacity for abstract thought, thus distinguishing them from the more linguistically advanced species. But most importantly the 'picture' renders, as no other device could, the life of the senses and instinct, since the impression the reader receives of the outside world is of a series of still images. Thus we are confused and frightened in a way which we cannot analytically grasp. For example, fearsome suspense and tension are built into the description of the New People's last activity on the terrace as they try to escape, precisely because − although there is intense and concentrated action − it is seen by Lok as a series of stills, each devoid of motion like moments caught in past time. They appear to be random events without the causality of one action leading to another: 'The fat woman was screaming [...] The old man was running [...] Chestnut-head was coming from where Lok was' (p. 210). Each short sentence, by way of excised agency, conveys the impression of arrested speed. Yet each operates like the beginning of a tale − an action caught immediately and seemingly frozen in time present; in fact, the sentences recall the beginning of *The Inheritors* itself: 'Lok was running as fast as he could' (p. 11). One action is apart from another; each is finishing and static; none is connected to another, nor even by the simple connective 'and'. Consequently, there is nothing Lok can imagine to do to either connect the actions together or stop them. Tanakil is dropped by Lok. Chestnut-head is traveling through the air, 'fitting the delicate curve of descent' (p. 211) over the fall. Marlan is flinging an arrow. Fa is jumping at the gully. A canoe is falling and splitting in two.

Of course, the actions are all too rigorously connected but, lacking the rational point of view that makes a pattern of seemingly random events, they impress the reader as individual assaults. As Lok and Fa slowly begin to formulate − and, as I shall argue, this is most wonderfully done during the episode of the ritual stag dance − *The Inheritors* can depict, by making the reader bring into focus the foregrounded meaning of the story, the nature of innocence and of the fall from innocence. We not only experience a consciousness that late twentieth-century Western individuals have lost, where instinct, intuition, and pictorialization once predominated, we also participate in that loss. When Lok, the man with few pictures, discovers like, similitude arrives and simultaneously metaphor empties. Piteous Lok must come to apprehend what has happened to Liku.

As with *Darkness Visible* and *Rites of Passage*, *The Inheritors'* effort is to implicate its readers in the experience of, and responsibility for, a loss of innocence. Its ideographic structure forces us to know that the innocence changed (and so lost) is our own, just as in *Pincher Martin* we will come to know the Purgatorial state. We proceed within the innocent's consciousness as it is forced to change until the penultimate chapter, where, in the narrative corridor of clean objectified authority, erasure of agency reduces Lok to an 'it', after which we enter the New People's mind. Such a movement brings pain. The knot binding the People together 'by a thousand invisible strings' (p. 104) has been supplanted by the 'strips of skin' (p. 208) tying the groaning men to their log/canoes and by the 'long piece of skin' (p. 159) which lashes Liku to Tanakil. In the fragmentation of what is described as 'inside-Lok' and 'outside-Lok', which intensifies his alienation from himself and Fa, we readers are meant to be provoked into considering contemporary dissociated, pluralized identities. This, of course, is the nature of change, as imagined in this fiction at least: once upon a time, Cro-Magnon's gain in intellectual grasp and apprehensive imagination involved the loss of Neaderthal's intuitive, if disconnected apprehension.

An ironic evolution then from People to New People, from a kind of pre-lapsarian to a post-adamite, from a primitive to a contemporary mentality: this is one shape in *The Inheritors*. The readers' comprehension is forced to emerge from Lok's mind to that of Tuami's, thereby arriving with the Neanderthal People at 'the place of the fall', from which we leave with *Homo sapiens*. Biological evolution would seem to be moral devolution, as ironic a turning as the Wells epigraph or the biblical beatitude referred to in the novel's title that 'the meek shall inherit the earth'. The New People's departure from the islanded forests is a final rupture with innocence. Is then the light of dawn that touches the sailors as they depart, like the new spring and new age that the melting ice hail, essentially bleak?

V

> But I quite agree that the parallelism between intelligence and evil does
> come out in my books because it is our…particular sin – to explain away
> our own shortcomings rather than remedy them.
>
> Golding to Tiger, Personal Communication

A new kind of darkness shadows the world; as the passage above
suggests, with manipulative intelligence comes the capacity for each of
us to avoid our essential nature or what lies in each of our 'darknesses'.
For example, see how the two species are contrasted in *The Inheritors*:
'Lok felt himself secure in the darkness' (p. 185), while the new
creatures are terrified of and by it. The point is fundamental, I think, to
Golding's moral diagnosis: individuals abstract from their own
shortcomings and project them as a fear of something Other, which
will haunt or destroy. In *The Inheritors*, the mythopoeia is often
developed imagistically, thus implicitly – certainly never as explicitly as
in *Lord of the Flies*. As Vivani stands fearfully, stroking the new one, the
others attempt to alleviate their own fear by stoking the fire, which is
already excessive; they all face '*outward* at the darkness of the forest' (p.
185, my italics). But their Promethean fire itself metamorphoses
darkness, making the island so impenetrably dark that the night-sight
of Lok and Fa is temporarily lost. In Lok's mind the fire and the fall
become associated so that the clearing below the tree is beaten with 'a
fountain of flame' (p. 171), not warm light but 'fierce, white-red and
blinding' (p. 171). The firelight – by extension intellectual consciousness
– intensifies the darkness, conjuring devils who 'live in darkness under
the trees' (p. 233) and then tries to destroy the fantasies thereby created.
Yet this fear of 'tree darkness' is a force that drives forward, the very
basis of the New Men's strength, as Lok understands when he knows
'the impervious power of the people in the light' (p. 185).

From a stasis of calm description at the novel's opening to the frantic
and confused dramatic action at the close, the reader comes gradually to
experience imaginatively the loss of innocence and the genesis of guilt.
First, Lok's incomprehension is our incomprehension; then Tuami's
doubt is our doubt. The book's central confrontation, where Lok sees a
'thing' in the water, dramatizes the sudden conjunction of this
innocence and its perfect opposite: consciousness. Reading the moment,
in a sense, we actively participate in the emergence of the mythological

ogre in the primitive mind, a mind emerging into consciousness.

Hanging from what will be the tree of knowledge, having already learned a new knowledge from it, Lok leans out over the dreaded water, trying to reach towards the island and the kidnapped Liku. He strains and balances, noticing that the water under him darkens as he stretches forward. Just as he hears the waterfall, the branches begin to bend under him. Gibbering in fright, he sinks and a 'Lok-face' (p. 107) comes up at him as the water appears to rise. It is the moment when the unknown, something dark and autonomous, confronts Lok's mind. The entire episode is projected through a defamiliarizing technique whereby we are locked in the primitive mind and hence without the interpretation that attends a similar scene in *Lord of the Flies*, where Simon confronts the head of the pig. Pictures, even fear, disappear, yet Lok cannot connect the Lok-face with himself; it is simply some dark spectre released from his mind and now compulsively, independently, capable of harming him. Lok sees something foreign which we know is also himself, but to him it is a threatening image of 'teeth grinning in the water' (p. 108). It gradually fuses with a new terror, the result of the waterfall and its implicit Fall:

The weed-tail was shortening [...] There was a darkness that was consuming the other end. The darkness became a thing of complex shape, of sluggish and dreamlike movement. Like the specks of dirt, it turned over but not aimlessly [...] The arms moved a little and the eyes shone as dully as the stones. They revolved with the body, gazing at the surface, at the width of deep water and the hidden bottom with no trace of life or speculation. A skein of weed drew across the face and the eyes did not blink. The body turned with the same smooth and heavy motion as the river itself until its back was towards him rising along the weed-tail. The head turned towards him with dreamlike slowness, rose in the water, came towards his face (p. 108–09).

It is the old woman Lok sees drifting towards him, like one of the logs that keeps falling off the fall. The body is a nighmarish thing in dark water, and its once knowing eyes are scraped and affronted by the weed-tails. The eyes that sweep across his face 'looked through him without seeing him, rolled away and were gone'; the eyes that once saw into the mystery of things no longer have any power in the technological world *Homo sapiens* has created and used against her.

Innocence, which before had been characterized by wholeness, becomes aware of deep water within itself, some part of the self inescapably fragmented from itself and uncontrollable. The encounter then results in a psychic fragmentation not unlike similar confrontation scenes in *Lord of the Flies*, *Free Fall*, and *The Paper Men*, which, however, bring about psychic unification.

While there are similarities between this and other confrontation scenes, here the episode reverberates, for the reader, with a kind of energy and terror that cannot be clearly explained in rational terms. For something horrendous happens in Lok – and us – as well as to him. It is as though 'a formless thing disengages itself from the depths of the mind, becomes a dark specter, rises with dreadful slowness [...] reveals sudden intimations of terror; hides them. Then slowly, relentlessly, it turns towards us in the full horror of its face.'[31] Certainly we respond primarily to the rhythm of nightmare: the same disturbing motion was used to describe the bowing corpse and the bouncing head in *Lord of the Flies*. In *Pincher Martin* there is a toy doll, a 'Cartesian Diver', whose motion is similar. In *The Spire*, Jocelin atop the spire waves left and right with the same dreadful slowness as does the blasted ship in the Antarctic ice in *Fire Down Below*.

The entire episode seems a radically compressed summation of *The Inheritors*' thematics since it connects the two psychic conditions of innocence and guilt and shows how the latter emerges from the former, as indeed Cro-Magnon emerged from Neanderthal – at least, in Golding's and Wells' representations. But its resonances function at a level not analytically obvious. Certain motifs, simple physical phenomena, inhabit the scene: 'wetness down there, mysterious and pierced everywhere by the dark and bending stems' (p. 107), the pillars of spray from the fall, the rising water – Lok's weight pulls the tree to the water but his experience is that the water comes to him – the fluttering weed-tails that regularly emerge, the stuff rising towards the surface, turning over and over, floating in circles as his own teeth grin in the water. 'He experienced Lok, upside down over deep water with a twig to save him' (p. 108). But each of these motifs operates with a kind of total recall because it has been prefigured in the narrative texture and will later be reiterated. Actual phenomena – river, tree, water, weed – are invested and charged with an energy that operates at a synaesthetic and symbolic level although they still maintain physical credibility.

Lok's incomprehension becomes finally our comprehension. If, like the presentation of the Pharaoh in the short story 'The Scorpion God', Colley in *Rites of Passage*, and Wheeler in *Close Quarters*, the presentation of the New People is indirect, then that indirection is dehumanizing. We see them less ambiguously as the tale proceeds until finally we are ripped away from the People's perspective in the coda. We look at inexplicable events from the inside and the outside. The reader, as I have been arguing, is expected to deduce significance and so connect details into meaningful constructs that the witless Lok is incapable of formulating. Thus as Lok and Fa stare incredulously, we deduce, in what is perhaps the most obscure chapter of the book, the magic-religion of the New People, the totem religion of the stag. We begin to appreciate that, although we discover the rituals of the totemic stag cult, in particular the sacrifice of a brave's finger to that magic, from the vantage point of 'tree-bound innocence' by way of the passive uncorrupt sense of Lok, our proper station is below. Our corrupt consciousness' place is at the Dead Tree's base. The entire episode, with the fall droning in Lok's ears, the wood pigeons pecking, the light of the fire blinding, the water shivering, has an imaginative power characteristic of the best in Golding's fiction. At the very basic level there is a simple wonder in the concrete, since it is Lok's screen-rendering of sensuality: Vivani 'lifted her arms to the back of her head, bowed, and began to work at the pattern in her hair. All at once the petals fell in black snakes that hung over her shoulders and breasts. She shook her head like a horse and the snakes flew back till they could see her breasts again' (p. 154). Then, in turn, we can discover ourselves below and understand both the sour-smelling 'wobbling animal' and the complicated and engrossing pleasure 'hunted down' by the Bacchanals. Using our corrupt consciousness, we even guess the most shocking event in the book: Lok will smell Liku all around the abandoned campfire because she has been killed and eaten.

Golding – surely, ingenuously – described the putting to sleep of Lok just at this juncture of the narrative as an example of his ability to make the best he could out of the limitations of the fabulist's art. It is, of course, no fabulist's gimmick, but rather a stellar example of what became a characteristic strategy of delayed disclosure. For, inasmuch as we guess from Fa's 'dead eyes' what has occurred, we in a sense share in the acts of murder and cannibalism by discovering the acts. The point is fundamental to Golding's moral critique: knowledge implicates us. The guilty may make a darkness, some blank fear or some totem of fear, but knowledge is recognition and it brings with it the necessity to acknowledge 'the beast' in our own natures. The problem that *The Inheritors*, *Lord of the Flies*, *The Spire*, and *Darkness Visible* raise is the contemporary gap between such knowledge and it being put into action, the whole ethos of a creature who transforms the darkness of the unknown into a threatening ogre or devil or enemy.

VI

What nonsense to say that man is reduced to insignificance before the galaxies. The stars are a common brightness in every eye. What 'out there' have you that does not correspond to an 'in here'? The mind of man is the biggest thing in the universe, it is throughout the universe... We are a foolish and ignorant race and have got ourselves tied up in a tape measure.

Golding, 'All or Nothing'

With the exception of *The Pyramid* and *Rites of Passage*, *The Inheritors* was the novel that Golding would reread: it was his 'favourite' and 'my finest'. For me, the curious history of its invention brings once again into radical question the received notion of Golding as an allegorist writing only from moral hypotheses that determine the shape of the fiction. For *The Inheritors* is no allegorical fable, a mode he regarded as being 'an invented thing on the surface'. Rather he intended it to approach the fictional equivalent of myth, 'something which comes out from the roots of things in the ancient sense of being the key to existence, the whole meaning of life, and experience as a whole.' The first draft of *The Inheritors* differed significantly from the published novel. It contained no last chapter, concluding at what is now the objective transition, and had very little exploration of the divided consciousness. Most significantly, it had no waterfall. Like *Lord of the Flies* it started as a simple argument with the smug-nineteenth century doctrine of progress and proceeded to imagine, through the tragedy of the People alone, the erasure of the mythological monster. After finishing the first draft, Golding made an inspired discovery; he began to see what the tale was really about and started again from scratch. Within a month he had completed the present and final version.

Two different, but metaphorically associated, strains brought about the re-conception and rewriting. First he found himself considering how the second law of thermodynamics – which claims that when change, such as the transfer of heat energy, occurs in a physical body the succession of changes results in the return of a substance to its original condition – had a peculiar inverted relevance to the psychological climate of the mid twentieth century, at least as he experienced it. Secondly he brooded on the law's great example: water, the energy of which moves from a state of high organization to a state of low organization. Concomitant with this was the certainty – as he once said to me – that humans are 'the local contradiction of this rule'; in them, 'the cosmos is organizing energy back to sunlight level.'

In a later essay, exploring the fact that Yeats' last poems burned through with a majestic ferocity, Golding was to use the same analogy from physics:

> The Satan of our cosmology is the Second Law of Thermodynamics, which implies that everything is running down and will finally stop like an unwound clock. Life is in some sense a local contradiction of this law [...] we should be cheered when life refuses to submit to a general levelling down of energy and simply winds itself up again.[32]

Such commingling of data from physics, anthropology, or archaeology with the insights of the poet's craft would come to typify Golding's method. In *The Pyramid*, chemistry jostles with music for the attention of Oliver, and we see the autobiographical boy in 'The Ladder and the Tree' caught between the solicitude of a scientific father and the lures of mediaeval romances. In the sea trilogy, the battle between the two lieutenants, cautious Charles Summers and innovative Mr Benét, over the best method for mending the damaged mast restates the relationship, while in the posthumous *The Double Tongue* there is the non-acrimonious contest between the Pythia, Arieka, and the temple's priest, Ionides. As *The Inheritors* was germinating, the recasting of the scientific law gradually became linked to another general precept: one informing Heraclitus' philosophical dictum that multiplicity and unity, the existence of opposites in eternal flux, depends on the balancing of the motion of 'the way downwards', while harmony and peace lead back to unity by 'the way upwards'. From this mulching it was to become clear to the imagination, Golding once explained, that the downward path of the innocent was essentially related to the surmounting path of the guilty: for nature is constantly dividing and uniting. An ultimate and, by extension, constant dynamic exists between phenomena and epochs. Death is never the final defeat.

All this imaginative brooding settled down, he again once explained, into 'the perfect image' of the law: a 'river with a fall', a log going down the fall and men with huge ganglia and enlarged skulls traveling up the river over the fall, pushed by some new intensity, some vision. As Lok, the prelapsarian, amazedly discovers: 'They did not look at the earth but straight ahead' (p. 143) when he sees the post-adamite New People swaying upright: 'It was as though something that Lok could not see were supporting them, holding up their heads, thrusting them slowly and irresistibly forward' (p. 144).

To these images was added that of an island, reared against the fall, because (as Golding was to tell me) it was technically necessary for the New People to leave the impenetrable dark shelter. They had to retreat up the slope 'as though the river itself were flowing uphill' towards the plains and the mountains. At the novel's beginning, for example, the bulk of the island – which is shielded by loathsome falling water – seems to Lok as remote as the skies. 'Only some creature more agile and frightened' (p. 41) than the People could reach it. Some larger creature with larger intelligence would explore its strangeness, a creature whose daring and power would be inconceivable to limited innocence. Perhaps, as in *Lord of the Flies*, the island becomes a macrocosmic image of human nature: divorced by its enlarged skull from brute nature, isolated at the foot of the Fall, divided by two falls from the mainland and forest. Perhaps the island is a symbolic image of the 'People of the Fall' who will go against the Fall.

The final extermination of the People would occur at the waterfall. In a river of blood, Fa drops over the fall as indifferently as the logs that repeatedly drop over, sitting limply among the branches of 'a whole tree from some forest over the horizon...a colony of budding twigs and branches, a vast half-hidden trunk and roots that spread above the water and held enough earth between them to make a hearth for all the people in the world' (p. 212).

Golding takes this woman of the 'hearth' to the edge of the fall; she can never pass beyond it because her nature – changed though she has had to be – cannot apprehend those weapons of destruction and tools of survival that the New People possess. Thus the last Oa-priestess, seen against the rituals of a male-dominated totemic religion, destructive river, and murderous Fall-nature, is caught in a Dead Tree whose relentless power she cannot avoid. Drowned, she is carried back below the fall. But the evolutionary life force drives the New People upwards – the word which always attends their description in the book – and forward, at a higher level of energy than that which the People possessed. Something thrusts the New People up the river, some pained need to widen the world as well as manipulate it.

Our last view of Fa is of her rolling over and over in the river while the fall's current thrusts her back and down to the sea. The whole 'dreamlike' motion and direction superbly repeats that of the old woman's frightening log-like descent to the sea in the deep waters of the river. In contrast to both, the New People's dugout canoes, the '*logs*' which Lok first sees on the river pointing '*up towards the fall*' (p. 115, my italics), can remain stationary, fighting and victorious over the current that urges them downstream. The navigators move steadily upwards, away from the sea, up beyond the fall, meeting as they ascend toward the plain avalanche-thunder like an angry god, which heralds the end of the Ice Age. The fear-driven Tuami feels 'as though the portage of the boats…from that forest to the top of the fall had taken them on to a new level not only of land but of experience and emotion. The world with the boat moving so slowly at the centre was dark amid the light […]' (p. 225). The New People have moved to yet another new level. The water now conquered, a new complexity, a new violence, and perhaps a more refined civility and creation are set afloat.

VII

The Inheritors is by no means the only Golding novel to project this visionary hope for the future […] Yet *The Inheritors* in its perfection of theme and structure remains the crown jewel of the canon.

B.R. Johnson [33]

It is possible to abstract from *The Inheritors* its author's conviction that where humanity is godlike is precisely where it can fall. The old community possessed love and reverence, not hatred, and they were irrevocably drawn by dread and joy to the New People in the latter's capacity as blazing fire and terrible water: the honey 'repelled and attracted', like the People. Lok, because his nature is innocent and loving, could not obey Fa and ignore Liku. Even when Fa had worked out a hostage strategy, he had to ask Tanakil where Liku was. He kept being drawn to his destruction as he knew the old woman, Ha, and Nil had been. Both 'outside- and inside-Lok yearned with a terrified love as creatures who would kill him, if they could' (p. 191). The New People had ochre and hunting spears and a potent honey drink, but the artistic images could be used for savagery, the weapons could be thrust into men's flesh, and the drink could intoxicate. Their complex power, like the rationality of Pincher on his island or Wilfred Berkley's imagination as he too suffers on an island, is both creative and destructive, just as is Jocelin's dream of a four hundred foot spire for his beloved cathedral.

That the sources and means of power and active creation are also the sources and means of destruction is (for Golding) humanity's long and tragic tension: an individual's primary nature is given (again, according to Golding's surmise), and where it seems most formidable it may also be most vulnerable. A relatively simple conviction, of course, but the process whereby Golding arrived at its fictional expression in *The Inheritors* is a more complex, indeed more compelling, matter, giving the lie to the notion of Golding's practice being that of the assured religious allegorist. As I have noted, certain images – call them pictures, in fact, since that is how an unblemished, newly apprehended image operates – and clusters of images grew after Golding's (gestating) thinking coalesced around the waterfall as the image of the recast dynamics of the Second Law of Thermodynamics. So the People's first displacement occurrs because a 'fallen log' has been removed from its habitual place across a river. The People's first knowledge of 'a new thing' comes to involve the Tree. Mal makes them run over – it is described as '*falling* across' (p. 17, my italics) – a new log. As with many of Golding's descriptions, the descriptive technique here operates on two levels – that of the realistic and that of the symbolic – with the intent that the reader should choose a reading: ignoring one or combining the two. Running is, in a way, a falling, since the body is hunched forward while pressing against the atmosphere. Similarly, the drone of the fall inhabits the People's ears when they first stop by the Dead Tree, which becomes the place where, the droning of the fall in their ears, Fa and Lok watch the antics of the Fallen People.

The Tree, the Fall, the Water: such tropes can be read as symbols embedded within the tale. They were not invented, as their author observed, so much as discovered by him. One can say, for example, that the water-world in *The Inheritors* is a destructive world, and the fall's moaning the insinuating of this destruction. At one level *The Inheritors* seems a network of things, of actions repeated, reintroduced and expanded so that, packed into a single phrase – the people are 'like the river and the fall, they are a people of the fall; nothing stands against them' (p. 195) – is something like a total recapitulation of the book's mythopoeia. Phrases have become charged with expressive force because they echo previous passages. They share a kind of micro-macrocosmic force, not because they are deliberately denoted that way – for this would make them signs – but because they image that which the reader would ascertain to be human nature. These hologram-like symbols compress the theme, yet have concrete and dramatic value; as in a dream or dream-odyssey we are guided through experience on the way to insight. Lok's first view of the tribe from his perch on the river's edge across from the island is a splendid illustration of this narrative process. Here all kinds of resonances from all kinds of stories about fear converge to create – in Lok and in the reader – a moment of sheer terror:

> The blob of darkness seemed to coagulate round the stem like a drop of blood on a stick. It lengthened, thickened again, lengthened. It moved up [...] with sloth-like deliberation, it hung in the air high above the island and the fall. It made no noise and at last hung motionless (p. 79).

The darkness that spells fear, the blood that causes revulsion, the motion of thickening and lengthening that brings to mind the snake, the picture of it hanging above the island and even the fall, identified with the two but somehow stealthy enough to transcend the two – all reverberate atavistically. Finally all occurs in silence and from a limited point of view that reports action, step by step, without interpreting it. The action, in turn, seems arrested, stilled. In fact, the passage illustrates the sensuous flexibility of the novel's language: restricted to a relatively narrow range of tropes – Tree, Fall, Fire, Water, Darkness – it moves from the literal to the symbolic to the literal without any sense of strain. Language is condensed so that several relevances become implicit in these limited words. Possibly Golding's conscious myth-striving in *The Inheritors* achieves specificity precisely because of a tight condensation.

The Inheritors, I think, finally arrives at a mythopoeic perspective in which a fable of the fall approaches a 'myth of total explanation'. The abstract movement upwards of the New People and the motion downwards of the People mirror another cosmic rhythm, that of birth and death. One episode quietly realizes this, functioning (for me) as a kind of epiphany of the mythopoeic perspective. At the death of Mal we see, in the burial ground, the evidence of all ages. Digging, the group comes across skulls and bones that have faded beyond their emotional interest. Liku plays with skulls at the side of the grave; Mal's body is folded in a foetal position, and he returns to his home. Oa takes him into her belly. The new one, playing at the side of the grave, extracts 'itself arse backwards from the hole' (p. 88). The skull is as much a plaything as the root-shaped toy that resembles Oa – life and death are brought to the point at which each out-stares infinity. Appropriately, at his end Lok draws himself quietly back into (what we readers know to be) Oa's belly. 'It made no noise, but seemed to be growing into the earth, drawing the soft flesh of its body into a contact so close that the movements of pulse and breathing were inhibited' (p. 221). Such promise of wholeness is held out to the New People too. As they move to the 'new level of experience and emotion', Tuami and the tribe laugh with a kind of fear and awe as the new one extracts himself from Vivani's hood – surely recalling Ha's fur where the new one earlier hid – 'arse upwards, his little rump pushing against the nape of her neck' (p. 233).

The solution that the fear-haunted artist Tuami gropes towards shaping in ivory at the novel's close is, in a sense, manifested already in the reader's own experience throughout. For if structure is ideographic, so too is point of view. Judgement is kept at bay so that we readers can grasp with (one trusts) our whole imaginative selves what are unanalyzable mysteries – the drone of the fall, the stink of honey, the ultimate cannibalism that even Fa turns dead eyes on. This reconciliation of opposites is impossibly difficult to embrace imaginatively, but that very difficulty is a deliberate and instructive strategy and one that will continue in Golding's practice. Two sets of actions are set before us here without authorial intervention. Events take place in the landscape and within the protagonist Lok's mind. We alternate between one and the other. Using Lok's eyes we see what he sees. And more. Later events take place in the landscape and within the protagonist Tuami's mind. The real matter, then, is that which lies between Lok's perception and Tuami's perception: we can share the tidal waves of terror and pain, the two tidal waves that enter the doubled protagonists. As Golding commented: 'We are like them [the Neanderthals] and as I am a propagandist for Neanderthal man it is…it can only work so far as *Homo sapiens* has a certain amount in common with Neanderthal man.'

Egotistic communication and communal life are two of the alternatives that are dramatized in *The Inheritors* as the tension between two different stages of human growth. The opposition would become a fragmentation within a single human being in *Pincher Martin* and *Free Fall*, and the comedic, ultimately sorrowful, connection between supercilious Talbot and the inept, needy Reverend Colley in *Rites of Passage*. It is the tension in *Lord of the Flies* between those who think and talk yet fail, and those who act yet hunt: between Piggy and Jack. But in *The Inheritors* the tension is sustained in the structure of the narrative. Its ideographic structure pictures both guilt-consciousness and innocence. We share Lok's disconnected pictures for most of the time and then see him from the outside as a grotesque red creature. The focus shifts to the newer tribe, and the final objectification of Lok is meant to distance him from us at the same time as winning enormous sympathy for his dying. Later our sense of Tuami is similarly modified. The effect is to deliberately complicate the possibility of us choosing between the two communities: the sensuous innocence of the clown and the intellectual guilt of the artist, so that the reader experiences both the sense of loss and the sense of gain. By means of ideographic structure, defamiliarizing focalization, and confrontation scene, the reader encounters dark and light, moving beyond simple experience/guilt or simple innocence/love to an apprehension of some future possibility of reconciling binary opposites.

Endnotes

1   Janet Burroway, 'Resurrected Metaphor in *The Inheritors*', *Critical Quarterly* 23 (1981), p. 55.

2   Jeanne Delbaere-Garant, 'Lok – Liku – Log: Structure and Imagery in *The Inheritors*', in Jeanne Delbaere (ed.), *William Golding: The Sound of Silence*, Liège, English Department University of Liège, 1991, p. 62.

3   David L. Hoover, *Language and Style in* The Inheritors, New York, University Press of America, 1999, p. 13.

4   Fantasy literature abounds, as J.K. Rowling, C.S. Lewis, and
     J.R.R. Tolkien demonstrate. Comparing the latter with Golding,
     Daniel Timmons argues that Tolkein 'encourages us to immerse
     ourselves fully in the work's world [...] where readers are scarcely
     conscious of the interpretative act of reading' ('Sub-Creation in
     William Golding's *The Inheritors*'; *English Studies in Canada* 22,
     1996, p. 400). While I agree that Golding 'deliberately puzzles', I
     would argue the bafflement is intended to provoke readers into
     constructing meanings.

5   That Lok is a fiction maker and thus in the long line of Golding's
     myth-makers, first Adam to the decidedly unparadised paper man
     Wilfred Barclay, cannot go unremarked. 'When the old woman
     puts the responsibility on Lok to act like a leader – "Let Lok
     speak" – Lok,' as Burroway so aptly points out (in the article cited
     above), 'does the only thing he can do, he *makes a story*' (op. cit., p.
     58). The tribe's foolish clown, we watch him mimicking,
     parodying, and (importantly) imitating, so that he can
     imaginatively identify with that which is imitated.

6   'Anyone who has read *The Inheritors* and wants to play literary
     detective,' write Bernard S. Oldsey and Stanley Weintraub in
     their 1965 summary of parallels, 'can find plenty of clues in the
     drawings and figures reproduced on pages...of *The Outline*.
     Items: ivory and bone knife points – of the sort Tuami makes at
     the novel's close; a large horned animal – of the kind Tuami
     draws on the ground; an antlered stag head done on ivory – like
     the totemic device of Marlan's tribe; and a small rotund female
     figure ripened as though in pregnancy – resembling the Oa
     figure of Lok's tribe' (*The Art of William Golding*, New York,
     Harcourt, Brace and World, 1965, p. 50). Palaeontologist
     Marcellin Boule, who first excavated a *Neanderthalis* in
     Dusseldorf in 1856, was responsible for the misconception that
     Wells repeated, since the shambling gait that Boule determined
     has since been seen to be arthritic limbs, an irony Golding would
     have enjoyed. What he could not have known is the (eerie)
     matter determined in 1970 by linguist Philip Lieberman and
     anatomist Edmond Cretin that Neanderthal's tongue and larynx
     prevented complex modern language.

7   Frank Kermode, 'The Case for William Golding', *The New York Review of Books* (April 30, 1964), p. 4.

8   Stephen Prickett, 'Inheriting Paper: Words and William Golding', *Journal of Literature & Theology* 6 (1992), p. 152.

9   Golding to Biles, Jack Biles, *Talk: Conversations with William Golding*, New York, Harcourt, Brace & Jovanovich, 1970, p. 105.

10   See in this context, Elizabeth Black, 'Metaphor and Cognition in *The Inheritors*', *Language and Literature* 2 (1993) pp. 37–48; and Marie Nelson, 'Two Narrative Modes, Two Modes of Perception: The Use of the Instrumental in Golding's *The Inheritors*', *Neophilologus* 70 (1986), pp. 307–15.

11   M.R.A. Chance, 'The Nature and Special Features of the Instinctive Bond of Primates', *The Social Life of Early Man*, S.L. Washburn (ed.), Chicago, University of Chicago Press, 1961, pp. 29–32.

12   'The triad of trees' which Pierre François considers – *The Inheritors*' dead tree where Lok hides, the oak tree upon which he and Liku swing, and the oak tree in the 'Balder and Aricia tree – seem to convey the same religious notion that ambivalence is not felt to be evil provided cosmology lays the emphasis on rebirth from death', 'The Rule of Oa and *The Inheritors*' in Delbaere (ed.), op. cit., p. 82.

13   Tuami's 'knife-haft that was so much more important than the blade' is ingeniously linked to Beowulf bringing 'back from his battle the hilt of the sword which, beneath the mere survived, not the blade. The blade melted away like icicles but the hilt told a story of triumph over death and fear' (Nelson, op. cit., p. 314), as it is suggested, will Tuami's carving at *The Inheritors*' conclusion.

14   Timmons, op. cit., p. 410. *The Inheritors* has also suggested a 'modern allegory' (L.L. Dickson, *The Modern Allegories of William Golding*, Gainesville, University of South Florida Press, 1990, p. 27) to some, 'a fable' (James R. Baker, *William Golding: A Critical Study*,

New York, St Martin's Press, 1965, p. 29), a 'myth' (V.V. Subbarao, *William Golding: A Study*, New York, Envoy Press, 1987, p. 35), and a 'fantasy' (David Pringle, *Modern Fantasy: The Hundred Best Novels*, New York, Bedrick, 1989, p. 2) to others.

15 B.R. Johnson, 'William Golding's *The Inheritors*: Dualism and Synthesis', *Southern Review* 19 (1986), p. 177.

16 See, for example, Samuel Hynes, *William Golding, Columbia Essays on Modern Writers*, 2nd edition, New York, Columbia University Press, 1968.

17 Hoover, op. cit., p. 6.

18 I, for one, was intrigued by this use of Golding's fiction and even more intrigued to learn that in the battle between scholars of style and those 'reader response' critics that 'one of the most often anthologized examples of the [former] school' (Hoover, ibid., p. 19) was an article on the functional theory of language by M.A.K. Halliday entitled 'Linguistic Function and Literary Style: An Inquiry into the Language of William Golding's *The Inheritors*' in *Literary Style: A Symposium*, Seymour Chatman (ed.), London, Oxford University Press, 1977, pp. 330–68.

19 Mark Adriaens, 'Style in W. Golding's *The Inheritors*', *English Studies* 51 (1970), pp. 16–30; Halliday, ibid.; D. Lee, '*The Inheritors* and transformational generative grammar', *Language and Style* 9 (1976), pp. 77–92.

20 R. Fowler, *Linguistic Criticism*, Oxford, Oxford University Press, 1986; G. Leech and M. Short, *Style in Fiction: A Linguistic Introduction to English Fictional Prose*, London, Longmans, 1981.

21 Hoover, op. cit., p. 13.

22 Khandkar Rezaur Rahman, *The Moral Vision of William Golding*, Dhaka, University of Dhaka Press, 1990, p. 53.

23 An authorial voice intrudes occasionally, interrupting the Lok

point of view in order to offer an abstracted explanation beyond that character's capacity to so generalize, as James Gindin has observed (*William Golding*, New York, St Martin's Press, 1988, p. 31). To my mind, Golding's strategy here can be likened to Austen's then innovative technique of free indirect discourse, especially as adopted in *Emma*.

24   James Gindin, 'Gimmick and Metaphor in the Novels of William Golding', *Modern Fiction Studies* 6 (1960), pp. 145–52.

25   Ian Gregor and Mark Kinkead-Weekes, *William Golding*, London, Faber and Faber, 1967, p. 67.

26   Naming is a consistent strategy in Golding's work as a wedge through which layered suggestions can be exposed. While the invaders here bear names like Tanakil, Vakiti, and Tuami, which correspond to their species' linguistic complexity, the others – Fa, Ha, Nil, and Mal – possess names whose monosyllabic simplicity accentuates the People's lack of intellectual guile. Onomatopoeic shading also operates: Liku, the small Neanderthal, is indeed 'like-you', and Tuami is 'one you love'; it becomes the burden of the narrative to make these puns pertinent.

27   'The last image of the book has frequently been interpreted as "the line of darkness has no ending". Golding does not say that. He says that Tuami cannot see whether it has an ending or not.' (Burroway, op. cit., p. 69).

28   For me, the scene is one of the most poignantly realized in the book, perhaps because it relates to the author's pictorial conception of the origins of myths, where he sees tribes sitting before their fires, joined in, and tied to, stories that are sifted and resifted, told and retold, adapted through successive stages of rejection and coalescence, in his phrase 'mulching' down in the very fabric of the each community's existence.

29   Gregor and Kinkead-Weekes, op. cit., p. 73.

30   The total submission to Lok-other, a subjection of selfhood (if

that term can be employed when discussing such a pre-rational mentality), is a recasting of Simon's faint before the head, where the 'darkness' or the knowledge of the destructive principle is simultaneously a losing of personality and a capturing of the other. Simon becomes the head, as later in *Free Fall* Sammy, by encountering the darkness of the cell, becomes Sammy-other, thus breaking open the prison of selfhood. Such submissions are those of the priestess (portrayed in *The Double Tongue*'s Arieka as she speaks Apollo's words), mystics, and, it goes without saying, the writer as he inhabits his imagined world.

31   Gregor and Kinkead-Weekes, op. cit., p. 89.

32   William Golding, 'Irish Poets and their Poetry', *Holiday* (April 1963), p. 17.

33   Johnson, op. cit., p. 182.

Pincher Martin

[T]he sea appeals to the English on at least two levels. It attracts the adventurous practical men who make a career out of it until the sea becomes known and ordinary. But it also attracts the other pole of our character, the visionaries, the rebels, the misfits who are seldom conscious of their own nature. It is these [...] who have a grudge or an ideal.

Golding, 'Our Way of Life'[1]

Much more markedly than *The Inheritors*, *Pincher Martin* reveals, as *Darkness Visible* would do later, Golding's idiosyncratic conception of contemporary consciousness and its condition of Being, treating in this fable a more explicitly theological subject than in *Lord of the Flies*. Unlike *Free Fall* and *The Paper Men*, where religious claims are secularized so that the reader can choose between spiritual and material explanations, *Pincher Martin* offers a detailed programme of the necessity for religious belief. Unlike in *The Spire*, however, this religious truth is presented through calculated distortion. As Golding himself once commented to me: '*Pincher Martin* is based on not merely a psychological impossibility but a theological one too.' It is about a dead body and a seemingly indestructible consciousness; yet the protagonist's particular history of guilt and greed was intended to stand as a fable for mid twentieth-century Western culture with its erasure of mystery and the transcendent.

Saying that for him it was a book of colour – 'a pair of red claws locked against black lightning' – first inspired by an image of a man drowning in the sea, Golding transmuted his own familiarity with the sea, his intimations of dread at sea, even his own childhood nightmares, into a contemporary Promethean fable about human nature. An ironic universality is suggested by linking the eponymous hero to figures from literature and myth. Thus the protagonist is associated with Lear and Hamlet; Scandinavian culture enters through Thor's lightning, Greek through allusion to Ajax, Roman through allusions to the Claudian well, Hindu by way of the *Rigeveda*'s Fisher King and Christian by way of Augustinian precepts and the hero's name. The fiction can also be seen as a grim parody of *Prometheus Bound* as well as a parodic inversion of *Robinson Crusoe*. Even an evolutionary context can be posited in the

91

hero's evolution from the sea; his emergence on the rock is depicted as though he has emerged from the birth canal. However ubiquitous these referents are, the fable's focus was a bleak and radically delimited one, for it studies a man alone on a rock in mid-Atlantic.

Much slighter in terms of plot than even *The Inheritors*, the tale concerns a naval officer blown off the bridge of a destroyer during World War II and his struggle with the Zeus of his own universe: the natural stupidity of water, the indifference of rock and sky and sun and rain. For the first time, Golding had fashioned a protagonist who is an adult male, his stamp and identity economically suggested by his nickname: Pincher. It is a clever emblematic invention as all Martins in the British Navy are called Pincher, just as all Clarks are nicknamed Nobby. The course of the novel revolves around the illumination of this Pincher's thieving and cosmic greed.

We first encounter the protagonist flailing about in a black sea. Our primary imaginative experience is of the physical stuff as experienced by a man immersed in water; he struggles to inflate a life belt, trying to keep the salt sea from his screaming mouth and to stay afloat. Almost immediately he is dashed against a barren rock: 'A single point of rock, peak of a mountain range, one tooth set in the ancient jaw of a sunken world, projecting through the inconceivable vastness of the whole ocean' (p. 30).[2] At enormous pain and with enormous difficulty he crawls up this rock using limpets as climbing pegs. The water beats against him washing him back mercilessly, but with a final titanic thrust he pulls his body into a rocky trench:

> The man was inside two crevices. There was first the rock, closed and not warm but at least not cold with the coldness of sea […] his body was a second and interior crevice which he inhabited. Under each knee, then, there was a little fire […] He endured these fires although they gave not heat but pain (p. 48).

For seven consecutive days Pincher struggles to survive; struggles to maintain sanity and health; struggles to tame the barren rock. First he raises a pillar of stone in the hope that it will be seen by possible rescue ships; this he calls the Dwarf. He proceeds to civilize the landscape; a prominent ledge he calls Lookout, a lower ledge Safety Rock; where he finds mussels to eat he calls Food Cliff; other points in the map he names Piccadilly, Leicester Square, and Oxford Circus. A good British sailor, he even provides himself with a pub, the Red Lion.

On the rock Pincher can gradually solidify his identity, reassuring himself of his own precise existence with a faded identity disc and using the photograph to give back his own image as in civilian life he used mirrors. When he cries triumphantly, 'Christopher Hadley Martin. Martin. Chris. I am what I always was!' (p. 76), the rock diminishes from an island to a thing, a simple, meaningless mechanism. But as strong as Martin's conscious determination is, he cannot maintain life alone on the island; his own ego is not sufficient to overwhelm the rock and what the narratorial voice calls 'the globe' begins to be invaded by imagined horrors. Panic, fatigue, memory, and hallucination appear to merge.

As the narrative proceeds, it depicts a protagonist gradually dissolving into fragments: a rational mind, itself divorced from its knowing 'centre', and around all a pain-racked body. Memory flashbacks torment and invade. He relives a childhood experience where he dared to descend steps into a cellar at night, there to encounter the feet and knees of some appalling god-like effigy. The Dwarf fuses with the cellar god and a confrontation occurs between the apparently mad Pincher and some kind of godhead with 'immovable, black feet' (p. 196). Pincher – like Simon before the speaking head – hears this god say, 'Have you had enough, Christopher?' These are, by the way, the first true lines of direct speech in the narrative, fourteen pages before the fiction's end. But Pincher resists, yelling demonically, 'I shit on your heaven' (p. 200). A storm begins to overwhelm the sailor, who still resists.

Although the third-person story of survival on the rock finishes with Chapter XI, the narrative is not yet complete: a fact now understood by even the most desultory reader of Golding's fiction. True to the characteristic strategy of what I have called the ideographic structure, the last chapter (Chapter XII) offers a coda to *Pincher Martin*, with its change in perspective. We find ourselves on a remote island in the Hebrides where two men are talking; a body has been washed ashore. Having lived beside the rotting corpse for a week while awaiting the official who will record its identity, Campbell, a crofter, sadly asks: 'Would you say there was any – surviving? Or is that all?' (p. 208). Officer Davidson instantly replies that Martin (for the corpse bears Pincher's identity disc) could not have suffered, if that is what Campbell is wondering, since 'he [Martin] didn't even have time to kick off his seaboots' (p. 208). In the first chapter, free indirect discourse informs that Pincher kicks off his seaboots to avoid drowning and later tears apart his already inflated life belt to give himself a Wagnerian enema. On the last page it is observed that Martin drowned *after* he had inflated the life belt, but before he had time to kick off his boots. The survival tale has been a post-mortem narrative, its events taking place in the consciousness of a dead man.

II

> Golding's reputation, like that of any artist, was created not simply by what he wrote or intended but also by the prevailing mentality of his readership, and often a single work will be selected by that readership as characteristic or definitive. Writer and reader conspire to sketch a portrait of the artist that may or may not endure.
>
> James R. Baker[3]

Clearly, *Pincher Martin* remains one of the more vigorously experimental of Golding's novels, numerous critics having found it formally and intellectually one of the more impressive as well.[4] 'Golding has brought something new to mainstream European literature in his endeavor to represent the horror and searing power of divinity fiction,' one critic has observed.[5] However, its initial reception was a good deal less happy, and right from the start the familiar source-hunting occurred. Thus a technical device of having memories sweep through a dying man was thought to have its origins in Ambrose Bierce's *An Occurrence at Owl Creek*.[6] But Golding – in his then much practiced habit of providing authorial interpretations for *Pincher Martin* – declared emphatically that it was not his intention to explore the legend about seeing one's whole past in the moment of death – Pincher drowns on page two of the tale. Other intertexualities have been suggested,[7] but for me the most ingenious – and still the soundest – excavation is that Golding had again subverted another popular novel, *Pincher Martin* being a recasting of a 1916 survival tale, *Pincher Martin, O.D.*, by Taffrail, the pseudonym for the now unremembered novelist Henry Taprell Dorling.[8] Taffrail's Pincher is torpedoed, as is Golding's; flung into the sea he remembers his seaboots and, as he removes one, death comes. Not only is he obedient to his fate – one he automatically assumes is predetermined by his 'Maker' – but Taffrail's Martin experiences 'a feeling of relief' that 'the struggle' in the sea is 'hopeless'. Taffrail writes: 'Pincher Martin committed his soul to his maker[…as] the most trivial events and the most important happenings of his short life crowded before him onto his overwrought brain'. In an identical situation, the responses of the two Pinchers are directly contrary. A similar opposition occurs at the conclusion of each fiction. In Taffrail's story, Martin is rescued by a fisherman: in Taffrail's hackneyed phrase, 'from the very jaws of death Pincher Martin stepped ashore'. In Golding's revision, another sort of Fisherman tries to bring about another sort of survival, but there is none.

Over the years, the most persistent dissatisfaction with the novel has been with the astonishing revelation that the coda imparts, readers having considered it a gratuitous puzzle which trivializes a triumphant work.[9] Following Golding's several (and, it must be said, doctrinaire) exegeses of the book's meaning, critics became more willing to explore the thematic *and* narrative legitimacy of the coda. 'When *Pincher Martin* was first published, many critics were unhappy with what they saw as a "trick" ending,' Kevin McCarron has noted, 'but there is no shortage of signs pointing to Martin's death. That the reader of *Pincher Martin* no more chooses to recognize the implications of these signs than the character does, forms part of Golding's assault on rationalism.'[10] And in a similar critical welding together of reader response and authorial intent, the coda came to be defended 'as a kind of necessary *peripeteia* and *anagnorisis*, a reversal and recognition, for the spectator [reader] of Christopher's drama, so that he [the spectator/reader] can clearly see'.[11]

In the context of narratological theory, *Pincher Martin* maintains itself as a fable allocating Golding's perennial religious theme – the necessity of vision as a preliminary step to salvation – in the purgatorial moment. Martin's 'present' struggle is intended as a recapitulation of his 'past' career on earth, while the 'present' resistance to death is intended as an eschatalogical prognosis about Pincher's 'future' career in eternity. To reiterate Golding's cryptic aside: 'Just to be Pincher is Purgatory; to be Pincher for eternity is Hell.' But Golding was imaginatively exploring the moment of Purgatory – a moment that contains the present, the past, and the future – in order to make a simple fabulist's point about the 'ordinary universe, which on the whole I believe likely to be the right one'. Thus the tale was intended as only an analogue for the real world. Pincher's inability to achieve salvation should have been read as an excessive warning on contemporary men and women's inability to achieve any kind of spiritual vision. Using the ideographic structure to make its religious comment, contradictory perspectives were turned on the one circumstance of the shipwrecked sailor. First, we have Martin's view of his own horrendous plight, then, in the coda, Davidson's and Campbell's views of it. These differ in their implications. We are moved from the fevered world of Pincher's consciousness to the apparently objective and sane conversation about the 'lean-to' (p. 208). Here, the naval officer interprets survival as a question about physical suffering while the crofter's bewilderment suggests that, in his view at least, there might be some spiritual dimension to it. He makes the point – significantly and by understatement – that Officer Davidson does not know about his 'official beliefs' (p. 208).

The perspectives of the rock-narrative and the coda were never intended to contradict each other. By evidence of the seaboots, the sailor is certainly not physically alive on Rockall during seven days of diminishing strength. Most certainly he is not just a corpse either. He most certainly suffered and – according to the fable's theological mythopoeia – this suffering will now continue eternally. It would be continuing in some other dimension as the crofter and officer brooded over the corpse. It was the intention that the reader would build the bridge between the contradictory views and discover by imaginative extension that humanity is both more than Davidson's literalism would decide yet less than Pincher's monumental endurance would seem to indicate. Should such a process of understanding take place, it would do so outside the fable proper. Readers would then snap the several 'official' views across each other, assembling all the views to arrive at something approaching an eschatologically inclusive perspective in which the 'sad harvest' to which Mr Campbell sadly alludes would gently and brokenly become significant.

III

[T]o achieve salvation, the *persona* must be destroyed. But suppose the man is nothing but greed? His original spirit, God-given, the *Scintillans Dei*, is hopelessly obscured by his thirst for separate individual life. What can he do but refuse to be destroyed.

Golding to Campbell

No tale of a shipwrecked sailor on a solitary rock, *Pincher Martin* is a report of a soul in Purgatory, with its protagonist creating the rock out of the memory of a once aching and now missing tooth and groping to control what is in fact a delusion. As the children in terror of themselves formulate the beast, as the New People make the People into hairy demons, and as Talbot in *Close Quarters* makes the drag rope scraping from the ship's bottom into a leviathan with head and monstrous fist, so Pincher – out of fear of death – creates a demonic Adversary: the sea, the rock, the sky, even a dreadful Theophany. The naturalistic story is effectively recounted in Chapter I : the protagonist's immersion, the few flickering impressions he has as the gun's tracer explodes and 'green sparks flew out from the centre' (p. 7), the water thrusting in '*without mercy*' (p. 7, my italics), and the moment of death. 'The green tracer that flew from the centre began to spin into a disc. The throat at such a distance from the snarling man vomited water [but] the hard lumps of water no longer hurt. There was no face but there was a snarl' (p. 8). The last chapter confirms the death, when a corpse is collected.

Because readers have a peculiar access to Pincher's consciousness, we can decipher hints that Pincher keeps turning away from. Every time Pincher comes close to awareness of his death, he turns aside – at one point he leaves a sentence unfinished: 'Strange that bristles go on growing even when the rest of you is–' (p. 125), and we supply the conclusion 'dead'. Similarly, he repeatedly flinches from calling the trailing rocks 'the Teeth' (p. 91), since again 'to lie on a row of teeth in the middle of the sea–' (p. 91) is to be 'dead'. On another occasion he mutters, 'the process is so slow it has no relevance to–' (p. 78), and, again, we supply 'death'. Another variation on this narrative strategy of delayed comprehension provides equally strong evidence for the protagonist's death. Pincher's post-mortem experience of himself is unmistakably made present in certain repeated clues, particularly those involving guano, red lobsters, rock/teeth, as well as certain reiterated motifs including a maggot-box and a curious experimental tool.

The technique is the characteristic strategy of deliberate obscuration, but with a difference. Whereas in *The Inheritors* readers have to make intelligible Neanderthal perceptions, here we are further limited by way of distortion with the tormented hero's consciousness shrinking and expanding, his senses reporting and distorting, his memory intermittently corrupting. Despite the fact that we assemble clues he refuses to recognize, we are never – until the coda – fully outside his focalization; most often we stare through the windows of his eyes, 'curtains of hair and flesh' (p. 161). Towards the end of the survival narrative, delirium invades Pincher's consciousness and crushes his identity; the reader suffers the distortion. But at a special vantage point.

As is the case in *The Inheritors*, when point of view is so handled that readers, peering down with Lok at the Bacchanals, recognize themselves in the figures in the clearing, so in *Pincher Martin* we are both inside and outside the consciousness of the protagonist. We experience the classic battle of man against the elements and acknowledge Promethean nobility while we simultaneously know at another level that such Promethean energy is cosmically irrelevant. Despite the elementary achievements of building a shelter, designing a water trough and using his one weapon, a knife, to get food and drink, and all that these represent of the expenditure of will and the strenuous assertion of intelligence, there is not enough evidence to support Martin's conviction of the uniqueness and superiority of his individuality, which, given his lack of faith in any other values, he is compelled to assert throughout.

The survival narrative of the rock begins and ends at the moment of physical death. Past, present, and future all are tied into an image of all-time (or no-time). I would argue that in this novel time is not a sequence but a simultaneity, with past, present, and future existing at the same instant, a paradoxical invention that gives the fable both its subject and its form. Pincher's experience on the rock, his ostensible present, exactly parallels the pattern of his past life. Memory flashbacks keep cutting across the present, and at certain points what I would term 'Time-Past' is gripped in 'Time-Present'. Similarly, his future pricks at his consciousness. Nathaniel Walterson is a friend from the past, but his spiritual lectures, when recalled, insinuate the very 'Time-Future' that possesses Christopher Hadley Martin. The hands which, on Rockall, Pincher mistakes for red (therefore illusory) lobsters are the fists that grabbed 'the penny and someone else's bun' (p. 120), back on civvy street. They represent symbolically the rapacious nature which the black lightning at the end of Chapter XI plays over and pricks at, 'prying for a weakness, wearing them away in a compassion that was timeless and without mercy' (p. 201).[12] As Lok was reduced to perception, the 'inside-Lok'; as Jack was reduced to savagery, the 'furtive thing'; as *Free Fall*'s Sammy Mountjoy will be reduced to irrational terror, the 'frantic thing'; as *Darkness Visible*'s Sophy will be reduced to 'darkness at the end of the tunnel' so Martin is reduced to the abstraction Greed, the two claws. All the paths of the fable lead back to his 'centre', the *ding en sich*, the irreducible Being that constitutes this man's nature. Yet there is still another option, a terrible one: 'The terrible option is up to him,' Golding insisted to me early on, 'choice between Purgatory and Hell.'

Christopher Hadley Martin's life can be viewed from three distinct temporal angles; each angle possesses an appropriate narrative technique and operates from a separate temporal perspective. For the remainder of this chapter I shall look at the action on Rockall in terms of three distinct temporal strands or time-modes. Then I shall examine the narrative techniques by which these modes are set in motion: the first, 'Time-Present' in Section IV; the second, 'Time-Past' in Section V; and the third, 'Time-Future' in Section VI. Finally, I will argue in Section VII that all three strands are to be seen in individual episodes where the supposedly real situation on the rock is mixed with memories of the past and fears about the future.

IV

'Time-Present'

We experience the Purgatorial moment at first as an accumulation of physical details, but details as experienced by a man in a state of fragmentation where, physically exhausted, he lies squinting through a damaged eye at an alien shape, inches from his eyeball. 'He came upon the moldering bones of fish and a dead gull, its upturned breast-bone like the keel of a derelict boat' (p. 59). The landscape seems radically dislocated. Furthermore, we are intended to grope through underlexicalized words like 'window', 'wall', 'globe', and 'centre' with their attendant effect of defamailiarization whereby that which one normally imparts to humanity is figured in non-human terms. Thus it is 'the centre' which knows that 'Christopher and Hadley and Martin were fragments far off' (p. 162), while 'a curtain of hair and flesh' obscures the rock and the sea. Thoughts, for example, are described as pieces of 'sculpture' hidden in the inward weather of the inner-skull, but 'in front of the unexamined centre' (p. 162).

After his ascent up the rock, physical pain, 'a deep communion with the solidity' (p. 25) of the crevice, brings the protagonist back to a single unit. Pain organizes into physical unity but not conscious awareness. Then, like a furred creature, consciousness must poke around meaningless impressions. At an enormous effort which approximates physical action it must dispense with some fragments to discover the few significant ones: 'among the shape-sounds and the disregarded feeling […] *it* was looking for a thought […] *It* found the thought, separated it from the junk, lifted it and used the apparatus of the body to give it force and importance' (p. 32, my italics). 'A valuable thought' in Time-Present is one that 'gives him back his personality' (p. 27). If Pincher's gropings towards some mode of rational perception imply something more severely disturbed than Lok's stumblings through 'pictures', then when *it* can say 'I am what I always was' (p. 76), Pincher can stop being isolated 'inside of the globe of his head' and extend normally through his limbs. The omniscient narratorial voice describes him as beginning to live 'on the surface of his eyes' (p. 76), not behind windows and shades. The rock appears to become a coherent object, diminishing – in his phrase – from 'an island to a thing' (p. 77). Thus Pincher makes the island rationally coherent and, in his terms, civilized: 'I am busy surviving,' he intones, 'I am netting down this rock with names and taming it […] What is given a name is given a seal, a chain. If this rock tries to adapt me to its ways I will refuse and adapt it to mine' (p. 86). So the ultimate truth of things is physical rock: wetness, hardness, and movement 'with no mercy but no intelligence either' (p. 115). Pincher believes that – like the New People in *The Inheritors* – he can survive by his linguistic appropriation of the world. Reduced to a thing, this island is no threat to his carefully 'hoarded and enjoyed personality' (p. 91). But the island is actually only an 'I/land', in Kevin McCarron's happy phrase.[13] Central to Pincher's situation in Time-Present is the dislocation of mind and body, matter and spirit, sensation and perception, dislocations which he admits exist – 'I was always two things, mind and body. Nothing has altered' (p. 176) – while at the same time resisting the implications of such divisions, for to acknowledge those would be to admit some truth about his own body's state. A 'silent indisputable creature' sits at the innermost centre of Pincher, looking out from his 'dark skull' into the 'inscrutable darkness' of the rock landscape. The technique of transitivity – an inanimate object becoming the subject of a transitive sentence – takes over as *it* stares through a window. At other times, Pincher's consciousness is described in metaphors appropriate to a creature immersed in water, the irony being intentional. As the third-person narrative summarizes, '*it* floated in the middle of this globe like a waterlogged body' (my italics). Consciousness is balanced between two pressures in the manner of the ingenious doll recalled in a memory flashback – a symbolic trope to be examined at the end of this chapter. It is sufficient here to note that the ineradicable 'isness' of the Pincher character is suspended in his physical body and – from the suggestions in comments about Nat – everyone contains such an observational point. Like Pincher, Nat's centre is disconnected from his body as well; we learn that at the binnacle of the destroyer Nat rests not outside in the physical world, but inside, 'attached by accident to life with all its touches, tastes, sights and sounds [...] at a distance from him[self]' (p. 51). Brooding and bemused, Pincher once decided that Nat's centre inside 'prayed and waited to meet his aeons' (p. 51).

In Time-Present on Rockall and when in pain, Pincher is described as striving for 'some particular mode of *inactive* being' (p. 49, my italics). This kind of interior balance (analogous, ironically, to Nat's submission) allows him to 'float' inside 'the bone globe of the world' (p. 48) and his own 'globe' or cranium. Pincher is depicted as striving for just that suspension between pain and passivity, consciousness and nothingness, that will neither eject him back into the world of the Time-Present fever-fire nor thrust him away from his 'hoarded personality'. Such an 'interior balance', such an inactive mode, compellingly defines what a waterlogged body would be known to sustain, another ironic inference to be grasped by the reader. The following passage, describing Pincher's efforts as he tries to sleep, marks another of Golding's most emphatic uses of defamiliarization, the reader being made to encounter more than a couple of layered thematic correspondences.

> He became small, and the globe larger until the burning extensions were interplanetary. But this universe was subject to convulsions that began in deep space and came like a wave. Then he was larger again, filling every corner [...] and the needle jabbed through the corner of his right eye straight into the darkness of his head. Dimly he would see one white hand while the pain stabbed. Then slowly he would sink back into the centre of the globe, shrink and float in the middle of a dark world. This became a rhythm that had obtained from all ages and would endure so. (pp. 49–50).

This could describe the delirium of bruised fever-ridden flesh which trembles involuntarily; the sense of delirium is conveyed by the inanimate metaphors of 'globe'; limbs which extend and then contract; a body so engaged in its pain that it seems a universe subject to arbitrary motions of nature. At the same time as rendering a feverish state, the passage is a fine description of a waterlogged body. The convulsions which begin in deep space wash through the globe with a rhythm 'that had obtained from all ages and would endure', very like the relentless 'minute rise and fall of the sea' which Ralph in *Lord of the Flies* had stared at numbly. The reader here is positioned to operate in the simply physical world (as Pincher tries to) or detect that this physical world is no more than the protagonist's extension of his own spirit.

Gradually, however, the centre forces itself to encounter its knowledge of death. Pincher's mouth may 'quack' about meaning and lecture ease but 'the centre was moving and flinching from isolated outcrops of knowledge' (p. 173). Pincher may try to dodge the knowledge but then he is forced back again, haunted by something he makes into a hag, haunted by all the rational answers the intelligence provides. In Time-Present, each step towards intelligent acquisition on the rock makes him remember his true state. Nagging elusive pictures of eating float through his memory: Chinese boxes, death again as he associates the maggot-box with a coffin. When he decides he will call the Rocks 'the Teeth', he is suddenly terrified and must run from the incipient knowledge that 'to lie on a row of teeth in the middle of the sea' (p. 91) is to be dead. At every stage, even in the sanctuary of madness, an intelligent action brings him back to the unreality of Time-Present.

Nor can he sleep, realizing with horror that he is afraid to sleep, for sleep is a 'consenting to die' in which the centre may slip into unconscious bleakness. At one point towards the fable's end Pincher (recalling Ralph and Simon in different circumstances and presaging Sophy's species of syncope before a Rorschach test in *Darkness Visible*) 'falls into a gap of darkness' (p. 167). 'It was a gap of not-being, a well opening out of the world' (p. 168). Coming back to consciousness the centre knows that 'something' has started to emerge, a pattern that he does not want to obey, a pattern of another sort than he can control, which his intelligence cannot dominate. Suddenly Pincher recalls a childhood dream of – an again unspecified – something coming out of a cellar corner and 'squeezing, tormenting darkness, smoke thick' (p. 138) into which he descends 'three stories defenseless, down the dark stairs [...] down the terrible steps to where the coffin ends were crushed in walls of the cellar – and I'd be held helpless, on the stone floor, trying to run back, run away, climb up' (p. 138).

Clearly the cellar world carries heavy symbolic freight representing (as Golding was to explain to me) 'a whole philosophy in fact –

suggesting that God is the thing we turn away from into life, and therefore we hate and fear him and make a darkness there'.[14] A marked feature of his religious speculation is how powerful and dangerous he construes that numinal night world to be, where terror cannot heal, but only destroy. Authorial paraphrase aside, the critical question posed is whether such terror is conveyed by the fiction itself. Examine, for example, the following passage, depending for its meaning on the very impact it produces, since here the reader has no point of view outside that of the protagonist's indirect discourse.

> Out of bed on the carpet with no shoes. Creep through the dark room not because you want to but because you've got to [...] No safety behind me. Round the corner now to the stairs. Down pad. Down pad. The hall, but grown. Darkness sitting in every corner [...] every thing different, a pattern emerging, forced to go down the meet the thing I turned my back on [...] Past the kitchen door. Draw back the bolt of the vault. Well of darkness. Down pad, down. Coffin ends crushed in the wall. Under the churchyard back through the death door to meet *the master*. (p. 178, my italics)

'The master' from whom the child tries to escape is an 'unknown looming' (p. 178), 'the heart and being of all imaginable terror'. The ambiguous night world is created through unspecific – underlexicalized – words, such as 'pattern' and 'the thing', being set within an apparently specific house where the descent occurs. Then there is the rhythmic repetition of 'down pad' as the reluctant child/man, victimized by an urgency he does not understand, creeps down past the paraphernalia of ghost tales: coffins, vaults, and churchyards. Recalling Lok's first view of the other, the encounter here operates in silence so that the drawing back of the bolt seems to resound in the black emptiness before the death door and 'the master'. The atavistic encounter, declares the narrative voice (or is it Pincher's declaration?) is 'a pattern repeated from the beginning of time' (p. 179), the approach of an 'unknown thing' from which the dark centre turns away. Is the pattern the thing that created it and from which it struggled to escape? And is the conflict between the remembered cellar and the opaque centre the essential conflict of the fable's religious vision? Certainly 'Time-Present' extinguishes any conception of Promethean man patterning a hostile nature into civilized shapes; this castaway Crusoe cannot control.

V

'Time-Past'

To fully understand the meaning of the cellar we must turn to Pincher's past. The purgatorial Time-Present contains Time-Past for, as Pincher is busy netting down the rock, the past strikes across the protagonist's efforts with intermittent clarity. Increasingly Time-Past becomes associated and intermingled with Time-Present. Running beside the Time-Present survival tale is the Time-Past morality play. 'Pincher,' said Golding, 'isn't [just] a man, really; he is Greed. That's why he's called Pincher. It's a straightforward morality play.' From the second temporal perspective we have another view of Chris Hadley Martin, a particular man, from his past actions. Memory flashbacks reveal episodes in the life of what could only have been an arrogant and profoundly greedy man. Pincher *was* a pincher, a robber, a thief, for he had eaten everything he could lay his hands on. He was 'born with his mouth and his flies open and both hands out to grab' (p. 120), as a rival actor once remarked. Chris's particular sin – embodied in the Chinese maggot-box trope – is that of gluttony. The producer of a morality play first made the identification as he introduced Chris to the masks of the seven deadly sins and the one he would wear: 'Chris – Greed. Greed – Chris. Know each other' (p. 119).

The memory flashbacks depict him as just such a grasping devourer: he maims a friend to avoid losing a motorcycle race; he steals another man's woman and invites the former to watch her in his own bed; he tries unsuccessfully to seduce a woman called Mary. As an actor in civilian life, Chris Martin also manoeuvred for success and this willed domination and greedy assertion have been what all his adult life has expressed. The only value in the world was his own personality; that which did not serve him, he tried to dominate. Moments before his submersion in the sea, his true criminality appeared. Aboard the *Wildebeeste*, he decided to effect the drowning of the generous friend, Nat – whom he had never been able to control – by having the destroyer turn suddenly. The irony of the matter is that the order 'Hard a-starboard' (p. 186) was the right order, for at exactly that moment the *Wildebeeste* was torpedoed. One possibility the reader is permitted to ponder here is that Chris might perhaps have been the only victim of the sea, for the rest of the crew might have survived, with Nat Walterson among them.

The bridge of a ship, 'an order picked out across a far sky in neon lightning' (p. 26), a woman's body, a boy's body, a box office, and, most important, 'a man hanging in the sea like a glass sailor in a jam jar' (p. 26): these are the memories that plague Chris in the Purgatorial Time-Past. Not only is an isolated man's delirious state appropriately constructed out of these fragmentary snapshots or memory fragments (where the past bombards, but the impressions appear as sets of stills), but also a past history is depicted that goes some way toward explaining the particular nature of Chris Martin.

The introduction of the protagonist's past through the characteristic Golding device of the 'picture' is both dramatically justified and technically skilled. At the fable's opening when the sailor is flung into the sea, turbines scream and the '*green* sparks' (p. 7, my italics) of a bomb tracer puncture the blackness of the seascape. The only lights cutting the night's darkness, then, are those from the tracer. As he dies, the brain/centre 'lit a neon track' (p. 8), and the green sparks merge with 'luminous pictures' (p. 8) that shuffle before him like a bundle of memory snapshots, 'drenched in light' (p. 8). The green tracer continues to flicker and spin and Pincher's centre, terrified of nothingness, clings to these tracers as, when thrust against the imagined pebbled island before him, it clings to the 'pattern in front of him that occupied all the space under the arches' (p. 23). Inside his head pebbles seem to shake; outside at the right side of his face pebbles nag like 'an aching tooth' (p. 24).[15] As we have seen, Pincher then proceeds to construct an illusory Time-Present out of the memory of this missing tooth. From the tracer lights he constructs Time-Past.

The 'random trailers' are just that: disconnected snapshots that remain unexplained, as do the Chinese box and the suspended doll. It is left not to the protagonist to connect the pictures impinging so randomly but to the reader, who comes to forge a coherent pattern, first about Martin's nature, his determined Being, and by extension about the nature of the universe imagined in *Pincher Martin*. By way of delayed disclosure and hidden cruxes, the text engages the reader in attending to and reconstructing what the protagonist is deliberately made to ignore.

Buried internal evidence in Time-Past indicates that Chris – despite his hardened criminality – had been attracted to goodness. Had he on any of these occasions when grace-abounded acted from charity rather than greed he might well have been granted the consolation of companionship, perhaps love. Several of the memory trailers focus on two important individuals from Chris's past: his spiritualist friend, Nathaniel Walterson, and the woman Nat married, Mary Lovell. Mary was a magnificent but contradictory figure to Chris. As her emblematic name suggests she was both sensual and virginal, like her successor, Beatrice Ifor in *Free Fall*. Yet Chris could never possess Mary and her unconquered mystery obsessed him, eating away at him just as Beatrice's mystery torments Sammy Mountjoy. Chris associates Mary with 'summer lightning' (p. 151) – Golding's rather too neat inversion of the black lightning which plays such an important part in the fable's mythopoeia. Her eyes and impregnable silences made her 'a madness, not so much in the loins as in the pride, the need to assert and break' (p. 148). He cannot understand why she should occupy his centre when the only real feeling he had for her was hate. Occupying his cherished centre, she challenges his whole egotistic view of life.

So too does Nat, to whom other pictures revert. Walterson, with his lectures on 'the technique of dying into heaven' (p. 70), is *Pincher Martin's* saint figure. Like Simon in *Lord of the Flies* and, later, Matty in *Darkness Visible*, he carries the fable's vision of the numinous. We see him both on the *Wildebeeste* and in Martin's digs at Oxford where we are made to understand that Chris loved him 'unwillingly…for the face that was always rearranged from within, for the serious attention, for love given without thought'.[16] At the same time, Martin hates him 'quiveringly […] as though he were the […] enemy' (p. 103). Then there was his sermonizing. Since their contemporaries lacked vision, Nat argued, and were unable to image their *Scintillans Dei* in an affirmative mythological context, the sort of heaven that might be posited would be construed negatively. It would be without form or void, Nat instructed – 'a sort of black lightning, destroying everything that we call life' (p. 183). Chris, of course, ignored Nat's sermonizing; yet he was overwhelmed by the generosity of the man: 'evidence of sheer niceness that made the breath come short with maddened liking and rage' (p. 55). At a deep level, Chris was offended by Nat's notion that Chris had 'an extraordinary capacity to endure' (p. 71), then repelled by Nat's gnomic prediction that the still youthful Chris would soon die. Above all, Chris realized with spite that both Nat and Mary stood 'in the *lighted* centre of [his] darkness' (p. 158, my italics). Because the dark centre had been lit and because he had been drawn to their warmth, each interrupted the consistent pattern of his malice. The autonomy of his greedy ego so challenged, he had to destroy that goodness or be destroyed himself. As he repeats to himself, 'But what can the last maggot but one do? Lose his identity?' (p. 184).

Other textual clues point towards the choices Chris was consistently offered. If, despite himself, he was drawn to goodness in the past, when he is flung into the water the sailor – pointedly – starts to swim not towards the darkness, but towards the light. That 'riven rock *face* with trees of spray' (p. 22, my italics) toward which he swims might have been the implacable visage of a compassionate god. And the spraying thunderbolts splaying from its hand might well have been the golden bough of Aeneas which could have taken the wanderer to the earth's belly and brought him back. In my reading there would seem to be more than partial evidence for this bough in the elaborate description of lightning as a tree, which (towards the end) the 'mad' Pincher pretends is an 'engraving'. In the following passage, presented by way of the protagonist's free indirect discourse, note in particular the appearance of a blossom:

> It was like a tree upside down and growing down from the old edge where the leaves were weathered by wind and rain. The trunk was a deep perpendicular groove with flaky edges. Lower down, the trunk divided into three branches and these again into a complication of twigs like the ramifications of bookworm. The trunk and the branches and the twigs were terrible black. Round the twigs was an apple blossom of grey and silver stain (p. 177).

But Pincher can no more read the engraving as a golden bough than he can in Time-Present – or could in Time-Past – accept a potential My-godness in himself. Thus at the end of Chapter I Pincher is described as interpreting the 'pattern in front [...] which meant nothing' (p. 23) to be the merciless Rockall, beaten by seawater and lost in Atlantic waste. At the Purgatorial moment, Love All becomes Fuck All.

In Time-Past, Chris was offered ways of breaking his own pattern of greed; he is offered this in Time-Present as well. Confronted with choice, he chooses not to break his pattern. In Time-Past as well as Time-Present, his torture is self-inflicted: a point of the utmost importance since the island is his own invention. Furthermore the pressure which he feels and the black lightning which descends to extinguish him become the heaven he will now choose in Time-

Future. Bereft of love, he turns away from love, making a darkness there; his body decays, but the god-resisting centre survives to tear at its own self, rather than submit.

VI

'Time-Future'

The third temporal perspective of *Pincher Martin* is the projection into an unrealized but nevertheless infinite future. Technically Time-Future is realized through memory flashback merging with certain symbolic episodes, which themselves have been modified by hallucination and stream of consciousness. Chief among these is the descent into the cellar: the recurrent memory of which merges with Pincher's past as an actor and his illusory present – his fever-ridden body sweating in the crevice of an illusory rock. The following passage, for example, effectively interlocks the three temporal perspectives that make up (in Golding's view) the Purgatorial moment: memories of childhood, the greed of the actor, the actual death, the bleak rock, the centre's combat, the fear of the future, all are bound together. On the level of Time-Present, the passage depicts the hallucinations of a man lying in the crevice of a rock and being drenched in his own sweat, which he translates into tears being shed, Pincher self-indulgently imagines, for him:

> They wept tears that turned them to stone faces in a hall, masks hung in rows in a corridor without beginning or end. There were notices that said No Smoking, Gentlemen, Ladies, Exit […] Down there was the other room, to be avoided, because there the gods sat behind their terrible knees and feet of black stone, but here the stone faces wept […] Their tears made a pool on the stone floor so that his feet were burned to the ankles. He scrabbled to climb up the wall and the scalding stuff welled up to his […] knees. He was struggling, half-swimming, half-climbing […] The tears were no longer running down the stone to join the burning sea. They were falling freely, dropping on him […] He began to scream. He was inside the ball of water that was burning him to the bone and past. It consumed him utterly. He was dissolved and spread throughout the tear an extension of sheer, disembodied pain (pp. 144–45).

Here in Time-Future, Christopher is re-enacting escape from death. From Time-Present's weeping figures, memory curves back to the various theaters of Time-Past and then farther back – to the recurrent terror of the cellar where black-booted gods haunted his childhood. Simultaneously he looks forward in 'the feet of black stone' to the insistent black seaboots he will see on a figure with whom, in Time-Future, he will speak. Abruptly, he is reminded of the fact of his corporeal death, so he proceeds to try to escape again by climbing up the faces. As he climbs, the fever-sweat/tears metamorphose into water and again he re-experiences his drowning: 'the tears were no longer running down [...] but dropping on him'. What identity still remains is 'sheer *disembodied* pain' (my italics).

As we well know, the centre is intent on avoiding what will obliterate it, with Time-Future positing that the centre must suffer eternally just this effort of escape from death. Only when the coda so corroborates does it become manifestly clear that *Pincher Martin* is about the paradox of eternal dying. Theologically antecedent to the narrative's ideographic structure, however, was the author's premise that the Augustinian view of the world might still be a relevant one for fictional purposes. Such a doctrinal blueprint was provided when Golding wrote me the following: 'Given a cosmos of physical and spiritual duality, God (love) creates man in his own image – since love needs an object. Man, who is free because he is God-like, can either turn outwards or away from this love.' Put another way, the created being can long for charity or lust for greed. From the evidence of Time-Past, Chris obviously adopted lust; turning towards himself he became – as Golding continued to explain – 'Greed which has no spiritual sight'. Thus in Time-Present he creates his own unprovidential isle which in Time-Future 'love tries to destroy [...] Love appears to Pincher as black lightning for Pincher has perverted his original spirit and what is light is darkness, what is heaven the black lightning – is hell.'[17]

But this is an authorial paraphrase of a religious mythopoeia, one which not only posits the duality of spirit counterpointing body but also a related moral antimony between one fictional character's nature and his god-nature, his My-godness. Although the fable does not show Chris as anything but the prototype of Greed, the religious scaffolding underpinning the narrative would posit that Christopher Hadley Martin's nature is so intermingled. My discussion has named the protagonist Pincher when examining Time-Present, Chris when examining Time-Past, and Christopher when examining Time-Future. This is mindful of Golding's exegesis that (although he was Pincher because of what he did to people) 'Christopher, Christopolus – he who bears the Christ in him – was what he was at the hands of God'.[18] Time-Future has him so addressed when a seabooted figure questions: 'Have you had enough, Christopher?' (p. 194).

From such a deployment of obscure, slight dialogue (the first direct discourse in the entire text) the reader is intended to surmise that Pincher is being offered – even at the last moment of his desperate escape-from-death – the choice of operating from his My-godness. Just as he had refused to confront the cellar-god in the past, just as he had refused to accept the dying-into-extinction that Nat taught, so in Time-Future he rejects this last mercy, yelling his satanic dismissal of divine pattern: 'I spit on your compassion!' (p. 199). And the compassion, doctrinally posited as love, must attack and destroy.

> The lightning came forward. Some of the lines pointed to the centre [...] waiting for the moment when they could pierce it. Others lay against the claws, playing over them, prying for a weakness, wearing them away in a compassion that was timeless and without mercy. (p. 201)

So concludes the penultimate chapter. Now reduced to his essence – claws and centre – the protagonist will suffer eternally, never to be destroyed, since this divinity cannot violate the given free will. And Christopher Hadley Martin has left Purgatory and entered Hell.

Hell, Purgatory, free will, compassion? We may fairly ask whether this theology has been rendered fictionally or whether it became accessible only after considerable authorial paraphrase. Readers detect some kind of powerful force interfering in the protagonist's petty designs, although we encounter no familiar or traditional visualization of that force. Described by the narrative voice as a 'pattern' or an 'engraving', it amounts – as Pincher is made to admit, in terminology as minimalized as that of the narrative voice – to 'a split in the nature of things' (p. 177). Pincher himself makes several images, all of them horrendous and malignant. 'She [the old hag] is loose on the rock. Now she is out of the cellar and in daylight' (p. 192), he screams to himself, knowing simultaneously that this hallucination is none other than the Dwarf with the silver head, a pile of stones energized by atavistic dreams of childhood and delirium, an all too ironic signal for rescue. The old hag is the cellar master as well, a threat which looms in opening darkness, the Adversary that lies in the cellar, the only sort of god that Pincher would be capable of imagining. In a final trumpeting blasphemy, he seizes the might of *Genesis*' Jehovah to create the godhead in his own image; facing his own face he yells: 'On the sixth day he created God. Therefore I permit you to use nothing but my own vocabulary. In his own image created he Him' (p. 196). The confrontation scene which follows is more dreadful than that of *The Lord of the Flies*; because the man here is so cunning, he can claim that the apparition is a projection of his own mind.

Yet it may be more. There is evidence in the figure's description that it could be intended to represent the godhead, but met in 'the accidents of Pincher's own culture'. Note first that Pincher observes the figure as being dressed in the garments of a sailor:

> The clothing was difficult to pin down [...] There was an oilskin – belted, because the buttons had fetched away. There was a woollen pullover inside it, with a roll-neck. The sou'wester was back a little. The hands were resting one on either knee, above the seaboot stockings. Then there were the seaboots, good and shiny and wet and solid. They made the rock behind them seem like a cardboard, like a painted flat. (p. 195)

Obviously this is Pincher's garb. And the labored point of the seaboots and their unmistakable presence indicates that Pincher is encountering his real (i.e. dead) self in the apparition, a point made all the stronger since the seaboots make Rockall behind into the 'painted flat' which actually it is. The encounter, then, re-orchestrates the interview between Simon and the head. As Simon before him, Pincher confronts the truth of his condition.

But the seabooted figure carries other – and more elaborate – valences, for Christopher Hadley Martin comes to the appalled realization that he could not have 'invented' the question addressed to him when the figure asks whether 'Christopher' has had enough. In dismay, Christopher stares fixedly past the boots and knees to the face:

> The eye nearest the look-out was bloodshot at the outer corner. Behind it or beside it a red strip of sunset ran down out of sight behind the rock [...] You could look at the sunset or the eye but you could not do both.

You could not look at the eye and the mouth together. He saw the nose was shiny and leathery brown and full of pores. The left cheek would need a shave soon, for he could see the individual bristles. But he could not look at the whole face together. It was a face that perhaps could be remembered later. It did not move. It merely had this quality of refusing overall inspection. One feature at a time (p. 195).

The features, like the clothing, suggest the apparition is in Pincher's own image, with the bloodshot eye referring back to the protagonist's own eye where a needle seemed to be nagging whenever he dipped into the water trough. And the figure's left cheek (behind which would have sat the significant missing tooth) grows the bristle which Pincher commented upon earlier, while the leathery brown skin could well be his own flesh in a decomposed state. Indeed the passage's three features recapitulate what have been clues to Pincher's death.

The figure, therefore, is exactly like the dead Christopher Hadley Martin, but with one exception. The total face is conspicuously absent; the dominant quality of the face — according to Pincher's focalization — is that it 'refuses overall inspection'. Pincher fixes on certain features, the sort, given his illusory world, he would focus upon. Yet he realizes that 'you could not look at the eye and the mouth together'. Nor could the sunset and the eye be seen together; one erases the other. 'It was a face that could perhaps be remembered later.' Could it not be the case then that the ineluctable and hidden face — if seen with other eyes, the eyes of the spirit — is the face of the Living God, whose place is the setting sun? No matter how discerning readers might have been in deciphering Golding's characteristic strategy of buried codes here, to fully comprehend the religious implications we would still have had to rely upon the author's own explication. Questioned as to the matter, Golding provided me the following lifeline:

My intention was to make this a visualization of the thesis that God can be known only in part. Dionysios Areopagitikos says that no matter how profound contemplation is, or how perfect the beatific vision is, there remains that secret part of God that can never be known.[19]

The protagonist's vision is partial, indeed; however, what he does not see, by choice and by nature, the reader is intended to infer. Pincher may see the godhead as a sailor and thus in the accidents of his own culture; nevertheless, what the reader can apprehend is that Christopher Hadley Martin is being offered the choice of making Thor's black thunderbolts into the setting sun of the Fisher King.[20]

VII

> Like a tormented corpse foretasting hell
> He lay eternities stretched out, and stark
> Swore like a mangy parrot 'til he fell
> Into the stinking limbo of the dark.
>
> Golding, 'Baudelaire'

Much more emphatically than any of the other novels, *Pincher Martin* tries to insist on the spiritual dimension, its coda confirming what undercurrents during the survival-narrative have moved towards. The implications of the three temporal perspectives —Time-Present, Time-Past, Time-Future — suggest that Pincher-dead is Pincher-alive. As Ian Gregor and Mark Kinkead-Weekes argued so convincingly, *Pincher Martin* is in no sense concerned with Becoming, but rather with Being. Its starting point was not the past life of Christopher Hadley Martin and how he became greedy, but the given nature of Pincher, the Maggot, and the demonstration of that nature in the past, in the present and in the future.

Among the many discomforts this fiction provokes is its declarative erasure of what is commonly expected in realistic narrative: a protagonist's developing awareness. Here narrative knowledge comes from readers' recapitulation and recognition of truths that already exist. The consciousness depicted *re*-examines static moments in the past which themselves are sometimes intimations of the future, with the reader being given access to information that the protagonist himself rejects. The characteristic technique of the coda insists on a new interpretation of the survival-narrative, earlier clues having been gradually assembled by the reader.

As tightly constructed and built pictorially as *Pincher Martin* may be, it was designed to demonstrate the relevance of the Augustinian view of the world in order to make the larger fabulist's point about the necessity for vision. The narrative works through a series of static images which, by juxtaposition and association and above all compression, inform the three temporal perspectives simultaneously. Thus the elusive Chinese box which comes from a story applied to Chris by one of his friends – it contains one huge maggot that has fed on all the others, but will itself be eaten – summarizes not only Pincher's view of the universe but Chris's demeanor on stage in Time-Past. It reveals him in Time-Present as Pincher-like he nets down the island and in Time-Future as he grasps his own claws, refusing the mercy of extinction. Through such static images, the three orders of time collapse over one another, revealing – like the Chinese boxes that fit into each other – one chemically pure state of Being: the cosmic maggot. A baleful vision of human nature, indeed!

Density of suggestion is achieved not by rich embroidery of image upon image, but – as was the case in *The Inheritors* – a tight condensation where one trope can operate successfully at different levels. Take for example the first 'picture', which Pincher sees while he is still struggling for breath in the sea.

> The jam jar was standing on a table [...] one could see into a little world there which was quite separate but which one could control. The jar was nearly full of clear water and a tiny glass figure floated upright in it. The top of the jar was covered with a thin membrane [...] The pleasure of the jar lay in the fact that the little glass figure was so delicately balanced between opposing forces. Lay a finger on the membrane and you would compress the air below it which in turn would press more strongly on the water [...] and it would begin to sink. By varying the pressure [...] you could do anything you liked with the glass figure, which was wholly in your power. (pp. 8–9)

Although not identified as such in the text, the ingenious toy described above is an experimental tool used for testing degrees of pressure in suspension, sinking, and floating, known as the Cartesian Diver. At one level, therefore, its presence in *Pincher Martin* permits an ironic sublation of the Descartes dictum, *cogito ergo sum*. But hindsight also permits the jam jar to encapsulate much of the fable's thematics. It focuses obliquely and importantly on Being, with Pincher forced to comprehend that the Cartesian Diver's predicament represents his own reality. As the figure floats, sinks, and rises 'in a little world that was quite separate', Pincher's consciousness floats in the globe of his skull; his waterlogged body floats in the sea: 'down it would go, down, down'.

He is forced to descend atavistically down, down, down to some cellarage in his own mind and then struggle towards the surface. One can also see in the jam jar's peculiar isolation Pincher's physical experience on the imagined island where he feels pressed down upon by the atmosphere (the membrane of the jar) and pressed into and up by the riven, harsh, hard rock (the water of the jar). And ultimately the delicate balance of the floating figure could represent humanity's condition *sub specie aeternitatis*, at least in the context of this fable's religious mythopoeia.

Humanity floats between two forces – the pressure of some divine cosmic power and the pressure of the merely mortal. Humanity is controlled inasmuch as it operates within 'a little world'. 'You could let it struggle towards the surface, give it almost a bit of air, then send it steadily, slowly, remorselessly down and down' (p. 9). The reader is positioned to discover that all the memory flashbacks, all the symbolic tropes – even the cosmic symbol of man alone on a rock surrounded by sea – are pictorial definitions of a creation whose essence is to be 'delicately balanced between two opposing forces'. Indeed, the reader is positioned to discover what Christopher Hadley Martin, as well as Davidson and Campbell, cannot know. The Antagonist's 'pressure' is not simply a 'remorseless' cruelty; it might easily be a merciful compassion. And the 'sad harvest' (p. 208) would be harvest indeed.

Endnotes

1   'Unpublished BBC talk, December 15, 1956, quoted in Virginia Tiger, *William Golding: The Dark Fields of Discovery*, London, Calder & Boyars, 1974, p. 102.

2   'As readers now know, Martin calls this rock Rockall not only because that is a real rock [off the Hebrides] but because he remembers a poor joke turning on a word that is a bad rhyme for Rockall and which is the obscene work for "nothing"'(Frank Kermode, 'The Novels of William Golding', *International Library Journal* III, 1961, p. 23).

3   James R. Baker, 'Golding and Huxley: The Fables of Demonic Possession', *Twentieth Century Literature* 46 (2000), p. 313.

4   See L.L. Dickson, *The Modern Allegories of William Golding*, Gainesville, University of South Florida Press, 1990; Patricia Merivale, '"One Endless Round": *Something Happened* and the Purgatorial Novel', *English Studies in Canada* 11 (1985) pp. 438–49; Kenneth Russell, 'The *Free Fall* of William Golding's *Pincher Martin*', *Studies in Religion, Sciences Religieuses* 5 (1975/6), pp. 267–74; Eleanor Wikborg, 'The Control of Sympathy in William Golding's *Pincher Martin*', in Mats Ryden and Lennart A. Bjork (eds), *Studies in English, Philology, Linguistics and Literature Presented to Alarik Rynell*, 7 (1978), pp. 179–87.

5   Leon Surette, 'A Matter of Belief: *Pincher Martin's* Afterlife' *Twentieth Century Literature* 40 (1994), p. 209.

6   See James Gindin, 'Gimmick and Metaphor in the Novels of William Golding', *Modern Fiction Studies* 6 (1960), pp. 145–52; Frederick Karl, 'The Novel as Moral Allegory: The Fiction of William Golding' in *A Reader's Guide to the Contemporary English Novel*, New York, Noonday Press, 1962, pp. 236–55; Vijay Lakshmi, 'Entering the Whirlpool: The Movement towards Self-Awareness in William Golding's *Pincher Martin*,' *The Literary Criterion* 17 (1982), pp. 25–36; Bernard S. Oldsey and Stanley Weintraub, *The Art of William Golding*, New York, Harcourt, Brace and World, 1965.

7   Among those suggested are Ballantyne's *The Coral Island* (Dickson, op. cit.), Conrad's *Nostromo* and *Victory* (S.H. Boyd, *The Novels of William Golding*, New York, St Martin's Press, 1988), Poe's short story, 'A Tale of Two Ragged Mountains' (Lea Tanzman, 'Poe's "A Tale of Ragged Mountains" as a Source for Golding's Post Mortem Consciousness Technique in *Pincher Martin*' *Notes on Contemporary Literature* 25, 1995, pp. 6–7), Hemingway's *The Snows of Kilimanjaro* (Dickson, ibid.) and – by way of ironic inversion – Defoe's *Robinson Crusoe* (Boyd, op. cit.; Lawrence S. Friedman, *William Golding*, New York, Continuum, 1993; Gabriel Josipovici, *The World and the Book: A Study of Modern Fiction*, Stanford, Stanford University Press, 1971; Kevin McCarron, '"In Contemplation of my Deliverance": *Robinson Crusoe* and *Pincher Martin*,' *Robinson Crusoe: Myths and Metamorphoses*, Lieve Spaas and Brian Stimpton (eds), New York, MacMillan Press, 1996, pp. 285–93.

8   Ian Blake, '*Pincher Martin*, William Golding and Taffrail' *Notes and Queries* (August 1962), pp. 309–10.

9   Donald W. Crompton, *A View From the Spire: William Golding's Later Novels*, edited and completed by Julia Briggs, Oxford, Blackwell, 1985.

10   McCarron, op. cit., p. 291.

11   Lee M. Whitehead, 'The Moment Out of Time: Golding's *Pincher Martin*' in James R. Baker (ed.), *Critical Essays on William Golding*, Boston, G.K. Hall, 1988, p. 57.

12   The density of cross-references and juxtaposition of similar motifs in dissimilar context that comprise the verbal surface is seen here. When the sailor falls into the sea, as Pincher is suspended 'between life and death', the water is described as pushing in 'without mercy', the exact phrase that will close the survival tale.

13   McCarron, op. cit., p. 289.

14   See as well the Golding letter quoted in John Peter, 'The Fables of William Golding: Postscript', *William Golding's* Lord of the Flies*: A Source Book*, William Nelson (ed.), New York, Odyssey, 1963, p. 34, and his response, when asked to comment on the cellar, that it was an effort to represent a theological concept. If men were given free will, they would obviously have the choice either to turn to God or away from Him. 'When you turn away from God, He becomes a darkness; when you turn towards Him, He becomes a light, in cliché terms' (Jack Biles, *Talk: Conversation with William Golding*, New York, Harcourt, Brace and Jovanovich, 1976, p. 74).

15   Thus the importance of the island/Teeth, a trope explored by most critical commentaries. When Pincher's tongue feels along the barrier of his own teeth – the pinchers in his eating mouth – he feels a gap. 'His tongue was remembering. It pried into the gap between the teeth and re-created the old, aching shape. It touched the rough edge [...] traced the slope down [...] towards the smooth surface where the Red Lion was [...] understood what

was so hauntingly familiar and painful about an isolated and decaying rock in the middle of the sea' (p. 174). Rockall's entire topography is the remembered tooth in the mouth of the ravenous Pincher.

16   In contrast to Pincher's face, one rearranged on the outside, Nat's face is rearranged on the inside, one more feature of his saintliness. The notion of someone's 'face' as, on the one hand, the disguise that can be rearranged whatever the treachery behind and, on the other hand, as the very seat of truth will come to be used in *The Pyramid* and *The Paper Men*.

17   Golding to Tiger, op. cit., p. 26.

18   Golding to Kermode, op. cit., p. 26.

19   Golding to Tiger, op. cit., p. 138. As will be seen in the final novel, *The Double Tongue*, Saint Dionysios the Areopagite long gripped Golding's imagination. An Athenian Christian in the first century A.D, he was converted by St Paul (*Acts* 17:34). Tradition has it that he was a martyr and first bishop of Rome; in the Middle Ages he was erroneously revered as the author of Neoplatonic treatises, which influenced medieval scholasticism, particularly through St Thomas Aquinas.

20   The figure in the seaboots can be linked to various transcultural representations of the godhead as well as the wise old man who asks questions for the purpose of inducing self-reflection. As Fisher King, the figure is associated with *Rigeveda*, the Hindu book that praises different gods, as well as the Rock at Scylla and its companion, the Charybdis–fig tree. In the legends of the Holy Grail, the Fisherman King dwells in the Castle of the Holy Grail, where the holy vessel is enshrined.

Free Fall

I

> Is our willingness to still keep the word 'saint' in our lexicon a crack in
> the matte wall of one of our important understandings of the world?
> Does the word create the possibility glimpsed and urge a quick discard
> of action beyond self-interest?
>
> Mary Gordon, *Saint Joan*

Pincher Martin, as we have seen, implied, and sought to demonstrate, the
presence of a spiritual reality, an unseen world that interpenetrates the
visible one. But it was the nature of the protagonist's cosmos that we
had to infer its presence negatively. With *Free Fall*, changes in
technique, focus, and authorial stance – for here Golding approached a
more conventional reader/author relationship by narrating the tale
from the first-person point of view of an unreliable narrator – all
combined to allow a narrative rendering of the moments of vision in
religious ecstasy. Thus *Free Fall* offers one vision of sanctity, not merely
the 'heaven of sheer negation', which could be construed from the
blackness of Christopher Hadley Martin's hell. To achieve that 'heaven',
Pincher had to surrender his own personality to a godhead's love and
pity: the purgatory that he occupies is a specifically theological one,
albeit unorthodox. *Free Fall*, on the other hand, posits the possibility of
another mode of existence, a world of magic and terror, spirit and
miracle to which Sammy Mountjoy, the protagonist, can direct what he
describes as his 'need to worship' (p. 109). Furthermore, the novel tries
to provoke this imaginative mode in the reader.

Looking back from *Free Fall* to *The Inheritors* and *Pincher Martin*, one
could see their author to have been a pattern-maker for whom pattern
was inadequate, structural pattern having been used to invalidate
thematic pattern. By setting up a tension between two contradictory
and inadequate patterns – one of which had been represented in the first
narrative movement while the other was represented in the coda's
reversal – structurally both texts created an ideogram for differing
truths. While, after *Lord of the Flies*, the novels forbade any simple or
'right' reading, the emphases in all three were on the inadequacies of

human nature. With *Free Fall*'s appearance in 1959, definitive changes occurred. A neat progression from collective criminality, which *The Inheritors* dramatized, to the perdition of Being in *Pincher Martin* narrowed further still in *Free Fall* to the exploration of one guilty person, enigmatic and individual. In contrast to its predecessors, this novel concerned itself with the rehabilitation of a divided soul, whose division was linked to a mid twentieth-century scepticism, even pessimism. Tracing, as it does, 'the process through time of one social and historical man becoming representative of contemporary manifestations of evil,'[1] *Free Fall* nevertheless never fully realized its promise.

The failure to achieve artistic coherence may well have rested on the very nature of its ambitious intention. As Golding remarked early on, he was trying to incorporate into this work 'the immediacy of inexplicable living', his goal being 'to give a picture of the patternlessness of man's existence in the west at the moment'. It was his sense at mid-century that no system of reference, no spiritual gravity, no creeds or codes operated to sustain the individual. 'I am a burning amateur, torn by the irrational and incoherent, violently searching and self-condemned' (p. 5), observes the narrator as he explores his condition of free fall. And he concludes: 'We are neither the innocent nor the wicked. We are the guilty. We fall down' (p. 251). While the mythic landscape is unmistakable – the nature of fallen man, Adam unparadised, the loss of innocence – the novel counterpoints at least two explications, that of the scientific juxtaposed with that of the religious. Its title alludes not simply to Milton's *Paradise Lost* ('Sufficient to have stood/But free to fall') but to the physical condition of free fall, one of unrestrained motion in a gravitational field. Taking as its focus the circuitous reflection – and *written* record – of a mid twentieth-century painter upon the events of his past, the novel involves a socio-cultural texture that was then new to Golding's fiction. It was as though he had 'deliberately set out in his fourth novel to counteract the critics' assessment of his fiction as simplistic parables demonstrating man's inherent (and irredeemable) evil.'[2]

Critical response to *Free Fall* has, for the most part, been lukewarm, even antagonistic; the immediate reception was extremely negative. Commenting upon the chronological irregularities, reviewers interpreted these distortions as proof of a penchant for obscurity and fortuitous cleverness. If gaps in the narrative were first judged wilful, later and more sustained analyses of the complex chronology came to grapple with its intent.[3] 'A man's life is an elaborate synthesis of [...] two time-scales and Sammy's cannot be properly understood unless we keep in mind both the chronological sequence of events and the way in which memory has reorganized it.'[4] Critical consensus agreed that *Free Fall* had its roots in *Pincher Martin*,[5] several suggesting that *Free Fall* was 'a kind of reverse *Pincher Martin* in that the protagonist brings his intelligence and creativity to bear on the task of finding rather than avoiding truth.'[6] Yet, although *Pincher Martin*'s verbal texture with its multiple shifting meanings had been commended in the past, stylistic innovations in *Free Fall* were frequently read as blunders or meretricious showmanship, especially in the mock-heroic parody of language of courtly love involving the young lovers, Sammy and Beatrice. My sense was always that the novel's mixtures of style – colloquialisms are often poised between scientific jargon, sensuous images, and lyrical cadences – were intended, like the disjunctive chronology, as verbal and structural counterparts to the thematic distinction drawn between the world of flesh and the world of spirit. Recognizing the departure from the remote settings of the earlier narratives and *Free Fall*'s social specificity,[7] many scholars and critics have continued to find the right pigeonhole for its narrative mode.[8] Whatever narrative formula one accepts as most accurate, however, whichever source one determines as most influential, their combined responses suggest how provocative *Free Fall* has been and underscores my feeling that, while a difficult work, it came to be rewarding and enigmatic in new ways. In fact, Golding insisted long ago that with *Free Fall* he had been 'moving much more towards novels where I don't understand what everything is about', an early declaration of a lifelong temperamental distrust of conceptual categories and what would become an increasing admiration for 'inconsistency': 'it's the only stance or stances in a shifting, incomprehensible, ambiguous, sliding-away-from-me-totality.'[9] So as early as the mid-1950s there was his affirmation of metaphor and myth as vehicles which find, but do not impose, order and coherence. And a narrator was created – certainly a surrogate for its author – seeking desperately to find pattern, not to impose it. And the narrative's project became one of avoiding the imposition of pattern while creating a metaphor that would imply the order of mystery.

If the 'crucial difference between *Free Fall* and the previous three novels [...] resides in the first person narration,'[10] it is instructive that the novel takes as its protagonist an artist who has 'hung all systems on the wall like a row of useless hats' (p. 6), having worn a Marxist eye-shade, a Christian beret, a rationalist bowler, and a grammar schoolboy's cap, and then thrown them all away. Despite this indifference, in what will be a crucial encounter with a Nazi psychologist (a demonic/angelic Interrogator much reminiscent of *Nineteen Eighty-Four*'s Inquistitor O'Brien) in a POW camp in Germany the soldier/artist is driven – by his own nature, that 'mystery' that the interrogator believes to be 'opaque' (p. 145) – to find 'some indications of a pattern that will include me, even if the outer edges tail off into ignorance' (p. 9).

From the quest for a pattern, a quest determining the fiction's spiritual outline, and the experience of a patternless world, the story emerges. Once again Golding's strategy was one of indirection; against the narrator's 'assertion of uniqueness and discontinuity we have to set the patterns, the elaborate echoes, the profoundly organized plotting of the novel itself. Between what the hero says and what the book says there is a relation which you might call contrapuntal.'[11] The narrator is brought back to the point where he could have chosen freedom, a freedom he had lost in young adulthood when he chose freely, because of his given nature, to commit a damaging, possibly sinful, act. Later in the chapter I shall examine this apparently contradictory view of developing behaviour and given being. It is sufficient here to point out that one of the consequences following from the narrator's new-found freedom is the discovery of a pattern emerging from the events of his past, a pattern whose shape the fiction's structure follows. And the pattern is one of guilt.

II

I have walked by stalls in the market place where books, dog-eared and faded from their purple, have burst with a white hosanna. I have seen people crowned with a double crown, holding in either hand the crook and flail, the power and the glory. I have understood how the scar becomes a star. I have felt the flake of fire fall, miraculous and pentecostal. My yesterdays walk with me. They keep step, they are grey faces that peer over my shoulder. I live on Paradise Hill, ten minutes from the station, thirty seconds from the shops and local. Yet I am a burning amateur, torn by the irrational and incoherent, violently searching and self-condemned (p. 5).

Free Fall's opening paragraph sounds, with Verdi-like bombast, the thematic dichotomy between the world of flesh and the world of spirit that the book will explore. 'To get the point of this paragraph,' as Gregor and Kinkead-Weekes observed, 'is to get the point of the whole book.'[12] The world of empirical observation and the world of imaginative vision: both exist and both are real. The narrator has perceived hosannas and pentecostal fire; he has witnessed the miraculous transmutation of scar into star; yet he lives 'ten minutes from the station, thirty seconds from the shops and local'. The stylistic counter-pointing of this secular colloquialism with those biblical echoes and rhythms of alliterative phrases such as 'I have felt the flake of fire fall' presents the discontinuity between the worlds. In childhood, as the narrator comes to understand, the two worlds interlock. For the adult Sammy, however, the past follows to condemn like grey faces forever unreconciled. There is no bridge. There is no forgiveness; the world of the spirit is experienced only as a condemnation of guilt, not as holiness or wholeness.

The formal carapace of the retrospective reminiscence consists of seven sequences, each involving pictures from the past. Chapters I to III deal with early childhood: when Sammy Mountjoy had freedom. Chapters IV to VI involve his youth and young manhood, when he lost his freedom. The conclusion of both sequences presents the same dilemma: once there was freedom; once it was lost. Chapters VII to IX involve the central confrontation of the book and Sammy's life; it is itself subdivided into three panels, with the outer two concerning Sammy's interrogation in the German prison camp during World War II and his terror-stricken experience in a dark cell. The triptych's middle panel reverts back to his childhood and deals in preparation for the following chapter with the question, one that held Golding's imagination in a life-long grip: 'How did I come to be so frightened of the dark?' (p. 154). Chapters X to XII give the climax of the narrative proper, moving from a transitional episode in the prison yard back to Sammy's early tutelage under the two grammar school teachers, Nick Shales and Rowena Pringle. Chapter XII outlines the act that cost him his freedom: the choice of physicality. Chapters XIII and XIV elaborate the 'everything' (p. 236) that his choice had sacrificed and in the coda gives the reversal that gathers the whole text together. Throughout the narrator returns to the present: the writing of his story. One system of rhetorical leitmotifs – 'Here? Not Here' – makes the transition and marks the climax of the narrative quest for the point at which Sammy physically crossed the bridge to East London and lost his freedom: a loss of the bridge between the flesh and the spirit. Various running images bind the fragments as well, chief among which are those associated with Sammy's coveted fag-cards: the kings of Egypt. As for Golding in the memorial essay 'Egypt from My Inside', so for his artist persona where the heroic aspect of humanity is conveyed by a traditional metaphor of royalty. So 'abashed before the kingship of the human face' (p. 150), Sammy captures the transfigured prison camp and its prisoners in his 'smuggled sketches of the haggard, unshaven kings of Egypt' (p. 188). Chronology, of course, has been deliberately, but not wilfully, distorted. Unscrambled, the story involves the childhood of Sammy Mountjoy, born of a woman of more than easy virtue in a Kent slum, Rotten Row; his schooling and friends; his adoption – hence social ascent – by the Church of England rector, the homosexual Father Watts Watt; his seduction of the beautiful, Chapel-going Beatrice Ifor; his betrayal of her and marriage to a Communist comrade, Taffy; his experience in a German POW camp; and finally his post-war experience when he returns home to encounter the mad Beatrice and revisit his 'spiritual' (p. 194) parents, the schoolteachers Nick and Miss Pringle. In temporal chronology the final 'event' is the narration of the story as Sammy's 'darkness […] fumbles at a typewriter' (p. 8). The novel closes, however, with a flashback to the prison and a German Commandant's ambiguous 'Sphinx's riddle' (p. 253) and a reference to Dr Halde, the interrogator, who in the words of the novel's very last sentence 'Does not know about peoples' (p. 253).

III

> When I make my black pictures, when I inspect chaos, I must remember that such [merciful] places are as real as Belsen. They, too, exist, they are part of this enigma, this living. They are brick walls like any others […] But remembered, they shine (p. 77).

Time shifts and chronological discontinuities as well as elaborate verbal echoes and the strategy of doubling – as well as the double (Sammy being to Beatrice what Halde will become to Sammy) – are all used in *Free Fall* to show the religious significance of one man's life. 'Signpost characters'[13] – the spiritual parents Miss Pringle/Nick; the two Eves of paradisal Rotten Row Ma/Evie, the two school chum tempters Johnny/Philip; the two Communist comrades Alsopp/Wimburg; and the two lovers Beatrice/Taffy – contend oppositionally for Sammy's soul. At the same time the narrative design is meant to account dramatically for the representative mid-century loss of the world of miracle. That the result is ultimately flawed rests on the issue that two independent quests operate throughout the novel: the quest for Being *qua* Being and the quest for the bridge between the worlds of the flesh and the spirit. Put another way, one can see that the resolution implied by the (characteristic) confrontation scene as well as the (characteristic) coda reversal relate thematically, but not dramatically, to the work's religious core. Consequently the novel's vision never coalesces and in the end becomes mere notes towards a problem, not the solution of one. *Free Fall's* primary quest involves Sammy's search for spiritual freedom in a climate of mid twentieth-century cynicism and scepticism. This is particularized as an effort to discover the bridge between the world represented by the indestructible burning bush in *Exodus* and that represented by the laboratory's bell-jar, where matter is neither destroyed nor created. Thematically the quest has affinities with other religious patterns of transformation, like those in Dante's *Vita Nuova*, to which *Free Fall* relates ironically and contrapuntally.

Once again there has been the intertextual inversion of a literary model, although in *Free Fall's* case the model, not its subversion, is taken as the right explanation whereas its recasting is intended to show the wrong explanation. The major quest is overtly theological – although unorthodox in nature – and in a sense the impasse to which this journey finally comes is a rational one. The suggestion – and this is at thematic level only – is that since freedom is experienced as well as guilt, there may be some place where the two worlds intersect, a place 'sometimes open and sometimes shut, the business of the universe proceeding there in its own mode, different, indescribable' (p. 187). This place is closed to the eye of logic. In my reading of the fiction's conclusion, the riddle posed in the coda is intended to resurrect this dead eye of logic in order to make the reader – not the unreliable narrator – cast a new eye of the spirit back over all that has occurred before the riddle was posed. Is that difficult task accomplished? Perhaps, perhaps not.

Other weaknesses flaw the work. Some are minor, such as the 'hackneyed' depiction of the German interrogator. 'If one feels a certain familiarity about Dr Halde, it is because he has appeared before in countless disguises as the articulate, dispassionate Nazi in World War II movies, the kind usually played by Erich von Stroheim, who abhors his present occupation but rationalizes it as expedient.'[14] Of a more serious nature is *Free Fall*'s aim to merge two methods of narration by grounding the inexplicability of felt life in some search for cosmic value. Thus Sammy Mountjoy is given a strong and specific social context. We see him at school with Philip fighting for his beloved fag-cards of the kings of Egypt; we see him playing bombers in the hop fields of Kent with another friend, Johnny. We watch him swagger histrionically before the lower middle class Beatrice Ifor as she leaves a training college in East London. Golding, however, would have Mountjoy's particular repudiation of the spiritual in his desecration of Beatrice identified with both its historical implications – World War II, to give one huge example – and its cosmic one as well. So the episode between Mountjoy and Halde in the POW camp re-orchestrates the interrogations Beatrice suffers under Sammy's fervent questionings: 'Don't you feel anything?' demands each interrogator. Answering Halde's crucial probing as Beatrice answered his, Mountjoy mutters the most paradoxical of seemingly empty of phrases, the very one given by Beatrice to her tormentor Sammy years earlier. 'Do you feel nothing?' Halde questions and Sammy replies 'Maybe' (p. 142): a more than valent phrase, given the connection being sought. For the implication of this reverberating 'maybe' is that Sammy's failure to accept responsibility and his inability to live within a coherent world is that of his mid twentieth-century contemporaries. 'For maybe was sign of all our times. We were certain of nothing' (p. 108):

> I welcomed the destruction that war entails, the death and terror [...]
> There was anarchy in the mind where I lived and anarchy in the world
> at large, two states so similar that one might have produced the other.
> The shattered houses, the refugees, the deaths and torture – accept them
> as a pattern of the world and one's behaviour is little enough disease.
> (pp. 131–32)

So one has an ambitious novel where psychological motivations war with the formal demands that the narrator's pursuit imposes upon the structure. Several times Mountjoy appears to be engaged in social, as well as moral, dilemmas whose outcome is in the balance. His fortune appears to be affected by recognizable social gradations (removal from

Rotten Row to the rectory brings social class promotion as well as physical comfort but a loss of creature comfort) and yet he seems to be influenced by forces beyond his immediate understanding. Still, social matters are often overshadowed by symbolical explanations, which function as a kind of authorial underscoring. This is especially true when Sammy chooses, rather than the uncharitable Miss Pringle's miraculous universe, the kindly Nick's rational one. The world of symbols, especially the trope of the door, formulates Sammy's predicament, as though an omniscient authorial voice were speaking alongside that of the narrator:

> This was a moment of such importance to me that I must examine it completely. For an instant of time, the two worlds existed side by side. The one I inhabited by nature, the world of miracle drew me strongly. To give up the burning bush, the water from the rock, the spittle on the eyes was to give up a portion of myself, a dark and inward and fruitful portion. Yet looking at me from the bush was the fat and freckled face of Miss Pringle [...] I hung for an instant between two pictures of the universe; then the ripple passed over the burning bush and I ran towards my friend [Nick]. In that moment a door closed behind me. I slammed it shut on Moses and Jehovah. I was not to knock on that door again, until in a Nazi prison camp I lay huddled against it half crazed with terror and despair (p. 217).

The conventions of actuality are twice violated by a deliberate blurring of action with narrative method, shifting between auto-biographical meditation, where character remembers event, and dramatically atavistic episodes where ego confronts psychic darkness. If *Pincher Martin*, in alternating 'Time-Past' and 'Time-Present', placed greatest emphasis on the latter by striking fragments of memories across Pincher's efforts to survive, then *Free Fall* exactly inverts the method. Sammy's past dominates his present writing although its presentation as a set of 'pictures' is no more than a development of the montage effect of *Pincher Martin*.

Again in *Free Fall* – as is the case in the earlier novel – the character is revealed in retrospect as a state not a process. Limited and unreliable as his narration may be, Sammy is no more self-creating – that is, capable of molding his own consciousness – than Pincher had been seen to be. The change in Sammy after his 'sin' is not an alteration of what previously existed, but merely the fulfilment of a latent possibility.

'Now I have been back in these pages,' writes the narrator, 'to find out why I am frightened of the dark and I cannot tell. Once upon a time I was not frightened of the dark and later on I was' (p. 165). Reality in *Free Fall* is a closed and static system; individuals carry their destiny within them and acts externalize that nature. Yet Sammy is looking beyond those closed walls and doors, seeking the freedom that is experienced and known as acutely as 'the taste of potatoes'. As he puts the matter:

> What men believe is a function of what they are; and what they are is in part what has happened to them. And yet here and there, in all that riot of compulsion comes the clear taste of potatoes, element so rare the isotope of uranium is abundant by comparison (p. 212).

IV

> And who are you anyway? Are you on the inside, have you a proof-copy? Am I a job to do? Do I exasperate you by translating incoherence into incoherence? (p. 8)

Like other self-reflexive authors concerned with writing about writing, Golding has his surrogate author/artist Sammy forefront the creative process. The novel opens with a kind of prologue, reminiscent of a dramatic monologue, in which listener is directly confronted by speaker. Except in the context of writing in *Free Fall*, it is a listener who is summoned as a participant in the unfolding confession, invoked, hectored, cajoled and then asked to sit in judgement on actions. Sammy bluntly intrudes, 'My darkness reaches out and fumbles at a typewriter with its tongs. Your darkness reaches out with your tongs and grasps a book' (p. 8). As my discussion of *Pincher Martin* makes obvious, the trope of darkness represents the internal landscape of psyche. *Free Fall*'s first chapter is a logical development from the filmic technique of its predecessor, where Pincher while drowning sees the essential factors of his life as neon lights and expands them. A kind of modulated Pincher, Sammy shares with him several traits, especially egotistic sensuality.[15] However, in an early conversation Golding remarked to me that Sammy took off from the point where Tuami sat, brooding over his ivory dagger, which is the moment – we remember – when he plans to transform the death weapon into a sculptor's tool. So it was the baffling business of creation that also provoked *Free Fall*'s genesis where – unlike a Pincher who imposes pattern by naming things Piccadilly Circus and Regent Street in order to control – a sculptor, a writer, a painter, each creator seeks desperately to discover a pattern. So Mountjoy organizes and reorganizes past events, not as they occurred but in the order of their affective significance. As narrator and omniscient authorial voice both explicate:

> For time is not to be laid out endlessly like a row of bricks. The straight line from the first hiccup to the last gasp is a dead thing. Time is two modes. The one is an effortless perception [...] The other is memory, a sense of shuffle, fold and coil, of that day nearer than that because more important, of that event mirroring this, or those three set apart, exceptional and out of the straight line altogether (p. 6).

The distinction – well within the Plotinus tradition, involving as it does the affective memory – gives *Free Fall* its principle of composition and, not unexpectedly, its metaphor for truth.

Except for its final event – the writing of life past in the present – the narrative proper is all retrospect. Instead of submerging character in development, presenting Sammy Mountjoy progressively, various snapshots of his character at various ages are displayed. In one sense, the reader, in juxtaposing the motionless images, experiences the effect of the passage of time as the narrator has experienced it. Take, for example, the sequence at the end of the novel when Sammy faces the insane Beatrice and surveys the consequences of his abandoning her. The asylum stands at the peak of, the not inconsequentially named, Paradise Hill, yet it has around it the sense of institution like the '*greyness* of a prison camp' (p. 238, my italics).[16] Originally it was the General's 'magic house' (p. 45), whose apocalyptic cedar tree, fairy lights, and dark Gardens of Persephone had bathed the young interlopers, Johnny and Sammy, in wonder as they 'wander[ed] in paradise' (p. 45). Now it is merely 'the grey house of factual succession' (p. 237), unredeemed by spirit because denied of spirit, where a wholly physical Beatrice pisses on the floor. Just as the consequences of denying a spiritual dimension had robbed the mansion of its beauty, the mid twentieth-century denial of the spiritual dimension had diseased the epoch with shattered houses, torture and death. So too the consequences of choosing physical lust with Beatrice – 'I could not paint her face; but her body I painted' (p. 123) – reinforce the reality of physical life and make it more contemptible. The middle-aged Sammy sees Beatrice's now sagging face shadowed by her body; only 'a little light was reflected from the institutional wall and showed some of the molding' (p. 242). The analogy here between the architecture of a building and that of physiognomy both erases human agency and neatly juxtaposes present with past.

Since the narrator – in writing himself – is commenting upon and assembling episodes, time is arrested in another sense and the protagonist can be viewed as a continuous being. In contrast to stream of consciousness strategies in Woolf or Joyce, for example, the 'pictures' of the past are not altogether random. Surveying his experience Mountjoy concludes:

> They are important simply because they emerge. I am the sum of them.
> I carry round with me this load of memories. Man is not an instantaneous creature, nothing but a physical body and the reaction of the moment. He is an incredible bundle of miscellaneous memories and feelings, of fossils and coral growths (p. 46).

For this reason, the narrative method is retrospective meditation. It consists in brooding on some instance which will bring about a total recall of a certain epoch, not as a faint memory but as a vividly relived experience containing its own significance. Take, for example, the writing Sammy groping to capture the essential nature of Ma, whom he experienced as 'warm darkness' (p. 15) and a blocking of 'the tunnel' (p. 15), and observing to his reader/narratee: 'And now something happens in my head. Let me catch the picture before the perception vanishes' (p. 15). He proceeds then to reconstruct the Epic Bog Brawl when Ma defends her 'throne' (p. 21), her voice bouncing 'off the sky in brazen thunder' (p. 19). And he concludes, 'I have no memory of majesty to match that one from Rotten Row' (p. 21).

When he sets aside theoretical categories, Sammy can glimpse in such a static image as this some rounded aspect of a whole truth, unfragmented and unabstracted. Or he can try to. Thus the comic yet awesome death of the Rotten Row lodger is seen through 'the mind's eye' (p. 29) when the adult Sammy stoops to knee height and becomes the small child, 'the empty bubble' (p. 29), who confuses the lodger's death with the cessation of a clock ticking. Like Ma and Evie, the lodger is an agent of imagination and hence a bridge to the world of miracle. Thus Sammy is suddenly haunted by a 'moustache of white swan's feather' (p. 76) when he is cringing in the cell, but he cannot be armored against death any more than he could be in Rotten Row. 'And the shape of life loomed [in Rotten Row] that I was insufficient for our lodger's thatch, for that swan-white seal of ultimate knowing' (p. 29). He is – as Golding puts it many times in *Free Fall* and will again of his protagonist Oliver in *The Pyramid* – 'on the pavement'. Sammy believes testimonies of miracles, he sustains a 'worried faith in the kings of Egypt' (p. 149), but as an adult he is insufficient to inhabit that world.

On the other hand, Mountjoy is given the capacity to live in a divided and double world. He is – as he himself realizes before Halde – 'not an ordinary man. I was at once more than most and less' (p. 150). The lesson the '*mind's eye*' (p. 29, my italics) seeks to discover is the point at which his inadequate being opted for one of those two worlds.[17] The implication is that Mountjoy might have always kept his double vision but that he was free to decide for egocentric and carnal reasons that it was unimportant. As he remembers his headmaster advising: 'If you want something enough, you can always get it provided you are willing to make the appropriate sacrifice [...] But what you get is never quite what you thought; and sooner or later the sacrifice is always regretted' (p. 235). Sammy Mountjoy makes the appropriate sacrifice; wanting Beatrice Ifor's white body he closes the door to the world of the spirit, losing his freedom and ability to experience both worlds.

V

[A]gain this is trying to move on a level of revealed religion, a rather sordid kind of twentieth-century beginning which might lead to a pilgrim's progress. But the pilgrim has got his feet in the mud. There are no trumpets sounding for him on the other side: the trumpets are a long way off.

Golding to Biles

Although the narrator may justify it as the logical outcome of his adopted materialism, the attentive reader understands that Samuel Mountjoy's worship of beauty is a worship of holiness and manifestation of his inherent spiritualism. He purposely disregards the spirit in seducing Beatrice, deciding that right and wrong are relative, but is shown trembling to contact her beyond 'the shoddy temple' (p. 108) of sex: '[A] sadness reached out of me that did not know what it wanted; for it is part of my nature that I should need to worship, and this was not in the textbooks, not in the behaviour of those I had chosen and so without knowing I had thrown it away' (p. 109). What the attentive reader also discovers is that the protagonist is made to deny the spirit by means of the spirit, an ironic point illustrated neatly by Mountjoy's Tate painting celebrating Beatrice's body imaginatively in a way he never touched her physically. In fact, he captures her nature despite himself and despite his negation of it: 'I added the electric light-shades of Guernica to catch the terror, but there was no terror to catch... The electric light that ought to sear like a public prostitution seems an irrelevance. There is gold, rather, scattered from the window' (p. 124). In the very first instance of repudiation he adopts materialism and the relativity of moral codes as an expression of his heart's affection for the kindly Nick. Indeed it is Nick's kindness, not his materialist system, which makes Sammy forsake the world of the symbol made intolerable by Miss Pringle's obsessive cruelty, a cruelty which defiles her inspired intimacy with the Old Testament.[18] In the final instance, when Sammy's physical eye cannot function in the cell's darkness and the world of the senses — the world he has declared real — is no longer available, his mind's eye creates monster after monster. His own darkness is not still; it forces him to explore the center both of the cell and his own internal darkness. Ultimately he will cry out for mercy, a cry which is an affirmation of the Spirit.

The religious connotations of Sammy Mountjoy's name underscore the thematics of revealed religion. Fragments of biblical allusions are encoded, for example, in the first phase of his life. The Old Testament prophet, Samuel, was conceived by Hannah through the ministering of a priest; Sammy's parentage is associated with a cleric since Ma's favorite fiction (and the one the child Sammy finds most attractive) is that his father was a parson. Like the Old Testament prophet who was brought to the altar to do service, Sammy too is drawn to the altar, although by the bad influence of Philip who urges him to defile not honor it. If these biblical intertextualities suffer, in part, ironic inversion, Sammy like his namesake does at least become a judge over himself and a proclaimer of kings. That Sammy's nature will ultimately choose hedonism is a point well made by the pun associated with his surname. Here one kind of 'mount-into-joy' is replaced by another and, if the infant Sammy was banished from Paradise Hill, then the post-pubescent Mountjoy conquered (as Peter Green felicitously phrased it) the *Mons Veneris*.

In the second phase of Sammy's early life – 'the whole time of the other school' (p. 192) – a more significant intertextuality is ironically inverted. As is the characteristic strategy, again it is the character's name that becomes the wedge which introduces an alternate, yet analogous world. Beatrice's name in *Free Fall* more than hints at the Dantean pattern underlying the novel's quest for a bridge between two opposing worlds. First seen by Sammy before a drawing class, 'a palladian bridge' (p. 221) has been established by the authorial voice to be behind her transparent and illuminated face. Issuing from the girl's brow Sammy is made to perceive what was the connected world of mystery and matter, 'a metaphorical light that none the less seemed to me to be an objective phenomenon, a real thing' (p. 232). Living in that freedom that the novel defines as unconscious undifferentiated perception, the painter Sammy looks upon the model Beatrice and experiences two worlds simultaneously; they interlock and he experiences that connection.

Almost certainly, the 'metaphorical light' emanating from the depicted Beatrice is meant to reference the exalted Beatrice of Dante's *Vita Nuova*. For *Free Fall* can be viewed as an ironic inversion of Dante's sublime sequence, a collection of thirty-one lyrical poems celebrating the beloved woman, interspersed with a prose narrative which comments upon the course of the developing devotion. In addition to the beloved's emblematic name and the representation of Sammy's sensual desire as a parody of all the torments, intolerable ecstasies, and anguished mortification attendant upon a courtly lover's unrequited love, there are several scenes in *Free Fall* corresponding to ones described in the prose chapters of the *Vita Nuova*. Dante unexpectedly sees Beatrice for the second time since her girlhood as she walks down a street in Florence, accompanied by two women (III). Sammy, for his part, manipulates events so that he can happen upon Beatrice as she leaves the training college in South London accompanied by two girl friends. Dante, soon after, writes a *ballata* to justify his love in Beatrice's eyes (XII); Sammy sends a heady letter declaring his ensnarement. The crucial moment in the transformation of Dante's despair to active praise – which issues in the famous *canzone* 'Ladies who know by insight what Love is' – occurs as Dante walks in the country beside a stream of very clear water (XIX). Similarly Sammy's devotion undergoes a crucial transformation as he wades through cathedral-like woods; passing through a stream of 'providential waters' (p. 235), he feels his manhood strong and decides upon lubricity – 'the white unseen body of Beatrice Ifor' (p. 235) – not Dantean love.

As Beatrice is to Dante so Beatrice is to Sammy: a creature wholly superior to himself, wholly Other. For Dante, however, Beatrice becomes an instrument of contemplation, exaltation and finally salvation (in the *Paradiso*, as we know, she leads him through Heaven) whereas for Sammy Beatrice is solely an instrument of lust. He chooses to confuse her mysterious, baffling beauty with simple salt sex – 'I love you, I want to be you!' (p. 105) he intones. By a deliberate act of will he makes that foreignness a servant to his passion and a slave of his egotism: sex becomes his 'shoddy temple' (p. 108) of worship.

In an early conversation about *Free Fall*'s germination with his friend Peter Green, Golding explained that his experience of the mid twentieth-century ethos – an incoherent world where the war and its aftermath were intimately linked, in his view, to scientific relativism – forged what I am here naming as *Free Fall*'s ironic recasting of Dante's *Vita Nuova*, an identification he himself never explicitly stated:

> But where Dante, presented with a coherent cosmos, was able to fit her into it, Sammy's confused cosmos ended by putting her through the whole mill of seduction – a scientific, rationalistic approach so to speak, so that Beatrice who took Dante up to the vision of God becomes a clog to Sammy and a skeleton in his cupboard.[19]

In contrast to *The Coral Island*'s ironic inversion in *Lord of the Flies*, the Dantean analogue does not consistently shape the text, operating as it does in only one phase of the narrator's journey. Neither the confrontation scene with its purgation of the protagonist nor the coda's revelation is informed by the *Vita Nuova*. The intention was to have the reader look back at the Sammy of the Van Gogh seduction bedsit and re-evaluate the unreliable narrator's judgement about Beatrice's 'opaqueness' (p. 113), it being not at all the 'avoidance of the deep and muddy pool where others lived' (p. 112), but rather the clear presence of generosity. Like Simon before her and *Darkness Visible*'s Matty after, Beatrice represents another example of the characteristic figure of the 'holy fool' offering 'the fool's wisdom in her key word "maybe".[20] That connection, that intertextual excavation, rests on the reader's ability – or willingness – to construct such an edifice on so small a scaffold: the mere, if pointed, naming of a character whose fictional realization is, in addition, never achieved by any other kind of particularization than the symbolic.

Nevertheless, this Dantean inversion is posited as the answer to the book's overriding question, 'where did I lose my freedom?' as well as being given as the explanation for error. Inhabiting a culture less susceptible to the lures of materialism, Sammy might have taken Beatrice as the ideal and been led presumably to a twentieth-century mystic Rose. But he takes her, as Golding remarked to me, as the opposite: 'the very concrete present to be achieved, conquered and beaten'.

> What had been love on my part, passionate and reverent, what was to be a triumphant sharing, a fusion, the penetration of a secret, raising of my life to the enigmatic and holy level of hers became a desperately shoddy and cruel attempt to force a response from her somehow. Step by step we descended the path of sexual exploitation until the projected sharing had become an affliction (p. 123).

Whereas Dante placed Beatrice in heaven in his last vision of her, Sammy, in words recasting Milton's Satan –'Musk, shameful and heady, be thou my good' (p. 232) – decides his heaven will be sex. And since Beatrice is, by upbringing, social class, and conformist convention, frigid, she becomes Sammy's hell, not his heaven at all.

Mountjoy, unlike his friend Johnny Spragg and Nick, is no innocent. Nor is he, like Philip or Halde, one of the wicked. 'The innocent and wicked live in one world' (p. 252); each operates in mutually exclusive, but existentially inclusive, spheres. Mountjoy belongs to a third category; he is one of the guilty and his sentence is to live in both worlds, suffering 'the mode which we call the spirit' (p. 253) as self-condemnation:

> Cause and effect. The law of succession. Statistical probability. The moral order. Sin and remorse. They are all true. Both worlds exist side by side. They meet in me. We have to satisfy the examiners in both worlds at once (p. 244).

There is no bridge.

VI

What we know is not what we see or learn but what we realize (p. 149).

Yet the sources and means of depravity are also the sources and means of power and active creation; Sammy's shabby victory over Beatrice paradoxically complements his mysterious victory over the bleakness of the prison cell with its dark center. Each manifests his special power, that reverence for beauty, that intense sensitivity, that 'nightmare knowledge' (p. 28) that lets him 'see unusually far through a brick wall' (p. 133). In earlier chapters, I argued that both *The Inheritors* and *Pincher Martin* conclude with a kind of mythopoeical positing that the point at which individuals become godlike is precisely the point at which fall could occur. In this context, what makes a specific action 'good' or 'bad' is what one individual affirms or denies; what, in fact, one individual does with the ideal. The People, we recall, can do nothing but love while Pincher can do nothing but desecrate; yet both are drawn by an ideal – one in the figures of the New People of the Fall, the other in the persons of Nathaniel and Mary. The implication is that there would be a certain crucial occasion where a test occurred and what individuals had carried within would confront them by way of the lineaments of choice. And *Free Fall* seems to suggest that at such a point there is evidence – does then its author take this literally? – that freedom exists. At such a point one is not determined by one's predetermined nature: one is sufficient to have stood but free to fall. Thus Fa, unlike Lok, can understand that the New People are dangerous, so that remaining awake she witnesses their transgressions. Lok, in contrast, cannot obey Fa's instruction to ignore Liku's absence and recapture only the new one. Remaining with his given nature, he is unable to imagine the New People could be destructive enough to sacrifice Liku and consequently his innocent nature contributes to Fa's death, his own, and, by extension, that of the Neanderthal species. Similarly Christopher Hadley Martin's particular power is his ability to survive; and it is precisely Christopher's endurance (under the aspect of Christopolus, the Christ bearer) that Chris Martin (under the aspect of Pincher) corrupts. Both *The Inheritors* and *Pincher Martin* offer this mythopoeia in structural terms, as I also argued earlier, with their coda reversals supplying the means by which the reader can revise initial responses. In *Free Fall* such an ideographic strategy is present in both coda and confrontation scene; however, the strategy of reversal plays no part in revising the reader's conception of the narrator's early childhood. The important question that Sammy poses to himself in the nightmarish experience in the cell – why he has come to grow so frightened of the dark – is not answered. Golding himself may regard darkness as the spiritual dimension of which the twentieth-century Western sensibility is incapable of conceiving except in terms of guilt and malignancy. But *Free Fall* as narrative does not locate the reason why darkness should suddenly be something that terrifies; why darkness should be imagined as malignant. It just *is*.

As twentieth-century pilgrim, *Free Fall's* protagonist is meant to typify his confused historical time because he comes to experience spirit only as guilt. Why then is he permitted to escape from 'the forcing chamber of the cell' (p. 190) into a kind of merciful – if momentary – freedom? I put the question to Golding, who remarked that the flashback at the novel's close is like the 'handprint on the canvas that changes the whole thing', bringing it all into a true focus. The 'key to it was that the door of the cell opened. I suddenly saw that, and it became the first genuine passion I felt about the book.'

Another investigation can be detected in *Free Fall*; this second pursuit seems to me to be the one to most vividly engage its author's imagination, for, as in *Pincher Martin*, it grew from a radically anti-historical view of human nature. As the inverted, perverted Dante, Sammy Mountjoy represents a mid twentieth-century man living in a recognizable English landscape where sexual prudery and the constraints of social class influence behavior as well as misbehavior. But at the interrogative heart of the novel, 'the forcing chamber of the cell', the protagonist is a being facing some kind of godhead, that inevitable thrust or bar of steel, what *The Pyramid* later terms that 'god without mercy', which operates in and on.

In the POW camp, Sammy is deprived of institutions, society, even memories, and is reduced under Dr Halde's persecutions to psychic elements: fear and conjecture. As Halde puts it to Sammy: 'For you and me, reality is this room' (p. 140), a comment which the protagonist enlarges upon symbolically when he is made to mutter in the cell:

I? I? Too many I's, but what else was there in this thick, impenetrable cosmos? What else? A wooden door and how many shapes of walls? (p. 169–70)

And given Sammy's adolescent choice of a material world, all that the cosmos is can be imagined as an impenetrable dark prison with a wooden door and no exit. Here in the confrontation scene action flows inward as Sammy is made to retreat into himself to explore his fear.

It is a quest for Being *qua* Being that occupies *Free Fall*'s center, in my judgement, and not the quest for a philosophical bridge between two worlds. Although the terms are deliberately underlexicalized, recalled imagistically is the purgatorial surrender that Pincher repudiates and later in *The Paper Men* Wilf Barclay will resist. Like Sammy's definition of art, *Free Fall*'s quest for Being *qua* Being is 'partly communication but only partly. The rest is discovery' (p. 102). For Sammy the experience proceeds out of what he has called his 'painful obsession with discovery and identification' (p. 103). And the journey bears similarities to archetypal journeys underground and the tropes of door, wall, darkness and encirclement are all metamorphic: they suggest that a total change of perception follows when the separating medium between interior identity and the Other is broken through. It is a process which involves stripping down a protagonist to that very last thing which cannot be destroyed. This, it would seem at least in *Free Fall*, is what its author takes as a definition of the human: an impenetrable target that will not buckle under pressure.

Following his inability to answer the questions from the Gestapo interrogator about escaped compatriot prisoners of war, Sammy is threatened with death and thrust into a locked cell. In the dark, Sammy finds some comfort in the wooden door that his back rests against, since it is a still and familiar point in the maze of imagined walls. But once he discovers that the shape of the confining space is a room with four walls, he realizes that the door, although wooden, only allows him to suffer in a recognized corner. If the cell is an objective metonymic counterpart of the material cosmos that exists beyond it, then, even if the door is breakable, no escape follows its collapse: outside the cell waits the avenging judge, Halde, and 'prison inside prison' (p. 171). To have the door unlocked is not to escape as Christian and Faithful do from Giant Despair's dungeon in *The Pilgrim's Progress*, for – in a century of disbelief – it is matter, not a supreme and merciful principle, which supports the world. To get outside the cell's door is simply to return to where one has started. And with vistas turning back on each other Sammy admits 'total defeat', knowing that such a view of life both blights human 'will and [is] self-perpetuating' (p. 171).

Yet being imprisoned in a dark cell is but the first step in Sammy's torture, a torture he comes to realize will be self-inflicted. Although he cautions himself not to move away from the known door, some interior thrust compels him to leave its wooden angle and investigate the cell's center: 'The centre was the secret' (p. 173). He understands another kind of prison now encircles him – and this one wholly immaterial, wholly psychological. 'One way you take the next step and suffer for it,' he berates himself. 'The other way, you do not take it but suffer on your own rack trying not to think what the next step is' (p. 177). He begins to populate the dark cell's center with imagined demons, for he cannot just remain by the door; he must deduce that something lies in the center and forces himself to guess, wonder, invent. It boils with imagined shapes. Then 'compelled, helplessly deprived of will, sterile, wounded, diseased, sick of his nature, pierced' (pp. 173–74), he stretches out his hand. He touches something wet, imagines: snake, acid, coffin, dead slug, gnarled body, then – sum of all terror – a dismembered phallus.

Sammy Mountjoy screams. He screams, expecting nothing beyond the threshold of his own consciousness but pain and perhaps its cessation, accepting 'a shut door, darkness and a shut sky' (p. 184). The center's wholly physical organ makes him scream in terror. It is the instinctive unconscious scream of a rat or captive animal but it becomes a human plea (the text claims) because it is directed towards some place, for 'the very act of crying changed the thing that cried' (p. 184). Instinctively 'the thing' or point of consciousness that is Sammy searches for a place where help may be found and that pursuit *Free Fall* posits as a unique characteristic of the human.

Since the external and substantial present offers only a twitching body and the concrete of the cell, 'it' (a defamiliarizing way of representing the point of consciousness through what has already become an habitual technique of transitivity) looks with 'not physical eyes' into an interior world. But the internal and insubstantial world offers no comfort either; if the present is only 'the physical world…and no escape' (p. 185), then the past, against which 'the thing' pitches, holds 'some forgotten thing' layers and layers below, which cannot be unearthed in the urgency of terror. A 'thing' against 'an absolute helplessness', screaming for mercy, 'it' can only pitch towards the future, hurling itself along a purgatorial furnace, experienced as a flight of steps from horror to horror. Flesh, language, thought, present perceptions and past memories, rind by rind, the identifying skins of Mountjoy's person are pared away; finally even the refuge of madness (which for Pincher, one recalls, was the last proof of identity) is destroyed. Then, at this point 'the thing' comes up against something which does not capitulate, an 'entry where death is close as darkness against the eyeballs' (p. 185). And breaks through that veil: 'And burst that door' (p. 185).

Free Fall is deliberately guarded about the cell door's opening, leaving the matter to readers, depending on their sensibilities, to decide. A Commandant comes 'late', we are told, opening it physically, but in one sense Sammy has opened it already by way of his spirit: the physical fact that it is closed is no longer relevant to a purged Sammy. From darkness, then, 'it' appears to escape through the veil into a world transfigured by spiritual freedom where a transformed Sammy can momentarily be clothed in the promissory garments of his name, as Samuel, the chosen servant of God, mounts into joy. With altered eyes, he perceives the camp prisoners as burning bushes and the dust and camp buildings as brilliant and fantastic jewels; Sammy accepts its spirit whose source is 'a place […]I did not know existed but which I had forgotten merely' (p. 187): a Traherne-like cosmos, its door is 'sometimes open and sometimes shut' (p. 187), but always there.

But this 'thing' – what Samuel sees as 'the human nature inhabiting the centre of my awareness' (p. 190) – has not been extinguished. 'To die is easy enough in the forcing chamber of a cell,' the narrator tells the narratee:

> But when the eyes of Sammy were turned in on myself […] what they saw was not beautiful but fearsome. Dying, after all, then was not one tenth complete – for must not complete death be to get out of the way of that shining, singing cosmos and let it shine and sing? And here was a point, a single point which was my own interior identity, without shape or size but only position. (p. 190)

Although the Allies have now been proven to be victorious, for this is the Commandant's implied news as he lets Officer Mountjoy out of the cell, and a world war has now been formally concluded, Sammy – like all the violated and violating nations once engaged – must accept living with that 'unendurable' (p. 190) history. Burst open as is the spiritual and physical door of the cell and opening back as it does on to the world of mystery, the inadequate Being that is Sammy's center still persists.

Take the cell then with its valent center as a metonymic representation of the carnage of the century. Take it too as a metonymic representation of Sammy's interior landscape. The Nazis, Sammy had conjectured, were psychologists of suffering and appropriated to each man the terror that would be 'most helpful and necessary to his case' (p. 173). For such a hedonist as Sammy has been, it would be appropriate for a phallus to occupy the darkened middle. In this imagined horror, central to the cell, Sammy recognizes his own interior identity: it becomes an objective counterpart for his own center, an odious and corporeal organ. In the coda at the end, however, when the temporal chronology has again been shifted, we learn that, as the Commandant was releasing the prisoner from the cell, the narrator turned backwards and noticed a wet rag in the cell's center, that terrifying cell being nothing more than a broom closet.

The method, characteristic of the ideographic structure, amounts to a delayed disclosure; in the coda's flashback, the reader discovers that the cell's center is quite innocuous: a damp floor cloth. Circumscribed in the cell, Sammy's imagination had invested the fragment with shape and infection – he had decided it would be a mutilated penis when he concluded that Halde would choose an appropriate punishment for such a hedonistic man as he. Readers now must judge (as Sammy himself has not been allowed by the narrative's end, itself the present writing of the retrospective reminiscence) that what Sammy had perceived as his unendurable identity – when he turned the eyes of the spirit inwards – might be similarly innocuous. Further, depending on how Sammy – both as individual and as representative of twentieth-century Western malaise – judges himself, he might discover some release from guilt, from darkness, some opening door. If he is not blinded by his own guilt – his conviction of his unendurable identity – he might see the Redeemer in the Judge.

Then what of the Sphinx's riddle which closes the novel – 'The Herr Doctor does not know about peoples' (p. 253)? Should we translate this gnomic fragment as a shorthand negation of mechanistic assumptions about morality which ignore the fact that even creatures as guilt-ridden as Sammy can experience moments of freedom, still could be offered release from the cosmic prison by creatures apparently as guilty as Halde? While the coda's puzzle – along with its reversal of fact and so of perspective – no more operates back upon the entire narrative than does the *Vita Nuova*, it recontextualizes the atavistic journey. Yet it hardly answers whether a bridge connects the two worlds.

Of course, the bridge between the grey world of flesh and the golden world of spirit might well have been the darkened cell with its reductive process, a kind of whipping which releases energies from their paralyses. Reminiscent of the nightmare fragmentation of Pincher's illusory 'Time-Present', the atavistic exploration in *Free Fall* does concern itself with the darkness that spells magic, terror and awe that Sammy the younger (like the boy whom the memoirist remembers in 'The Ladder and the Tree') 'inhabits by nature' (p. 217). It is the source of the artist, Sammy Mountjoy's real creativity: 'Sometimes I would feel myself connected to *the well inside me* [...] There would come into my whole body a feeling of passionate certainty [...] Then I would stand the world of appearance on its head, would *reach in and down*, would destroy savagely and recreate' (p. 102, my italics). Decidedly this darkness, and its mysterious connection with creation and destruction, bears little relation to 'the world of miracle' (p. 189), the Traherne-like singing universe. Nor is it the detached, understandable, and usable universe of cause and effect. It simply *is*: 'it reveals though we can't explain what it reveals'.[21] And both the narrator and his author would leave the discovery there. In my mind *Free Fall* does not achieve the 'miracle of implication' which Sammy/author Golding cites as the aesthetic end of any portrait where 'the viewer's eye' and not the artist's pen creates a completed line and brings itself 'slap up against another view of the world' (p. 102). On the other hand, I find it no mean example of 'laborious portraiture', a confession of failure and a confession of growth.

Endnotes

1   James Gindin, *William Golding*, New York, St Martin's Press, 1988, p. 49.

2   B.R. Johnson, 'Golding's First Argument: Theme and Structure in *Free Fall*' in James R. Baker (ed.), *Critical Essays on William Golding*, Boston, G. K. Hall. 1988, p. 65.

3   See L.L. Dickson, *The Modern Allegories of William Golding*, Gainesville, University of South Florida Press, 1990; Avril Henry, 'The Structure of Golding's *Free Fall*' *Southern Review* 8 (1976),

pp. 92–124; David Higdon, 'William Golding's *Free Fall*', *Time in English Fiction*, London, Macmillan, 1977, pp. 51–56; Johnson, op. cit.; Philip Redpath, *William Golding: A Structural Reading of his Fiction*, London, Vision Press Limited, 1986.

4   Jeanne Delbaere-Garent, 'Time as Structural Device in *Free Fall*' in Jeanne Delbaere (ed), *William Golding: The Sound of Silence*, Liège, English Department University of Liège, 1991, pp. 92–93.

5   See S.H. Boyd, *The Novels of William Golding*, New York, St Martin's Press, 1988; Lawrence S. Friedman, *William Golding*, New York, Continuum, 1993, John Peter, '*The Fables of William Golding*', *Kenyon Review* 19 (1957), pp. 577–92.

6   Johnson, op. cit. p. 53.

7   See Bernard F. Dick, *William Golding* (revised edition), Boston, Twayne Publishers, 1987; H. McKeating, 'The Significance of William Golding', *The Expository Times* 79 (1968), pp. 329–33; Clive Pemberton, *William Golding*, London, Longmans Green & Co, 1969.

8   Categories have included 'detective story' (Friedman, op.cit); 'fable' (Peter, op. cit.; Walter Sullivan, 'The Fables and the Art' *Sewanee Review*, 1963, pp. 660–64; Margaret Walters, 'Two Fabulists: Golding and Camus' *Melbourne Critical Review* 4, 1961, pp. 18–21); 'allegory' (Dickson, op. cit.); 'confession' (Peter Axthelm, *The Modern Confessional Novel*, New Haven, Yale University Press, 1967; Friedman, op. cit.); 'autobiography' (Dick, op. cit.); '*kunstlerroman*' (Johnson, op. cit.); '*bildungsroman*' (Boyd, op. cit.; Donald W. Crompton, *A View From the Spire: William Golding's Later Novels*, edited and completed by Julia Briggs, Oxford, Blackwell, 1985; John Whitley, '"*Furor Scribendi*" Writing about Writing in the Later Novels of William Golding', *Critical Essays on William Golding*, James R. Baker [ed.], Boston, G.K. Hall, 1988, pp. 176–93). Joyce's *A Portrait of the Artist as a Young Man* was the work most frequently cited in the latter context, although the familiar excavation of possible intertextual allusions or influences extended to Sartre's *Nausea* (Friedman, op. cit.; James Gindin, *William Golding*, New

York, St Martin's Press, 1988); Camus' *The Fall* (Friedman, op. cit.); Poe's 'Pit and the Pendulum' (Redpath, op. cit.); Dante's *Divine Comedy* (Inger Aaseth, 'Golding's Journey to Hell: An Examination of Prefigurations and Archetypal Pattern in Free Fall' *English Studies* 56, 1975, pp. 3–15; Arnold Johnston, *Of Earth and Darkness: The Novels of William Golding*, Columbia and London, University of Missouri Press, 1980) and his *Vita Nuova* (Boyd, op. cit.; Friedman, op. cit.; Johnson op. cit.; Tiger, op. cit.).

9   Golding to Baker in James R. Baker, *William Golding: A Critical Study*, New York, St Martin's Press, 1965, pp. v–vi.

10   John S. Whitley, '"*Furor Scribendi*" Writing about Writing in the Later Novels of William Golding', in James R. Baker (ed.), *Critical Essays on William Golding*, Boston, G.K. Hall, 1988) p. 177.

11   Frank Kermode, 'Adam's Image', *The Spectator* (October 23, 1959), p. 564.

12   This passage's relation to the novel is discussed in detail in Ian Gregor and Mark Kinkead-Weekes' 1960 article, 'The Strange Case of William Golding and his Critics', although their point that 'the first paragraph presents 252 of *Free Fall*'s 253 pages in miniature' (p. 118) is too sweeping, since many motifs – notably the darkness trope – do not enter the paragraph.

13   Whitley in James R. Baker (ed.), op. cit., p. 179.

14   Bernard F. Dick, *William Golding* (revised edition), Boston, Twayne Publishers, 1987, p. 59.

15   At one point in *Free Fall* there is a verbal echo of *Pincher Martin*; elucidating the conservation of energy to the young Sammy, Nick says it holds both mentally as well as physically: 'You can't have your penny and your bun' (p. 216).

16   The encounter is seeded with many of the motifs established in earlier episodes. Beatrice's mad nittering recapitulates a lodger's bird-like breathing, which, upon its secession, the young Sammy

had imagined not death, but the stopping of a clock's ticking: 'She was jerking round like the figure in a cathedral *clock*' (p. 243, my italics). The major re-orchestration is the madness itself, for lust-struck Sammy had pretended madness in order to seduce the chaste Beatrice. 'You mustn't ever say such a thing, Sammy' (p. 240), he remembers her having cautioned, as he watches her in the asylum.

17   In contrast to Sammy, Nick is an innocent even though he believes in the world of matter; in other words, his nature remains complete even though his vision is confined to one mode. Sammy alone extends the materialism to its moral field.

18   A persuasive case for Miss Pringle being responsible for Sammy's later desecration of Beatrice has been made. 'She instils guilt in Sammy about two things, two areas about which she seems herself deeply disturbed and unhappy: sex and class [...] her sense of religion [being] horribly entangled with her sense of class' (Boyd, pp. 74–75). Such warped respectability is 'a very prominent feature of Golding's English landscape', as one sees in *The Pyramid* and *Darkness Visible* alike.

19   Golding to Green, Peter Green, 'The World of William Golding', *Transactions and Proceedings of the Royal Society of Literature* (1963), p. 55.

20   Boyd, op. cit., p. 72.

21   Ian Gregor and Mark Kinkead-Weekes, *William Golding*, London, Faber and Faber, 1967, p. 255.

The Spire

I

> It is not too much to say that man invented war at the earliest moment possible. It is not too much to say that as soon as he could leave an interpretable sign of anything, he left a sign of his belief in God.
>
> Golding, 'Before the Beginning'

If *Free Fall*'s final page challenges the limitations of pattern while remaining bifocal in vision, ambiguity, rather than prescription, ultimately informs the divided world its narrator inhabits. *The Spire* takes that paradox – that any scheme is self-contradictory because in some sense it is a metaphor – as its generating subject. The world this novel invokes (as well as evokes) is pluralistic, multi-layered, intermingling, complex. Yet it places a wilful and unrelenting pattern-maker as its central intelligence. Out of the confrontation and inevitably intense collision of the two emerge what was once described as 'one of the most ambitious and fascinating novels of the century'.[1]

Critics now agree that *The Spire* marks the completion of one phase in the novelist's development; in my view, it recapitulates many of the features of the earlier works. Once again character is presented not only in torment but also through torment. Once again a central crisis brings about the meeting of two worlds, a meeting which is figured in a confrontation scene. As before so here, with conscience and circumstances fusing in judgement of crime. In the painful purgation that follows there is the elimination of all but the essential *ding an sich* of the protagonist: that bar of identity that does not buckle. And, like unreliable agents before, the 'refracting consciousness'[2] seeks explanations and justifications for troubling actions.

The story concerns a Dean of a fourteenth-century English cathedral who is convinced that he has been chosen by God to cap the magnificence of his cathedral with a four hundred-foot spire. The plot is simple enough and, like the narrative that extends chronologically over a two-year period, moderately straightforward. To this extent, the novel represents a return to the method of *Lord of the Flies* while resembling *Pincher Martin* and *Free Fall* by way of its action being steeped in the inner consciousness of its leading character, although presented from the third-person point of view rather than the first. '*The Spire* is a perfect example of what Wayne Booth calls a third-person narrator-agent novel; that is, a third-person novel whose central character exerts such an influence on the action that he or she seems to be telling the story.'[3] Taking their shape from the gradual erection of a cathedral spire, early episodes show an economy that is in marked contrast to the language of excess that characterizes the protagonist's extreme self-absorption.

Isolated temporally as well as spatially, *The Spire*'s events occur in a setting almost as delimited as that of the island in *Lord of the Flies*, for it is confined within the cathedral walls, its Deanery and Close and, in particular, the expanding stone flesh of the rising structure. One bare brief account – less than a summary paragraph in length – has the Dean leave his Cathedral Church of Our Lady to preach to haggard congregations in country churches of his gift, to urgently talk about the spire's construction in the churches of the city where he is archdeacon and to assail another congregation worn gruel-weary from rain, flood, death, and starvation in the Church of Saint Thomas. Enacted events, however, move out beyond the Close and into the village only after the spire's erection has been completed, and then sparingly in the coda of the narrative. Within the increasingly unreliable consciousness of the protagonist, Dean Jocelin, developing action becomes more and more circumscribed, rendered as much of it is through his inner voice. But if the events that comprise the plot line are blurred by the focalizing strategy of his dominating indirect discourse, other things are indelibly present. The mechanics and mess of medieval construction are fiercely rendered: the rubbing, scraping, chipping of oak boards; the hoisting then erecting of scaffolding as workmen climb from level to level; their shouting and cursing and singing; the clanging and banging of their tools; the dropping, pulling and snaking of ropes; the hod-carried stones dragging past transepts; the hammering of nails; the cutting, carving, shaping of stone; the searing of steel bands for the rising tower; water dishes choked with wood slivers to test the possible movement of stressed pillars; glass cutters and stone masons sculpting gargoyles; planks, plinths, rivets, cables, besoms, adzes, ladders, crowbars, chisels, mortar; T-squares, plumblines, stone dust, dirt, wood shavings. Golding's commanding hand in his imaginative construction of a medieval spire – with its lights and octagons and grisaille squares – would only once more be matched in an equally triumphant creation of an early nineteenth-century wooden vessel in the later sea trilogy.

Minor characters – and a number are sketched, including a dumb sculptor, a jabbering, clacking wife, a flippant courtesan, and a self-righteous sacristan – exist as they pass in and out of Jocelin's obsession. Thus his daughter-in-god is no more than blazing red hair while the solicitous chaplain, Father Adam, seems to have no face at all and is so clothespeg-like that Jocelin dubs him Father Anonymous. If the huddled roofs of the town are viewed solely from the spire's high vantage point, shrugging their shapes into it, then the spire and its builders are looked at almost completely from Jocelin's perspective. And although the social and religious tempests of the late medieval period are hinted at – with 'Jocelin's story [being] seen to be part of a larger socio-cultural process, the awakening of forces that led England from the Middle Ages into the Renaissance'[4] – social context in the manner of *Free Fall* has been largely abandoned. Which is not to say that the novel is not grounded historically. For example, Jocelin's 'renovation project is part of a larger trend in medieval architecture: the transition from the Romanesque to the Gothic'.[5] Yet when the reader sees Jocelin from the outside, as one does at several important junctures, it is with the sense of jolted strangeness that recalls the objective transition to Tuami's view of Lok in *The Inheritors*. As the narrative continues these jolts become more and more powerful, since we have been occupying Jocelin's consciousness, which is itself increasingly hermetically closed.

The narrative is built on two movements: Chapters One to Ten and Chapters Ten to Twelve. The building of the spire is followed by an examination of motive. On the completion of the spire's construction a dramatic reversal occurs which shatters the protagonist's illusions. Jocelin is forced to review his own motives and acknowledge his own deceptions. The inspection comprises the novel's second movement, where Jocelin comes up against the 'cellarage' of his own mind, those things which he has deliberately repressed. If one looks at *The Spire*'s ideographic structure, this movement is an extension of the characteristic concluding coda that the earlier works posit could provide a kind of mythic integration that might be accomplished by the reader should various clues be reassembled. Peculiar to *The Spire* is the protagonist's own realization of the full import of his actions; the hero Jocelin accomplishes the fusion of alternate explanations. In a last cryptic cry, '*It's like the appletree,*' the division between pagan and

Christian, the distance between cellarage and sky, the dueling dualities set in motion metaphorically, are brought into essential relationship.

But what of the earliest stages of an engagement, one described as a 'model of Aristotelian structure [whereby] Jocelin moves from [...] prideful eminence to reversal and discovery, the whole action arising from his essentially admirable yet flawed nature'?[6] One morning early in his Deanship (so his written account records) Jocelin had a vision when – lying at the church's crossways – he felt himself being initiated into a 'newfound humility and newfound knowledge'. This he sensed physically as a fountain bursting with 'flame and light, up through a notspace, filling with ultimate urgency and not to be denied [...] an implacable, unstoppable, glorious fountain of the spirit, a wild burning of me for Thee' (p. 193). At the novel's opening, a physical spire – what Jocelin calls his ultimate 'diagram of prayer' (p. 120) – is in the very first stages of construction. The nave is filled with dust, a hole has been torn in the cathedral's side to bring through beams and stone and Jocelin is laughing in 'holy mirth' (p. 8) while the sunlight throws the colored refraction of the Abraham and Isaac window on his ecstatic face.

Jocelin soon meets opposition to his plan from both his friend and confessor, Sacrist Anselm, and from the master builder, Roger Mason, who finds that the foundations are scarcely adequate for the cathedral's existing structure. By force of Jocelin's will the spire continues to be constructed, although now against the judgement of the clergy, the teams of workers who risk their lives at each level, assorted townsfolk threatened by the singing pillars, the congregation cursing that (even in the Lady Chapel) services have been suspended and, above all, Roger, who counsels the folly of the enterprise. Jocelin is reflective in his remark, one intended to will the master builder to continue: 'The net isn't mine, Roger, and the folly isn't mine. It's God's Folly' (p. 121):

> The building is a diagram of prayer; and our spire will be a diagram of the highest prayer of all. God revealed it to me in a vision, his unprofitable servant. He chose me. He chooses you, to fill the diagram with glass and iron and stone, since the children of men require a thing to look at (p. 120).

Monomaniacal will overrules pragmatic counsel, although it is never a simple matter of faith's conquest of common sense, since Roger, responding inventively to perilous architectural conundrum, develops new and inspired technical solutions. Indeed, his is 'a system of engineering so new that many of the processes Roger invents and uses are unnamed, vague and only under partial control.'[7] Jocelin trusts his vision, is reassured by a warmth at his spine that he calls his guardian angel and finds encouragement in the promise of a Holy Nail that his Bishop will have sent from Rome. Upon opening a pit at the cathedral's crossways, it becomes clear that foundations do not exist. If there had ever been any Christian faith among Roger's mostly heathen army, it breaks down, coinciding with the threatened destruction of the cathedral. Riots ensue and the Verger Pangall vanishes.

Jocelin's fanaticism is now so intense that he deliberately exploits the master builder's desertion of his wife and adulterous attachment to the Verger's wife, Goody Pangall. Jocelin ruminates:

> […] Goody and Roger, both in the tent that would expand with them wherever they might go. And so distinct that it might have been written […] there was the thought. It was so terrible that it went beyond feeling, and left him inspecting it with a kind of stark detachment, while the edge of the spire burned into his cheek […] 'She will keep him here' (p. 64).

Goody's bloody death in childbirth, the master builder's drunkenness and attempted suicide, even the changed countryside whose landscape is altered by the tower 'laying a hand' (p. 107) and enforcing a new pattern of streets, roads, migrations – 'The countryside was shrugging itself obediently into a new shape' (p. 108) – all are the costs and the sacrifices and the lessons of the holy exploit. Or is it not an unholy exploit?

With the arrival of ecclesiastical authorities from Rome to investigate the complaints against the Dean, a second narrative movement begins. A Visitor brings the Holy Nail. Seeing Jocelin deranged, his clerical cassock tied high for climbing, his decanal and pastoral duties wantonly deserted, the obligatory sacrament of confession abandoned now for two full years, his hair disarrayed and full of wood shavings, the Commission indicts him and relieves him of his Deanship. Jocelin's sole concern is that the spire should be nailed securely to the heavens. In the midst of a raging storm he ascends the tower and performs his last act of faith by hammering in the Holy Nail at the spire's apex. For him, securing the spire is the sacred 'equivalent of Roger's steel hoop, not a physical stay but a spiritual one.'[8]

The narrative's first major movement has concluded. Bent and ungainly as it has become, the completed spire stands at four hundred feet. In the extended coda, Chapters Ten to Twelve, menacing facts begin to emerge. Jocelin finds his decanal appointment was due not to the customary election by the cathedral chapter but rather to a debased aunt, the mistress of the King. He discovers his canons dislike and dismiss him by way of his Deanship's irregular origins, while his deacons loathe his arrogance, grandiosity and excessive emotionalism. Father Adam denounces the record of his original vision of the spire as spiritually naïve. Even the mighty pillars are hollow; they were filled not with solid stone, but rubble by 'the giants who had been on the earth in those days' (p. 188). The world now appears corrupt: a whirligig of grinning, noseless men. In despair Jocelin flings himself down on the crossways, his place of original vision and 'his place of sacrifice' (p. 189). There, like a broken snake, he is scourged: 'Then his angel put away the two wings from the cloven hoof and struck him from arse to head with a whitehot flail' (p. 188).

But his angel may be a delusion too – spinal tuberculosis has been wasting away his body. During the six months left him to live, Jocelin inspects the falsity of all that has gone before. The two sorts of cellars, his hidden nature and the pit at the spire's base, are surveyed. Slowly he acknowledges a repressed lust for Goody that made him marry his daughter-in-god to the impotent, aging Verger. He acknowledges Pangall's murder, for the pagan workmen had used the Verger as a ritual scapegoat for their fears, burying him in the pit at the crossways, along with the four sculpted heads of Jocelin. Jocelin then knows himself responsible for the death of a stonecutter in a fight, the fall through the air of a carpenter and four ruined lives. All that remains is the spire, 'an ungainly, crumbling thing' (p. 193), a monument to his error, once an act of devotion, then the repression of sexual energy and the crude expression of lust, now a cruel hammer of vengeance pressing down on the world. Crawling back from the New Street den of the now inebriate Roger, the townsfolk attack him, just as Pangall had been reviled by the workmen:

> […] a storm of voices [struck him], all shouting and laughing and making hound noises. He got up by the wall, but the noises swirling round him […] brought hands and feet and dim faces at his own […] He heard his gown rip; he could not lie down for hands held him up. The noises began to bray and yelp. They created their own mouths, fanged and slavering (p. 215).

However, moments before his death and the giving of the Last Host, Jocelin suffers another vision. Through his sickroom window he glimpses a thing surpassing in beauty any other vision. 'It was slim as a girl, translucent. It had grown from some seed of rosecolored substance that glittered like a waterfall, an upward waterfall. The substance was one thing, that broke all the way to infinity in cascades of exultation that nothing could trammel' (p. 223). It is the spire, still standing, and the novel takes this as one moment of meaning as Jocelin, dying, whispers his beatitude: *It's like the appletree.*

II

[A] host of memories were like sentences from a story which, though they left great gaps, still told enough.

The Spire

[*The Spire's*] style is precious and at times bewildering: there are brilliant images, but there is an obliqueness, in narrative method as well as in style, that often seems to have little purpose except to tantalize.[9]

Few reviewers committed themselves solidly in support of *The Spire* when it first appeared in 1964. At the time, the book's appearance amounted to a reality check for its author's reputation, a verification or negation of the earlier accomplishments, a kind of test case for a writer who had been too hyperbolically cast as the 'white hope' of the mid twentieth-century British novel. Several years intervened between its publication and that of *Free Fall*, although Golding wrote a substantial number of reviews and articles for British and American journals. With the increasing popularity of *Lord of the Flies*, he had sought distance, refusing interviews by the media and generally avoiding the kind of literary conviviality expected of a distinguished writer, a practice he was to follow intermittently throughout his working life. *The Spire* accordingly received the kind of attention that placed it in an area between notoriety and critical recognition: a best seller, grudgingly credited but often discredited. For example, a critic no less astute than the late V. S. Pritchett would write in the *New Statesman* that Golding had succumbed to the 'underworld of fashionable paranoia' – the consequences were 'obscurity, monotony and strain'.[10] Style was assailed as needlessly constricted, the key descriptive terms being 'labored' and 'obfuscatory'; that Gothic excess operating in the novel as an ironic analogue of character came only to be understood in later discussions. Nor has there ever been the kind of close analysis of style that *The Inheritors* received, even though *The Spire* shows some interesting innovations appropriate to the book's medieval period and spirit.[11]

Although criticism has since shifted towards detailed analysis of the roots of Jocelin's pride,[12] early critics misapprehended the increasing egotism of the obsessive Jocelin, reading his isolation and, in turn, the novel's themes as necessitated by Golding's inability to present human relationships. A related point – Golding having in the early years been charged with being inhibited from handling any but adolescent or pre-adolescent relationships – was that *The Spire* sacrificed both the integrity and inviolability of individual consciousness to the interests of abstract ideas. We now know, however, that Golding abandoned whole sections of narrative devoted to the early relationships between Jocelin and Anselm and Jocelin and Alison in a strict paring down of the fiction's structure. Thus, both characters are relevant not to Jocelin's past but his depicted present and become agents for the ironic reversal of the protagonist's fortune and then his discovery: as in classical drama, *The Spire*'s coda weds peripeteai to anagnorisis. In the novel's final version, of course, Jocelin discovers that his appointment to the Deanship was not one elected by God; its origin, like that of the funds, was soiled by human corruption, a matter he is made to learn only after the spire's construction is completed. Enmeshed for ten chapters in Jocelin's self-absorption, the reader experiences a distancing from that intensity, as the third-person limited point of view expands to suggest the more objective viewpoints of Alison, and especially the Papal Visitor.

In early discussions of *The Spire* it was less structure that was examined and more often historical/literary source. It having been assumed that since the earlier novels subverted literary ancestors as one starting point, then *The Spire* might well be a reversal of some other writer's version of hubris attendant on cathedral construction. Many interwoven intertextualities have been suggested – most sharing the commonalities of building and a fall from pride of place.[13]

While Golding adamantly denied any literary precursor – 'no work comes out of another unless it is stillborn,' as he once insisted – my sense is that a sharper distinction should be drawn between generating source, intertextual allusion, and literary/historical association. For example, consider the author's remark to me that Trollope's Barchester series was 'sewn in negatively' to the extent that the medieval mind had at is forefront precisely that which Trollope's secular age ignored: 'Trollope included everything but the church.' Instead of Trollope's concern with secularized religion and ecclesiastical careerism, 'we have the age of faith, just as disedifying, when Christianity was still in rivalry with pagan devil-worship and when worldly desires sublimated into religious zeal could have terrifying consequences.'[14]

It was wondered at the time of the novel's publication where Golding had boned up on the facts about the mason's craft, it being assumed there must have been some 'useful' point of technical departure.[15] In point of fact, an architectural book on tower building from Harvard's Weidner Library was briefly consulted, then set aside since – as he told me – Golding preferred to use his own (considerable) knowledge of seamanship. As he would later in the creation of *Fire Down Below*'s creaking, stinking wooden hulk *Britannia*, so in *The Spire* he 'did the whole thing in sailor's terms'. He continued:

> Seamanship has been defined as the art of moving heavy weights – with the implication that you only use the most primitive means: blocks, tackles, levers. I know about that.

This accounts for one system of tropes – where the cathedral is a 'stone ship' fitted with a mast, its pillars 'float', its foundation a 'raft' on which the 'ark' rests. However, the strategy hardly suggests the detailed dexterity with which ongoing engineering stages are described: from 'the construction and placement of beams and cross-beams, the carving and heavy placement of stone and the various means designed to shore foundations and forestall the creeping of the earth underneath.'[16] The following passage, where the master worker is warning the Dean against the feasibility of building any higher, reveals a writer engaged not in the formulation of simplistic theses but the rendering of historical detail, in short:

> We've nothing but a skin of glass and stone stretched between four stone rods, one at each corner [...] The stone is no stronger than the glass between the verticals because every inch of the way I have to save weight, bartering strength for weight or weight for strength, guessing how much, how far, how little, how near [...] I've clamped

the stones together but still I can't make them stronger than stone. Stone snaps, crumbles, tears (p. 117).

The sustained critical attention to symbolism and imagery that *The Spire* has received over the years[17] has shifted towards considerations of its recreation of an historical period. Certainly it depicts the great century of medieval corruption by reference not only to Aunt Alison, whose money builds the spire, but also the near illiterate Ivo, a minor character who is made chancellor simply because his father owned the forests from which the cathedral beams were constructed. The text alludes to this corruption by having Ivo's installation occur ironically in the qualified sunlight cast through the cathedral's St Aldhelm window. The historic St Aldhelm was a seventh-century Bishop celebrated for insisting that faith was only granted in the tradition of the Roman Catholic Church and that the duty of accepting derived solely from St Peter and the tradition of the Roman church. A glancing reference is also made to Malmesbury Abbey where 'a spire comparable in height collapsed in the fifteenth century', the reference reinforcing the historic fact that 'structural collapse was a regular event in medieval Europe, as builders' ambitions outran their technical skills.'[18] And then there is the matter of the Holy Nail. No matter how much an obsessed Jocelin believes it to be the Holy Church triumphant, it is, as the worldly Alison registers, a cheap enough substitute for the costly funds that the Dean's Bishop might have persuaded the Roman ecclesiastics to provide: one more sign of the widespread corruption of the Roman Catholic Church's self-serving hierarchical institution in the period. For it is not only the Dean who can be charged with dereliction of duties; his Confessor and 'Sacrist [is] a time-server who runs a small business within the walls of the Temple'.[19] The Dean's own Bishop – residing in worldly Rome for the two years – is guilty of neglect, a cathedral being the official seat of a diocesan bishop.

III

The truth is we have a primitive belief that virtue, force, power – what the anthropologists might call mana – lie in the original stones and nowhere else… Our old churches are full of this power. I do not refer to their specifically religious function or influence. There is a whole range of other feelings that... coagulated around them... The historians of religion might mutter about the stones that they were 'relics by contact'. But contact with what? It *was* mana, indescribable, unaccountable, indefinable, impossible mana.

Golding, 'An Affection for Cathedrals'

While no simple source or scenario underpins *The Spire*, one can detect those diverse fragments that contributed to its genesis, coalescing according to the logic of the imagination from whose soil the novel grew organically. The autobiographical essay 'The Ladder and the Tree' – with its antitheses represented by the ascending ladder to the tree-house and the dark fearsome graveyard at its base – influenced directly the symbolic opposition of pit and tower in *The Spire*. Climbing away from the crossways' stirring earth to divest himself of its 'confusion' (p. 100), Jocelin is described as feeling 'the same appalled delight as a small boy feels when first he climbs too high in a forbidden tree' (p. 101). Similarly encoded is the cellar trope from *Pincher Martin*; as one recalls, this multivalent trope suggests the morbid terror beneath the conscious mind, an invocation that *The Spire*'s coda reinscribes when Jocelin is described as 'a building about to fall' (p. 222). Interrogating the drunken Mason about the contents of the cathedral's pit, he asks, 'What's a man's mind, Roger? Is it the whole building, *cellarage* and all?' (p. 213, my italics).

Minor works were germane as well, including an occasional essay reviewing an antiquarian's book on an early twentieth-century hermit in the English countryside and an unpublished BBC radio play, *Miss Pulkinhorn*, and the short story from which it was derived, originally published in a 1960 issue of *Encounter*. The latter showed an author much preoccupied with the intermingling of faith and guilt several years before *The Spire*'s appearance, but nevertheless during its gestation. Juxtaposing a conventionally religious but perniciously bigoted spinster with a religious eccentric who prays ecstatically before the red sanctuary candle and beside an illuminated window, the play explores the seemingly inevitable opposition between orthodox belief and the unaccountable certitude the mystic possesses, which defies reason, reasonableness, and the data of the empirical world. It is not without relevance to *The Spire* that the church in which *Miss Pulkinhorn* is set, and to which all of the play's action is restricted, was Salisbury Cathedral, its Abraham and Isaac stained glass window having a role in the emerging thematics of the sacrificial figure. The scapegoat and sacrificial victim become amplified in

The Spire, as I shall argue; indeed, the novel's very first paragraph announces their presence when a complex image describes Dean Jocelin's face illuminated by the Abraham window:

> He was laughing, chin up [...] God the Father was exploding in his face with a glory of sunlight through painted glass, a glory that moved with his movements to consume and exalt Abraham and Isaac and God again (p. 7).

It is not too speculative a point to make that other motifs from *Miss Pulkinhorn* came to be knitted through *The Spire*'s fabric, including the metaphor of the growing tree to represent the entanglement of human motives and the early English hymnal 'Tomorrow Must be My Dancing Day' with its enigmatic refrain, 'Sing O my love, O my love, my love, my love/This have I done for my true love'. As in the play, so in the novel the refrain is made to alternate between traditional verses from the ritual of the Eucharist, although with less thematic justification in *Miss Pulkinhorn* than *The Spire*, where the ironic interweaving nicely reveals Jocelin's confusion of motives and love objects. The rendering of the religious eccentric would also come to be rethreaded. While he is a simplified specimen of the Simon/Nat visionary and prototype for *Darkness Visible*'s Matty and especially Reverend Colley in *Rites of Passage*, his refiguring in the person of Jocelin issues in that singular kind of believer, self-deluded, living on the very fringes of lunacy, but adamant about belief. Unless an innocent by nature – as is Miss Pulkinhorn's victim and as are Colley, Matty, Simon, Nat – such a man of faith can be very dangerous, indeed.

Mentioned above is another occasional piece that, in my judgement, came to be sewn into the cloth that became *The Spire*: Golding's 1960 *Spectator* review of an amateur antiquarian's book, *A Hermit Disclosed* by Raleigh Trevelyan. Showing considerable insight into the innocent Jimmy Mason, the hermit whose diary the antiquarian had unearthed, Golding's review is pervaded not only by a kind of lyric lucidity but a singular interest in Jimmy Mason's religious conversion. Yet the sole portion of Jimmy's diary that Golding's review quoted (an entry Jimmy Mason wrote when he was bewilderingly attracted to a neighboring woman) was the following passage:

> Went to bed at half past eleven, and not lain many minutes before felt something so strange come down from heaven. It seemed as if come so

many times and would never go away. How bad it made me feel I cried and prayed to God. Directly it went I felt no more. It would never be any evil, but good as one of the angels of God. [20]

The recorded dream/vision's prose rhythms – spontaneously eruptive, since Mason was an unschooled country laborer – seem sexual and phallic, as the experience itself might well have been. Considering the singularity of the passage, I was prompted by the striking similarities to make the connection between it and Jocelin's first phallic dream. Waking in loathing, Jocelin is described as lashing himself 'seven times, hard cross the back in his pride, one time for each devil' (p. 65). Could it have been that brooding upon Jimmy Mason's diary opened the way for the dramatic possibilities of making his sexual naïf Jocelin feel physically his vision as the angel of God at his spine, a delusion which would allow the alternate motifs of sexuality and spinal tuberculosis to enter the story and so function as alternate explanations for vision? Another imaginative seed for the raven-like egotism of Jocelin is more certain. Golding once mentioned to me one of Viollet-Le-Duc's gargoyles, which perches on the balustrades of Notre Dame Cathedral in Paris. Known as the Le Stryge gargoyle, it has been made memorable by Charles Meryon's 1853 etching. A grimacing inhuman bird-man with a half-human lean face, enormous wings, and its chin resting on folded hands, it stares sternly over the city, flocks of ravens reeling past it and swirling round city towers, chimneys and roofs.

The host of legends and historical facts surrounding Gothic cathedrals in England – the country which experienced the apotheosis of medieval construction – could not help but be absorbed as part of the novel's imaginative mulch. It is a matter of historical record that in 1322 the tower of Ely fell. Canterbury Cathedral's builder, William of Sens, fell from scaffolding and broke his back. In 1646 the central spire of Lichfield Cathedral was demolished by Royalist forces, such was its symbolic arrogance. The spire of Chichester fell in 1861, tumbling in February after the congregation's singing during the Christmas services. Peterborough Cathedral was built on a peat bog, and Bath Abbey in the vicinity of ruins of successive Roman baths. Carlisle has two streams flowing beneath its tower; Wells ascends from a ring of pools; and Salisbury Cathedral, the country's tallest and most extraordinary spire surmounting its top, rises from marshlands. So it is likely these legends, or known fragments of them, had – to use Golding's own figure – rotted to compost, 'mulched down' in the imagination's fertile soil. Recall, for example, the essay about Salisbury and Winchester that he wrote the year following *The Spire*'s publication, which shows his affectionate familiarity with many of their chronicles. Describing Salisbury Cathedral's legendary origins, he seemed to be celebrating both the victory of faith and the triumph of engineering invention. According to legend, as readers remember:

> Round about the year 1200, Bishop Poore was standing on a hill overlooking the confluence of the local rivers [...] when the mother of Jesus appeared to him, told him to shoot an arrow and build her a church where the arrow fell. The arrow flew more than a mile and fell in the middle of a swamp. There with complete indifference to such things as health, foundations, access and general practicability, the cathedral was built. Eighty years later with a technological gamble which makes space travel seem child's play, the builders erected the highest spire in the country on top of it, thousands of tons of lead and iron and wood and stone. Yet the whole building still stands.[21]

Furthermore, the author of *The Spire* passed much of his adult life close to Salisbury Cathedral, teaching – as it were – under its tower, so it may well have been one possible – if not, *the* – historical model for Dean Jocelin's 'bible in stone'. The fictional cathedral has been given some of the details that attended the construction of Salisbury's spire. Begun in 1220, a 404-foot tower (the Cathedral Church of the Blessed Virgin Mary's stretches four hundred feet) was added a century later, its apex topped by a capstone. It rests on four pillars whose diminishing thickness thrusts appalling weight into a marshy bog on which the whole edifice is supported. As happens in the fiction, one of Salisbury's pillars slipped out of perpendicular, despite thick iron bands which had been used to strengthen the spire's structure: 'It leans. It totters. It bends. But it still stands.'[22] Until the mid twentieth century the whole structure was a source of considerable anxiety, but it is now known that this watery meadow conceals one of the strongest weight-bearing geological formations in the world. Nevertheless, the builders' faith (or foolhardiness) and their astonishing engineering feat still amount to little less than a miracle, since they could not possibly have suspected such a stratum. 'It is a miracle of faith,' Golding once declared: 'A definite act of faith.'

Not far from Salisbury Cathedral itself lies Old Sarum. A rather formidable symbol of continuity, it has been the site of (possibly) a Roman camp and of Saxon and Norman towns. Its cathedral was the bishopric of two twelfth-century bishops, whose names were Jocelin and Roger, and at the end of the fourteenth century the cathedral stones were raised to provide materials for the building of the magnificent Salisbury Cathedral Close. Earlier stern straight roads crossed Salisbury Plain and converged at what used to be a prehistoric metropolis whose 'cathedral' (Golding's word) was Stonehenge. The high chalk Downs of Wiltshire surrounding the two monuments are also alight with legends, even artefacts, from thousands of years of historical activity. Europe's largest neolithic stone circle, the Avebury Stone Circle, is close by as is the West Kennet Long Barrow, the largest chambered collective tomb in England and Wales. Then from the Bronze Age there is the enigmatic Silbury Hill, the largest man-made megalithic structure in Europe, its stepped cone rising from Wiltshire chalkland near Avebury; nineteenth-century Chalk Horses at Alton Barnes, Halckpen Hill, Broad Town, and Marlborough; the Celtic field system at Burderop Down used well into the medieval period; the churchyard of Ogbourne St Andrew with its round barrow once used for pagan burials dating back to the Saxon period. It little surprises that Golding remarked, 'Wiltshire is not a place so much as a kind of palimpsest of various generations and centuries.'[23] The area is thick with the bones of ancient peoples: Roman, Celt, Saxon, Dane, Norman.

Wiltshire's archaeological sites, its monuments, their ruins and annals and legends, the soil itself represent a rather complicated metaphor for human effort, it would seem. Take one example: that of the Sarsen Stones, so redolent with history and human use over the ages. Known to some as 'druid stones', these pieces of siliceous sandstone are abundantly present in the Marlborough area, giving by way of their size and greyness the impression of grazing sheep. They have been used from the palaeolithic period to the Bronze Age for the making of axes and other tools. From the Saxon period to the mid nineteenth century they were used for the constructing of houses, garden walls, paving stones; from the 1850s through the 1940s for the building of tramway sets and pavement curbs for cities like Swindon in Wiltshire. For me they confirm mutely what I take to be at the heart of *The Spire*'s enterprise: an ancient repetition of creation and destruction in historical as well as geological times. Like Salisbury Cathedral's spire, their presence speaks both of the anonymity of human enterprise and its essential autocratic origins, so much so that: 'The very stones cry out.' They contain *mana*.

IV

It was so simple at first. On the purely human level of course, it's a story
of shame and folly – Jocelin's Folly, they call it. I had a vision, you see, a
clear and explicit vision. It was *so* simple! It was to be my work. I was
chosen for it. But then the complications began. A single green shoot at
first, then clinging tendrils, then branches, than at last a riotous
confusion. (p.168)

I have suggested that *The Spire* represents a departure from the earlier
novels in the way generating associative strands, rather than literary
subversion, fed its growth. Furthermore, its structure allows, unlike in
the earlier codas, the new perspective to come from the enlightened
viewpoint of the protagonist himself as *he* looks back upon events with
different eyes. In as much as no other consciousness views events,
readers are made to adopt the protagonist's perspective throughout.
And yet a 'master of manipulating the limited point of view, Golding
has specialized in creating narrative consciousnesses which are
notoriously unreliable',[24] and *The Spire* was no exception.

In fact, I would argue that the reader is again being relied upon to
make connections that the protagonist cannot yet make. 'We learn of
Jocelin's failings both through the direct evidence of his interaction
with others and his thought and also by reading the book rather as a
medieval might have read the symbolism of forms and images of a
cathedral.'[25] Certain ironic asides, the juxtaposition of dialogue with
recording consciousness, the symbolic patterns certain phrases assume
as they are reiterated through the text, each is intended to hint at
Jocelin's folly: the cupidity of his dedication and the complexity of his
motives. Among these the tent, the mayflower, the kingfisher and raven,
and, above all, the burgeoning tree are relevant in multivalent ways, the
latter especially so since one of the book's major thematic
preoccupations is the nature of the generative process. Readers then
can interpret Jocelin's dreams in their sexual context whereas Jocelin
himself deliberately denies them their sexual origin, even when the
buried creatures come to haunt him.

Consider, for example, the careful identification of Goody with her
double, the dumb stonecutter Gilbert, where the red-haired 'devil' of his
dream's 'uncountry' hums from an empty mouth. Both Goody and
Gilbert – as the doubling of their names implies – are objects of Jocelin's

suppressed desire, silent servants to his prurience and prudery. He, however, prefers to interpret them as bewitchments or bad angels; thus he creates a demon from the stuff of his own mind, in the manner of the New People and Pincher before him. An analogous identification between the cathedral and a man's body, with the obviousness of the spire's phallic coding, is drawn – on the whole fairly decorously – at several junctures in the novel. The very first chapter has Jocelin surveying the small model of the cathedral, which resembles, he thinks:

> a man lying on his back. The nave was his legs placed together, the transepts on either side were his arms outspread. The choir was his body; and the Lady Chapel [...] was his head. And now also, springing, projecting, bursting, erupting from the heart of the building, there was his crown and majesty, the new spire (p. 8).[26]

Although tellingly Jocelin does not observe it, any cathedral's cruciform shape is first and foremost emblematic of Christ's crucifixion, an outward and visible sign of an inward and spiritual meaning. Too soon the cathedral/corpus equation will shift, the spire dangerously becoming the phantom penis of Jocelin's loathsome masturbatory and copulatory dreams:

> It seemed to Jocelin that he lay on his back in his bed; and then he was lying on his back in the marshes crucified and his arms were the transepts with Pangall's *kingdom* nestled on his left side. People came to jeer [...] Only Satan himself, rising out of the west, clad in nothing but blazing hair stood over his nave and worked at the building [...] (pp. 74–75, my italics).

It would be an oversimplification to interpret the spire's projection as 'the phallic sublimation of Jocelin's repressed yearning for the red-haired wife', as *Time* magazine reported. The erection lends itself to a wide range of metaphoric treatment, for 'Golding rarely works with a monovalent image'[27]; it is successively the 'mast' of a ship, 'a dunce's cap', a 'stone hammer' waiting to strike and the stone diagram of the highest prayer of all. The observation that 'it gives one some idea of the nature of this writer's gift that he has written a book about an expressly phallic symbol to which Freudian glosses seem irrelevant'[28] seems much to the point, for phallicism operates as just one aspect of the primordial, that ritual terror, barbarism, and magical awe that exist within the civilized psyche. The whole ambiguous continuum is figured here by the pit/cellarage where, as in earlier works, the trope of seething water and darkness conveys the horror implicit in death, decay, and destruction. A female space, the pit also is 'a fitting counterpart to the huge stone *phallos* that rises over it'.[29] For Jocelin – with both his medieval misogyny and his medieval sensibility – it is 'Doomsday coming up [...] the damned stirring or the noseless men turning over and thrusting up' (p. 80).

During the crucial episode at the pit, the symbolic dimensions of the cathedral model assume this larger relevance when Jocelin 'in an apocalyptic glimpse of seeing' catches the impotent Pangall being mocked by a workman, who dances with 'the model of the spire projecting obscenely from between his legs' (p. 90). Jocelin turns away in disgust, alarmed by any relationship between flesh and spirit. 'Renewing life' (p. 58) horrifies him – it is like mud covering his body. Rachael Mason is 'a furious womb [that] had acquired a tongue', woman – or in the words of the novel 'Beldame'[30] – strips the sparkling honeybars and phantom light of existence down to where 'horror and Farce' take over. He tries to escape into free air and light, away from darkness and marsh, where creation is 'not the burgeoning evil thing, from birth to senility with its complex strength between' (pp. 62–63).

Although Jocelin tries to move away from 'all this confusion', each new level brings a new effect, a new cause, a new lesson. A funnel is built over the crossways, the pit is filled in, yet a new pit emerges on the higher level in the swallow's nest that Goody and Roger come to occupy. There is a lesson for each height; like 'dark waters in his belly' he feels that he brings 'essential evil' (p. 106) with him all the way to the 'stork's nest' (p. 124), a third kind of pit at the head of the tower. Yet something new is learned with each pit, something that could not have been predicted. 'We're mayfly. We can't tell what it'll be like up there from foot to foot; but we must live from morning to evening every minute with a new thing' (p. 117). Although Roger insists that Jocelin should 'look down [...] look down' (p. 117), the bird in flight dreads the dreary factual pavement. He longs to be the raven 'that knows what the sunrise is like' and have 'some knowledge of yesterday and the day before' (p. 117).

To evade them, Jocelin suppresses the memories of red hair, mistletoe, wolf-howl, and burning fires. The reader's understanding suffers a similar suspension. What, at mid-point in the narrative, is the hideous obscene berry Jocelin scrapes from his boot? Why does the memory of the pit – 'a grave made ready for some notable' (p. 13) – erupt in his memory as he scans the shuddering bale fires in the Valley of the Hanging Stones? What 'devils from hell' torment him, swooping with scaly wings past his spine as he mounts the corkscrew stairs? What plant with strange flowers and fruit, complex, twining, and caught with red hair does he see? Obviously these fragments are the imaginings of an obsessed mind, but their very insistent repetition and elaborate interweaving with each other suggest 'a pattern' (p. 187) that Jocelin is depicted as deliberately ignoring. 'There it came again,' Jocelin ponders, 'the notsong, the absence of remembering, the overriding thing' (p. 166).

Focalization is managed so readers must experience the terror before understanding it; we are confined within a confining mind. The physical sense the novel imparts is more arduous still since we, at times, have access to the wider angle of the third-person limited point of view. Whereas, for example, our view of Goody Pangall is his – her being 'synecdochally reduced to her blazing hair'[31] – other things also come only marginally into focus, so that we get exactly the same impression of Alison's face as does Jocelin. To him – to us – she appears enormous, this emissary from the secular world. Yet we have our own perception, point of view having been managed so that the reader can construe some of the social and uncharitable implications of Jocelin's obsession as he himself cannot. The sharp tap and wet star on Jocelin's shoe is Pangall's tear. Roger is terrified of heights and is being driven by an unrelenting will; his wife is churlishly dismissed when she requires sympathy. Aunt Alison is no more or less wanton than the Dean, whose position she established by a boudoir giggle. Father Anselm's 'stately head' is steeped in petty malice.

On the other hand, readers are made to identify so strongly with the protagonist that when Jocelin's motives are inspected by his interrogators it is impossible not to find the questions repellent in their simplicity. During these interrogations readers find themselves sharing Jocelin's total conviction of the inadequacy of words to explain the entangled course of events: 'That's too simple, like every other explanation. That gets nowhere near the root' (p. 195). We understand Jocelin's point that there seems no way of tracing all the complications back to their root, no way of disentangling the anguished faces from the concrete construction. Readers are caught – and this is a frequent trope in the book – between the outside of things and the inside of things, unable to make a judgement. We are never allowed to settle into one view.

Everything in the novel is made to glance two ways. The workmen are 'good men' yet infidels and blasphemous. The cathedral is rich with the 'Fabric of Constant Praise' (p. 165) yet seems a 'pagan temple' (p. 10); Goody is as godly as her name implies, yet this good child is an adulterous adult; Roger is a masterful master builder yet suffers from vertigo. Jocelin is a brutal self-deluded egotist; nevertheless, when exalted by vision – whether God-inspired, flesh-inspired, or disease-inspired – he accomplishes the concrete construction of a spire that 'joins earth to heaven' (p. 69). Its very stones are windows by which men look at the infinite, yet 'they cry out' (p. 223). The allusion here to *Luke* 19:40 – 'I tell you if these [disciples] were silent the very stones would cry out and rejoice' – is a motif woven through the novel's verbal cloth as part of the complicated metaphor for human effort that is the book's major preoccupation. In a sense, Jocelin himself becomes such a stone monument in death: he is a 'building about to fall' (p. 222), his ribs are like the stone vaulting that he inspects during delirium. Breathing, he pulls himself 'down into the stone mouth, [which] would break up the stone and eject a puff of shaped air' (p. 218). And, of course, his death effigy sculpted by Gilbert is a stone skeleton lapped in skin: a *momento mori* and a *momento vivere*.

Everything in *The Spire* is like this: protean, ambiguous. An ostensibly sturdy Christian cathedral rests on the uncertain foundations of 'the living pagan earth' (p. 80). Its four pillars are less majestic saints than human lovers; they dance over slime and stirring grubs. An exultant prayer is supported by the corrupt money of an adulterous aunt and a murdered man, who 'crouched beneath the crosssways with a sliver of mistletoe between his ribs' (p. 222). Creation brings with it violence and death. The man of God rejects God: '*How proud their hope of hell is. There is no innocent work. God knows where God may be*' (p. 222), Jocelin cries out on his deathbed, convinced of his own guilt. Moments later we learn that a sexual explanation for sin is as inadequate as any despairing one. Jocelin fumbles towards a formula for his folly and decides his spire was nothing but 'a great [phallic] club' lifted towards a tangle of hair blazing in the sky. He mutters aloud, 'Berenice,' but no single conception of corruption suffices either, for it is the fiction's effort to try to insist that the physical and spiritual are perpetually intermingled. Golding makes this point – very obliquely and far too minimally for many readers – by having Father Adam (who is set upon helping Jocelin into heaven) read the Berenice of the Catullus poem to whom Jocelin refers as Saint Berenice, a most obscure early Christian martyr.

Seconds later, at the moment of his death, Jocelin glimpses the physical spire through the window, a physical sight that the text intends should lead him towards the spiritual vision with which the novel would close. In a reworking of the narrative strategy of confrontation scene (where dramatized oppositions are meant to be resolved) it was intended that Jocelin might be read as being released from a burden of considerable guilt. *Pincher Martin* places Pincher before a stone erection called the Dwarf, *Free Fall* places Sammy Mountjoy before a rag, *The Spire* places Jocelin before that object also emblematic of guilt: for the cleric, it is the 'stone hammer' that he had 'traded for four lives' (p. 221). In contrast to Sammy and in contrast to Pincher, however, Jocelin is pictured as experiencing – in his moment of confrontation – not just purgative panic but also astonishment and joy, which the text inscribes as 'split[ting] the darkness' (p. 222). Also intended was that readers accept that mystery as being experienced not as malignancy, but as terror-and-joy. Before Jocelin's eyes, there is an object which he perceives – the third-person limited point of view endorses this perception – as something rushing towards infinity, yet glittering like a fountain that falls. It is an 'upward waterfall', and that paradox is intended to figure forth a multifarious dynamic reality where some pattern might be perceived. The truth embodied is one composed not of sets of opposition – profane/sacred, sexual/ascetic, physical/spiritual, innocent/guilty – but as a suspension of perpetually fused antinomies: a bluebird/over/panic-shot darkness, to borrow the novel's multi-layered metaphors. Extending the vision to a moral context, human acts may be seen to have elements of innocence and guilt, each modifying, each creating the other. And as is the case in *Free Fall*, pattern emerges; it cannot be imposed.

We must assume that it is for this reason that the novel has the Church immediately translate Jocelin's affirmation of the spire and all that entails in his final cry '*It's like the appletree*' into a gesture of Christian assent when Father Adam reads the whisper and joy on the dying man's lips as '*God, God, God*'. The protagonist, on the other hand, seems to be bringing into connection the upward unstoppable thrust of the unruly member to the seething underside, panicshot darkness to struggling kingfisher. Like the Original Tree itself, the 'long, black springing thing' (p. 204), Jocelin had noticed among the scatter of angelbuds is blighting plant, but bursting apple blossom too.[32]

Conclusion seems much too strong a word for the notions about terror-and-joy that close this novel. By the necessity of Golding's craft, one relying on the oblique and the compressed, a sensuous resolution is intended to be invoked by the ongoing rhetoric: 'In the tide, flying like a bluebird struggling, shouting screaming to leave the words of magic and incomprehension' (p. 223). The rubric's meaning cannot be decoded and put into conceptual terms. As seems the case in most representations of intense illumination, conceptual terms are inadequate to portray the felt experience. Words that seek to embody 'magic and incomprehension' can only be presented through metaphor, by some linguistic ultimate that will invoke all the earlier associations that were planted to grow.

V

[R]eligion[s] came in layers, each age super-imposed on an obscurer and more savage one. The layers existed together, since nothing is as conservative as religion. Dig down, and just below the surface you come on human sacrifice and, at the bottom, traces of cannibalism.

Golding, 'Delphi, The Oracle Revealed'

As I have argued, if there is an inheritor of integrated vision in *The Spire* one sees him in the figure of Jocelin with his commingling of kingfisher/over/deepwater. Before such achieved insight, disclosures that have been delayed until the novel's extended coda have to be revealed, specifically the delayed disclosure of Pangall's death which coincides with Jocelin's realization of his own repressed lust. We recall that, throughout the spire's construction, Jocelin tries to avoid the 'whole train of memories and worries and associations which were altogether random' (p. 95). When urgent memories are buried, he is happy: for example, perched at the top of the spire. However, when he looks four hundred and more feet down at the pit, 'unlooked for things come [...] things put aside from the time when the earth crept' (p. 105) at the crossways.

Pangall is significant, in ways readers come only slowly to intuit. At a dramatic level the connection between Pangall and Jocelin is clear enough – Pangall's mismarriage to a young woman, arranged by Jocelin himself so as to keep his daughter-in-god pure – is the springboard for one of the book's major complications: the liaison between Roger and Goody.[33] Furthermore, as opposing doubles, the counterpointing of a celibate Dean with an impotent Verger has a certain deft economy in a novel investigating the varieties and ironies of progeniture. Yet more than dramatic function is at work, the Pangall character being foregrounded rather more strongly than a minor character would ordinarily be expected to be. Indeed, the novel insists upon locating Pangall's significance in the distant past. He is the last of a line that has served the Cathedral Church of the Blessed Virgin Mary for four generations; he is connected through these ancestors to oak out of which the beams were fashioned and, not incidentally, the wood on which mistletoe flourishes when the tree is green. Thus Pangall's early warning about unseasoned and burning wood has a symbolic, as well as a dramatic, relevance when one recalls the omnipresent trope of a plant with 'strange flowers [...] engulfing, destroying, strangling' (p. 194).

Then there is the matter of Pangall's cottage resting against the Cathedral side – a matter the text reiterates in one of Jocelin's masturbatory dreams. Why is it a 'kingdom'? And why is it described as being built – as it came to be – 'against the architect's intentions' (p. 17) like 'a monument'? In fact, some of its piecemeal construction predates the Cathedral and the Normans themselves by over 'a thousand years'; presumably, fragments of Saxon and Roman origin are sewn into its decaying fabric. Reconsidering the richness of Wiltshire's palimpsest, Golding elaborated in conversation upon the historical underpinnings:

> The intention was that the Pangalls picked up what was lying about and also 'won' building materials. The Saxon wayfarers, by the way, used Roman ruins as shelter, thus calling them Cold Harbours. Where you get the name, Cold Harbour, you get or had got a ruin, probably Roman. There are, for example, reused Roman tiles in a Mildenhal church near Marlborough [Wiltshire]. I put a Cold Harbour in *The Spire* to render the whole concept critic-proof. (Golding to Tiger)

In this context, one is forced to remember not only the historical density of the landscape, but also the long-standing proximity of the two 'monuments', the Christian cathedral of Salisbury and the pagan place of worship, Stonehenge. It is Pangall's kingdom of time that is actually invaded by the workmen – 'murderers, cutthroats, brawlers, rapers, notorious fornicators, sodomites, atheists' (p. 167), to a one – as they taunt Pangall and insolently pile the rubble of construction around the cottage. It is this kingdom that is vanquished, as the dimensions of a cathedral, the shape of a landscape and a whole town undergo a convulsion of change, with new roads and a 'New Street'. Like other vanquished kingdoms, Pangall's shares that regrettable loss that is implicit in the nature of change itself. One way of life lost, another grows from its place; Pangall and his line testify to that ancient repetition of rise and fall, growth and decay-and-growth. He and his kingdom's line witness the cycle figured in the paradoxical 'upward waterfall', which Jocelin is made to affirm at the novel's close.

From the outset Pangall, dusty brown and 'dung coloured' (p. 20) with his devil-broom and deformity is associated not just with the crippled Hephaistos of myth and but also with the earth that Jocelin rejects. As the poor knave sheds tears of humiliation, sunlight draws the Dean's eye away from the 'sharp tap on the instep of [his] shoe' (p. 20), an incident adroitly prefiguring the crucial episode at the pit. Here Jocelin scrapes from his instep the brown obscene berry of mistletoe and tries to close eyes and ears to the long wolf-howl and 'hunting noise of the pack that raced after' (p. 90) the vanishing Pangall. In fact, Pangall has not fled from his kingdom and the persecutions there but has been murdered and then buried in the pit's earth. As readers know, the whole incident is handled as covertly as those earlier ritual murders in *The Inheritors* and *Lord of the Flies* of Liku and Simon, both of whom function as religious scapegoats sacrificed to ensure group solidarity.[34] Drawing on the evidence of Pangall's death by mistletoe, an early analysis maintained that the Norse Balder myth was as essential to *The Spire*'s construction as the Grail Legend to Eliot's *The Wasteland*, arguing that – by way of what we would now term its intertextual influence – it could be seen to underlie the meaning of Pangall's murder.[35] Just as one discerns Tennyson's Arthurian enchanter Merlin in *The Inheritors*' Marlin, the witch doctor of the totemic cult of the stag, so Balder can be found in Pangall. During a struggle for possession of the exquisite Nanna, Balder is slain by his rival Hodhr with an arrow constructed out of mistletoe, the one thing to which he is vulnerable.

It is true Pangall is convinced he will die as some kind of scapegoat for the workmen's vengeance and superstition and their dismantling of his kingdom. Remembering, however, that Jocelin makes the pointed connection between the obscene berry and Pangall's disappearance on the evening of the Solstice, it seems also likely that Golding had in mind more general folklore than one particular myth. He specifically employed the site of Stonehenge (Stangheist or Hanging Stones), where it is believed the sun was worshipped and the oak tree was venerated, its mistletoe performing a specific part of ritual attached to the monument. The sacred oak could not be felled nor a human proxy slain before a ritual cutting of mistletoe from the tree on Midsummer's Eve. Describing how any religious impulse might be seen in its slow metamorphosis, Golding remarked to me:

> The fact is primitive religion is all, of course, really contradictory and at the same time conservative. So the religion of my masons would have much in common with whatever went on at Stonehenge – and indeed with what went on in caves and clearings; but its systematizations would be partial, shifting. The workmen would kill Pangall [...] because of a generalized feeling that he might make a good guardian of the foundations and a conservative feeling that the job can only be done really decorously with flint or mistletoe.

On such a subject, both Frazer and Graves long ago argued that, cross culturally, such ritual cutting of mistletoe and sacrifice symbolized the emasculation of an old king by his successor.[36] In the anthropological as well as the mythic context, the death of deformity and sterility would appear to constitute the necessary antecedent to a release of generative powers in a new kingdom. In such a reading, *The Spire's* Pangall would be both scapegoat and fertility god with the terrors of the cellarage containing their own paradoxical joy, the grave possessing the power to renew.

With his death the pestilence is not entirely dispelled, however. Only the painful transition from one religious variant to another occurs, although this transition might involve a measure of fortunate advance. Perhaps a refinement begins to evolve; as one impulse becomes superimposed on another more obdurate one, primitive scapegoat comes to be supervened by Holy Fool. And while Pangall is murdered, Jocelin is merely taunted. High in the 'wooden dunce's cap' (an appropriate site and synecdoche for any fool), the masons adopt Jocelin as their totemic figure. He will ward off their superstitious fears about heights: 'no one at the top tried to drive him off, and he could not think why this was, until one day he asked Jehan who answered him simply:'"You bring us luck"' (p. 151). In some sense Jocelin already supports the spire as much as Pangall's crouched corpse does, for the first set of his sculpted stone heads had been flung into the pit to steady the foundations. From the first it was planned that he would be 'built into' the cathedral, the four effigies of Jocelin originally being intended to surmount the spire, exhibiting on four corners a 'Nose like an eagle's beak. Mouth open […]' (p. 23) proclaiming the Holy Spirit (as a profligately ecstatic Jocelin once ordained) day and night till doomsday, spouting their Hosannahs as the gargoyles spout rain. The burial of these carvings in the earth's seething bowels clearly has the narrative value of prefiguring the (necessary) eradication of Jocelin's wilful pride. In addition, a whole set of linked, associative metaphors cluster around Jocelin's physiognomy, figure, and motion. To Anselm he seems to be 'flying like a great bird' (p. 201); to Alison he resembles 'a great bird hunched in the rain' (p. 184). Most frequently the image of the raven jostles that of the eagle, as the latter appears under the traditional guise of Devouring Will. Jocelin believes Gilbert – at work sculpting the first effigy of the Dean's head – is carving a stone image of an eagle, the creature associated with St John the Evangelist in *Ezekiel*. Up in the rising tower squatting among ravens, the bird traditionally associated with the devil by way of its black plumage, Jocelin mutters as one more dark bird wings by: 'as far as I'm concerned it's an eagle' (p. 107).[37] Deaf as he is to worker Jehan's insistence that the swooping bird is not eagle but raven, so too is Jocelin blind to the carving, less eagle in likeness than gargoyle.

Importantly, in fact, Jocelin is associated with this primordial figure of disintegration and decay, for his physiognomy does resemble what are described as the 'diseased' (p. 67) gargoyles that spout rain continuously from Christmas to Lent during that season's floods and plague and deaths and rot and ruin. With straining mouth and blank eyes they appear to 'yell soundless blasphemies and derisions in the wind' (p. 67). Yet built into the cathedral (as surely as Pangall came to be), the gargoyles perform a purgative role, 'some infinite complexity of punishment' (p. 97), that Jocelin himself will come to adopt:

> […] with what accuracy and inspiration those giants had built the place, because the gargoyles seemed cast out of the stone, burst out of the stone like boils or pimples, purging the body of sickness, ensuring by their self-damnation, the purity of the whole (p. 67).

That purgative role – and thus the symbolic conflation of the protagonist's visage with those of the gargoyles – is dramatized in the narrative when Jocelin is attacked by the townsfolk, an attack clearly meant to duplicate Pangall's persecution and his ritual function. Lying in the filth of the gutter, his stinking rotten body stripped of clothes, Jocelin hears 'hound noises', baying and yelpings with the (tribe-like) mob creating 'their own mouths fanged and slavering' as it pounds its beast into the earth. Saved from Pangall's fate, however, Jocelin becomes not scapegoat but rather Holy Fool.

Hindsight now shows that central to Golding's vision has always been an eschatology of the sacrificial victim – deity, mystic, saint, scapegoat, or fool – who performs the necessary exorcism of fears. Contemplating 'that man who reached out both arms and gathered the spears into his own body', *Free Fall*'s narrator (and thus, as fictional surrogate, Golding's spokesperson) suggested tentatively that 'the nature of our universe is such that the strong and crystalline adult action heals a wound and takes away a scar, not out of today but out of the future. The wound that might have gone on bleeding and suppurating becomes healthy flesh' (*Free Fall*, p. 75). Meeting the fate of those who remind society of its fears and guilt and terrors, time after time and in culture after culture, such individuals – having become the objectification of those fears – are maligned, hated, and destroyed. Thus in the person of *The Spire*'s Jocelin actions are performed at his life's end, actions that go beyond personal gain so that such a figure would become an instrument not of his own egotism, but the executor of a larger and more implacable pattern.

The Spire, it had been said, is about 'vision and cost'. In the mind's cellarage are both creator and destroyer. Creation involves bloodshed, sacrifice, and murder; the crossways over which the spire grows is 'a grave for some notable' yet 'a pit to catch a Dean'. It is the place of sacrifice, yet the place of vision too; 'here where the pit stinks, I received what [vision] I received' (p. 58), as Jocelin ruminates. As *The Inheritors* had, and as the (unfinished) *Double Tongue* would, *The Spire* dramatized a chronicle of one phase in what can be understood as the ancient repetition of rise and fall – and rise again; one phase in humanity's 'upward waterfall'. Remember that its first page opens on a substantial manifestation of both triumph and sacrifice, as the visual text of the Abraham and Isaac window fuses with the joy on the Dean's face. And *The Spire*'s last page closes on another substantial manifestation of triumph and sacrifice in Jocelin's sight of the spire, whose perceived rose colour is both emblem of mystic rose and blood sacrifice. From Jocelin's perspective, and through the indirect discourse that marks his mode of perception, we have his final near-consolatory vision of this his spire:

> It was slim as a girl, translucent. It had grown from some seed of rosecoloured substance that glittered like a waterfall, an upward waterfall. The substance was one thing, that broke all the way to infinity in cascades of exultation that nothing could trammel (p. 223).

It is a vision – Jocelin's and ours, should readers, after witnessing such costs, share such vision – where an Homeric extended simile almost connects material and spiritual, primordial and divine. Like the shorthand that is perhaps Jocelin's sense of similitude, the vision is compared to an apple tree seen earlier on approaching Roger Mason's valently named den, Letoyle, there to seek forgiveness. Stumbling forward, the now withering Jocelin notices a still miraculously flowering apple tree with a 'long, black springing thing' (p. 204) at its center. Is it meant then that Jocelin is able to fuse apparent opposites, balancing vision with its cost: so many lives disheveled, Pangall's kingdom destroyed, a new-born infant dead, and other lives also lost?

The novel's closing page answers this question obliquely, Jocelin's vision of the spire as an upward waterfall being crucial, if gnomic. It is instructive here to compare *The Spire* with *Free Fall*, there being a marked difference between the two. Before the rag, Sammy remains burdened with a conviction of his own guilt. In *The Spire*'s second narrative movement, Jocelin also experiences the world of the spirit as self-condemnation. The structure's coda with its series of disclosures forces Jocelin to accept his own cellarage; he admits his responsibility for the anguished faces that cannot be disentangled from the riotous confusion of the spire's growth. While he purges his spiritual arrogance and seeks contrition from the harmed Roger he despairs of his own guilt and abandons the possibility of merciful miracle. As were Sammy Mountjoy's, so are Dean Jocelin's eyes turned in upon his own darkness:

> Heaven and hell and purgatory are small and bright as a jewel in someone's pocket only to be taken out and worn on feast days. This is a

grey, successive day for dying on. And what is heaven to me unless I go in holding him by one hand and her by the other? (p. 222).

So we may fairly ponder whether 'the salvation of Jocelin is left as doubtful as the fate of the spire'[38], which may or may not continue to stand. The lack of closure, of course, is deliberate, the narrative strategy being one that provokes the readers, putting them into the positions they have chosen to adopt. That 'Jocelin destroyed the cathedral as the house of God and the chapter as a community in order to achieve his megalomaniac vision'[39] can be one legitimate reading. Just as legitimate is another reading where Jocelin's last vision is seen as redemptive, amounting to 'a statement of Faith. Although it is not "God! God! God!" in the way Father Adam means, it is, one suspects, "God! God! God!" in the way Golding means, and in its love and exaltation has its own inclusive charity.'[40] Since the Host is laid upon the dying man's lips, the reader can also conclude that Jocelin, unlike Sammy, is granted forgiveness: sinners at the last minute may be saved, for (to borrow a forceful maxim from Graham Greene's *Brighton Rock*) 'between the stirrup and the ground there is hope.'

In my view, the confrontation scene on the novel's last page can be read as a release from punishment as Jocelin's primary guilty perception of the spire transforms itself into one of transfigured astonishment. In Jocelin's initial perception of the spire being like two eyes looking at him, 'an eye for an eye' (p. 222), is encoded an implicit allusion to 'Eye for eye, tooth for tooth, hand for hand, foot for foot/Burning for burning, wound for wound, stripe for stripe,' and the vengeful punishing Judge of *Exodus*. In encountering those merciless eyes Jocelin might be said to be encountering his own loathsome judgement upon himself, with forgiveness impossible.[41] As Jocelin concentrates, the two eyes seem to slide together to become the figure of the physical spire. And it is possible that we are watching the Judge metamorphose into the Redeemer, experienced as triumphant 'flashes of thought which split the *darkness*' (p. 223, my italics). Jocelin's last words, which relate his exultation to the apple tree may be interpreted – although in a different context – in the way in which Father Adam interprets them: as evidence of Jocelin's atonement and God's mercy. As *The Inheritors* offers the hint of positive change on the plain beyond the Fall, as artist Tuami sculpts from the death-weapon the new life-image, so at *The Spire*'s conclusion there might be, in the stone fabric of the 'upward waterfall' connecting heaven and earth, the promise of a new heaven and a new earth. So: does the spire of the Cathedral Church of Our Lady continue to stand?

Endnotes

1   Donald W. Crompton, '*The Spire*', *Critical Quarterly* 9 (1967), p. 64.

2   David Skilton, 'Golding's *The Spire*', *Studies in the Literary Imagination* 2 (1969), p. 53.

3   Bernard F. Dick, *William Golding* (revised edition), Boston, Twayne Publishers, 1987, p. 72.

4   Arnold Johnston, *Of Earth and Darkness: The Novels of William Golding*, Columbia & London, University of Missouri Press, 1980, p. 75.

5   Margaret Hallissy, '"No Innocent Work": Theology and Psychology in William Golding's *The Spire*', *Christianity and Literature* 47 (1997), p. 46.

6   Johnston, op. cit., p. 69.

7   James Gindin, *William Golding*, New York, St Martin's Press, 1988, p. 52.

8   Donald W. Crompton, *A View From the Spire: William Golding's Later Novels*, edited and completed by Julia Briggs, Oxford, Blackwell, 1985, p. 40.

9   Laurence Lerner, 'Jocelin's Folly; or, Down with the Spire', *Critical Quarterly* 24 (1982), p. 12.

10   V. S. Pritchett, *The Living Novel and Later Approaches*, New York, Vintage Books, 1967, p. 13.

11   The novel's medieval ethos, the ideological context of the fourteenth century – and especially 'the theology of sin' – have been usefully explored where the distinction drawn is between

the twentieth-century psychological reading of pride as 'excessive self-esteem [...] remedied by increased self-awareness' and the fourteenth-century theological reading of pride as a 'deadly sin, requiring not merely recognition but repentance, specifically by means of the sacrament of penance' (Hallissy, op. cit., p. 37).

12 E. C. Bufkin, 'The Nobel Prize and the Paper Men: The Fixing of William Golding', *Georgia Review* 39 (1985), pp. 55–65; Crompton, op. cit., 1985; Laurence Lerner, op. cit., 1982; Walter Sullivan, 'The Fables and the Art', *Sewanee Review* (1963), pp. 660–64.

13 These have included Ibsen's *The Master Builder* (Hallissy, op. cit.; Bernard S. Oldsey and Stanley Weintraub, *The Art of William Golding*, New York, Harcourt Brace and World, 1965), Sophocles' *Oedipus Rex* (Dick, op. cit.; Lawrence S. Friedman, William Golding, New York, Continuum, 1993), Melville's *The Bell Tower* (Hallissy, op. cit.) and Browning's *The Bishop Orders his Tomb at St. Praxed's* (Oldsey and Weintraub, op. cit.) where both texts have priests named Anselm. In the latter case my hunch was Golding intended the name for his scrupulously correct Sacrist to be an ironic echo, not of Browning, but the name of a twelfth-century Archbishop of Canterbury who was attacked as a hypocrite. Other proposed sources for *The Spire*'s tower and tale have been as various as T.S. Eliot's *The Rock*, Carlyle's *Past and Present* and even Dorothy L. Sayer's *The Zeal of Thy House*.

14 David Lodge, 'William Golding', *The Spectator* (April 19, 1964), p. 490.

15 Frank Kermode, 'The Case for William Golding', *The New York Review of Books* (April 30, 1964), p. 3.

16 Gindin, op. cit., p. 51.

17 Richard S. Cammarota, '*The Spire*: A Symbolic Analysis', in Jack I. Biles and Robert O. Evans (eds), *William Golding: Some Critical Considerations*, Lexington, University of Kentucky Press, 1978, pp. 151–75; Jeanne Delbaere-Garant, 'The Evil Plant in William Golding's *The Spire*', *Revue des Langes Vivantes* 35 (1969), pp. 623–31; Sue Thomas, 'Some Religious Icons and Biblical

Allusions in William Golding's *The Spire*', *Journal of the Australasian Universities Mode* 64 (1985), pp. 190–97.

18 Hallissy, op. cit., p. 46.

19 S. H. Boyd, *The Novels of William Golding*, New York, St Martin's Press, 1988, p. 89.

20 Golding quoting from the diary recorded in Trevelyan, *Spectator* (March 25, 1960), p. 48.

21 William Golding, 'An Affection for Cathedrals' *Holiday* (December 1965), p 36.

22 *Ibid*, p. 39.

23 Golding to Biles, Jack Biles, *Talk: Conversations with William Golding*, New York, Harcourt, Brace & Jovanovich, 1970, p. 94. The Wiltshire landscape – rechristened Barchester in *The Pyramid* and foregrounded in *The Spire, The Pyramid, Darkness Visible*, and *The Paper Men* – seems as much mythic landscape to Golding as Wessex was to his predecessor Hardy, and no less complex in its imaginative influence.

24 Johnson, op. cit., p. 68.

25 Boyd, op. cit., p. 90.

26 Two transepts only were required to figure forth this corporeal shape, thus another reason why the actual cathedral at Salisbury was modified in the fictional depiction.

27 Dick, op. cit., p. 77.

28 Kermode op. cit., p. 4.
29 Boyd op. cit., p. 85.

30 The point is well taken that the vocabulary here is 'surely a disaster', *beldame*'s meaning not being sex but great grandmother

or remote ancestress; old woman, especially an ugly old woman, and thus is 'comically inapt' (Lerner, op. cit., p 14).

31   Dick, op. cit., p. 72.

32   The apple tree here carries not only those associative strands from *Genesis* but draws together all the other trees and growing plants so abundantly present in the novel, including the oak and cedar trees brought by Ivo and by which his position is secured. Another tree is relevant; at the book's opening Jocelin stands by a window and sees sunlight as 'an important dimension' (p. 10). The figure used to describe the sun blossoming against the workmen and the dust-filled nave is that of a branching tree.

33   Such a January–May liaison has a long literary life with the inevitable triangle: a lame husband, a neglected wife and a blandishing, strong suitor. Here the Greek smithy Hephaistos is very much an intertextual glance, in my judgement. Married to Aphrodite, who played him false with Ares, Hephaistos – so went the bard Domodocles in Book VIII of *The Odyssey* – lamented that 'Aphrodite [...] holds me in little favour because he is handsome and goes on sound feet while I am misshapen from birth.' Piteous Pangall, however, never makes the treacherous snare of spider webs, the net having already been spun by Goody and Roger's attachment.

34   In *The Spire*, 'Misshapenness and Impotence are ritually murdered. The sacrificial victim is built into the pit to strengthen the inadequate foundations,' as was first observed by Ian Gregor and Mark Kinkead-Weekes (*William Golding*, London, Faber and Faber, 1967, p. 211), with other discussions building on their lead (Howard S. Babb, The Novels of William Golding, Columbus, Ohio State University Press, 1970; Boyd, op. cit.; Cammarata, op. cit.; Delbaere, op. cit.).

35   Crompton, op. cit., p. 66.

36   'The killing of the king and the scapegoat ceremonial appear to have been originally distinct, but it seems probable [...] that when

the scapegoat was human, he might prove an economical substitute for the king and so the two ceremonies would sometimes be confused with one another,' as Enid Welsford's *The Fool* so describes in Boyd's useful quote from her history of folly (Boyd, op. cit., pp. 99–100).

37 It is here that the Meryon etching of the Le Stryge gargoyle comes into play as one of the imaginative seeds for Jocelin's raven-like egotism, for the etching includes the swirling black ravens.

38 Hallissy, op. cit., p. 54.

39 Lerner, op. cit., p. 11.

40 Gregor and Kinkead-Weekes, op. cit., p. 235.

41 Recall here Simon and Pincher each brooding before a face which is both his own and that of a god, for Jocelin's confrontation at *The Spire*'s close is a re-orchestration of the earlier theophanies.

Darkness Visible

I

> And I saw in the right hand of him that sat on the throne a book written within and on the back side sealed with seven seals [and] in the days of the voice of the seventh angel, when he shall begin to sound, the mystery of God should be finished.
>
> *Revelation* 5.1–10

> We're all mad, the whole damned race. We're wrapped in illusions, delusions, confusions about the penetrability of partitions, we're all mad and in solitary confinement.
>
> *Darkness Visible*

Its oxymoronic title trumpeting thematic clashes between dark and light, *Darkness Visible* orchestrated on a symphonic scale what had persisted in being a textual preoccupation for its author. Borrowed from Milton's description in *Paradise Lost* of hell as a place of 'no light, but rather darkness visible', the title is highly resonant. In the context of Golding's work, it goes back to the phrase 'the darkness of man's heart' in the grieving last line in *Lord of the Flies*. There in the first fiction (and with increasing narrative flexibility in the eleven novels which followed) the method of fabular structure provoked critical analyses that privileged religious readings. Golding's previous works had been so shaped as to make imaginatively visible what to the closed eye of the contemporary seemed problematic: the presence of the spiritual realm.

Described by one critic as 'undoubtedly William Golding's most puzzling and enigmatic work',[1] *Darkness Visible* marks an especially valuable site from which to investigate the affiliation of narrative strategy and the reader's construction of meanings. This is precisely because the novels written by William Golding continued to be interpreted as religious allegories.[2] But from the perspective of current critical taxonomies, with an author like Golding there is need to define and delimit, separating the practice of literary interpretation from the act of reading. The specific intent of my discussion in this chapter is set within this critical context. I shall register the significant place of doublings, pairings, oppositions, the novel's oxymoronic title signaling a practice that informs both its themes and structure. What is characteristic of Golding's project is that naming and numbering strategies conspire to engage readers in acts, not so much of interpretation, as apprehension.

In a literary period that deconstructed the interpretative habit of valorizing transcendental signifiers just as it deposed authorial intention, Golding's wider religious project seemed especially problematic. 'How does one read a book that is so spattered with clues and signs, clotted with symbols and puns, from the lewd aptness of [the Australian Aborigine] Willy Bummer's name to the [dream] figure with the sword in his mouth straight out of *Revelation*?' wondered A.S. Byatt.[3] To many of its reviewers the novel's religious project seemed unfashionable. Joyce Carol Oates, for one, declared that Golding's 'pristine allegory' could be likened to a vehicle whose use was 'mainly to instruct, to teach; our habit with vehicles [however] is to disembark once we have reached our destination'.[4]

Some critics stressed what they took to be the work's metafictional tendencies and its intertextuality.[5] One proposal (more ingenious than persuasive, in my view) informs the first chapter of *The Coincidence of Opposites: William Golding's Later Fiction* where Kevin McCarron suggests that, in addition to Milton, the secondary sources for *Darkness Visible*'s title can be found in John Clare's satire *The Parish*, Walton Hannah's 1953 treatise *Darkness Visible: A Revelation of Freemasonry*, Aldous Huxley's utopian fantasy *The Island* and Elizabeth Gaskell's industrial novel *Mary Barton*, each of which contains the oxymoronic phrase. Pre-eminently (and bizarrely, in my view), McCarron argues, there is Pope's *The Dunciad*. 'As any reader of *The Dunciad* is made immediately aware, Pope continually parodies *Paradise Lost* throughout his own poem and is certainly doing so at the opening of Book Four, where the phrase "darkness visible" occurs.'[6]

Numerous though the intertextual strands may seem to be, the novel as a whole gains by being linked back to the 1840s and 1850s and compared parodically with the then distinct narratological genus: the Condition of England Novel. Variously known as state-of-the-nation or social-problem novel, this sub-genre was distinguished by its focus on the nation's social, material, and moral health as well as the related controversies that accompanied the expansion of factory production in mid nineteenth-century Britain.[7] It was C.F.G. Masterman, a radical journalist and Liberal MP representing the distressed riding of East London in Lord Asquith's 1909 government, who resuscitated for public-minded Edwardians the valent phrase, first used by Carlyle in *Past and Present* (1843). *The Condition of England*, Masterman's 1909 book of social criticism, was central to the tradition, being a treatise on the ideological contradictions of middle-class liberal humanism – especially Edwardian attitudes to the Industrial Revolution's dislocation of the traditional structures of English society.

Placed by way of its subversive use of the tradition of the Condition of England novel, *Darkness Visible*'s spiritual critique engages by erasing the social and economic critiques that are explicit in its Victorian and Edwardian predecessors.[8] It can therefore be situated – albeit slantingly – as one more speaker in a continuous cultural debate about the place of spiritual values in a nation given over to materialism; a debate sustained in England since the Industrial Revolution and given past centrality in both Matthew Arnold's *Culture and Anarchy* and Raymond Williams' *Culture and Society*.

So panoramic in its portrayal of twentieth-century English society that it possesses characters – indeed, events – enough to embarrass a Russian realist, *Darkness Visible* spans some four decades, depicting (although eccentrically) diverse places. London under World War II aerial bombardment is followed by a sweep across the Australian outback. Arrival in Sydney is followed twenty years later by a return to a Wiltshire town, depicted earlier, whose sedentary Old Bridge shakes from lumbering lorries as they continue past a posh public school where a planned kidnapping of an 'Arab prince' will be thwarted by a dervish-like whirling inflamed figure. Polyphonically, *Darkness Visible* orchestrates a medley of narrative voices where characters are made to speak with various national, regional, colloquial, age-specific, and social-class vernaculars. Also included is the steady authorial voice of third-person descriptive rectitude. So readers listen to a loony liberal schoolmaster, a plaintive grandmum, a rhetoric-wedded terrorist, a hurting, enraged daughter, a cranky spiritualist, a down-on-his luck toff with resilient accent and fading expectations, indignant townswomen gossiping self-righteously, vexatious officials with Australian flat vowels, and swinging sixties pub crawlers popping black pills. Such interweaving of various voices posits, of course, the idea of nation, which itself becomes a presiding and investigated character. As in Shakespeare's histories, multifarious voices from that commonweal become as much the stuff of instruction about England's estate as the rebarbative colloquies of Falstaff's knaves, fools, and bawdy friends. Like those history plays, contemporary and past Condition of England novels 'invite us to consider England as a social organism whose health is suspect'.[9] An image of both its own milieu and of earlier developments, *Darkness Visible* shares much with this literary genre. It is also, of course, the work to which Golding referred when he told me he was going to write a novel 'not about Britain, but about England'.

Yet even when he seems intent on fostering the illusion of actuality, he gives us a social world unpopularly insistent upon the spiritual so that *Darkness Visible* can still be profitably 'regarded as the climax of [Golding's] attempts to create a religious novel for our times'.[10] In it the forces of light and darkness are once more found to be counterpoised, carried principally by the two characters that act as their representations. In one sphere there is Matty; literal, guileless, Bible-saturated, and solitary, he believes himself to be Elijah, servant of God. In the other sphere sits Sophy; nihilistic, disloyal, treacherous, her mind plugged into the cacophonous snarls of radio waves, she shares with Matty a sense of spiritual difference – one she dedicates to 'outrage' (p. 167). Their ensuing narrative convergence (whether accidental or predestined, the text itself refuses to confirm) makes visible the thematic of darkness' visibility, the fiction closing as it opened: with flaming fire. Yet the novel is so elusive and allusive, fissured and ambiguous it seems to have resisted readings that claim firm interpretative closure. 'Conceived on a massive scale, it seeks to create a religious dimension…by asking what does it mean for a writer to have a religious imagination in the violence of late twentieth-century life,' Ian Gregor and Mark Kinkead-Weekes temporized, for example, before going on to conclude that conclusions are themselves questions. 'What,' they added, 'will it mean to introduce "a holy man" into a world of global crime and hijacking?'[11]

I argue that *Darkness Visible* provokes a range and variety of critiques. In so saying, I want to underscore the point that the several enterprises of a Golding work can seldom be exhausted by any single approach. A critique of autobiographical enactment in his novels would produce yet another – and certainly lively – reading, for example. In the figure of the chess player[12] and that of the bookseller in *Darkness Visible* can be detected disguised – and partial – autobiographical portraits.[13] Seen from another critical perspective, the work is helped by being placed in the Judaeo-Christian apocalyptic tradition, internal evidence suggesting how it recasts, as one among several embedded narrative codes, fragments from the *Book of Revelation*. Like its predecessor (written to urge an infant Christian Church against despair) the contemporary text issues gnomic warnings about judgement. Elliptical allusions and cryptic clues, especially those inscribed in the textually interleaved Matty's journal, reverberate with the kind of figurative phraseology, astral imagery, symbolic numbers, winged seraphim and witnesses characteristic of such ancient apocalyptic texts as *Ezekiel, Isaiah, Daniel*, and, of course, Matty's favourite Biblical reading: *Revelation*.

II

God knows why one should look further than England for monsters; but yes, there must be English monsters and Gaia my chief character.

Golding, Letter to Tiger, 1968

I feel my identity like a lump of stone; feel wholly, irredeemably ignorant; sometimes meditate upon the monster with a sense of inadequacy, dumbness, ignorance, but not despair. The search will be desperate; but fascinating, exciting, when at last I lumber into some sort of movement.

Golding, Letter to Tiger, 1968

Published in 1979, *Darkness Visible* occupies a valent place in the Golding canon, and not simply because its author was said to have been 'profoundly disturbed by what he had produced'.[14] First of all it appeared twelve years after *The Pyramid* (1967), an especially uncharacteristic gap for a novelist whose first three books, one remembers, appeared in three consecutive years and whose eighth novel, *Rites of Passage* (1980), followed *Darkness Visible* by a single year, there then being published in quick succession *The Paper Men* (1984), *Close Quarters* (1987) and the final volume in the trilogy, *Fire Down Below* (1989). Secondly, it is a novel about which he steadfastly refused to comment. However, my sense is that at an early stage Golding had called the germinating donnée for his novel 'about England' *Here Be Monsters*: an intuition supported by the placing of the word 'monsters' in *Darkness Visible*'s penultimate page where the book's over-riding thematic of judgement is resolved by a redemptive character's last – and morally passionate – comments. By way of reference to *Here Be Monsters* (and what later he would describe as 'the terrible disease of being human'), Golding once remarked that one of the things he most wanted to do ('very much – very much') was 'to describe evil so it could be seen, so you knew it existed'. Meditation upon 'the monster' he elsewhere compared to the diver's leap, the simile suggesting just how corporeal an imagination's birthing must be: 'It's like the decision to dive off a high board, breathless, heart thumping, hysterical until the brave moment when one puts pen to paper.'[15]

During those twelve years when the novel was in gestation there were other (occasional) publications, plus a daily journal, one which reportedly anticipated postmodernist strategies with 'Dream Ego' (a fictive dream character), a fictive day character, and a fictive journal writer commenting on the three interleaved accounts. Volume after volume was written, most recording dreams, ideas for essays, novels, a screenplay for *Pincher Martin*, character sketches of friends. 'I [...] find myself justifying the wide spacing of my novels,' he observed at a University of Kent lecture two years before *Darkness Visible*'s publication, 'by the thought that all the time I am writing these millions of words...I feel guilty if I miss a day and that seldom, or almost never happens, sick or well, rain or shine.'[16] This diurnal exercise – carried through to the end of his life, for a last entry was recorded on June 20, 1993, the night before his (unanticipated) death – may have functioned as a way of jumpstarting the stalled novelist's engine, so giving modes of comfort to the blocked writer. However, hindsight shows this period of silence to have been a time also marked by three casualties, one so grievous that it surely fueled much of *Darkness Visible*'s pain.

Nevertheless, it should also be remarked that *Darkness Visible* is Golding's seventh novel. In the symbolic numerology of *Darkness Visible*'s parent text, *Revelation*, the number seven, signifying plenitude or perfection, is especially important. For example, the lamb has seven horns and seven eyes; there are seven churches, spirits, trumpets, thunders, vials, blessings, and – importantly – seals. The breaking of the last and seventh announces the dreadful Day of Judgement: 'And when he had opened the seventh seal, there was silence in heaven about the space of half an hour' (*Revelation* 8:1).

What must be observed is that *Darkness Visible* itself teases elusively with the number seven: a Mr Hanrahan has seven daughters: after saying a sentence of seven words, a spiritual enthusiast becomes overwhelmed by a beatific 'memory of sevenness' (p. 205). Two of the novel's most antagonistic, yet thematically reverberative words – 'freedom' and 'entropy' – are each constructed from seven letters. Indeed, the 'memory of sevenness' the enthusiast muddles through is an apprehension of the sung sound 'freedom', the word the novel's redemptive character hears, although not in human speech, on the novel's last page. Then there is the silent Matty – whose middle name Septimus is derived from the Latin for seven – who spends seven days ritually arranging a mound of matchboxes and later dances joyfully to Beethoven's *Seventh Symphony*. A mark of Sophy's malevolence is her response to some repeated digits in a day's date, insisting the numerical repetition is evidence neither of plenitude nor coincidence but 'deliberate' entropy. The date she so interprets is 7/7/77. At one level, Golding's seventh novel can surely be construed as a Book of (contemporary) Revelation. So seeded is the system of sevens that Golding provides one example of what will be several exuberant intertextual jokes. Here the comedic deflation involves describing Frankley's, an ancient and almost continuously reconstructed ironmonger's, as it shuffles into its last repair on the occasion of the 'visit of His Majesty King Edward the Seventh' (p. 38).

Seen from another critical perspective, that of the reader's necessary piloting past narrative gaps, *Darkness Visible* can be situated in a different context. Golding has frequently – and the seventh novel is no exception – practiced 'a withholding or delaying of information, a delicate and deliberate veiling of meaning'.[17] To this end, novels which enjoyed obliquity in narrative method, point of view and style became Golding's strategy for implicating the skeptical reader – all in the service of participating in not just an imaginative, but a religious construct. For not the least of the demands in reading Golding is the insistence that readers be producers (rather than consumers) of textual meaning. As I have earlier argued, the first five fictions adopt what I call an ideographic structure, each work offering two contrary views on one situation through a coda reversing expectations built by the narrative's first movement. The effect of this dyadic structure is to make the novel what we now (following Barthes' terminology) call 'scriptible', the reader having been positioned so as to assess binary oppositions and make complementary that which first insists itself as contradictory. In addition, the ideographic structure was Golding's way of having – to quote a contemporary, Doris Lessing – 'the shape make its own comment, a wordless statement'.[18] Not only did the shape force the dislodging of rigid interpretations, it also worked to disrupt religious dualities and the either/or equations enforced by terms frequently used in Western descriptions of the religious: saintliness/sinfulness; innocence/guilt; spirit/matter.[19]

In contrast to the first fictions, *Darkness Visible* has broken down/through the dyadic partitions of the early ideographic structure by dividing itself into three discrete parts. 'Structurally, the work is a trinity through which dualism is both asserted and denied,' one commentator has observed,[20] borrowing Christian terminology for the triadic structure which in the secular Hegelian model (equally relevant to a discussion of *Darkness Visible*) is described as thesis, antithesis, and sublative synthesis. The effective outcome of *Darkness Visible*'s triadic framework is dramatic as well as thematic, allowing the storyteller in Golding (excelling so in lean, rapid action) to bring into vivid convergence in Part Three of *Darkness Visible* the two major characters separated by the part each inhabited and embodied thematically. In the third convulsive part, the two plots of Matty and Sophy join several multivocal subplots of the novel's final section to wash together and over the reader like a fiery tidal wave. As ebb tide, one slight shift of focus, a single paragraph, concludes the novel.

III

The Second World War […] uncovered […] areas of indescribability […] The experience of Hamburg, Belsen, Hiroshima and Dachau cannot be imagined. We have gone to war and beggared description all over again. Those experiences are like black holes in space. Nothing can get out to let us know what it was like inside […] We stand before a gap in history. We have invented a limit to literature.

Golding, 'Crabbed Youth and Age'

Part One concerns the life of Matty. It begins in the literal inferno of the London Blitz as a boy miraculously emerges, unconsumed – to borrow the allusion to *Exodus* 3:2 here encoded – from what would seem to be an all too unholy 'burning bush' (p. 9) of flames. Hideously disfigured (one side of his face is light, the other dark, twisted, with a shrunken maroon ear), the child is tagged and so given the (magical) number seven: Septimus. But he is soon called Matty, the title given to

Part One of *Darkness Visible*. Indeed, the child's name is the primary device through which the novel's thematics are wedged, slantingly – Golding practicing here his consistent habit of veiled meaning. Of major significance is the association the reader deduces between the given name Matty and *Matthew*, the New Testament's first gospel, which differs from the other three in its focus on Christ as an awaited Messiah-King of Israel. Matty's interleaved diary – the gospel according to Matt(y)hew – might also be read as anticipating this event. In the penultimate lines recorded in his journal, Matty writes, 'That child shall bring the spiritual language into the world and nation shall speak it unto nation' (p. 101). These lines reveal the destiny that the literalist Matty believes has been revealed to him: guardianship of a child who, to Matty's (literalist? obsessed? mad? spiritualist? spiritual?) eyes, is the anticipated Messiah.

Matty's first name carries at least two other prerogatives. Matthew also means 'gift of God', and so Matty would seem with 'no background but the fire' (p. 17). Coupling his Christian name with Septimus, his assigned middle name, could refer to:

> Matthew, chapter 7, whose opening verse provides what is to be a major theme of the book: judgement, both in the straightforward sense provided by the verses themselves – 'Judge not, that ye be not judged'– but also in the sense of final judgement, the judgement day promised in St John's Revelation.[21]

In hospital the burnt babe[22] is bundled by charitable yet indifferent hands, almost given the surname 'Windup' until another charitable hand makes a merciful substitution. 'The name had first jumped into his mind with the curious effect of having come out of empty air' (p. 17), the authorial interjection hints. The image of 'a rare bird' quickly follows, directing the agile reader to the conclusion that the name might have been Windhover. This recalls the Egyptian god Horus, pictured as a falcon, and used most powerfully in Gerald Manley Hopkins' mystical poem as a symbol of Christ and the Ignatian rule of disciplined submission of selfhood.[23] The hospital supplies a new substitute for Windhover and Windup. The altered version, however, takes on its own unstable life, the text never stating nor stabilizing the final intent of this puzzle.

The surnames by which Matty is variously called throughout the novel are saturated with a signifying fluidity: Windrave, Windrow, Windgraff, Windy, Wildwave, Winsome, Woodrave, Wildwort, Wheelwright, Wandgrave, Windrap, Windwood, Windgrove, Windrove. Transformed through this repetition-with-variation they announce that Matty – the child born of the burning bush – is, at one level, to be taken for spirit – as in the Greek '*pneuma*', meaning both wind and spirit. Inflected in the shifting name with its near-stable sign, 'wind', is a disguised sacred script:

> The wind bloweth when it listeth, and thou hearest the sound thereof, but canst not tell when it cometh, and whither it goeth: so is everyone that is born of the spirit.
>
> *John* 3:8

Matty's shifting surname figures, by way of its mutable immutability, the agency of the Holy Spirit, that Comforter whom Christ promised would guide the apostles after His death, as described in *John* 15.26. Naming, with its attendant cloaked clues, is once again the means by which the text can endorse (in a skeptical time) as comprehensive a definition of the numinous as that present in the Fourth Gospel, to which *Darkness Visible* is here indebted.

But is this realm real? 'Is Matty really a prophet who can see through the surface of things, or is he merely naive? Are his apparitions perhaps projections of a tormented, simple mind?'[24] For tormented Matty profoundly is, sliced through with guilt for what the reader, unlike literalist Matty, takes to be an ambiguous role in the accidental (or suicidal) death of a schoolmate, the epicene beauty Henderson, by whom their pederastic schoolmaster, Sebastian Pedigree, has been much besotted:

> Matty's throwing of a gymshoe, an enactment of a phrase from the *Psalms* ['Over Edom will I cast out my shoe' *Psalms* 60.8; 108.9] contributes by physical or magical force to Henderson's fatal fall. Matty [...] feels that he was putting a stop to 'Evil', but there is nonetheless [...] a strong element of jealousy and rivalry for the love of Mr Pedigree, for Matty is in need of love and has mistaken some sarcastic remarks of Pedigree for affection. Mr Pedigree [...] puts all the blame on poor Matty: 'You horrible, horrible boy! It's all your fault.'[25]

Knowing as well that his face is repellent, one side darkened while the other is bleached white, Matty flees from his guilt and his lust for 'the daughters of men'. Sexuality for him is, of course, the rapt adoration of beauty. Self-exiled in Australia, he reads his Bible, takes on silence, study, and solitude and performs rituals derived literally from *Ezekiel* and *Revelation*. These include heave offerings; wave offerings, dust shakings of feet; the knocking three times on doors; a construction, (presumably an enactment of *Ezekiel* 7.24-25) of a matchbox tower, whose 'great flame licked across the wasteland' (p. 70). Then an elaborate task where he immerses himself in dank, dark, glutinous, and weedy water, weighted down by clanking wheels while bearing aloft a lamp:

> The water rose past his waist and to his chest [...to] the man's chin and then suddenly, higher. The man floundered and the water washed [...] he was out of sight and there was nothing to be seen...but an arm and hand and the old lamp with its bright white globe [...] Down there underneath he was thrusting strongly into the ooze [...] and he got his head up and grabbed a breath. After that he rose steadily towards the other side and the water ran from him and from his hair and his wheels; but not from the lamp. Now he stood and [...] began to shudder, shudder deeply, convulsively[...while] thirty yards away, across the water, a huge lizard turned and loitered off into the darkness (pp. 75–76).

The passage, quoted at length, is another exemplary use of the Golding textual strategy of a confrontation scene, that moment of dreadful psychic and physical danger where characters encounter their fear of negation or nullity, experienced as a fear of darkness. Here in *Darkness Visible*, 'the man' descends, in darkness, metaphorically into his own darkness, sustaining aloft a lighted lamp that he will soon be described as 'heav[ing] four times at four points of the compass'; then blowing out its wick. Interpreted quite frequently as an 'epic descent to the underworld that the hero undertakes so he can return, renewed, to pursue his mission on earth',[26] the 'purification', 'sanctification', or 'initiation' ceremony depicted[27] is made deliberately opaque by way of its external narrative focalization, a technique that challenges the reader to make sense of this wordless behaviour. Idiotic or idiosyncratic? Meaningless or meaningful? Fool or Holy Fool?

As with my earlier point about naming and numbering strategies, each of which places the reader in the centre of narrative production, the reader can be so badgered by such baffling puzzles that he either resists – itself a mode of constructing meaning – or determines some of their implications. Additional deciphering shows that Matty's shifting surname – Windrave, Windgraff, Windgrove, Windrove, etc. – metamorphoses fourteen times; thus the sacred number seven (7 + 7 = 14) is re-invoked. Another indication of just how scrupulously the text rests significance on a covert cross-referencing of numberings is the initial appearance in *Darkness Visible*'s Chapter 7 and subsequent interleaving in *Darkness Visible*'s Chapter 14 (7 + 7) of Matty's diary. As 'eruptive, revelatory, but uncomprehended by the narration outside'[28] as this record of Matty's hallucinatory delusions or mystical visions is, its own organization is arranged to resonate internally. Once again, the valent trope is the signifying number seven. For example, the diary has 47 entries: the first entry is dated May 17, 1965 while the last is May 13, 1967. Most importantly, Matty's tutelary spirits – 'one was in blue and the other in red with a hat on. The one in blue had a hat too but not as expensive' (p. 86) – appear in 14 (7 + 7) of those 47 entries. Obscure as the individual diary entries seem, their language not so much borrowed from as stamped by *Revelation* (the sacred text Matty is presented as knowing best), the interlaced journal's account of spiritual progress is meant (in the words of a skeptical bookseller Sim Goodchild) to 'throw some light' (p. 261). Of course, these cranky conversations with the spirits (where he is instructed to return to Greenfield for his fate is to be there and linked with a child) may be 'the product of fasting, loneliness, and skewed religiosity'.[29] Because the journal revels in its first-person point of view, (a major shift from the free indirect discourse of the rest of the narrative) the reader has access only to Matty's belief that he is 'near the centre of things' (p. 91). In the battle between good and evil, his destiny is to 'guard a child and heal Mr Pedigree and my spiritual face' (p. 235).

Thus when Matty's surname finally settles (by repetition-without-variation) into Windrove, it is of central thematic significance that it does so by having been woven, according to my count, seven times through that portion of the text. (The only other name-variation privileged by numerical repetition is Windgrove, appearing four times in the text; the grove of winds, the metaphor implicitly embedded by this variant Windgrove, provides the place where the droving of winds will find their grove.) The seven insistent repetitions of Windrove occur at *Darkness Visible*'s penultimate representation of Matty, where he is described as ceasing to be material, his body becoming wind-swept, swirling spirit. During the terrorist attempt to abduct the son of an Arab sheikh from an exclusive boarding school, a planted bomb explodes, setting afire the room where Matty is working. Whirling round and round, he directs his 'shape of flame' (p. 248) towards the kidnappers running away with the blanketed boy. The child is dropped, and thus saved, while Matty expires. He has become the 'burnt offering' (p. 238), the destiny Matty had recorded in his 17/6/78 journal entry as being the destiny given him by the 'white spirit' – the Christ figure from *Revelation* 1.16 – 'with the circle of the sun round his head…and the sword proceed[ing] out of his mouth' (p. 23). In *Darkness Visible*'s naming and numbering strategies, Matty has come to fulfill his textual destiny. Finally and fully, he enacts the many meanings of his (God-given) name: Matthew Septimus Windrove.

IV

Original sin […] I'm convinced of original sin. That is I'm convinced of it in the Augustinian way […] I think the root of our sin is there, in the child. As soon as it has any capacity for acting on the world outside, it will be selfish; and, of course, original sin and selfishness – the words could be interchangeable. You can only learn unselfishness by liking and loving.

Golding to Carey, 1986

If Part One, 'Matty', is narrated from Matty's obfuscatory perspective as it traces his ascent into light, Part Two, 'Sophy', is seen from its eponymous protagonist's clever perspective, tracing Sophy Stanhope's descent into darkness. We watch the angelically beautiful Sophy (and Toni, her fairer twin) from their tenth year: motherless, dismissed by a manically self-obsessed father, solitary, bonded and yet in silent warfare against each other, the two girls grow into young womanhood in a provincial English town, Greenfield.[30] Beyond Greenfield's Old Bridge and farther out in the greener fields of the country is Wandicott House School to which Matty, following the years of self-imposed exile, comes to work as an odd-jobs man. Casually, the text notes the chance passing of Matty and Sophy, their near encounter, then seamless separation. This convergence happens on three separate occasions (pp. 101, 132, 175), the number three here being assuredly relevant. Until Part Three, the odd couple's convergence seems coincidental. Sophy watches a man – whom the reader alone recognizes as Matty – pass by Greenfield's High Street and (characteristically) she sees 'a horrid two-tone face' (p. 175). Meanwhile, having noticed the twins entering Goodchild's book shop, Matty (characteristically) describes them in his diary as 'so beautiful, like angels' (p. 101), puzzling whether they are the children whom his spirits have said need protection.

Sophy certainly needed protection. And mostly from herself. Always in rivalry with Toni – and especially for her father's attention – Sophy is driven by his rejection and impassive abandonment ultimately 'to an incestuous lust which is also a desperate call "a sign as if it had been shouted". The Miltonic reminiscence, "hurling her away from the column room" secures the metaphoric link with Henderson's fall, "Hurled headlong flaming from th'ethereal sky" [I, 35].'[31]

Unlike Matty, Sophy experiences her loveless loneliness as an internal darkness. In early childhood, something so seemingly accidental as the stoning of a dabchick initiates her into the perverse pleasures of sadism. Denied the real stuff of love, in early adulthood indiscriminate, manipulative sex with strangers becomes one way of forcing her being, her will, upon others. So for Sophy, the meeting of flesh against flesh is loveless, sexless even. Orgasm, when first experienced, comes by way of the excitement of pushing a penknife into the shoulder of her copulating companion. Listening to a radio programme on entropy – 'the universe running down' (p. 131) – she decides she not only believes in that principle, but that she wants to speed the uncoiling: 'the long, long convulsions, the unknotting, the throbbing […]of space and time on, on, on into nothingness' (p. 167).[32]

Like Matty's full name, Sophy Stanhope's is menacingly emblematic, conflating the *hope* upon which she could *stand*, following Paul's injunction to the Corinthians – 'And now abideth faith, hope, charity, these three: but the greater of these is charity.' *Corinthians* (13.13) – with wisdom, that being the translation of the Greek word *sophia*.[33]

The ironic inversion is pointed, Sophy Stanhope's nature being a nullification of her name's spiritual obligations. One recognizes in Sophy's chosen reality – 'your own self sitting inside with its own wishes and rules at the mouth of the tunnel' (p. 123) – the attribute both *Pincher Martin* and *The Paper Men* assign to solipsistic egotism. That is, its capacity to pervert what in another context was termed one's *Scintillans Dei*, one's God-given spirit. In *Darkness Visible's* thematics, each character works out a gesturing discourse – on the other side of language – to express the needs his or her nature demands. Thus Matty's visions propel him to love and protect, while Sophy's visions direct her to hate and desecrate. When emblematic numbers appear, Matty expects on 6/6/66 – since in *Revelation* 13.18 the number 666 is the 'number of the beast' – the appearance of the apocalyptic Antichrist and the securing of destruction, as has been figured in *Revelation* 17.13–14. 'Many people will know the carnal and earthly pleasure of being alive this day and not brought to judgement. No one but I have felt the dreadful sorrow of not being in heaven with judgement all done' (p. 89), he writes at day's end, having borne the awful number (inscribed with his own blood) through the streets and into churches and chapels. To Sophy, on the other hand the numerical congruence of 7/7/77 spells not coincidence, but deliberate pattern:

> Everything's running down. Unwinding. We're just – tangles. Everything
> is just a tangle and it slides out of itself bit by bit towards something that's
> simpler and simpler – and we can help it. Be a part (pp. 166–67).

This is hardly plenitude (as *Revelation* 5.10 promises of the number seven): hardly even promise – so withering at the roots are faith, hope, and love in her stony, frightened, and needy nature.

Drawn (despite her self-sufficient egotism) to a dimension larger than a single 'mouth-of-the-tunnel' (p. 123) reality, Sophy chooses to hear not the airy firmament with its ancient symphony, but 'the voice of the darkness between the stars, between the galaxies, [as] the toneless voice of the great skein unravelling and lying slack' (p. 173). In a universe so regressive, and one in which she colludes, Sophy nevertheless dreads the extinction of her hoarded self. This fear is dramatized in a rather obliquely rendered confrontation scene where, having stared at 'a black shape' (presumably, a Rorschach-like 'blotch of ink' (p. 157)), she screams, in terror. And screams and screams; then faints. However, the heavens and their musical spheres – all the long pull of history with its rounds of creation and destruction – remain for her just noise in the sky. Order is 'weirdness' (p. 132) in her sight.

Static, the transistor blur and buzz she fastens on to, *is* static – in its sense both of jarring discontinuity and sluggish inertia. Acts of momentum are thus needed to set in motion what she requires and calls 'the simplicity of outrage' (p. 182).

Venomous fantasies become an eroticized way of sculpting the terrorist agenda: Sophy's experience of outrage's simplicity. Outrageous public actions will make 'her inner darkness visible to the daylight world' (p. 249). Not for nothing is Sophy's orgasmic release described as an apocalyptic 'black sun' (p. 252). Her final outrage – a delusive hallucination of castrating the kidnapped child, a boy she fantasizes being bound to a stinking toilet, there to weep blood from the penile wound she has inflicted – can be likened to the moment in *Revelation* 6.12 when the sixth seal of the book of life is opened, and the 'sun became black'.[34] So Sophy commits herself – as obsessively as does Matty to his spiritual venture – to what she believes must quicken and express the entropic process, her gospel of gratuitous decadence and degeneration. Of course, it is Sophy who masterminds the botched kidnapping whose outcome is a child's safety and Matty's horrible death. Is his quietus accidental, coincidental, or providential? In a time of 'mouth-of-the-tunnel' skepticism, the novel permits its readers to review Matty so that his naming and associated numberings, his gestures and eccentric performances can speak with confusion and/or clarity. It is in *Darkness Visible*'s third part that such transmutations occur; it is in *Darkness Visible*'s third part that the reader is left to resolve such conundrums.

V

> Time and time again people bring to my notice parallels, oppositions, appositions, levels, of which I was unaware. The writing of a novel is at once simpler and more complicated than what people say about it after it is written.
>
> Golding to Haffenden

The very presence of Part Three is disruptive of *Darkness Visible*'s play with doublings, pairings, and binary oppositions, and resolutely so. For the pattern of doubled perspective is systematically present from the start, first punctuating – by way of numberings – the novel's opening paragraph, in which there are two streets, two pubs, and two shops. Chapter Two, in turn, begins with:

> two trade unions, two historical foundations, two years, World War II and two boys. The third chapter introduces a [Greenfield] ironmonger and a [Greenfield] bookstore and the fourth chapter a Melbourne ironmonger and a suburban Melbourne bookstore. Matty comes into the possession of two books, each of them a Bible.[35]

As a thematic, the dyadic code informs both the novel's major symbols and the signification of its major characters. Doubles emerge: frequently as opposites and less frequently as forms of oxymoron. Thus, in a story which has rivers of flame beginning and ending its calamitous plot, fire is both purgative and destructive, while water – the book's other importantly foregrounded symbol – is both cleansing and cloacal. Visionary Matty imagines his beloved nurse is two people, while he himself – damaged by fire – shows a divided face to the world, dark on one side and light on the other. Her face as light-bearing as an angel's, Sophy is darkness. Furthermore, she experiences herself as dual with a ravenous 'inside' and compliant 'outside'. Greenfield's Edwina and Edwin Bell (coupling or as a couple) are all but sexually interchangeable, while the Stanhope twins are 'as different as night and day' (p. 105), separate yet together, dark and fair. Schoolteacher Edwin Bell and the bibliophile Sim Goodchild are doubled partners in the middle-aged thirst for authenticity, while Sophy and the London layabout Gerald pair by way of deviousness like incestuous brother and sister. Matty's sometime double is a pederastic schoolmaster, an unexpected doppleganger. No more identical than the Stanhope twins, Matthew Septimus Windrove and Sebastian Pedigree are twin-like, mutually resonant. 'Pedigree was like Matty and dedicated to one end only. But unlike Matty he knew only too well what that end was' (p. 85), the text carefully interposes. In fact, in a work concerned with transcendent heaven and entropic hell (and the connections between those two immensities), the Matty/Pedigree dyad is wonderfully instructive. As the text wryly observes about their first encounter: 'They could be said to have converged on each other, although Matty was going up and Mr Pedigree was going down' (p. 21).

Structurally as well, *Darkness Visible* is shaped initially by the principle of the oppositional dyad. Seen from the challenge of Part Three, Part One and Part Two are opposed doubles, diverging like their representatives, Matty and Sophy, in convergent ways; Part One, 'Matty', and Part Two, 'Sophy', are also twin-like, thematically linked in a subtle, yet significant, manner and so achieving an uncanny balance of similarity-with-variation. A shoe is cast and a stone thrown. A skyring glass is wordlessly studied and a transistor radio is brooded upon. A man in black and a dark creature both pass down a shared High Street, while a dark pool and an inkblot mark the commonality of two otherwise bizarre immersions. The parallels, conclude Ian Gregor and Mark Kinkead-Weekes, responsible for identifying these correspondences, 'are as striking as the differences'.[36] Thus Sophy is both Matty's opposite and his dark double.[37] Hers – the great skein unwinding – may be a nihilistic universe, yet her thirsting for that chosen spiritual dimension matches Matty's hunger for his. Matty, in fact, intuits her capacities, but is deeply confused by her duality, wondering whether she is a good spirit or disguised as an angel of light. Writing about how oddly she accepted the loss of her 'jewel' (both literal and symbolic), he adds: 'it took…all day to see she knew about signs and how to show them' (p. 236). Recording what he believes his spirits have told him, Matty notes in his diary's last entry: 'Many years ago we called her before us but she did not come' (p. 238).

As so often in Golding the buried, always oblique, clue becomes the locus for textual meanings and the reader's engagement with paradox. Thus Sophy's inscribed 'hunger and thirst after weirdness' (p. 132) – a grim recasting of Christ's benediction: 'Blessed are they which do hunger and thirst after righteousness' (*Matthew* 5.6) – is that character's perversion of her capacity to worship: her jewel. One among many of the text's appropriations of scriptural metaphors for the famished, thirsty soul, the allusive reference is also – and exuberantly – recast in an incorporated joke: 'men had all kinds of thirst in all kinds of desert. All men are dypsomaniacs. Christ himself had cried out on the cross [I thirst!]' (p. 32), Pedigree mutters as he tries to rationalize his own longings. Comically inverted here is *John* 7.37, where Christ advises that 'he that believeth in me shall never thirst'. But if *Darkness Visible* sometimes divulges its themes in comic mode, to what do such jokes lead as the narrative's temper switches from the near allegorical to the putatively odd, comic, and yet ominously significant?

VI

[T]he novelist offers his work in the automatic expectation of its being accepted [...] we rely on the readiness of people to perform an operation every bit as mysterious as the writing. It is our nature to receive writing. I [...] use a phrase of my own and hold up my hands in outright astonishment at what I will call the reader's instinctive complicity. It is his, it is our ability, unconsciously to accept the scraps, the hastily gathered observations, the leaps and gambols of language and thereby share some level of reality.

Golding, 'Belief and Creativity'

With a text so markedly conscious of binary doubles, the introduction of a third term demands then to be interpreted throughout as a determined gesture, one that implicitly queries the reductiveness of binary frames. In, for example, the apparent insignificance of a character's enthusiasm about a planned séance – as one of three compatriots remarks, 'So it'll just be the three of us' (p. 235) – the number three is to be construed as an informative trope. Indeed, the number three plays throughout the text. In Chapter Three, Matty receives his calling when he gazes into the skyring glass. Hanrahan's house (with his seven daughters) has three walls. In Australia, Matty passes 'three decaying houses', 'the low hump of three trees' (p. 61), and presses his car's starter three times at the end of the ritualized immersion, after which he plays with three pebbles in another ritual. Leaving Australia, he repeats the ceremony of shaking the dust of the land from his feet three times.

Then again Part Three – unlike Part One, 'Matty' and Part Two, 'Sophy' – takes its title 'One is One' not eponymously, but provocatively. 'One is One', a refrain from a medieval religious mnemonic 'Green Grow the Rushes O',[38] could well have been completed by the next lines, 'And all alone/And evermore shall be so', whose absence in *Darkness Visible* amounts to an implied presence. The contemporary world so ironically named by Part Three's title, 'One is One', is fully the medieval song's opposed double. Neither unitary nor unified, the England of the late twentieth century presented in this section is multivocal, polyglot, inchoate, cacophonous, as jets scream and juggernauts snarl down Greenfield's High Street and over the Old Bridge. Whereas *Darkness Visible*'s earlier intertextual echoes were biblical and classical,[39] allusions in the third section are (intentionally) quite the antithesis of its title, 'One is One'. Muddles, messes, confusions, befuddled and isolated characters, all populate Part Three. References here are a tangle of religions, philosophies, polylingual scripts – spendthrift in their spiritual relativism. Skyring glass; *I Ching*; Tarot cards; Sartre's axiomatical vision of nihilism, *Huis Clos* being rehearsed by Greenfield's Little Theatre Group ingenuously in the church's north transept, the place traditionally reserved for the Christian Host; the *Bhagavad Gita*; Theosophy; Scientism; the Mahatma; the Dalai Lama; the Philosophical Society; Transcendentalism; the Great Wheel; the Hindu universe; skandhas; temple; mosque; and (with a title sardonically appropriate to the context here) Gibbon's *Decline and Fall* – that references as diverse as these should appear in Chapter Twelve alone gives some evidence of what Part Three suggests is the spiritual muddle of late twentieth-century faith. Religious profligacy matches metaphysical insolvency.

Part Three of the triadically structured *Darkness Visible* offers a third shift in perspective. The perspective – unlike those of Part One and Part Two, where a single witness is the lens through which events are focused – is itself triangulated since it is from the viewpoints of three elderly men: the bookseller Sim Goodchild, the schoolmaster Edwin Bell, and the pederastic Sebastian Pedigree. 'Their lives become connected with those of Matty and Sophy,' observes a critic, 'when they [...] arrange a séance together with Matty in the very room Sophy had intended to become the prison for the kidnapped boy, a coincidence occurs by which they [...] become involved in the plot centered upon the kidnappers.'[40]

Whenever such coincidences seem to occur so fortuitously in the authorially managed plot of a Golding novel, readers know that they cloak another design: for, at that level, coincidence becomes concurrence. In this context, Sim Goodchild's trajectory through the novel marks the text's spiritual thematic, his ambivalence being that middle ground where such extremities as Sophy's needy nihilism and Matty's autocratic otherworldliness might be played out. Goodchild's perspective – his skeptical weariness, the sense (which Sophy shares) that everything is running down – dominates 'One is One'. His especial participation in, as well as partial perception of, things in both the 'Matty' and 'Sophy' sections can be charted with the hindsight Part Three permits. At the novel's opening, a 'bookseller' is identified as one of the *three* volunteer firemen present, the numerical signifier and one of its representatives posed as such in the text's earliest pages. Through the bookseller's eyes the reader witnesses the infernal flames and, emerging from the pillars, the naked figure of a child, whose survival is – quite simply – a miracle. By way of this (initially) unnamed observer, the text, from its first pages, alerts the reader to the gaps – in this case the bookseller's misrememberings. Brooding, he is plagued by:

> a memory flickering on the edge of his mind and he could not get it further in where it could be examined; and he was also remembering the moment when the child had appeared, seeming to his weak *sight* to be perhaps not entirely there – to be in a state of, as it were, indecision as to whether he was a human shape or merely a bit of flickering brightness. Was it the Apocalypse? (p. 15, my italics).

The memory, flickering like firelight, might well have pulled before the bookseller's moral eyes what Golding places before those of the deciphering reader: *Ezekiel*'s vision of divine glory: 'And I looked, and behold, a whirlwind came out of the north, a great cloud, and a fire infolding itself, and brightness *was* about it, and out of the midst thereof as the colour of amber, out of the midst of fire' (*Ezekiel* 1.4). Even as the signifying memory is being misremembered and unexamined, a child solemnly walks from the midst of apocalyptic fire. A 'burning bush' before him, the bookseller's 'weak sight' focuses not on the miracle of the child – burning, yet not consumed – but on entropy, decline, devastation, de-creation: what Sophy will later come to celebrate. 'Nothing,' the unnamed bookseller concludes, surveying the lighted waste of the dockside and the 'flickering brightness' that *is* the unnamed child's being, 'could be more apocalyptic than a world so ferociously consumed. But he could not quite remember' (p. 15).

By its deposited hints, the text insists that this bookseller (one of three ordinary firemen irradiated nonetheless by the miraculous) be identified by the reader – remembering back from Part Three to Part One – as Sim Goodchild, owner of Goodchild's Rare Books on Greenfield's High Street. An average twentieth-century unbeliever and the novel's later representative of quotidian middle-aged, middle-class English manhood, Sim Goodchild lives 'among a whole heap of beliefs, first-class, second-class, third-class…right through to the blank wall of…daily indifference and ignorance' (p. 247). In his person is figured the workings of the mundane and diurnal world of the spiritual dimension, his quite ordinary life being the locus for warring armies of belief, disbelief, disinterest, then temptation. Like other fastidious agnostics, he is represented as viewing religious premises with the skeptic's slit eye.

By Part Two, Goodchild has settled down to his bookstore's business and (by way of symbol) the diminished business of England, the decade now being the 1970s, when the magnolia-like promise of the 1960s has bloomed and declined. Goodchild is altogether normative, uninteresting, representative: a man whose greatest memory consists not in the whirligig of flame and apocalypse, but in a recollection of an afternoon when he introduced to the Greenfield's Philosophical Society the high prophet of atheism, Bertrand Russell.

By Part Three, the elderly Sim Goodchild, his failing bookstore both emblematic and symptomatic of the near bankruptcy of English culture and its economy in the late 1970s, is neither lucid atheist nor untroubled agnostic. Nor can he be what Matty is: the literal believer. Washed by contrary beliefs, Goodchild experiences himself as a 'committee of discordant members', for so the text covertly puns. If the 'majority [were to] vote' (p. 225), it would endorse – Goodchild is made to observe – what could be termed partitions, those '[h]igh walls, less penetratable than brick, than steel, walls of adamant' (p. 83) that seal off person from person: separating, dividing, alienating.

Goodchild and Matty, Sophy too: each of Darkness Visible's three major characters is to be apprehended by the reader in the light of his or her thirsting beyond such partitions for some source which might quench a parched soul. Goodchild's spiritual thirst – and the text ensures that his longing for the beautiful begins in reverence – moulds itself all but as misshapenly as Pedigree's. A decade earlier, the bookseller had become intoxicated with the enchantment of his young neighbours, Sophy and Toni Stanhope. So much so that he put out bait, children's books in the shop window, to lure the twins away from their perambulations down the High Street and through the door into his store: so sadly named Goodchild's Rare Books. 'How exquisite they had been […] What a delight it had been to watch them grow; though no matter how wonderfully *nubile* they became, they could never surpass the really fairy delicacy of childhood, a beauty that could make you weep,' Goodchild reminisces (p. 213). As the matter is put later in Part Three, with its other revelations about One often being Not/One, Sim Goodchild's delight in little girls was, like Pedigree's aching for little boys, a perversion of spiritual need. Thus does his 'unruly member' (p. 226) regulate the warring spiritual self that makes up Goodchild's 'committee of discordant members'. Goodchild is alone – and evermore shall be so.

Yet 'One is One/And [not] all alone', for 'many cross associations move out from the enigmatic title'.[41] Like his namesake, Simon called Peter, Sim[on] Goodchild may thrice deny, and be part of, the unwinding process of separate, meaningless, ridiculous events that make up the daylight world of Greenfield and its High Street. Or he may be born again the good child – God's child – and experience himself as part of 'the whole cloth of what had seemed separate' (p. 48). Goodchild suffers such a revelation as barriers between the worlds of matter and spirit dissolve, and partitions are momentarily penetrated. In silence during a séance with Matty and the religious enthusiast Edwin Bell, the skeptical bookseller finds himself 'reading' his own hand:

> The palm was exquisitely beautiful, it was made of light. It was precious and preciously inscribed with a sureness and delicacy beyond art and grounded somewhere else in absolute health [...] Sim stared into the gigantic world of his own palm and saw that it was holy (p. 231).

In this ordinary, un-good man come together those opposite potentials that the murky Sophy and the luminiferous Matty represent: in Sim Goodchild the divergent paths of darkness and light converge. One is One.

I share the view that 'Golding…employs a tripartite structure to reduce an ostensibly binary opposition into the One.'[42] The destabilising principle behind the triadically structured *Darkness Visible* extends to include the disruption of polarized doubles and enforce a religious dimension, where 'One is One/And all alone/And evermore shall be so'. Thus, Edwin/Sim, one among several polarized dyads in the novel, dissolves to become a triadic unity – Edwin/Matty/Sim – when the three men ruminate together in Stanhope's ancient stable. They form a trinity, or triple unity, recalling as well the 'three rivals' of the medieval song. Again, numbering is foregrounded, three being sown throughout with another critic-proof joke being made: to improve his weak vision, Sim is given three pairs of spectacles. In addition to the Edwin/Sim dyad the twined dyad Toni/Sophy becomes the triad Toni/Gerald/Sophy, where their individual nefarious ambitions become crossed to embark on the kidnapping of the child. And cryptically transcribed, through the text's habit of naming and numbering, the polarized double Goodchild/Pedigree transforms into the triad Goodchild/Windrove/Pedigree. On Matty's convergent connection to the two, the good child's pedigree can wind up, recalling Matthew Windrove's never-name Windup, again becoming God's child.

VII

> [Sim] tried to imagine some deep, significant spiritual drama, some contrivance, some plot that would include them both and be designed solely for the purpose of rescuing Pedigree from his hell; and then had to admit to himself that the whole affair was about Sim the ageing bookseller or no one (p. 247).

Such disruptions as these of dyad into triad are at the heart of Golding's critique of binarism in the seventh novel. *Darkness Visible*'s doubling of Part One and Part Two (with their triangulation in Part Three) is conclusive, both thematically and structurally. As disrupted doubles, Part One = Part Two. Just as 1+2=3, (Part) I+(Part) II=(Part)III. Seen through a glass darkly, I is I(1) when 'One is one' – Part III of the triadic structure – triangulates the dyadic divisions of 'Matty' and 'Sophy' and makes not-ones One, III(3) being the numerical as well as symbolic summation of I(1) and II(2). I will conclude the chapter not with schematics such as these but with an examination of one more strand, yet another thread in a text all but overly patterned.

Greenfield, the dreadfully typical English provincial town is summoned before the reader by *three* perambulations, seemingly inconsequential and unconnected, yet naggingly repetitive. Why, we wonder, *does* the text accompany Matty, Sophy, and then Pedigree as each walks along the High Street past Frankley's, the ironmonger 'of character' (p. 42), Goodchild's Rare Books (filled with 'words, physical reduplication of the endless cackle of men'[42]), the solicitors firm, Sprawson's, across the Old Bridge over the canal with a public urinal at its root and then back to the towpath behind the old stable, close to which lies a rotting barge? Mr Pedigree, for one, is described as going 'widdershins round a circle that was in fact a rectangle [...] and in furtive triumph, the police car defeated, to the roots of the Old Bridge and the black urinal again' (p. 82). And in her one moment of childhood intimacy with a 'wooing' father, Sophy remembers being taken round the rectangle: 'Suddenly she understood. It was like taking a new step, learning a new thing, the whole place came into one' (p. 106).

Emanating back from the High Street and Sprawson's, where both Edwin Bell and Robert Stanhope have apartments, to the Stanhope twins' stable is, Goodchild discovers, a secret garden sown with every imaginable scent: rose, camomile, nettle, rosemary, lupin, willowherb, foxglove, Buddleia, old man's beard, veronica. 'This oblong of garden, unkempt, abandoned and deserted, was nevertheless like a pool of something, a pool, one could only say, of quiet Balm' (p. 227), muses Goodchild as he walks towards the stable and the prearranged séance. In the daily cacophony of Greenfield such a garden is holy, a Gilead whose hush − like balm − can heal the sin-sick soul. The clue here for the reader to decipher is the garden's camouflaged, yet penetrable, position, being linked to one of *Darkness Visible*'s major explorations: the piercing of partitions, the breaking down of barriers.[43] Hidden from each solitary walker who separately passes Frankley's, Goodchild's Rare Books, and Sprawson's is that these walls conceal this place of watery stillness, holy home to a 'still dimension of otherness' (p. 221). For as water was precious to the ancients in the desert so is silence precious to the noise-weary contemporary. The reader alone is positioned to see *through* Frankley's, Goodchild's Rare Books, and Sprawson's and determine that behind the walls of trade, learning, and law there exists, however 'unkempt, abandoned and deserted' a grove for the spirit's wind.

Invisible to Greenfield's High Street as is the protected garden, the 'black urinal' (p. 82), to which Pedigree is furtively drawn to 'worship', is both public and visible. Another spatial metaphor for the spiritual with which the reader must negotiate, the urinal's position over the water at the Old Bridge, amounts to a malodorous desecration of what was once practised. As Bell is made to explain to Goodchild, so precious was water once that it was worshipped as holy: 'They used to build churches by holy wells. Over them sometimes' (p. 222). Although never explicitly stated, the contemporary perversion of ancient rites inscribed here has the intended effect of reiterating the kind of inverted spirituality Sophy expresses in her 'hunger and thirst after weirdness'. The point is underscored by the description of ten-year-old Sophy poking her head round the stable dormer and staring down the garden towards the Old

Bridge to will a dirty old man (whom the reader alone identifies as Pedigree) to stay in 'the filthy old stinky-poo urinal' (p. 132). In pointed contrast is the description of a third walk. During *his* lonely perambulation, Matty walks across the Old Bridge and 'the iron loo at the root of the bridge flushed automatically as he passed. He stood, and looked down at the water of the canal in that age-old and unconscious belief that there is help and healing in the sight' (p. 47).

Seen from such a critical perspective, this little patch of Greenfield carries a considerable symbolic weight. Imaged here as well is the history that all Condition of England novels explore. 'The "unkempt, abandoned and deserted" garden whose riotous plants can be found in their first literary flowerings in Shakespeare's histories, emblematizes late twentieth-century England, as do the indeterminately ancient walls of the ironmonger, Frankley's. Some of the building's walls were of 'brick, some tile-hung, some lath and plaster and some of a curious wooden construction. It is not impossible that parts of these wooden areas were in fact medieval windows filled [...] with wooden slats and now thought to be not more than chinky walls' (p. 38). Explicitly described as 'an image in little of society at large' (p. 38), Frankley's piecemeal structure reveals 'building and rebuilding, division, reclamation and substitution, carried on throughout a quite preposterous length of time' (p. 38).

Building and rebuilding, division, reclamation and substitution: the words might well describe human history, certainly English history, as exemplified by *Darkness Visible*'s careful building: its strategies of naming and numbering; the various stratagems placed before the reader to aid in construction; its referential allusions and enigma-besotted clues; the shifts in point of view and its braided Christian and classical symbologies. Each of these indirections is directed towards the discovery of directions, this being the challenge the reader encounters always with Golding, whose textual intentions suggest readers embrace paradoxes of existence. So in the novel's penultimate scene, when the dying Pedigree imagines golden light emanating from what was once the disfigured face of the now immaterial Matty, Golding means readers to intuit that a maimed creature like Pedigree can be granted the possibility of salvation. Assenting to Matty's enduring love ('that it should be you, ugly little Matty, who really loved me') Greenfield's loathed scapegoat acknowledges the mote in his own nature, as those who malign him do not:

There've been such people in this neighbourhood, such monsters, that girl [...] Stanhope, Goodchild, Bell even and his ghastly wife – I'm not like them, bad but not as bad, I never hurt anybody – *they* thought I hurt children but I didn't [...] And you know about the last thing the thing I shall be scared into doing [...] just to keep a child quiet, keep it from telling – that's hell, Matty, that'll be hell – help me! (pp. 264–65)

And, resisting in terror, he nevertheless surrenders to a Matty transmuted into *Revelation*'s great, golden, plumed peacock whose stern, loving and terrible lips offer '*Freedom*'. 'The filthy old thing' that the park keeper in the novel's brief coda judges 'would never be cured' may be our human pedigree, suffering certainly from the incurable disease of being human. But beside one judgmental point of view we must put Matty's gnomic journal, news of which warms the grieving Sim Goodchild: 'Somehow and for no reason that he could find, Sim felt heartened by the idea of Matty's journal – happy almost, for the moment. Before he knew what he was about he found himself staring intently into his own palm' (p. 261). For Matty's journal, like *Darkness Visible*, successfully manages to 'throw some light' on the second half of a darkened twentieth century.

Endnotes

1   Glorie, Tebbutt, 'Reading and Righting: Metafiction and Metaphysics in William Golding's *Darkness Visible*', *Twentieth Century Literature* 39 (1993), p. 47.

2   See Bernard F. Dick, *William Golding* (revised edition), Boston, Twayne Publishers, 1987; L. L. Dickson, *The Modern Allegories of William Golding*, Gainesville, University of South Florida Press, 1990; Joyce Carol Oates, '*Darkness Visible*' *The New Republic* (December 8, 1979), pp. 32–34; and Brad Owens, 'Golding's New Morality Tale: Hard to Believe', *Christian Science Monitor* (November 28, 1979) p. 24.

3   A. S. Byatt, 'William Golding: *Darkness Visible*', *Passions of the Mind*, New York, Turtle Bay Books/Random House, 1992, p. 172.

4   Joyce Carol Oates, op. cit., p. 32.

5   See in this context Patricia Waugh, *Metafiction*, London, Methuen, 1984, p. 141. Some stressed *Darkness Visible*'s concerns 'for writing about writing' (John S. Whitley, '"*Furor Scribendi*" Writing About Writing in the Later Novels of William Golding' in James R. Baker (ed.) *Criticial Essays on William Golding*, Boston, G.K. Hall, 1988, p. 176) and its 'persistent questioning of language, the obvious reflexivity, the Biblical parody' (Tebbutt, op. cit., p. 48). Others engaged in the familiar habit of source hunting, variously citing as intertextual allusions and influences such works as Dante's *Inferno*, Mann's *Death in Venice*, Dostoyevsky's *Crime and Punishment* (Dick, op. cit., 1987, p. 95), Eliot's *Four Quartets* (James Gindin, *William Golding*, New York, St Martins Press, 1988, p. 70, Lawrence S. Friedman, William Golding, New York, Continuum, 1993, p. 123), and *The Wasteland* (Friedman, ibid., p. 123).

6   Kevin McCarron, *The Coincidence of Opposites: William Golding's Later Fiction*, Sheffield, Sheffield Academic Press, 1995, p. 18.

7   First defined by the French critic Louis Cazamian (*The Social Novel in England 1830–1850*, Martin Fido (trans.), London, Routledge and Kegan Paul, 1973), in the 1950s Kathleen Tillotson (*Novels of the Eighteen-Forties*, London, Oxford University Press, 1954), Arnold Kettle ('The Early Victorian Social Problem Novel' in Boris Ford (ed.) *From Dickens to Hardy*, London, Pelican, 1958, pp. 169–87), and Raymond Williams ('The Industrial Novels' in *Culture and Society, 1780–1950*, New York, Columbia University Press, 1958, pp. 78–109) identified the criteria for the narrative genus. For more recent studies see Ivan Melada, *The Captain of Industry in English Fiction, 1821–1871*, Albuquerque, University of New Mexico Press, 1970, Catherine Gallagher, *The Industrial Reformation of English Fiction 1832–1867*, Chicago, University of Chicago Press, 1985, and Rosemarie Bodenheimer, *The Politics of Story in Victorian Social Fiction*, Ithaca, Cornell University Press, 1988. Although Gindin's chapter on *The Pyramid* and *Darkness Visible* is titled 'The Condition of England', his intention is to describe 'the comprehensive social statement about his own world' (op. cit., p. 65) that Golding makes in these two novels, not

to characterize the two as heirs to the nineteenth-century discursive novel.

8   Some examples of the sub-genre would include Gaskell's *North and South* (1855), Kingsley's *Alton Locke* (1850), Dickens's *Hard Times* (1854), Eliot's *Felix Holt, the Radical* (1866), Wells' *Tono Bungay* (1909), Forster's *Howard's End* (1910). There are also post-war Condition of England novels – Lessing's *The Four-Gated City* (1969) and her *Memoirs of a Survivor* (1975), Drabble's *The Radiant Way* (1989), Barker's *Union Street*, Lodge's *Nice Work* (1989) and Byatt's *Babel Tower* (1997) among others.

9   The dislodging of the metaphor of malaise implicit in the metonymic phrase 'Condition of England' was effected by David Lodge, wearing at the time the literary critic's gown, not the novelist's cape in his chapter, '*Tono Bungay* and the Condition of England', *The Language of Fiction*, New York, Columbia University Press, 1966, p. 218. The chapter, to which I am indebted, appeared some 35 years before Lodge's fictional reworking of the literary theme in *Nice Work*, his comedic lambasting of contemporary commerce and culture.

10 Ulrich Broich, 'William Golding and the Religious Function of Literature', in Ulrich Broich, Theo Stemmler, and Gerd Stratmann (eds), *Functions of Literature: Essays Presented to Erwin Wolff on his Sixtieth Birthday*, Tubingen, Niemeyer, 1984, p. 317.

11 Ian Gregor and Mark Kinkead-Weekes, 'The Later Golding', *Twentieth Century Literature* 28 (1982) p. 93.

12 In conversation with John Carey, who described the novelist as 'a ferocious chess player', Golding remarked that he had 'always liked chess, and always known more about what was happening in the chess world than the man in the street' ('William Golding Talks to John Carey' in John Carey (ed.) *William Golding the Man and His Books: A Tribute on his 75th Birthday*, New York, Farrar, Straus & Giroux, 1987, p. 180).

13 Just as the protagonists of *Pincher Martin* and *The Paper Men* would reveal under such scrutiny not just the

sardonic play on letters which call to mind the heroic *Prometheus*, but also autobiographical projections by a writer rather too summarily read as absent from his allegorical fables. In this context, Golding's daughter, for example, observed that at least a couple of the characters in *Darkness Visible*'s town, Greenfield, were based on the family's neighbours in Wiltshire.

14 Obituary, The London *Times*, June 21, 1993, p. 17.

15 Golding to V. Tiger, personal correspondence.

16 William Golding, 'Egypt from My Outside', *A Moving Target*, London, Faber and Faber, 1982, p. 57.

17 John Coates, 'Religious Quest in *Darkness Visible*', *Renascence: Essays on Value in Literature* 39 (1986), p. 286.

18 Doris Lessing, *The Golden Notebook*, New York, Simon and Schuster, 1962, p. xvii.

19 '*Darkness Visible* is not concerned with the conflict between good and evil, but with humanity's insistence upon perceiving all experience in terms of duality,' writes McCarron (op. cit., p. 22), providing perhaps a rather too generalized assessment of the novel's several thematic projects. His analysis of 'triple sequences […] as a deliberate structural device', however, is extremely useful, particularly the analyses of their pervasive presence as a stylistic device in authorially reported action or description.

20 Hetty Clews, '*Darkness Visible*: William Golding's *Parousia*', *English Studies in Canada* 10, (1984), p. 323.

21 Donald W. Crompton, *A View From the Spire: William Golding's Later Novels*, edited and completed by Julia Briggs, Oxford, Blackwell, 1985, p. 96. An early and seminal analysis of *Darkness Visible*, an essay as invigorating as his (again seminal) essay on *The Spire*, Crompton's exegeses permitted many of us to reread/re-right/re-write Golding's book. (See, among others, S.H. Boyd, *The Novels of William Golding*, New York, St Martin's Press, 1988, Arnold Johnston, *Of Earth and*

Darkness: The Novels of William Golding, Columbia & London, University of Missouri Press, 1980 and Tebbutt, op. cit.) My one contention, a minor one, is Crompton's casting of Matty's progress as a re-enactment of the progress of Biblical history from the Old Testament, through the New to the Apocalypse. As Boyd observes, 'Matty may be a prophet and evangelist, but he is also a grotesque and a fool, a saint perhaps, but perhaps a religious maniac. Passing judgement on Matty and his career is no easy matter' (Boyd, op. cit., p. 130). Another lively knitting together of clues was provided by my graduate student, James Scheiner: 'The double sevens suggested by the two seven-letter names – or, if you like, Matty's initially being called Seven before receiving his more proper Christian name [Septimus] can lead the reader to Matthew 7:7: "Ask and it will be given you; seek and you will find; knock and it will be opened to you".' Given the novel's investigation of various kinds of spiritual longing, the reading seems effective.

22   Gunnel Cleve argues that Matty's appearance resembles the figure in Robert Southwell's poem, 'The Burning Babe' ('Some Elements of Mysticism in William Golding's Novel *Darkness Visible*' *Neuphilologische Mitteilungen* 83, 1982, p. 459). A more likely source is *Isaiah* 20:2, where the prophet is described as 'walking naked and barefoot'.

23   From myth to myth, culture to culture, the bird figures forth the soul. Consider a book Golding would certainly have known, the *Hieroglyphica of Horapollo*, the secret guide to Egyptian hieroglyphics; appearing first in 1505, it had some thirty editions, translations, and reprints over the next one hundred years alone. The 7th Hieroglyphic in Book I, a Hawk, emblematizes the soul, whose Egyptian name, Baieth, means soul and heart. The heart, according to these Egyptians, contains the soul. Striking as well in terms of apparent serendipity is the 29th Hieroglyphic of Book II, where emblematizing the Infinite or Fate is the figure of *seven* letters surrounded by two fingers.

24   Willy Schreurs, 'Darkness Visible: The Choice between Good and Evil' in Jeanne Delbaere (ed) *William Golding: The Sound of Silence*, Liège: English Department University of Liège. 1991, p. 135.

25   Boyd, op. cit., p. 132. Among several inscrutable moments in the text, this episode – generative of Matty's long and silent mystical vocation – brings to mind Golding's remark during a 1977 lecture on the novelist's craft: 'Conrad lays it down as a prime aid that the writer must know something about each character that he will not put in the book and will not reveal to any reader or critic' (*A Moving Target*, p. 140). Of course, the near impenetrability of the episode (a cunning test, in my view) has led readers and critics alike to quite various judgements. Compare, for example, McCarron's view that 'Matty is the only character in the novel to actually cause, directly or indirectly another character's death: a child's death' (op. cit., p. 31) to Dick's observation that 'Matty, who takes everything literally, cursed Henderson [...] by hurling his shoe, causing the boy to lose his balance and fall to his death' (op. cit., p. 103). Dickson's summary here is a balancing one: 'Though Golding's text is not clear about the exact circumstances of Henderson's death, for Matty's shoe is found under the body [...] there is an ironic implication established. Presumably Matty is connected with Henderson's fall, after literally "casting his shoe" at the suspected wrongdoer' (Boyd, ibid., p. 113).

26   Dick, op. cit., p. 105. Crompton writes, 'there are strong overtones of a descent into an underworld, whether classical or Biblical in Matty's ritual (op. cit., p. 109). Ian Gregor and Mark Kinkead-Weekes suggest that Matty 'not only bears witness to a light that shines on, transcending the passage through the underworld – he also proclaims the eternal glory of the wheeled cherubim of *Ezekiel* and the *Apocalypse*' (William Golding: A Critical Study, London, Faber and Faber, 1984, p. 282). It is *Ezekiel* 1.21 where the Old Testament prophet is given the mission 'to prophesy to the Israelites' (Friedman, op. cit., p. 129). McCarron suggests as relevant passages from *Revelation*: '"And I saw an angel coming down out of heaven with the key of the abyss and a great chain in his hand" (20.1–1) and also "And the city has no need of the sun or of the moon to shine upon it, for the glory of Gold lighted it up, and its lamp was the Lamb" (21.23–24)' (op. cit., p. 39).

27   For use of these three terms, see Friedman, op. cit., p. 129.

28   Stephen Medcalf, 'Bill and Mr Golding's Daimon' in John Carey
      (ed.), *William Golding, The Man and his Books: A Tribute on his 75th
      Birthday*, New York, Farrar, Straus & Giroux, 1987, p. 42.

29   Friedman, op. cit., p. 130.

30   Ironically named, Greenfield shares with *The Pyramid*'s Stilbourne
      a characteristically English kind of warped respectability. That
      novel's epitaph, drawn from the *Instructions of Ptah-Hotep*, offers an
      informative gloss here as well: 'If thou be among people make for
      thyself love, the beginning and end of the heart.'

31   Thérèse Vichy, 'Tragic Experience and Poetic Innocence in
      Darkness Visible' in Frédéric Regard (ed.), *Fingering Netsukes*, Saint-
      Etienne, Publications de l'Université de Saint-Etienne in
      association with Faber and Faber, 1995, p. 130.

32   In the last devastating conversation between father and
      daughter, Stanhope supplies the term 'entropy' (p. 185) in
      response to Sophy's comment: 'You, Mummy, Toni, me –
      we're not the way people used to be. It's part of the whole
      running down' (p. 185). The entropic principle, of course,
      informs the Second Law of Thermodynamics, which Golding
      had characterized some fifteen years earlier as the 'Satan of our
      cosmology'(Golding, 'Irish Poets and Their Poetry' *Holiday*,
      April 1963, p. 17).

33   In her chapter on the novel, Byatt elaborated upon the allusion,
      writing that, by name, Sophy is also the 'Gnostic or Hermetic
      or Jewish Wisdom, who in some myths of the Creation and Fall
      was separated from God in the creation of matter, imprisoned
      in the latter and condemned to be incarnate as a series of
      women, daughters of men doomed to lust after the sons of God'
      (op. cit., p. 171).

34   In the context of this adaptive recasting of imagery, Matty's naive
      identification of Sophy with the Great Whore of Babylon of
      Revelation 20:14, who brings forth the 'second death, even the lake
      of fire', seems not so misogynistic.

35 Roy Arthur Swanson, 'Versions of Double Think in *Gravity's Rainbow, Darkness Visible, Riddley Walker*, and *Travels to the Enu*', *World Literature Today* 58 (1984), p. 205.

36 Gregor and Kinkead-Weekes, op. cit., p. 123.

37 'A curious likeness' is established between Matty and Sophy, with the former regarding his sexuality as 'sinful, dangerous and vile' while the latter 'cultivates the dangerous, violent and sordid' in hers (Boyd, op. cit., p. 134). Matty, however, comes to understand that the sexual 'defilement' of self is not something about which he has to 'be frightened or ashamed'. So, on discovering that he has not been gelded by the Australian Bummer, he shouts in joy: 'I am a man I could have a son' (p. 237), all the while dancing to Beethoven's *Seventh Symphony*.

38 I am indebted here to Crompton's exegesis; he observes that the song aided 'children in remembering some of the basic truths of the Church' (op. cit., p. 111).

39 The novel's epigraph, '*Sit Mihi Fas Audita Loqui*', for example, summons Virgil's invocation to the gods in Book Six of *The Aeneid* to embolden him to describe the terrors of the Underworld as he embarks on that voyage.

40 Broich, op. cit., p. 317.

41 Gillian Stead Eilersen, 'A Password for the Darkness: Systems, Coincidences and Visions in William Golding's *Darkness Visible*', *Critique: Studies in Modern Fiction* 28 (1987), p. 116.

42 McCarron, op. cit., p. 26.

43 Walls fall, as Chapter I dramatizes in its depiction of the blitz. The fireman Goodchild 'had watched a wall six storeys high fall on him all in one piece and had stood, unable to move and wondering why he was still alive'. Was it coincidence or miracle that made 'the brick surround of a window on the fourth storey [...] fit round him neatly?' (p. 11), the text teases.

The Paper Men

Golding and I [...] have both seen our work endlessly discussed, analyzed, dissected [...] victims of that characteristic twentieth-century mania for treating living artists as if they were dead – a process that may please teacher and student on campus, but which...does something rather different to the still-breathing subject on the anatomy table.

John Fowles, 1986

The writer [...] finds ways of evading [...] questions, or confusing [...] questioners, by masks, disguises, obliquities and ambiguities, by hiding secret meanings in his text – secret, sometimes, even from himself.

David Lodge, 1990

Narrative theory now instructs that the reader beware. There are no innocent accords between author and text, reader and text, context and text. Take titles, for a start. Although apparently paratextual in status, they mark the reader's first encounter with the text; indeed, the title of a novel amounts to the beginning of the text. Whether announcing a theme didactically as does *Pride and Prejudice* or inviting symbolic interpretations as do *To the Lighthouse* and *The Rainbow*, titles seek to shape the reception of a book's meaning at the very outset. Almost inevitably disguising an impulse to influence in an authoritative way the reading of that which is named, the authorial gesture of the chosen title constitutes what Derrida describes as a 'frame' or 'delimitation' that 'has enormous consequences'.[1]

It was not solely the titular framing of *The Paper Men* that would testify to the truth of Derrida's observation in the novel's initial provocation of a largely negative reception. While the title's embrace of intertextuality – a common appeal of both modernist and postmodernist titles – permitted reviewers to cite as allusive brother text, T. S. Eliot's 'The Hollow Men'[2] its trope carried both metonymic and metaphoric meaning.[3] The majority of reviewers neglected the metaphor, making much of the metonym: that writers are men of paper in the sense that they make their living by means of manuscripts, book proofs, notebooks, journals, newspapers, magazines. In writing a novel about a best-selling novelist being persecuted by an American academic, Golding had – those reviewers contended – written an *apologia pro sua vita*. The novel was an 'awkward testimony', indeed 'a public self-abasement'.[4] Viewing the narrative as though it were a direct portrait of the artist as an old man, another reviewer observed: 'There are signs in the novel itself that Golding is somewhat bothered by his apotheosis as Grand Old Man of English letters, and, in that sense, the book is ironically well timed'.[5] Appearing in February 1984, several months earlier than the originally scheduled autumn publication date, *The Paper Men* seemed to be positioned to take advantage of its author's recent receipt of the Nobel Prize for Literature.[6] The author of *The Paper Men*, already a critical, financial, and international success, whose work had so absorbed academics that an enormous body of scholarship had evolved, seemed up to his elbows in accolades. There had also been the 1980 Booker Prize for *Rites of Passage*, a selection that famously provoked disparaging remarks from its unsuccessful competitor, Anthony Burgess.[7] In one reviewer's chilly summary, the message of *The Paper Men* 'would appear to be made up of [...] a personal protest against the notion that writers are public property [...]'[8]

Was Golding announcing novelistically his frustration as a much investigated author, whose privacy had been all too frequently invaded, over the years, by intrusive academics in pursuit of their own professional purposes? Such an interpretation was presented in one essay by E. C. Bufkin, who argued that the:

> [...]impetus of this novel must have been private as well as public and professional... The origin may have been described in the preface to *A Moving Target*: 'I have always tried to resist this [critical interrogation about my work] and have always given way in the end so that at last I find myself talking about myself with the grossest liberality. This leads to nothing but self-disgust.'[9]

Certainly, *The Paper Men*'s title carries as acerbic an autobiographical comment on the literary marketplace as George Gissing's, when, almost a century earlier, he named the novel that described his own baleful experience in that work place *New Grub Street*. Several autobiographical nuggets are deposited in the Golding narrative. The persecuted novelist, Wilf Barclay, with a Bill Golding-like scrappy beard and an age-weary loathing of literary liming, winces with irritation at being made the subject of an 'academic light industry' ever since the success of his high acclaimed first novel, *Coldharbour*. The fictional W. B. (like the real-life W. G.) served in the Royal Navy during the war and afterward did some desultory fringe theater: intertextual traps that author William Golding must surely have enjoyed setting to snag an earnest critic or two.[10]

The Paper Men, therefore, adopts and adapts elements in common with the narrative strategy we call autobiographical, thus blurring the generic border between the rhetorical acts of fiction and those of autobiography. 'There is certainly amusement,' remarks Kevin McCarron, 'for the reader in noting those moments when Barclay's comments seem to echo beliefs that Golding has expressed elsewhere. Barclay's observation at the literary conference in Seville, "A few females appeared to be taking notes", evokes a rather sweeping statement Golding had made in one of his essays: "Like all women students, they are inveterate, comically obsessive note-takers." '.[11] At the same time, the novel blurs other generic borders; in its ridicule of the customs and practices of contemporary literary life it borrows and modifies that narrative strategy we call satire.[12] Here farce is the ruling force: 'I recognized uneasily the hand of what I sometimes thought to be my personal nemesis, the spirit of farce' (p. 11). The novel's opening chapter begins with a badger at the bin, the badger grubbing through the 'dustbin, ashcan, *poubelle*, what ever one chooses to call it' (p. 9) being Professor Rick L. Tucker of the University of Astrakhan. By my way of unscrambling, Astrakhan reads Trashkaan, and so it is farcically fitting that Tucker's University of Astrakhan/Trashkaan's T-shirt should read OLE ASHCAN, as Golding's text insists on several occasions.

Reductive artfulness of this sort is one of the features of the convention where names are never neutral, carrying as they do satiric significance. Golding's game in naming his alcoholic, atheist narrator Wilfred Barclay is one of inversion; 'Wilfred', Partridge's dictionary of slang informs us, means 'a teetotaller', a reference to the early twentieth-century M. P. and abstinence champion, Sir Wilfred Lawson.[13] And 'Barclay' is, of course, George Berkeley, the eighteenth-century Irish bishop and philosopher who argued that no subject exists apart from Mind, Nature being conscious experience and forming the sign of a divine universal Intelligence and Will.[14] As to the character Tucker, that naming may well be a mimic enactment. Blake Morrison's throwaway comment in the *TLS* review has the ring of possibility: 'There are no Rick L. Tuckers in my Golding bibliography, but I might well find the name too close for comfort if I were a scholar like James R. Baker, who has been interpreting and casebooking Golding since 1964.'[15] Nor does the satirist delineate characters with neutrality; often the treatment of social types follows a Swiftian practice of reducing figures metonymically to their corporeal features. Thus the dogged, indefatigable Tucker is first characterized by a densely hairy chest, 'then a narrower shrubbery leading down to an even more densely haired nest of privates' (p. 13). The event occasioning Barclay's glimpse of the Tucker-forest is the richly comic episode opening the novel. Rooting noises at the dustbin make Barclay suspect a badger, which he stalks airgun in one hand, the other clutching a torch and a sagging pajama bottom. The gun accidentally fires, the wounded badger gulps, a Professor caught in the act of rifling an ashcan for discarded authoriana. Falling pajama trousers are kicked aside, hairy nakedness, on inspection, reveals no injury: 'As if on cue, the kitchen door open[s], stage left' (p. 13). 'Could you two men make less noise about it?' Liz, the distinguished author's wife remarks.

A good deal later, the distinguished author decides to turn the tables on the badgering biographer, making the predator his prey by writing a satiric story, featuring the fellow as 'a comically loathsome figure' (p. 79). When author Barclay determines on selection, not invention, his choice is between metonym and metaphor, diegesis and mimesis. Puzzling over all the fictional possibilities, author Barclay remembers that:

> ...there were thickets in his arm pits, small images of the same in his nostrils – probably the hair extended down his legs to end round his ankles like the feathers on a cob or...a cart horse. It grew thick and close over his head, thick on his eyebrows... How much hair could the novelist get away with? Not quite so much – the bit down the front, the mop of black hair on his head, the eyebrows and eyelashes would be more than enough... It was sheer luck I knew he was as shaggy between the legs as a Shetland pony (p. 79).

Satirically encoded, critics are what their private parts display: a buffooning of animality summed up in *The Paper Men* by Wilf Barclay's description of Tucker as: 'bulging flies' (p. 90). Satirically ridiculed as well are self-dramatizing, self-loathing, and self-pitying novelists. If the critic is badger, ape, horse, and dog, then the artist is ragged journal, yellowing newspaper, fusty book, dog-eared manuscript. Glancing towards an inevitable mirror in an inevitable bar, Barclay sees not the expected 'red-faced Englishman' but rather 'some kind of leather that had been stowed in an attic for generations and was dusty and cracked' (p. 71). If in metonymic thrust the critic is dog, then the artist is aging, inconsequential paper.[16] More paper man – in the metaphoric sense of being one-dimensional – than his pursuing badger, he lacks what the badger possesses: considerable powers of potential persecution. In early nineteenth-century colloquialism, the word badger was low cant for river thief; after robbing, the badger would murder his victim and then throw him into the river.[17]

II

Who is in control of whom? Is the author the elitist figure demanding a sophisticated reader? Or is the inferring reader ultimately the one with the power, the power to ignore or misread the intentions of the [author].

Linda Hutcheon, 1985

Perhaps one faults Golding too readily in *The Paper Men*'s near misogynist presentation of Tucker's wife, Mary Lou. Another in a long line of passive females, whose vulnerable beauty tempts libidinous men, her satiric function in the novel is largely subsumed by the cartoon-like name and the lampooning detail that she 'majored in flower arranging and bibliography' (p. 65).[18] But then, on first reading, *The Paper Men* seems placed in the tradition of comic self-conscious literary novels like Vladimir Nabokov's *Pale Fire*, Robertson Davies' *The Rebel Angels*, Alison Lurie's *The War Between the Tates*, A. S. Byatt's *Possession*, Martin Amis' *The Information*, or Graham Swift's *Ever After*. Such novels mock the procedures of academic scholarship and literary practices. To the literary historian's eye, Golding's book participates in several of the rhetorical techniques of parody that works such as Kingsley Amis' *Lucky Jim*, Malcolm Bradbury's *The History Man*, David Lodge's *The British Museum is Falling Down*, and Mary McCarthy's *The Groves of Academe* deploy in their mockery of pedantry.

But there are very marked differences. That convention's common technique of literary pastiche seems in *The Paper Men* less a way of imitating (with a knowing grin) academic discourse than representing imitatively a character's consciousness, itself the object of that character's self-targeted satire. To borrow again the term Kristeva coined, the surface of *The Paper Men* is a tissue of intertextualities. James Gindin's lucid summation that 'literary reference is profuse and incessant…the references themselves function idiosyncratically and randomly, a world of verbal and cultural artifact without coherence or historical meaning'[19] is especially useful here. Although we may not articulate our reading experience in this way, the primary surface we are engaged by (or alienated from) when first we read *The Paper Men* exhibits textual appropriations. It also makes an exhibition of textual appropriation. Those readers already familiar with Golding's habit of encoded cues might well feel obliged to search beyond the text, using the quotations as clues to meaning – and many have.[20] On balance, however, the textual appropriations of various kinds of literariness, while they collude in being threaded through a text already sewn with autobiographical and satiric strands, inhibit interpretative acts. Many of the quotations hang suspended: inert. Allusions to allusions joggle partial quotations of quotations while unidentified references to, or misquotations from, canonical male writers like Shakespeare, Keats, Tennyson, Ibsen, Nabokov, Shelley, Dickens, Scott, T. S. Eliot, Johnson, and Milton jostle with clichéd renderings of discourses already themselves parodic.

It's as though an intertextual ventriloquist act is being performed; in the very first chapter Coleridge, Maigret, and Holmes crazily share the same microphone, while high culture taxonomies like Aristotelian 'peripeteia to end all peripeteias' squabble with comic-book sounds '*glug*' and '*gulp*'. If we recall that the strategies of mimicry, pastiche, and parody are discourses that Bakhtin categorized as 'doubly-oriented' or 'doubly-voiced', then *The Paper Men*'s staging of these doubly-oriented speech discourses could be sighted and identified, the text being so aligned. A passage midway through the novel, for example, borrows the discourse of the courtroom drama, illustrating that exaggerated mimicry that Bakhtin calls 'stylization', the burlesque of a hackneyed style we remember from countless written (never spoken) works. In the obligatory judge and jury assessment, prisoner Barclay, by way of his 'habit of scrawling lies on paper into a shape that the weak-minded have taken as guide, comforter and friend', is found guilty. 'I would remind you, m'lud, that the principal witness for the prosecution, the man Plato, is a foreigner […]'[21] opines Barclay, in defense of his own prosecution of himself for 'being a real bastard' (p. 47). Another passage borrows grandiloquent Churchillian rhetoric to fight the black hole of the drunk's amnesia – 'fight it on the beaches, in pubs and restaurants, clubs, bars, in travel, in the house, in the very damned delectable bottles themselves' (p. 8). This is what Bakhtin identifies as parody: the imitation of a style for purposes the reverse of those for which the discourse was originally intended. Another passage describing the inevitable crush of the British schoolboy imitates that mode of colloquial oral narration that Bakhtin calls the *skaz*: *'Jeffers is a frightfully good chap and I am keen on being his – it's marvellous being in the second with him – Jeffers caught a frightfully good catch off my bowling at first slip – I told him it was a frightfully good catch and he didn't seem to mind my speaking to him'* (p. 58). And twisting throughout, there's a mimicry of that nasal, diminished discourse Englishmen's literary ears construe as American English: 'Now, hon, it's time you got out of bed, we got to do St Peter's before one, hon' (p. 99). No American talks the way Barclay has Tucker talk. His is a discourse of clumsy, cliché-ridden writing about Americans that is burlesqued here, again the kind of doubly-oriented speech Bakhtin would define as stylization. Finally, for the purposes of this discussion, there is a most consistent stylistic band, one representing Barclay's consciousness, that plays through the novel. This is the style that critics have decried as 'designed to set the reader's teeth on edge [so] weary and wearisome, [so] cynical and cynically unconcerned at its own clumsy [...] nature'.[22] Read even with some degree of tolerance, the examples that follow still seem baleful testimony:

> The drink, such as it had been, was dying out of my brain and leaving a kind of sediment of irritation, vague discomfort and even remorse. It had not been – no, indeed – a *bender* or *booze up*. By the exercise of special pleading I could have persuaded other people that my evening's consumption had been no more than reasonable with regard to the duties of a host: an English author entertaining a professor of English Literature from overseas (p. 7).

Or:

> Yes, the girl. That's the thing about a flash. It blasts the life and colour out of a face, however delicate, so that this was not so much the Mary Lou who had adored her big strong man and tried as far as she could to

complete the magic circle – oh no! This was the doll, the plastic imitation of a girl...(p. 133)

And:

When it came to sex, Lucinda was a genius. If *she* chose to write her memoirs! Dear God, *Domine defende nos!* A book for none but the gallant investigators of the human farmyard... Folks, what you have been looking for, take it home with you, a present for the wife, the kiddies, the dear old folks in whose toothless caverns marge will not melt – something new! (p. 51)

One recognizes, by reason of one's irritation with these exclamatory textual performances, what Bakhtin would have diagnosed as the discourse of 'hidden polemic', *viz.* 'any speech that is...overblown, any speech that is determined beforehand not to be itself, any speech replete with reservations, concessions, loopholes'.[23] Such recognition does not change one's displeasure.

So the literary historian pauses to register how far short, in comparison with other comedies of academic manners, the comedic achievement of the Golding text falls. As one commentator summarized:

Wilfred Barclay, though he regards himself as one of nature's clowns, is a desperately unfunny writer of comedy. Barclay himself provides the appropriate response to the book's humour with the ubiquitous 'Ha etc.' with which he marks any near-miss at a witticism or comic turn of phrase on his own part. 'Ha etc.' is both an apology for a laugh and an apology for the absence of a laugh: there is certainly need of apology.[24]

But *is* there need of apology? And who should apologize: W.B. or W.G.? To declare *The Paper Men* a failed comedy is to neglect to see how cunningly it subscribes to that mode's discourses *without* endorsing its energetic hilarity or irreverent vitality. Deliberately foregrounded in *The Paper Men* text is the absence of what must be abidingly present in the travestying vision: the robust spirit of renewal, the kind of humor exposing authoritarian pieties that Bakhtin called the carnivalesque. Located in Greek satyr drama, Roman *Saturnalia* and medieval parodic travesties of sacred word and sacred liturgy, the carnivalesque preceded the novel.

However, the tradition of the parodic in fiction is, according to Bakhtin, one of multivocal, or 'dialogic' discourse whose energies celebrate heterogeneity of attitude and encourage heterogeneity of response.

Characteristically, double-voiced discourse belongs to that category of speech 'which not only refers to something in the world but also refers to another speech act by another addresser'.[25] Its effect is to extricate the various discourses that make up the polyphonic text that constitutes prose literature from the dominant frame of monologic authorial voice. As Bakhtin puts it: 'any and every straightforward genre…may, indeed must, have itself become the object of representation, the object of a parodic, travestying "mimicry"… Parodic-travestying literature introduces the *permanent corrective of laughter*, of a critique on the one-sided seriousness of the lofty direct word…'[26]

In sharp contrast, Golding's text lacks − and I would argue, deliberately so − such a positive regenerative power. Barclay's cartoon quack, 'Ha et cetera', pretty much sums up the book's intentional negation of laughter. According to Bakhtin's formulation in *Rabelais and His World*, the genus of humor one would detect in *The Paper Men* would be designated 'destructive humor', which he typifies as laughter 'cut down to cold humor, irony, sarcasm' that has ceased 'to be joyful and triumphant hilarity.'[27]

It is therefore important to recognize the implications of Bakhtin's argument: if the agency of destructive humor erases the joyous inverted world of the carnival, then the monologic voice comes to be reinstated, a matter very much relevant to Golding's strategy in, *The Paper Men*. Golding's deployment here of these 'double-voice discourses' and intertextualities most frequently acts to block, not aid, the reader's pleasure. Comprehension is similarly obstructed. Foreign phrases, for example, silt Barclay's narrative, appropriately enough for a writer on the run, traveling the road systems of Europe; its 'high roads, motorways, the autoroutes, autostradas, autobahns, autoputs from Finland to Cadiz' (p. 25). Depending on their familiarity with, for example, *gueule-de-bois* or *experientia docet stultos* (or autobahn, autoputs, autostrada), readers may be included or excluded from their resonances. The reader 'has to construct a second meaning through inferences about surface statements and supplement the foreground with knowledge of the backgrounded context'.[28] Yet the reader is confronted by intertextual cul-de-sacs that seem only to announce they are dead ends. The medley of exaggerated styles given to Wilfred

Barclay serves to counteract any plurality of perspectives. His voice imposes *his* interpretative authority on the story; characters, like Tucker, Mary Lou, and the homosexual Johnny St John John, are crude caricatures, speaking one voice: the narrator's, not their own. Examine, for example, Johnny St John John's conversation when he and Barclay meet on a Greek island. Johnny's colloquy is stippled with literary allusions to the writers Ambrose Bierce, Shakespeare, Sappho, Keats, and Blake; it even carries the Barclay tag, 'Quote, so human, unquote' (p. 107).

Since Barclay, as Crompton and Briggs argue, 'is the ostensible author of *The Paper Men*, the reader is faced with the problem that Golding's success in presenting the withdrawn and self-absorbed world of his hero, in recreating this mimetically from within, risks undermining the book's appeal'.[29] This, however, is a view rather miscalculating Golding's technique of establishing a parallel between theme and writerly act. The text insists on positing as theme the villainous self-absorption of its unreliable narrator, one who, admitting to dissipation on the first page, plunges further and further into self-loathing as he flees abroad, pursued – like Poe's William Wilson – by a mirroring doppelganger. Golding's intentions here are very much contrary to those of contemporary self-reflexive practices of writers like John Fowles, Umberto Eco, Margaret Atwood, or Donald Barthelme. Parody, pastiche, stylization, hidden polemic, satire, intertextuality, and autobiographical teasing, all of the apparatus behind *The Paper Men*'s textual performance comes to function like the intrusive omniscient narrator of a nineteenth-century 'classic realist text'. It amounts to no mean feat that *The Paper Men* uses many of the practices of postmodern fiction so as to position the reader in that very old-fashioned place. Invited, the reader can condemn on moral grounds the irascible, repugnant villain if they see him as such. Incapable of feeling, parasitic and derivative, Wilfred Barclay – perhaps also his nemesis, Rick Tucker – is repellent precisely to the degree that he experiences the world *only* through layers and layers of borrowed words and borrowed styles. Put another way, *The Paper Men* follows what I regard as a characteristic strategy in Golding's fiction: readers must assemble, even infer, data that self-absorbed narrators with their revelatory surface texts simply do not apprehend. The question, of course, is who ends up constructing the text: writer or reader?

III

A beginning, a muddle, and an end

Philip Larkin

I began this chapter by suggesting there was no innocent contract between a text and its reading and that *The Paper Men* is no exception to this rule. We have seen it to be a novel bristling 'with pre-emptive weaponry aimed at annulling every reservation we may have, by persuading us that the flaws are all deliberate'.[30] Perceptive critics have noted that its plot – in the Aristotelian sense – is circular. Starting with the clown's airgun performance and the badger's '*gulp*', it concludes with the unfinished word 'gu'. 'The story itself is perfectly symmetrical, beginning and ending at Barclay's Wiltshire home; in between, the two men vie for ascendancy over each other with the balance of power shifting first one way and then the other.'[31] Barclay is in feckless and fugue-like flight throughout the novel: to Italy and back, to Spain, to South Africa, to South America, North Africa, Finland, to Switzerland and back. In hired cars, on airplanes, motoring down asphalt wastelands, shoaling up at one hotel suite or another, driving past sunsets and sunrises, holed up in one bar or another, his identity finds confirmation in credit cards, *poste restante* mailings and delusions that have him imagine sighting his hairy hunter behind churches, beside fountains, in front of windows, alongside statues. 'Paranoid, he is persecuted. Acrophobe, he is exposed to heights. Suggestible, he recalls a hypnotic experience of his youth and an encounter with an Italian stigmatic.'[32] Although they meet on only three occasions, badger Tucker is in actual pursuit, needing to be named the official biographer now that his research is to be funded for seven years by a philanthropist, the mysterious Halliday. In a kind of symbiotic doubling, Tucker is also driven, giving truth to John Clare's 1836 poem 'Badger', 'When badgers fight [...] everyone's a foe.' This is demonstrated many times, particularly during their encounter in Schwillen when his strategy to obtain Barclay's permission includes offering the submissive, innocent May Lou as barter: 'To know myself accepted, endured not even as in honest whoredom, for money, but for *paper!*' (p. 75) Barclay rages as he ushers the vulnerable child-wife out the door. The next day after a fog-weighted alpine walk in Weisswald that results in Barclay falling through a broken railing and then being saved, Tucker's hand holding him 'by the collar' (p. 87) so as to draw the fright-filled author slowly back up the precipitous cliff, Barclay rages even more ferociously. 'First his wife, then when that ploy failed, my life [...] handed back to me, but now, as I saw, on conditions like the surrender of a city' (p. 93). Battlements reraised, Barclay escapes again: this time to fear that it is Halliday from whom he flees: 'Clearly Halliday was more dangerous than Rick. After all, with his sources of information he didn't have to guess. He simply knew my biography' (p. 110).

Barclay's account grows more and more unreliable, disconnected, out of control, maniacal as the flight narrative continues, although it becomes clear — even to him — that he is trying to escape from remembering his own biography. In spite of the alcoholic benders, buried memories flicker to the surface: a man killed in a hit and run accident, the germ for a novel purloined, indeed plagiarized, the abandoned wife and daughter, both unloved, the theft of incriminating letters. 'These memories, how they sting, scald, *burn*' (p. 47, my italics). He finds himself — so the reader must judge, although the viewpoint is by now disoriented by drink and delusion — isolated on an island[33] whose landscape Barclay not insignificantly reads as 'powdered pumice with knives of black glass sticking up through it like a feast of steeples' (p. 119). At one point, he walks down a corridor whose walls support 'ancient corpses': 'ha et cetera. Sicilian burial customs, q.v.' (p. 120), he japes. Heat and strain press inside him and appear to couple with the brassy light and swelter outside as he staggers up towards a cathedral, noticing on the horizon a 'plume of black smoke'. At that moment a volcano erupts and an earthquake — matching rhythmically his delirium tremens — begins rocking and wrecking, dislodging from the cathedral's ceiling a blue mosaic fragment that would have fallen just under his left foot were he to have trodden forward. 'You don't want to fall off the edge,' he mutters, recalling the terror of the alpine fall. With caution, he moves towards the north transept to find himself abruptly face to face with an enormous and alarming silver statue:

It was taller than I [...] and striding forward like an archaic Greek statue. It was crowned and its eyes were rubies or garnets or carbuncles or plain red glass that flared like the heat in my chest. Perhaps it was Christ. Perhaps they had inherited it in these parts and just changed the name and it was Pluto, the god of the Underworld, Hades, striding forward (p. 123).

In a confrontation scene as charged as any of those in the earlier novels, Golding once again depicts the encounter between an imagined implacable Other and a creature who envisages that imagined godhead through the smeared prism of his own nature. 'Surrounded, swamped, confounded all but destroyed, adrift in the universal intolerance, mouth open, screaming, bepissed and beshitten, I knew my maker and I fell down' (p. 123), Barclay iterates, as he (like Simon before the head, Pincher Martin before the Dwarf or Sophy brooding upon the black ink stain) collapses, insensate.

Unlike Martin, Barclay does not claim the apparition to be a projection of his own mind. There is evidence, however, that the features he selects he also chooses to interpret in their least benign symbology. Shimmering silver becomes adamantine steel, cerulean blue turns malevolent slate, the ruby red of the Christian passion declines into carbuncle, glass; the flaring heat inside his chest: merciful Christ is metamorphosed into menacing Hades. Thus does heaven become hell. Thus does Barclay in his own image imagine god: a 'universal intolerance'. Emerging from days of silence, Barclay struggles to give words to his conception that the steel Hades has created him, one of the 'predestinate damned', in its own image. And the phrase the paper man constructs consists of three singularly simple words. 'I. am. sin.' (p. 127).

Classic tales of the supernatural, as we well remember from the ghost stories of Edith Wharton and Edgar Allan Poe, must be capable of double interpretation, the narrative being able to sustain both a realistic and a supernatural explanation. *The Paper Men* follows this paradigm since Barclay is by his own boast 'very receptive to hypnotic suggestion' (p. 48). Already, his friend Johnny has advised him to find some kind of companionship, say a dog, otherwise he could well be locked up as a 'dipso-schizo'. Alcoholic, he is also diagnosed as having suffered a stroke, thus the many references to the pressure and heat inside his chest during the Sicilian episode, the collapse in the cathedral, and the efforts in the hospital to relearn language. Tellingly, he describes the laborious process of 'moving each syllable from here to there' as akin to an attempt to '*re*fashion a statue' (p. 126, my italics), surely a textual clue, given Barclay's first fashioning of the Lipari statue. Confined though one may be within the narrator's mind, there is sufficient textual evidence planted for Barclay's religious vision to be simultaneously read as an extreme manifestation of his solipsistic egotism: 'I saw I was one of the, or perhaps the only, predestinate damned' (p. 124). Having confronted and been converted to a wrathful godhead, 'divine justice without mercy' (p. 125), Barclay has created the conditions of his own hounding.

Golding's textual strategy frequently is one of defamiliarization, the deliberate elimination of the normal sequential narrative stream. Characteristically, a series of partial revelations function as much to mislead as guide understanding. Nowhere is this more in evidence in *The Paper Men* than in the chapters that follow Barclay's Sicilian conversion where, in the words of one reviewer, 'the prose [...] becomes overheated, allusive and hard to follow'.[34] Dreams, visions, and hallucinations infect, not so much offering alternative readings as equivocal riddles. The reader 'is continually made to suspect that Barclay himself is never sure of the precise point where his dreams may be distinguished from reality, and vice versa'.[35] Nightmares begin to invade the day. A recurrent one graphically illustrates the difference between being able to quote Mephistopheles from *Dr Faustus* –'why this is hell nor am I out of it, Marlowe, q.v.'(pp. 125–26)[36] – and inhabiting that fiery abode of visible darkness in one's day-to-day consciousness. I present the nightmare passage at length, it being useful to decode what the narrator resists. The text insists:

> This dream was I'd be in Marrakesh [...] running away from Rick [...] into the Sahara...the sand was very hot, oh very hot, oven-hot [...] how I had to move, dance, run, jump up and down! [...] However, using all my mighty dream-intelligence, I evolved a compromise [...] I bent down and endured my burning feet while with my hand I made a hole in the sand. It seemed logical at the time that this should result in a hole so deep and black it was sickening, like a hole in the universe, but it wasn't burning sand. If I bored enough holes I had a space to put a foot and escape the burning; at which point I would wake up (pp. 156–57).

Experiencing himself daily as one of the damned, Barclay now dreams daily, his 'intelligence' borrowing a fiery landscape as a conventional image for hell. In desert sand so hot it roasts the flesh, the dreamer invents not rain as relief, nor even Eliot's promissory thunder. For, of course, the dream episode calls to mind not just *The Wasteland* and 'The Hollow Men', but also Luke's account of Christ's forty days in the wilderness. The scriptural injunction with which Christ confronts the Devil – 'Get thee behind me Satan, for it is *written* Thou shalt worship the Lord thy God/and him only shalt thou serve' (*Luke*

4.2–8, my italics) may well be the 'strange language' the dreaming Barclay writes in the sand. However, the dream intelligence invents black holes, the trope of darkness being re-orchestrated just as, earlier in the novel, the crustacean imagery figuring Pincher Martin was used to depict Barclay's egotism. As symbol, *The Paper Men*'s 'deep black…hole in the universe' is the very negation of soothing ease, despite the dream fact that it gives succor. Paradoxical balm to the dreamer's burning feet, the negating black hole becomes the only kind of relief a man such as Barclay would be able to imagine.

IV

Some literary students and critics are likely to be worried by the idea that a literary text does not have a single 'correct' meaning, but probably not many. They are more likely to be engaged by the idea that the meanings of a text do not lie within them like wisdom teeth within a gum, waiting patiently to be extracted, but that the reader has some active role in the process.

Terry Eagleton

Typically, Golding's novelistic practice is seldom direct; often he draws readers away from his text's thematic course so that it takes one by (moral) surprise that one has become so dislocated and, in turn, implicated in constructing the meanings of the text. Rather than raising questions about the veracity of the novel form (as, for example, in the braided codes of A.S. Byatt's *Babel Tower*), metafictional strategies in *The Paper Men* function as interpretative devices. One clue to this intent can be discovered in the explicit manipulation of those metafictional devices that highlight the acts of authorship and readership. What follows are ten passages whose appearance in various of the novel's chronological chapters casts shadows, each item outlining *The Paper Men*'s external scaffolding. Put another way, these passages function as locks, arresting the narrative's uninterrupted stream of discourse. At each of these junctures, narrator Barclay seems to be interrogating previous judgements or experiences. Furthermore, the narrator openly addresses an inscribed reader or 'narratee'[37]; as in, for example, the overt challenge to '*Please* see the joke!' (p. 128), or the interjection

'Yes, I know you'll have forgotten Johnny's dog' and the injunction
that follows to 'Look it up' (p. 129). What is most striking about these
passages is that there is a marked change in their stylistic protocols.
Unlike the enervated, doubly-oriented meandering that typifies the
jawing Barclay, the interlocutory voice is distinguished by its
stability, even reliability.

#1 [I]f I bothered to leaf through that pile of journals out there that I am
going to burn, I could tell you the hour as well as the date […] (p. 8).

#2 You could call it a faint, a distant awareness of Liz: and I see now that
I've written it down that it wasn't that at all (p. 27).

#3 This isn't going to be an account of my travels. I suppose it's mainly
about me and the Tuckers […] It's about more than that, though I can't
really say what, the words are too weak, even mine; and God knows, by
now they ought to be about as strong as most words can be (p. 60).

#4 I have just examined what remains of my journal for that year – one
of those journals so soon to perish in the holocaust – and find the date
unusually full (p. 61).

#5 This isn't a biography. I don't quite know what it is, since there are
enormous gaps where I don't remember what happened[…also] the
attempt to get some kind of coherence into this mass of paper, the months
after Lesbos and Johnny are patchy because of the state I was in (p. 117).

#6 Now I have to tell you about that island although I don't want to, it
still gives me the jitters […] As a matter of fact I've been screwing myself
up to do it for some time and I can't do it sober […] Oh I know in the
morning I'll be going down to the kitchen to count the empties with
no […] Rick to go through the dustbin […] He's probably wandering
about outside somewhere to keep an eye on me […] I can look straight
across the lawn from where I'm sitting to the woods on the other side
of the river or I would if I could but I am not able, it being about three
o'clock in some morning (p. 118).

#7 [S]o for my biography I mean our biography you can find the exact
place and date. (p. 126)

#8 I haven't the heart or courage to reread that lot. It was a bad time and the very memory tempts me to the bottle, which I am anxious to avoid (p. 128).

#9 It made me laugh at the time though not now of course, not after what has happened since and being where I am. There's the faintest light of dawn behind the woods across the river. Soon there'll be the dawn chorus though I shan't hear it over the clatter of this wretched machine (p. 129).

#10 Yesterday I reread [...] the whole thing from Rick at the dustbin down to [...Liz's] wake [...] Putting aside repetitions, verbals, slang, omissions, it's a fair record of the various times the clown's trousers fell down (p. 189).

My suggestion is that the voice zone inhabited here in the ten passages I have quoted is one whose neutrality ensures reliability, even authority. With the changed stylistic protocols, superficial literariness has been erased. Language no longer serves as the object of mimetic representation, but serves to comment diegetically. Linguistic markers (#s 2, 3, 5, 9) combine with the use of the preterit verb tense (#s 2, 4, 8, 9) to call to the narratee's attention (#s 1, 2, 6, 7) the act of writing (#s 2, 3, 5, 7, 9) as an event within the story. The act of reading is thematized too, for the narrator observes (#s 1, 4, 8, 10) that he has reread what he earlier wrote. Like the numbered chapters – sixteen in all – that cut and control the narrative flow, these interruptions break the narrative's forward impulse to mark the text's compositional processes. The question is who speaks here? The implied author as narrator? To whom does he speak? The implied reader as narratee? Can simple-minded narratee become enlightened reader? Can unreliable narrator become gesturing author?

Linking together the passages I have described above as neutrally zoned interjections, one finds that the text bearing the title *The Paper Men* is a rather different construction from what its intertextual and autobiographical calisthenics first seemed to suggest. The novel's scaffolding, like carapace to insinuating inner worm – to borrow two of the book's pervasive metaphors – erects as ongoing the act of composition by one paper man. The textual present turns out to be not Barclay's continuing account of his travels, as seemed the case while the flight narrative pushed forward in chronological time. Rather, the textual present is Barclay before his loud typewriter, the dawn's song of birds in the Wiltshire meadows unfurtively declaring the day's beginning. He is near completing a project he set himself just before he left Rome in response to Liz's death-bed letter that he return to England, the project being 'not a journal but more hippty-hop' (p. 162) like a book 'picking a story out of a mess' (p. 163). A textual past is the narrator's mimetic record of events during the ten years that make up the plot of the interleaved paper men's lives, including the trail of memories and stream of consciousness erasures that ensue. Textual present and textual past may be spliced together by setting the figures of author Barclay and critic Tucker – with their interlocked fates – beside one another as doubles; for indeed, each paper man functions as the other's alter ego. At one pole, Tucker 'represents the surfacing of all Barclay wants hidden from himself and the world'[38] while at the other, Barclay represents the life Tucker himself does not have and can only possess by acquiring Barclay's life. During the years of aborted effort to trap his subject in 'his lobster pot' (p. 36) and become the authorized biographer, Tucker leaves his university position, gives away his wife apparently to the benefactor, Halliday, and travels hither and thither in search of Barclayana. When Barclay stops fleeing and begins preying, hunted and hunter exchange places. Critic and author, tempter Mephistopheles and tempted Faust, hairy Esau and cunning Jacob, exchange roles with the crafty Barclay plotting how to steal his brother's birthright. If textual clues to this symbiotic doubling are as scattered as in any scavenger hunt, nevertheless they do direct the reader to puzzle over why Tucker and Barclay slowly come to adopt each other's accent, even exchanging words – hence, for example, the ping-pong play on 'acclimatize' and 'acclimate'. Another technique employed to depict the locked, but doubling battle between the two paper men consists in the exchange of dialogue, presented without the speech tags that would have identified which character had spoken, the narrative effect of which is to have the reader place the combatants side by side. A more substantial likeness, however, is that Tucker comes to be infected with paranoid delusions similar to those that propel Barclay, imagining he has seen Barclay in places never visited, waving a signed authorization paper, then disappearing; or telephoning and then hanging up. 'You and Rick have destroyed each other' (p. 175), instructs Liz towards *The Paper Men*'s conclusion. It is a judgement the text has earlier and horrifically dramatized in two separate, but interconnected, episodes.

A mark of Golding's fiction is its enactment of a humiliation ritual wherein an individual is reduced to that station one defines as scapegoat, an individual persecuted to ensure a terrified group's belief system. *The Paper Men* deploys this pattern, but with especially interesting revisions. First of all, there are two humiliation rituals and two scapegoats, debasement being inflicted upon each paper man by his double. Secondly, since the novel represents itself – unlike *The Inheritors* or *The Spire* – as a realistic contemporary text, it must have the rituals performed in modes appropriate to its secular context. Thus, a scapegoat is less a sacrificial victim than an object of irrational hostility whose degradation consists in being diminished, degraded, and brought downward, being reduced to either a lower stratum of the body or a lower stratum of existence. On balance, the secular world depicted in *The Paper Men* is seen as one governed by gravitational forces and materialist explanations. The earth is but a ball, balanced between forces and hurtling though space. Hence the novel's reiterative presentation of Barclay's terror, implicit whenever he travels by airplane. And explicitly in Sicily and Switzerland where the facts of nature – its 'ghastly indifference' (p. 89) to human security – seem not so much suspended as reinforced. Earthquakes, volcanoes, tidal waves, even a mundane (spinning) saucer remind Barclay of 'the crazy ball flying through space which, if you care to think of it is an enormity verging on, no surpassing outrage' (p. 120). His solipsistic construction of the godhead as universal indifference leads him back to Weisswald where he has arranged a meeting with Tucker in order to perform a 'theologically witty' (p. 130) rite of passage. The day before he and Tucker are to meet, Barclay returns to the cliff from which he had earlier fallen, and where he had been saved from destruction, his putative biographer grasping his collar. His furious discovery is that Tucker had orchestrated a humiliation in which it was he himself who was the scapegoated figure. For there was not the slightest possibility of loss of life, as Tucker knew: 'There, just under where I'd hung in fog, a meadow stretching away, with cows in it' (p. 135). Suddenly remembering Tucker's 'smile of triumph' that afternoon, Barclay knows himself to have been humiliated and emasculated, degraded to collared dog. Indeed, mastered by slavish critic.

In store, however, is a second theologically witty ritual, Barclay's humiliation of Tucker. In exchange for being granted permission to be the official biographer Tucker must give an account of acting the pander in offering Mary Lou to both Wilf and Halliday. 'In fact, the biography will be a duet, Rick. We'll show the world what we are – paper men, you can call us. How about that for a title?' (p. 152) observes the writer/narrator, thus inserting in the text the title of Golding's text. Object of Barclay's hatred, Tucker is metamorphosed into a beast. He is made to beg like a dog, bark 'yap yap' and lap up wine from a saucer. The malice-filled parodic phrase, 'Good dog, Rick, good dog!' (p. 150), finally goads Tucker into action; he hurls the saucer (which drives past Barclay to end spinning decorously on the floor), collapses into a chair, then bursts into wrenching tears as he slumps forward, a deflated and degraded servile scapegoat. Completed, the ritualized exorcism is Barclay's harrowing way of showing himself to be one of the predestinate damned. 'I turned my attention back to the intolerance and insolently interrogated it. *How's that?*' (p. 150).

V

The worm of conscience still begnaws thy soul.

Shakespeare, *Richard III,* V. *3*

[You] have spent your life inventing a skeleton on the outside. Like crabs and lobsters. That's terrible because the worms get inside [...] My advice [...] is to get rid of the armour, the exoskeleton, the carapace [...] You could try [...] religion, sex, adoption, good works [...] Start at the bottom with a dog (pp. 114–15).

The passage immediately above where Johnny St John John diagnoses Wilf Barclay's egotism represents the sole occasion when one is able to see the book's unreliable narrator from the outside and with any kind of clarity. Located in a chapter at the novel's very midpoint, the passage contains important clues for unwinding this tale's several twists. Among the many modes it engages, Golding's ninth novel is certainly a fabular construction as well, striving to make eruptive the stuff of the numinous. 'The first-person confession of an agnostic artist transformed by an unasked-for spiritual experience,' summarizes one critic,[39] that unasked-for experience being the atavistic encounter with forces before which self-sufficient egotism must collapse. A 'theologically witty' fable in itself, *The Paper Men* deals with experiences it suggests as spiritually real. Its project then becomes one that compellingly seduces the reader's willingness to unravel knots, so as to sew new significances. Plainly put, the reader must do the work the narrator omits, avoids, or evades, constructing what the narrator's limited perspective cannot provide.

As Christ's precursor, St John the Baptist, did before him, Johnny *St John* John bears a message, his admonition being that Barclay rid himself of carapace, lest the worms of self-loathing 'begnaw the soul'. Metaphorically speaking, Barclay has to turn his exoskeleton *outside in*. And he should start, Johnny's advice concludes, with a dog. Armored anew by faith in Hades – the hellish god he created in his own image – Barclay feels compelled to make life hellish for others, transforming his slave, the hairy Tucker, into a dog.

Reverse the word dog, the text insists. Turn it outside in, and it becomes god, a theologically witty window through which to see the religious vision of *The Paper Men*. Take, as example, Barclay's denial of the Italian Padre Pio's stigmata – 'My driving force was a passionate need for there *not* to be a miracle' (p. 20) – and turn this negation outside in. One then has an explanation for the four fiery stigmata on Barclay's hands and feet towards the novel's end when – it appears – the black holes of the desert nightmare no longer staunch the burning. The strategy of reversal decodes other enigmas, transforming – importantly – the inscrutable Halliday. Cast as a sinister Mammon supporting second-rate academics and described as being 'very fond of ladies' (p. 66), Halliday never appears. Not so much an absent presence as, for example, Forster's deft incarnation of Ruth Howard Wilcox during much of *Howard's End*, Halliday is present by way of perpetual absence. Thus the empty page to which Barclay turns when consulting *Who's Who in America* for Halliday's entry fills the paper man with dread about its '*dread*ful significance' (p. 159, my italics).

Seen from outside in, Halliday may well be Holiday, as in Holy Day,[40] in which case his presumed collection of beautiful women, which includes the transparently *love*ly Mary Lou, could be seen with other than lustful eyes and construed as a gathering together of holiness. 'Defeated by holiness,' Barclay recollects while gazing upon Mary Lou's beauty, 'the medieval illuminators stood their saints in a world of gold' (p. 62).[41] And Halliday's observation – reported by Mary Lou – that Barclay has 'no capacity for love' becomes a significant insight into what Barclay himself will have to turn outside in.

Just such a spiritual reversal occurs when Barclay (now in Rome) suffers a mystical experience that amounts to a complete reconfiguring of that confrontation with the ghastly statue, then shaped as symbol of intolerance. The Italian sequence begins with vague references – all the more significant for their obliqueness – to:

> Rome, no, not religious Rome but hotel Rome. You get to Piazza what's-it with the fountain in the little boat and then up the Steps and the hotel is at the top. There's a church up there too but [...] the hotel [is] far, far preferable (p. 158).

Barclay's disclaimer aside, this is 'religious Rome'. The Piazza di Spagna has at its centre the Barcaccia fountain, a religiously valent symbol, shaped like a half-sunken boat (metaphoric vessel for those who, like Christ, are fishers of men) fed by waters from an ancient aqueduct, the Acqua Vergine, or holy waters of the Virgin. In turn, the Spanish Steps sweep upward to the Trinita dei Monte church, beside which lies the Hassler-Villa Medici, the luxurious hotel whose regal balconies command views of both sacred and secular Rome. Conspicuous by their absence is any reference to the Keats Shelley Museum House towards which one end of the Barcaccia faces. That paper man Barclay does not quote from the two poets here, nor for that matter allude to either the Hotel Inghilterra or Babington's English tea room on the Via Condotti, suggests that the secular realm has now been jettisoned.

Seated on one such Hassler balcony, Barclay is provoked first by an apparent hallucination when he sees a figure that readers must take to be Halliday, positioned, like Johnny's 'One Above', on the Trinita dei Monte church. The awe-terrified Barclay then intones: 'and my God he was standing on the top' (p. 160). Attentive readers, who note the omission of parenthetical commas in Barclay's statement, will be rewarded with the text's intention.[42] What follows occurs in a state described as 'more than a dream and more than being awake' (p. 160) where he joins Halliday; the two descended the Spanish Steps:

> [A]nd stood among the people with the patterns of jewels and the heaps of flowers all blazing inside and out with the radiance [...] They held hands and moved and the movement was music. I saw they were neither male nor female or perhaps they were both [...] What mattered was the music they made. Male and female was of no importance for me, he said, taking me by the hand and leading me [...to] a dark, calm sea (p. 161).[43]

The indeterminacy of the narrator's statement here – 'You could say that I dreamed' (p. 160) – enacts the passage's theme: interdependence. 'In this epic vision,' the critic Franz Wohrer has argued, 'Halliday eventually assumes the role of a spiritual guide to the gates of Heaven, bestowing on Barclay literally the gift of a Holy-Day.'[44] But Barclay's climax of insight is reached when his atomized individuality comes to be worn away, abraded to *extra*-linguistic coherence: 'For the singing and the song I have no words at all' (p. 161). In the search for ways to communicate ineffable reality, several strategies are employed. These include the merging of sensory images of music and light; the use of the subjunctive; the depiction of anonymous and androgynous creatures dancing; and the embedding of, as Wohrer has glossed, text from *Revelation* 5.9: 'And they sung a new song, saying, Thou art worthy to take the book and to open the seals thereof.' But on awakening Barclay simply uses the term 'asisness, *Istigkeit*' (p. 161)[45] to describe the *extra*-linguistic knowledge that has been burned through. Involuntarily, happiness descends. Barclay's newly attained awareness reveals that flight is no longer needed: the direction he faces, assuredly narrow, is assured.

Never reluctant to instruct through teasing intertextuality, Golding has Barclay amplify the *Istigkeit* nature of being mortal by the following cryptic aside: 'how it is to be human though a, quote, mere fish but queer fish, unquote' (p. 161–62). By now so familiar with Wilf Barclay's doubly-oriented stylistics, one might well disregard the ambiguous, incomplete phrase as more paper-posturing; attentive readers, however, are rewarded again. Turning back to the book's central chapter where the narrator can be seen from outside in, one discovers – Golding's text forcing this decoding – that the mildly entertaining doggerel Johnny St John John had published in the *TLS* has meaning beyond the first representation in the text, where its *double entendre* seemed one more example of homosexual camp:

> For man is a funniful fish, a mere fish but a queer fish, a holy roly poly fish, very particular where his milt (the queerest flesh of the fish) is spilt (p. 115).

Much more than mere mannered frivolity, the verse is a device through which the novel's eschatological thematic is obliquely wedged. Adopting the narrative strategy of reversal, the technique by which Golding's text has insinuated notions of the spiritual, Johnny's poem permits interpretation in a decidedly different mode from that artful wordplay suggested by his description of the piece as a *jeu d'esprit* (p. 115). Genuinely a *jeu d'esprit*, its play with spirit images man as strange, holy inhabitant of water, whose joy becomes paradoxically greatest when splenetic sources of terror are blasted/split asunder. Elusive and maddingly indirect as it is, the text's play here depends upon referential use of the most traditional of Christian symbology. Water is a cleansing and tributary element; the fish a constant symbol of Christ – the five Greek letters forming the word 'fish' being the initial letters of those five words: 'Jesus Christ God's Son Saviour'.[46] Just as fish cannot live except in water, the true Christian soul cannot live but through the waters of baptism. Johnny St John John had preached a secularized admonition on this theme to Barclay when instructing his friend that he should try some way to have his (dipso-psycho) sense of sin remitted. Without question, *The Paper Men*'s text has come to shudder forward, engaging the reader in its final quietus.

VI

In the midst of life, we are in death.

Office of the Burial of the Dead

Even by Golding's exemplary models, the coda to *The Paper Men* is hugely daring. For the novel's final line – 'How the devil did Rick L. Tucker manage to get hold of a gu' (p. 191) – makes us reconsider all that has gone before. *The Paper Men*, we discover, is not the unmediated confession of the life story of Wilf Barclay. It is a soon to be deceased man's retrospective record of the last fifteen years of his life, the composition of which, the neutral zoned interjections have allowed us haltingly to realize, he began on his return to England in his sixty-fifth year. It is also a composition that ends, with the closing of Barclay's story in his sixty-fifth year at the hand of his putative biographer, the *rifling* badger of the novel's first page. Hunter and hunted have exchanged places, the air gun of the first episode becoming the Bisley rifle of the last.[47] Critic Tucker certainly gets author Barclay's life, shooting dead a hitherto moving target. And Barclay owes Tucker his life in more ways than one. Appropriate to the intertextual issues characterizing its paper world, the book's conclusion marks a metafictional way of ending the novel, Golding creating an open rather than closed ending. His narrator is stopped in mid-word. Verifiably and physically dead at the book's conclusion, Wilf Barclay's spiritual future remains ambiguous. And Tucker? Since he 'only exists for us in the writing', one commentator argues that this paper man also vanishes. 'The text is therefore doomed always to incompletion because it always leads up to Tucker's pulling the trigger. We can describe *The Paper Men* as being an account of its own incompletion'.[48] A similar assurance informs another reading of the text's conclusion, one which states that the 'last word [...] goes to the author, but this last word is cut off, truncated, by the interpolation of the critic, and the author's final word is forever incomplete, forever amenable to interpretation'.[49]

Most critics, however, have felt at best uncertainty. Variously 'baffled, confused and disappointed', many share one assessment that Barclay remains 'fixed in a state of being in which even encounters with the Divine seem unable to alter his nature or direction'.[50] How else explain Barclay's egregious actions back in England where he leaves his wife to die alone, later to boast at her funeral about his stigmata: 'Four of the five wounds of Christ. Four down and one to go' (p. 188). Above all there is the seeming sadistic treatment of Tucker, the latter now a mad dog: literally, for at their random encounter Rick is squatting on the floor, grinning – his tongue lapped forward – and barking. Later, on hearing Wilf remark, 'You're not going to write that particular biography. I'm going to write it myself' (p. 182) Tucker howls, bays, then bites the betraying biographee's ankle. And Barclay? He continues on in quiet happiness, still embraced by his beatific vision of *Istigkeit* in Rome.

'Golding contrives [...] a denouement that renders the eschatological issue permanently inconclusive,' one critic determines,[51] while another argues that the novel, 'though eschatological, does not encourage us to look well to that last end which we must all face but rather shows us that heaven and hell are states we can create here and now within ourselves'.[52] As always, the reader must fill in gaps, constructing textual intentions. My own sense – by way of the text's neutrally zoned stylistics which foreground the compositional act – is that *The Paper Men*'s exoskeletal purpose is one that erases any bargaining or contest between ostensible oppositions: author and critic; narrator and narratee; present and future; matter and spirit; death-in-life and life-in-death. Barclay's premeditated present to Tucker represents what the narrator describes as an '*uncovenanted* mercy' (p. 190, my italics) precisely because such exchange would have no terms attached.

Handing over to Tucker what neutral zoned passage #7 called 'my biography I mean our biography' (p. 126), Barclay's gift of his freshly composed, uncensored life-record would be an act of free will. Its donation would amount to an experiencing of spiritual freedom, as the novel's penultimate page indicates. Shortly to set fire to 'the paperweight of a whole life', all the 'unnecessary correspondence, reviews, theses, financial statements, manuscripts, interlinears, proofs' (p. 190), Barclay writes he will give Rick:

> [T]his small sheaf of papers, all that is necessary, all that will be left, all that means anything to set over against the lying stories, the partial journals and all the rest. It will be a kind of dying. Freedom [...] (p. 190).

'A kind of dying. Freedom'; the suspiciously direct emphasis here prompts a re-examination of the post-visionary moment in Rome when it is determined Barclay must embark upon this writing enterprise. The indeterminacy of narrator identity is important here: 'I saw that...there was still a book that *I or someone* had to write, not a journal but more hippty-hop' (p. 162, my italics). It matches an equally significant indeterminacy of narratee identity: 'Then I'd consider the book I had to write, picking a story out of a mess. I'd consider its *recipient* and think how my feet and hands would stop hurting when I finished writing' (p. 163, my italics). Golding, of course, wants his readers to work to intuit matters, among them that these identities participate in that state that many years earlier Golding had called 'original spirit' as in '*Scintillans Dei*'. Seen from this perspective, the 'hippty-hop' story is gospel truth, hence Wilfred Townsend Barclay's gospel of good truth. Shedding carapace, and turned outside in by 'someone' who writes the good news, Barclay reaches out towards a 'recipient', someone with power enough to stem pain. It is Barclay's intention to relieve Tucker, since 'I have it in my power and what is more in my purpose to heal him' (p. 189), at which point what can well be construed as timely death intervenes. Just as he prepares to show compassion, acting thus from his god-given capacity as unskeletoned, funniful, holy fish – he who bears the Christ in him – Barclay is made to meet his end. He receives the last of the five identifying stigmata born by Christ as a gunshot wound. In the fable's religious eschatology, the verso of Intolerance has been turned outside in to the recto of mercy as a willing Wilfred (Will-freed) is helped into heaven.

And Rick Tucker? If a man as morally mutilated as Barclay can be saved from eternal damnation then his mirroring double might well be provided with the means by which to earn his end. Textual evidence – albeit distorted by Barclay's recording eye – has already shown Tucker's sensitivity to beauty, the novel's symbol for purity, sanctity, and holiness. Twice he is shown weeping, Barclay linking the drops of water to 'Virgin tears?' while musing, 'Probably in magic there was great virtue in such drops' (p. 153).[53] Most importantly, it is through Tucker's receptivity to sound – the novel's symbol throughout for music with its implied holiness – that one of the metaphoric doors to the fable's vision of the cosmos as interdependent/indivisible is opened. When, during the Weiswald walk, Tucker makes Barclay listen to a single stream's two voices, Barclay hears 'cheerful babble' and 'deep meditative hum'. The former represents 'a kind of frivolity as if the thing [...] enjoyed its bounding passage downward through space' while below this surface the latter 'sounded from some deep secret of the mountain itself' (p. 83). Generally, critics have interpreted the passage to represent what they take to be The Paper Men's two-level plot: 'Beneath the social parody...there is also, as always in Golding, a metaphysical level.'[54] A closer scrutiny of the complex symbol, however, disallows a simple binary separation of the two voices. First, each voice is named 'the thing'; it meditatively hums from the mountain at the same time as it sings its own cheer. That their entanglement is inextricable can also be apprehended by linking the first voice's shaped sound of 'bounding [...] through space' to the several images of the balled cosmos flying, supported only by gravitational forces. For nature here is no indifferent terror, sustained as it is by 'the deep secret of the mountain', the stream's second voice. To link, in turn, (the first voice's) shaped sound of 'frivolity' – its boundless joy in its bounding – to day-to-day happiness is to apprehend the diurnal joy that Istigkeit bestows.[55] 'I don't think there's a scientific explanation though if you're a scientist you may cook one up and if you've kept up your religion you may cook one up but hell I'm not dealing with fatuous abstraction like religion or science I'm dealing with life I tell you and asisness' (p. 161), as an impatient Barclay expostulates, much later on.

Revisiting that Swiss scene, one begins to hear many of the corded leitmotifs that have already come to represent the spiritual realm orchestrated once again.[56] Several suggest that Tucker possesses 'a divided nature' (p. 84), although Barclay dismisses the possibility that Tucker is anything but 'physical'.[57] Warning about the volatility of mountains, Tucker remarks, 'There's no knowing what might be going on *up above*', as in Johnny's the One Above. Listening to the rushing water with its double voice, Tucker observes, 'Isn't there something real queer about the sound' (p. 83), as in Johnny's queer fish. Describing the delight he experiences on listening to water and rook and to 'no noise, though that's rare nowadays [...] positive no noise,' he calls the quiet happiness 'just how living is' (p. 84), as in Barclay's *Istigkeit*. So even by Golding's exemplary models, *The Paper Men*'s shift of viewpoint on all that has preceeded is also hugely daring, it being the reader alone who – by seeing Tucker from a viewpoint other than Barclay's – constructs the second perspective on the novel's events.

If 'the wound Barclay is[...]a mark of salvation,'[58] what then of Tucker's final plight? I think the text, with its deliberate underscoring of the double nature of the two men's lives and its pointed balancing of the two men's names offers the reader its outside in reversal of the nature of ultimate things:

> Who knows? With intolerance backed right out of the light there is room for an uncovenanted mercy like the one that drives me to give Rick these papers: a mercy by which those unsatisfactory phenomena, Wilfred Townsend Barclay and Richard Linbergh Tucker, may be eternally destroyed (p. 191).

'Is this what keeps me happy?' wonders Barclay, the reader now assigned the grave task of writing Tucker's future.

Endnotes

1   Jacques Derrida, *The Truth in Painting*, Geoffrey Bennington and Ian McLeod (trans.), Chicago, University of Chicago Press, 1978, p. 69.

2   S.H. Boyd, *The Novels of William Golding*, New York, St Martin's Press, 1988, p. 182; David Lodge, 'Life Between Covers', *The New Republic* (August 16, 1984), p. 34.

3   I am indebted here to David Lodge's observation that 'Both Barclay and Tucker are "paper men" not only in the metonymic sense that they live off and by paper (in the form of books, manuscripts, letters,

etc.) but also in the metaphorical sense of being two-dimensional, incomplete human beings' (Lodge, ibid., p. 34). The distinction Lodge drew prompted my own structural analysis of the text's paradoxes and problematics.

4   Derwent May, 'A Spate of Sneers', *The Listener* (February 9, 1984), p. 23.

5   Eva Figes, 'All that Glitters' *New Statesman* (February 10, 1984), p. 23.

6   The Swedish Academy announced the award in October 1983; Faber and Faber published the novel some four months later.

7   Established in 1969, The Booker Prize changed from marking a modest success into 'the making of a myth', writes Martyn Goff, 'in 1980, the year in which William Golding won by a hair's breadth with *Rites of Passage* from Anthony Burgess' *Earthly Powers*. Whether it was the sense of two giants battling against each other [...] there is little doubt that the contest started to matter not just to literary circles, but to a huge number of ordinary readers' (Introduction, *Prize Writing: An Original Collection of Writings by Past Winners to Celebrate 21 Years of the Booker Prize*, London, Hodder & Stoughton, 1989, pp. 12–13).

8   Auberon Waugh, 'Wrap Up *The Paper Men* and Freeze It', *Daily Mail* (February 9, 1984), p. 7.

9   E. C. Bufkin, 'The Nobel Prize and the Paper Men: The Fixing of William Golding', *Georgia Review* 39 (1985), p. 64.

10 There are other self-referential threads; as one of many *poste restante* the itinerate Barclay is given the address 'The Confederate Hotel, Roanoke VA' (p. 98), an address amounting to an insider's joke since Golding spent one witless year as Hollins College's 1961–62 writer-in-residence in the then still patrician state of Virginia. And Barclay's 'quaint old house' (p. 43), which Rick Tucker, the would-be Barclay biographer, so admires for its *echt-* English atmosphere – surrounded as it is by water meadows and the Wiltshire Downs with their chalk White

Horses – resembles the thatched cottage in Bowerchalke near Salisbury where the Golding family lived for many years. Having spent time at their Bowerchalke home as a weekend guest, I recognize the fictionalized 'cottagey' (p. 173) guest room that Golding provides for his narrator's return to his Wiltshire house. The watery watercress meadows described in the novel are also autobiographical play; Mrs Golding's instructions to guests included the directive that one should find Ebble Thatch close to the cress beds.

11 Kevin McCarron, *The Coincidence of Opposites: William Golding's Later Fiction*, Sheffield, Sheffield Academic Press, 1995, p. 146. One can take issue with McCarron's understatement that Golding's misogynist remark in his essay 'The Glass Door' is 'a rather sweeping statement'. Golding's generalization is patronizing, at best. And while a male narrator like Barclay may be permitted the sexist perspective of a man reporting on female behavior, a male essayist may not so easily be allowed such stereotypical lenses.

12 A convincing case for reading (at one level) *The Paper Men* as a satire is made by Bufkin, who traces the techniques of satire present in the novel: low farce, verbal and physical vulgarity and animality, digressive plot, repellent characterization. 'Thus as the satirist writing out of disgust and indignation [Golding] will effect a change through the humor of exaggeration (farce) and boisterous laughter (low comedy), using the satirist's stratagem to attain the moralist's goal of correction for the sake of the good – or at least the better.' (Bufkin, op. cit., pp. 64–65).

13 Eric Partridge, *A Dictionary of Slang and Unconventional English*, vol. II, 1931, reprinted London, Routledge & Kegan Paul Ltd, 1970, p. 1511.

14 Once again, this contains an insider's joke: Golding found the American pronunciation of the University of Berkeley – much in the news during the student demonstrations in California in the 1960s as the University of 'Burkely' – comically resonant. Every Englishman knew the correct pronunciation of Bishop Berkeley's name was Bishop 'Barclay'.

15 Blake Morrison, 'In Death as in the Life', *Times Literary Supplement* (March 2, 1984), p. 215. Other names are given satiric twist. Two habitués of the Random Club's secular world of paper-worship – the Random being a writer's club – bear the names of holy saints; there is a Gabriel, whose talk hardly announces a miraculous birth. And the homosexual poet, Johnny St John John, although no forerunner of Christ, does appear to know about a force beyond material being: 'One Above' (p. 115).

16 Autobiography intrudes again; as early as 1966 Golding described 'William Golding, author' to me as 'the guy, the paper model, the man that never was'.

17 Partridge, pp. 27–28. One such badger is the 'varmit' Pip Pirrip meets (the boy hanging, perforce, upside down – inverted, like his palindromic name) in *Great Expectations'* first chapter; it is unlikely Golding would not have been familiar with this cultural/literary naming.

18 Barclay's exasperation and amusement with things American and academic here amount not so much to a parochial jibe as a derisory one. 'Rick and his wife are [...] walking, talking clichés, embodiments of a certain *de haut en bas* English view of the backwoods of American academia' in Boyd's view (op. cit., p. 186).

19 James Gindin, 'The Historical Imagination in William Golding's Later Fiction' in James Acheson (ed.), *The British and Irish Novel Since 1960*, New York, St Martin's Press, 1991, p. 115.

20 'Barclay peppers his narrative with references and allusions that send the critic scurrying to dictionaries of quotations,' writes Boyd, one such critic himself. As he explains, a partial quotation intoned by Tucker – '"Two voices are there, one is of the deep..."' – comes from the English light versifier J. K. Stephen, who wrote: 'Two voices are there: one is of the deep [...]/[...] and one is of an old half-witted sheep/Which bleats articulate monotony [...]/[...] And, Wordsworth, both are thine' (Boyd, op. cit., pp. 187–88). Stephen's verse is itself a pastiche of Wordsworth, of course. A further explication is offered when McCarron adds: 'the

issue is more complex; for the lines that J.K. Stephen parodies are a paraphrase of those that open Wordsworth's "Thoughts of a Briton on the Subjugation of Switzerland". Given that Switzerland is where the [Tucker/Barclay] incident is taking place [...] further parodic potential is contained within this title [...since] at this point *The Paper Men* is depicting the thoughts of a Briton who is himself being subjugated *in* Switzerland' (McCarron, op. cit., p. 166). It may not be wholly uncharitable to observe that this particular chase illustrates the rummaging the novel ridicules, what I would call a paradigmatic search and destroy mission.

21   This is another allusion, one amounting to a cultivated joke since Plato banished poets from the Republic because the skilled depictions of imperfect persons could have deleterious moral effects.

22   Boyd, op. cit., p. 184.

23   Mikhail Bakhtin, *Readings in Russian Poetics: Formalist and Structuralist Views*, Ladislav Matejka & Krystyna Pomorska (eds), Cambridge, MIT Press, 1979, p. 155.

24   Boyd, op. cit., p. 184.

25   David Lodge, *After Bakhtin: Essays on Fiction and Criticism*, London, Routledge, 1990, p. 33.

26   Mikhail Bakhtin, *Rabelais and His World*, Helene Iswolsky (trans.), Bloomington, Indiana University Press, 1984, p. 55.

27   Bakhtin, ibid., p. 38.

28   Linda Hutcheon, *A Theory of Parody*, New York, Methuen, 1985, p. 21.

29   Donald W. Crompton, *A View From the Spire: William Golding's Later Novels*, edited and completed by Julia Briggs, Oxford, Blackwell, 1985, p. 163.

30   James Lasdun, 'Bridges and Gods', *Encounter* (May 15, 1984), p. 65.

31   Sebastian Faulks, 'In Pursuit of a Subject', *Books and Bookmen* (February 1984), p. 21.

32   Frank Kermode, 'Superplot', *London Review of Books* (March 1, 1984), p. 15.

33   The island is unnamed, but embedded references suggest it is Lipari off Sicily's northern coast. See here Crompton and Briggs, op. cit., p. 176; Nadia D'Amelio, 'No Inheritors in *The Paper Men*' in Jeanne Delbaere (ed.), *William Golding: The Sound of Silence*, Liège, English Department of the University of Liège, 1991 p. 189; Jeanne Delbaere-Garant, 'The Artist as Clown of God: Golding's *The Paper Men*', Delbaere, ibid., p. 173. That the volcanic Lipari islands, Lemnos, once contained the ancient seat of the worship of Haphaestus, the god of fire and the forge, should not go un-remarked here. On Lemnos, a jet of natural asphaltic gas issued from Mount Moschylus, burning so steadily for so many centuries that it was still there during Alexander the Great's reign.

34   Faulks, op. cit., p. 21.

35   McCarron, op. cit., p. 184.

36   Golding's habit of recasting literary models seems once again present, in the view of several critics who amplify the Marlowe quotation by seeing the entire drama as the moral spine to which *The Paper Men* relates by way of repudiation. First suggested by Crompton and Briggs ('[T]hough Barclay echoes [...] Marlowe's Mephistopheles, his role in the fable is rather that of Faustus, and it is Halliday's agent Rick Tucker who has been cast as Mephistopheles' (op. cit., p. 166)), both James Gindin, *William Golding*, New York, St Martin's Press, 1988, p. 82 and Philip Redpath, *William Golding: A Structural Reading of His Fiction*, London, Vision Press Ltd, 1986, p. 193 adopt and endorse the gloss in their discussions. McCarron ingeniously argues that the tempted figure in Golding's work is given the tempter's line from Marlowe 'to break down the antithesis between the creative artist and the critic', a project he sees as central to the novel (p. 150). Despite the fact that both works

present a false Helen as agent in trying to tempt a Faustian figure into signing a pact, my own view is that *The Paper Men* does not structure itself upon one literary text. The significance of the embedded Marlowe line rests on its naming – as a paper man like Barclay would need to so inscribe – what it is to live a living hell.

37 Gerald Prince, 'On Readers and Listeners in Narrative', *Neophilgus* 55 (1971), pp. 117–22.

38 Redpath, op. cit., p. 188.

39 Jeanne Delbaere-Garant, 'Describing the Indescribable: The "Things of God" in Golding's Fiction', in Ortwin De Graef *et al*, eds, *Sense and Transcendence: Essays in Honour of Herman Servotte*, Leuven University Press, 1995, p. 134.

40 Although I arrived at this identification independently, Crompton and Briggs (p. 172) have also made this point.

41 Reiteratively, Barclay and Tucker, Tucker and Barclay declare that May Lou 'isn't physical'. To read outside in once again is to comprehend that Mary Lou *is* spiritual, as are 'purity, sanctity, holiness, beauty incomparable' (p. 109), all words used to describe her.

42 Barclay has already had some intimations concerning Halliday/Holiday/Holy Day, although characteristically he resists. When he and Tucker talked earlier about Halliday, Barclay ruminated: 'The lord giveth and the lord taketh away, cursed [*sic*] be the name of him whatever one he chooses' (146), thus deliberately inverting the phrase, 'Blessed be the name of the Lord'.

43 The 'more than a dream and more than being awake' had an autobiographical source some thirteen years before the publication of *The Paper Men*. Golding began the first of his journals with a character 'Dream Ego' in 1971, having had in sleep an emancipatory vision of a singer descending the Spanish Steps into darkness.

44 Franz Wohrer, '"Face to face with the indescribable, the inexplicable, the isness": Intimate Relationships with the Divine in *The Paper Men*', in Regard (ed.), op. cit., p. 169. Wohrer's essay, an exhaustive exegesis of Golding's use of the Christian mystical tradition, argues that 'the mystics referred or alluded to in the novel [...] include St Francis of Assisi, Meister Eckhart, Julian of Norwich, John of the Cross, the *Cloud*-Author and St Augustine' (p. 152).

45 Wohrer explains the term *Istigkeit* '(more accurately, "*Istikeit*"/"*Isticheit*") as the historical spelling of the original Middle High German'. It is a theological concept whose derivation comes from the 'Rhineland mystic Meister Eckhart [1280–c.1328] and refers to "the essence of life or being" which, in essence, [is] the same as the essence of God' (ibid., pp. 171–72).

46 My association that follows here may well be one the Golding text does not encode. However, I am struck by the Old Testament Apocrypha concerning Tobias, whose father, suffering from severe affliction of the eyes, sends his son in flight and movement accompanied by a faithful dog through a desert. An Archangel accompanies them and when a fish leaps out, ready to be devoured, Tobias is advised to save the heart, liver, and gall. The gall, a possible synonym for *The Paper Men*'s Johnny St John John's poetic 'milt', restores sight. 'As for gall, it is good to anoint a man that hath whiteness in his eyes, and he shall be healed,' the sacred text advises, bringing one up again against *The Paper Men*'s (probable) project of redemptive vision.

47 Textual evidence that the reader must assemble indicates that Tucker (who stayed in the Wiltshire guest room) stole the Bisley gun, so named for the Bisley Surrey shooting competitions of the National Rifle Association. Liz tells Wilf that her former husband, a game hunter, had 'scarpered' when her cancer began to 'gallop'. 'Left everything and ran, even left his Bisley gun and his big game books' (p. 169). Later, Barclay sees on the guest room mantelpiece the game books. 'Above them a horizontal shape of unfaded wallpaper showed where he had hung his "bisley" gun' (p. 173).

48   Redpath, op. cit., p. 190.

49   McCarron, op. cit., p. 193.

50   Crompton, op. cit., p. 174. One critic is outright in condemnation of the novel's ending: 'The conclusion, which looks more like a trial ending than a real denouement, is pathetic rather than tragic' (V.V. Subbarao, *William Golding: A Study*, New York, Envoy Press, 1987, p. 130).

51   Lawrence S. Friedman, *William Golding*, New York: Continuum, 1993, p. 169.

52   Boyd, p. 199.

53   For Christian mystics and the tradition of *'charisma lacrimarum* [...] tears are clearly tokens of grace', as Wohrer explains (p. 170), although in another context, since Wohrer was examining Barclay's weeping in Rome and not Barclay's thoughts about Tucker's tears in Switzerland. My sense is that the reader is intended to accept as significant the clue about Tucker that Barclay's egotism prevents him from following here.

54   Jeanne Delbaere-Garant, op. cit., p.16. See as well Kermode (op. cit., p. 15), and Redpath's discussion: 'The first voice [...] is surface existence, the daily life we lead [...] Beneath this is the meaning behind [...] the "deep secret", and in *The Paper Men* this is a meta-physical question of being, or, as Barclay calls it, of "isness"' (p. 183).

55   On his return to the Swiss mountainscape, Barclay hears 'only one voice', and 'this was the light, babbling one' (p. 135), his binary division here symbolizing one individual's state of spiritual negation. Barclay's negation is to make from a whole a diminished part. Having returned from the Lipardi confrontation, the cosmos for Barclay is intolerant and terrorizing, sustaining of mana only by the *via negativa*. Hence Tucker's thrown and rolling (flying) saucer is for Barclay an image of terror. And babble can be the stream's only sound.

56 'Thy life's a miracle,' exclaims Edgar to the blind Gloucester, who has been led to believe that he has fallen from a cliff at Dover, yet still survived death. Clearly Golding wants readers to review the first Swiss scene, seeing in it the allusion to *King Lear*.

57 Compare Tucker's comment to Barclay, 'I know how I must seem to you, sir. Just another sincere but limited academic' (p. 83) to Johnny's rebarbative – and parallel – statement, 'you think I'm an ageing queer in your categorizing way, and of course I am, among other things' (p. 115). Both statements say something important about Barclay's limited perception, as we see when we adopt the text's strategy of reversal.

58 Irene Simon, 'Vision or Dream? The Supernatural Design in William Golding's *The Paper Men*', in Jeanne Delbaere (ed.), *William Golding: The Sound of Silence*, Liège, English Department University of Liège, 1991, p. 185.

Rites of Passage

I

British seamen have long and justly been esteemed for a disinterested generosity toward others in distress.

Robert Finlayson,
An Essay addressed to Captains of the Royal Navy, 1824

Rites of Passage, borrowing its title from Arnold Van Gennep's classic study of initiation rituals,[1] plunges the reader into the Napoleonic era, just as the splendor of the spacious days of His Majesty's Royal Navy had begun to change. Lord Horatio Nelson, its heralded hero, now lay buried in St Paul's Cathedral with the nation's triumphant ship, *The Victory*, dry-docked in Portsmouth harbour. We readers are aboard a converted British warship whose passengers are bound for Australia, long the dumping-ground for criminals, bankrupts, and assorted undesirables. Stories set on ships at sea traditionally permit a host of literary associations, including those already present in Alexander Barclay's *Shyp of Folys* (1509), where the ship itself becomes a cautionary tale of good and bad government and the hard task of piloting a precarious society – both temporal and spiritual – through the shoals, rocks, wrecks, and storms of life. By locating his ship's sea voyage in the early nineteenth century – with its pervasive themes of hierarchical rank, social privilege, snobbery, true and sham gentility – Golding was able to investigate such subjects as justice, moral responsibility, the uses and abuses of authority, and social class.[2] The stratified world of his ship serves as a social microcosm, encapsulating as it does a whole society.

In *Rites of Passage* the ancient wooden vessel, constructed apparently long before the iron ballast frigates of the 1790s, carries in its stinking hull cargo, guns, animals, emigrants, and the shipmen of the fo'castle, including a shadowy purser who gives truth to Pepys' comment that 'a purser would not have twice what he got unless he cheated'. Commanding the quarterdeck at the other end of the vessel is the ship's absolute ruler, Captain Anderson, barking orders to his standing officers: Cumbershum, Deverel, and Summers. In the cabins of the.

privileged reside Mr Prettiman, a marine lithographer, claiming to have been the first in his field to portray the hero Nelson's death at Trafalgar,[3] and referred to as a 'notorious free thinker' (p. 93) and the caustic governess, Miss Granham, to whom he will become betrothed. Most significantly, aboard this 'wooden world' (p. 6) are the two characters whose respective journals will supplement each other to constitute the narrative of *Rites of Passage*: Reverend James Colley, a Church of England parson whose sad servility suggests he is very much the promoted peasant still, and – from the higher echelons of society – Mr Edmund Talbot, godson to the titled brother of the governor of Van Diemen's Land, Britain's colony in the South Pacific.

Golding first gives us Talbot's sea journal to his influential godfather through whom he has secured an administrative post in Van Diemen's Land. The journal smacks of obsequious flattery and confident ambition: 'You have set my foot on the ladder and however high I climb [...]I shall never forget whose kindly hand first helped me upwards. That he may never be found unworthy of that hand, nor *do* anything unworthy of it – is the prayer – the intention of your lordship's grateful godson' (p. 10).

Talbot, like Lord Chesterfield's son, is learning the patrician art of pleasing prettily for a purpose.[4] The complacent, fastidious, patronising, and utterly class-bound Talbot's awareness of his social rank combines with his sturdy vanity to assure him that the entire 'floating society' (p. 144) owes him homage. His voyage from England to the Antipodes, those rocky uninhabited South Pacific islands so named because they are as far south as Greenwich is north of the equator, is Talbot's initiation – both moral and geographical – into the underbelly of a hemisphere.

For all this, *Rites of Passage* is a funny book. Golding makes good his satiric intention to castigate social snobberies and vices in the manner of the picaresque voyages of Defoe, Fielding, Swift, and Smollett. His novel, like Sterne's account of his travels through France, parodies the voyage literature of that period, which tiresomely gives us so many of the unvarnished facts and so little of the living spirit of the journey. Clearly, Sterne's *Tristram Shandy* exerts an appealing influence on Golding, for Talbot, like Tristram, is both chronically indisposed and, when it comes to the art of storytelling, chronically self-conscious:

Good God! Look at the time! If I am not more able to choose what I say I shall find myself describing the day before yesterday rather than writing about today for you tonight! For throughout the day I have walked, talked, eaten, drunk, explored – and here I am again, kept out of my bunk by the – I must confess – agreeable invitation of the page! I find that writing is like drinking. A man must learn to control it (p. 29).

Eager though Talbot may be to write like 'lively Fielding and Smollett', rather than 'sentimental Goldsmith or Richardson' (p. 3), his journal – in its sudden starts and stops – echoes Tristram's digressive narrative: a resemblance which the Oxford-trained Talbot himself is quick to see. 'I wrote that yesterday,' Talbot scribbles to his godfather in reference to a brief, breathy complaint about his colic of the day before. 'My entries are becoming short as some of Mr Sterne's chapters!' (p. 72). Golding even mocks Sterne's famous chapter headings: Talbot, in an unsuccessful attempt to number his journal entries, scrawls Alpha, Omega, Beta, Gamma. And the hobby-horse upon which Talbot gallops full tilt is his absorption in the nautical tactics and language of the Tarpaulin, which he studies assiduously in his copy of William Falconer's *Universal Dictionary of the Marine*, a 1769 source book for the technical terms and phrases of the ship. Although he can little understand how ironic this entry will prove to be, Talbot notes early in his journal:

Summers is to explain the main parts of the rigging to me. I intend to surprise him with a landsman's knowledge – most collected out of books he has never heard of! I also intend to please your lordship with some choice bits of Tarpaulin language for I begin [...] to speak Tarpaulin! What a pity this noble vehicle of expression has so small a literature! (p. 74).

If Tarpaulin is the ship's language of trade, then Talbot's developing linguistic competence becomes one more feather in the cap of his abundant class confidence.[5] Convinced as he is of his birth's worthiness and his rank's right either to dismiss outright or condescend to social inferiors, he begins the voyage with no qualms about exhibiting his consequence. Demanding from his servant, the 'walking Falconer' Wheeler, an unusual degree of attention and many draughts of paregoric, he provokes Miss Granham's admission that she, the daughter of the late canon of Exeter Cathedral, was been obliged by distressed circumstances to take up the governess trade. He then cheerfully dismisses Lieutenant Summers' meritorious rise from the lower ranks with the patronizing remark, 'Allow me to congratulate you on imitating to perfection the manners and speech of a somewhat higher station in life than the one you was born to' (p. 51). In an early caricature of the Reverend Mr Robert James Colley, Talbot invokes his version of Aristotle's dictum that there is a natural order to which men belong by virtue of their physique. The parson's 'skimped and jagged' countenance recalls that of a peasant. By dint of some meretricious patronage, judges Edmund, himself the not unhappy recipient of patronage, Colley has been elevated beyond his station: 'Indeed, his schooling should have been the open fields, with stone-collecting and bird scaring, his university the plough' (p. 67). Patronage, patronized, patronizing: Talbot has a complacent, albeit youthful, confidence in the infinitesimal gradations of class distinctions that will come to be tested by the journey's events, events that will propel an inner journey from snobbery to partial enlightenment. Indeed, 'it is a very Austen-like ironic education, learning to detect the person beneath the social exterior, that Talbot undergoes.'[6] Never achieving the insight reached, for example, by Elisabeth Bennet when the heroine of *Pride and Prejudice* exclaims, 'Till this moment, I never knew myself', the hero of *Rites of Passage* learns – like another Austen heroine, *Persuasion*'s Anne Elliot – to distinguish between social worth and social station. True to the generic demands of the *Bildungsroman*, where it is required of either heroine or hero that a philosophy of life should begin to be learned, Edmund Talbot's growth to maturity involves being schooled in those lessons that match responsibility to rank. Fortunate by birth and prosperous by patronage, patronized and patronizing alike, Edmund may never fully don the garments of his name's suggestiveness (an old English personal name, Edmund codes protector as well as prosperity and fortune), but the future civil servant is learning. 'He learns very little, he changes very little, but that is the speed at which people learn and change. They don't become great good figures all at once, or great bad figures all at once. They learn their lessons painfully and slowly,'[7] as Golding observed: an observation I read to be a determined gesture to undermine the melodramatic and the theatrical, the allegorical and the fabular.

II

> *The French Lieutenant's Woman* and *Rites of Passage* please by a deliberate thematic and technical archaism, yet at the same time carry within them an awareness of technical change and the complex action of time on the authenticity of narrative. [*Rites of Passage*] is therefore an example of a number of complex relationships – of changes in the life of forms in art, changes in the relations of writer to reader.
>
> Frank Kermode[8]

As readers of *The Scorpion God*, *The Hot Gates*, and *The Double Tongue* will remember, Golding had always been much absorbed by history, cutting sweeps wide and assured into distant times, shaping and fitting historical detail like the timbers of a great ship to a moral purpose. *Rites of Passage*, so exuberant in its depictions of 'tones and attitudes we hear in the literature of the time, in Byron and Creevey, in Peacock and Leigh Hunt, in Theodore Hook and Pierce Egan,'[9] continued this legacy with its publication in 1980, an appearance soon after to be awarded the prestigious Booker Prize. On the face of it, a robust naval yarn, giddy with playing the seeming postmodernist game, with antic parodies of period fiction, with ebullient pastiching of nineteenth-century literary techniques, the novel became one of those rare works to delight the common reader, indulge the academic excavator,[10] and provide puzzles for cultural soothsayers. Interviews on radio and television and commentary in the British press marked a renewed interest in what had now been reconfigured as national monument: Nobel novelist, Sir William Golding. Of course, critical opinion was not entirely laudatory. For the many who praised a skilled reconstruction of an earlier epoch in what was termed an 'historical novel',[11] particularly its parodic imitation of then dominant literary genres,[12] other reviewers (predominantly American) found the habit of intertextual weavings wearying. There is 'a schoolmasterish streak in Golding inclining him towards the didactic, tempting him to embellish his work with literary references [...] and echoes,' lectured the *New York Review of Books*.[13] Another commentary underlined this criticism with the warning: 'There is the danger that the stylistic virtuosity [could] degenerate into an end in itself.'[14]

Rites of Passage, I would argue to the contrary, is not so much an accessible, if mannered, literary *jeu* as a canvas of grids, elusive riddles, enigmas, and troublesome obscurities as puzzling at first as any painting from Picasso's Cubist period. As in the earlier novels, it is not the least difficult aspect of reading Golding that he expects his readers to reassemble narrative shapes, a re-assemblage that always requires from the reader more than a measure of competence. If a 'novel is in one sense a game […] that requires at least two players, a reader as well as a writer,' in David Lodge's observation,[15] then any Golding novel, in which the responses of both reader and writer are carefully studied and anticipated, can be likened in a similar way to the game of chess. Convinced that the reader's activity is as mysterious as that of the writer, Golding would come to describe that participatory activity as 'the reader's instinctive complicity'.[16] Emphasizing the agency of the fiction reader while differentiating that active mode from the traditionally passive mode of a Coleridgean willing suspension of disbelief, Golding's formulation would seem to share the deconstructionist notion that readers comply with, as well as conspire in, to quote Golding once again, 'that extended co-operation that must go on between the novelist and the reader'.[17] In my view, this tenet quite interestingly informs *Rites of Passage*'s delaying strategies where narrative order disagrees with the chronological order of the story. Not only is the 'implied reader' solicited to complete the story initiated by the 'implied author'[18] – a characteristic Golding strategy – but there is also a doubled contract of complicity and conspiracy between the novel's two fictive narrators and its two fictive narratees.

Following in the tradition of early eighteenth-century letter-journals, *Rites of Passage* embeds in its narrative a fictive recipient, for whom the fictive missive is being written. But as readers well know, Golding's book has two narratees, Talbot's journal enclosing Colley's, which itself is addressed to a narratee inscribed solely *within* its textual world. The reader of the novel, *Rites of Passage*, thus has the vertiginous experience of *doubly* indirect access, as it were 'through' the figures of the implicitly designated narratees, Talbot's godfather and Colley's sister.

Juxtaposed with the eighteenth-century epistolary novel or, for that matter, such nineteenth- and twentieth-century framed tales as Brontë's *Wuthering Heights*, James' *The Turn of the Screw* or Conrad's *Lord Jim*, Golding's novel aggressively announces the relationship between teller and listener, narrator and narratee, author and reader. From the perspective of late twentieth-century Anglo–American narratological theoretics, 'foregrounding' such as this amounts to what is described as 'authorial awareness' of the 'problematics' of story-telling, a metafictional preoccupation with (and so anxiety about) the transmission and reception of meaning. To have readers pulled towards the fictiveness of the text (which, in Linda Hutcheon's formulation is determined to be the designing aim of metafictional narrative[19]) is to experience the effect created in exemplary ways, for example, by Doris Lessing's *The Golden Notebook*, whose blocked narrator writes in various notebooks about the fictionality of fiction. Hauling the reader over to confront the storytelling process, lecturing the captive reader on the arbitrary fictiveness of storytelling, debunking that reader's expectation that the created world has 'reality', to sever fictions from the traditional aim of 'classic realism' have each been seen as the discovery (as well as creative burden) of postmodernist writers, among them Pynchon, Gass, Barth, Kundera, Angela Carter, Bradbury, Martin Amis and Fowles.

Thus if *Rites of Passage* adopts Swift's *Journal to Stella* and Boswell's *London Journal*, both 'forms of correspondence written for recipients',[20] Golding goes one better than Boswell and Swift, extending their habit of addresser and addressee by incorporating two sets of correspondence, not one. This double staging could be read as evidence that Golding's absorption in language's capricious traffic weighed so heavily that he felt compelled to enact twice over his preoccupations with processes of communication. Without doubt, 'the journal form does reveal with particular clarity and immediacy the tricky, volatile relationship between language and experience, between the text and the imperfect elusive life with which it engages.'[21]

Certainly, the question of writing and reading, of learning to compose and decipher languages – including that of social class – is persistently thematized in *Rites of Passage*. 'Language and art itself, as both process and product, are central concerns of the novel,' as Kevin McCarron argues,[22] sharing the view of such commentators as Ian Gregor and Mark Kinkead-Weekes, who see 'linguistic focus' as a characteristic of the later fiction, although they insist that *Rites of Passage*'s delight in language is not a metafictional negation, but an affirmation of 'the power of writing as a rite of passage'.[23] So Whitley's cautionary note, for example, that 'the links between Golding and the creators of metafiction can easily be overestimated'[24] is a useful one, particularly when one keeps in mind the metafictional convention whereby 'texts introduce their author, or a thinly disguised surrogate for him or her, into the text itself in order to raise questions about the ethics and aesthetics of the novel form'.[25] So compromised is the contract between author and reader in such metafictions that the implied reader is made to accept the fictional world solely as 'an authorial construct set up against a background of literary tradition and convention'.[26] My sense is that Golding's kinship lies far away from metafiction and far closer to another tradition where a fictive narrator comments (either reliably or unreliably) upon his or her modest artistic competence, a tradition that includes James, Huxley, Faulkner, Proust, Gide, Cervantes, and even Sterne. Here, 'the narrator writes of the burdens of authorship [...] speaks freely of the need to push this narrative button, tip that lever, and apply a brake now and then, but it is clear that he is deeply *into* his story [...] and would not for the world disturb the reader's illusion that there really is [a] "somewhere"'.[27] In such works, the reader is pulled not (as in metafiction) into the fictiveness of the text – which in Hutcheon's formulation is the designing aim of metafictional narrative[28] – but forward, intrigued by the promise of progressive plots – with their duration, compression, peripeteia, anagnorisis – to make 'sense of those meanings that develop only through textual and temporal succession'.[29]

'Making sense' as well as 'to make sense of' are problematical in the late twentieth century, where nineteenth- or eighteenth-century narrative solutions, with their face-to-face omniscient relationship between author and reader, no longer serve. One convention, however, remains constant: the narrative exchange between writer and reader, which is essential to storytelling. I would also argue that it is one sustained today in much more manipulative ways than, for example, George Eliot's narrative apostrophizing of her reader when she delivers opinions and judgements, or E.M. Forster's more tentative asides. Golding would later remark, in a response to an observation by a *Rites of Passage* reviewer that, in the late twentieth century, the relationship between reader and writer lacked the easier nineteenth-century dispensation with its commonly shared grounds of discourse: 'I would accept abusing the reader to some extent... You've really got to be a skull-cracker today. It's a brutal situation in which to write... Everything's shifted. I believe in looking out from behind a couple of eyes and seeing what goes on'.[30]

III

'Mr *Summers!* Will you have the sternpost out of her?' Summers said nothing but the thudding ceased. Captain Anderson's tone sank to a grumble. 'The pintles are loose as a pensioner's teeth.' Summers nodded in reply. 'I know it, sir. But until she's rehung–' 'The sooner we're off the wind the better. God curse that drunken superintendent!' He stared moodily […] at the sails which, as if willing to debate with him, boomed back. They could have done no better than the preceding dialogue. Was it not superb? (pp. 260–61)

If *Rites of Passage* shows a preoccupation with language, there is also Talbot's – and abidingly Golding's – delight in Tarpaulin, the vernacular of the ship. A formidable example of its salt taste is provided in the passage above, made all the more comic for interrupting – with its spirit of farce – a moment of some seriousness: burial at sea. The language of the Tarpaulin has a 1769 source book, William Falconer's *Universal Dictionary of the Marine*, which Golding has evidently adopted in his characteristic paraphrase of the Old Masters. As many of the novelist's commentators have insisted, the novels have (in varying degrees) all had as part of their genesis a quarrel with another writer's view of the same situation. By deliberately subverting literary models, Golding intends his reader to judge the moral distance between, for example, Ballantyne's complacent view of small boys in *The Coral Island* and his own sombre recasting in *Lord of the Flies*. In *Free Fall* (as I argued earlier), this sublative technique undergoes something of a sea-change, but even there Golding uses Dante's *Vita Nuova* as an ironic model for Sammy Mountjoy's love of Beatrice Ifor. There is no such simple scenario underpinning *Rites of Passage*, a matter which need not surprise. Consider the novel's enormous treasure chest of allusions: Ariosto; Aristotle; Austen; Baxter; Chaucer; Cobbett; Copernicus; Defoe; De Quincey; Fielding; Fuseli; Gibbon; Goethe's *Faust*; Goldsmith; Homer's *Odyssey*; Kepler; Lesage's *Gil Blas*; Martial; Milton's *Lycidas*; Newton; Plato's *Republic*; Racine; Richardson; Saint Augustine's *Confessions*; Seneca; Servius; Shakespeare's *Much Ado About Nothing*, *Macbeth*, and *The Tempest*; Smollett; Sophocles' *Philoctetes*; Sterne's *Tristram Shandy*; Theocritus; Virgil's *Aeneid*; and – pre-eminently – Coleridge's *The Rime of the Ancient Mariner*.

Rites of Passage's provenance, however, is Wilfrid Scawen Blunt's two-volume work, *My Diaries: Being a Personal Narrative of Events, 1888–1914*, wherein Blunt mentions an acquaintance's reference to an episode in the 1790s involving the 'Iron' Duke of Wellington. En route to India, Wellington boarded an adjacent convoy, having been requested to buoy the spirits of a fellow seafarer sunk in deep lethargy. The Iron Duke's effort apparently failed – the man died.[31] 'I don't understand it. But it's something that deeply interested me,' Golding said of the incident, which clearly constitutes an intriguing, because inexplicable, determined death. '*Rites of Passage*,' Golding continued, was 'an attempt to invent circumstances [...] where one can see that this kind of thing can happen: that someone can be reduced to the point at which he would die of shame.'[32]

Of course, sea mysteries such as this long fascinated and appalled Golding; indeed, in both *Lord of the Flies* and *Pincher Martin* the sea lurks as a palpable presence and atavistic force. As we know, the ocean was no imaginative stranger to Golding, who commanded a British Navy rocket cruiser during World War II and participated in the sinking of the *Bismarck*. Except for the last twenty years, Golding had sailed for much of his life. He knew as well as any man that the sea is a graveyard of ships, the ocean floor a litter of wrecks, including the rusty remains of his own typewriter and all the rest of the gear from his ketch *Tenance*, shipwrecked off the shores of Southampton in the mid-1960s. That the sea frightened Golding at the same time as it dangerously drew him forwards should not be read as paradoxical. An exceptionally superstitious man in private (a legacy from his Cornish mother), the sea had a fierce hold upon his imagination, akin to that boyhood Marlborough house with its terrifying graveyard. So the life and literature of sea voyages, *The Odyssey* and *The Aeneid*, the poetry of salt water, naval logs, sea shanties, Napoleonic seafaring memoirs and history (which he had read vastly), navigation manuals, accounts both fictional and real, came – to use a figure of speech with which he would have felt at home – to mulch down. In their rich coalescence, *Rites of Passage* germinated.

Much has been made of specific sea literature sources, with Melville's *Billy Budd* and Conrad's *Heart of Darkness* being the two works most frequently put forward as texts re-engaged by *Rites of Passage*.[33] Seen from such a perspective, the parallels between Talbot's duplicitous letter to Colley's sister and that of Marlow to Kurtz's 'are strikingly similar in motive', while Golding's sailor, Billy Rogers, is 'a perverse echo of Melville's Billy Budd'.[34] Then there is throughout the novel the persistent threading of Coleridge's *The Rime of the Ancient Mariner*, with its now-hackneyed verse line 'Alone, alone, all, all alone'. That line is so startlingly juxtaposed with the novel's narrative eruptions as to restore its once rough magic. While the 'whole novel echoes the sounds of other men's art, Melville, Conrad, Richardson, Coleridge,'[35] my sense is that Golding has reworked not so much the nautical literature of Melville, Stevenson, and Conrad as the travel literature of Smollett[36] and, in particular, Marryat.

Peter Simple, Frederick Marryat's 1834 tale of a fool who rises up to become a gallant and capable officer in His Majesty's Service, may be one of the literary models Golding recasts in *Rites of Passage*. Marryatt's portrait of the frank, open-hearted tar whose fun-loving temper buoys him up in a sea of hard knocks is, as Golding once said of Wells' view of Neanderthal man, 'too neat, too simple'.[37] Literature may have it that the jolly tars of the fo'castle with their practical jokes were a fun-loving lot. In actuality, they were probably as ignorant, superstitious, and unruly as the tars Golding portrays in *Rites of Passage*. In his paraphrase of Marryat's resolute, generous and ever-courteous Captain Savage and the frigate world he commands (both a nursery and a school for the true spirit of British seamanship), Golding once again shatters such a smug view of human nature. His cleric-hating Captain Anderson – who licenses the tars' persecution of poor parson Colley – is a genuine, rather than counterfeit, Savage. Golding's sea story has, as Talbot himself writes: 'never a tempest, no shipwreck, no sinking, no rescue at sea…no thundering broadsides, heroism, prizes, gallant defenses, and heroic attacks' (p. 278). It does, however, sight an enemy, dark on the horizon: the guilt and shame gripping the heart of man.

IV

I was never made so aware of the distance between the disorder of real life in its multifarious action, partial exhibition, irritating concealments and the stage simulacra that I had once taken as a fair representation of it! (p. 110).

As a rule, in Golding's novels the sheer magic of the storytelling lulls us into unguarded enjoyment. Our innocent delight is then darkly undercut by an abrupt shift in narrative viewpoint; new revelations force us to modify our earlier sympathies and reconsider what – to our untutored hearts – had previously seemed innocuous. In this, *Rites of Passage* is no exception. Talbot's journal – which frames the story – disarms almost totally with its descriptions of the ship's pitching, thumping, and groaning, of passengers staggering across dripping planks or bedding down – sickened by the sea – in their foetid hutches. From Talbot's indeflectably patrician point of view, we see the ship's motley society. For society this wooden world most certainly is. The ship at sea has long represented a social microcosm. Here we glimpse a wider society whose social ranks duplicate its landlubber hierarchy. It is a pyramidal, yet increasingly porous, British class system, where the still feudal eighteenth-century Georgian world was giving way to the early nineteenth-century Regency period, with its changes in social arrangements associated with years of naval victories and prize monies as well as economic booms in manufacturing and trade in the wake of the Industrial Revolution and the Napoleonic Wars. Inhabiting its several decks are the vessel's various social classes in their descending levels. Officers and assorted specimens of gentry (and pseudo-gentry) breathe the upper deck's 'cool, sweet air' above the ship's *waist*; a painted white declarative line divides that waist from several lower decks, crowded with farriers, scriveners, clerks, typesetters, emigrants, 'people of all ages and sexes and smells' (p. 84). Further down rests the gun room with its warrant officers, midshipmen, a gunner, a carpenter, a sailing master. And deeper still, dark, sulfurously hot and stinking with rat excrement, bilge-gravel, and sand, lies the ship's *belly*, colonically filled with a crew of unruly deckhands. Little wonder that Talbot should invoke established order on asking the question of Cumbershum: 'How is order to be maintained? …Your crew is not all officers! Forward there, is a crowd of individuals on whose obedience the order of the whole depends' (p. 22).[38]

If Talbot's journal disarms, we will later join him in ridiculing the cleric, who cuts such a lamentable figure in his ecclesiastical finery:

> The surplice, gown, hood, wig, cap looked quite silly under our vertical sun! He moved forward at a solemn pace as he might in a cathedral […] But the sight of a parson not so much walking […] as

processing [...] amused and impressed me [...] He lacked the natural authority of a gentleman and had absurdly overdone the dignity of his calling. He was now advancing on the lower orders in all the majesty of the Church Triumphant [...](p. 106).

The class-ridden perceptions of a first-person narrator as unreliable as Talbot are decidedly narrow, and limited all the more by the absence of authorial comment and interpretation. Add as well the ideographic habit – with its practiced technique of calculated obscurity – which is very much in evidence in *Rites of Passage*. One result of this strategy is to 'limit the reader's epistemological basis by consistently withholding the means for a more clear-sighted analysis'.[39] Indeed, we must often piece together – even deduce – information that the self-absorbed Talbot simply does not apprehend. His myopia is with us from his first journal entry when he writes: 'The month or day of the week can signify little since in our long passage from the south of Old England to the Antipodes we shall pass through the geometry of all four seasons!' (p. 3). That he neglects to understand that the ship will, on passing through the seasons, cross the equator and so rest for some days in the equatorial belt of calms, marks an omission all the more telling since Talbot will frequently allude to Coleridge's *The Rime of the Ancient Mariner*, savouring the refrain: 'Alone, alone, all, all alone/Alone on a wide sea!' A more significant bafflement is over a snatch of Tarpaulin slang, 'badger bag', which Talbot hears sniggered in the ship's stinking belly with its fecal darkness, an area he visits in an effort to find a place for a possible concupiscent congress. 'I wonder what is meant by the expression "Badger Bag"? Falconer is silent' (p. 84). This alerts us again to the presence of another important missing clue.

Similarly, Talbot's confused registering of a creeper plant growing in the bilge's dark cellarage – 'its roots buried in a pot and the stem roped to the bulkhead [...] wherever a tendril or branch was unsupported it hung straight down like a piece of seaweed' (p. 78) – warns us that there may be yet another web of complex meaning somewhere beyond Talbot's comprehension, especially as he has just heard from the carpenter, Mr Gibbs, that the reason for the ship's sluggishness has been its weed-covered bottom, 'If they took the weed off her [...] they might take the bottom with it' (p. 82), Gibbs mutters, rather pointedly. Soon Talbot will visit the Captain's cabin and be astonished by the spectacle of this morose tyrant tending lovingly a rich garden of geraniums and

Garland vines: rows of 'climbing plants, each twisting itself around a bamboo that rose from the darkness near the deck' (p. 159). It is left to the reader, not Talbot, to make sense of the captain's 'private paradise' where the '[un]expelled Adam', Anderson, is positively amiable. His Eden's balmy air is perfumed by 'still innocent, unfallen' white Garland Plants, a species he cherishes as much for their earliest ceremonial use – with these waxen garlands 'the ancients [...] crowned themselves' – as for his own fancy that 'Eve so garlanded herself on the first day of creation'. The plants are all the more treasured since he has triumph-antly raised *two* of the three plants from seed. Sir Joseph Banks, Captain Anderson laughs, insisted that it would be impossible to grow Garland Plants from seed; then Anderson amusedly quotes Banks as saying to him: 'You might as well throw the seeds overboard' (p. 160).[40]

Then there is a geranium's 'disease' of the leaf, to which Anderson draws Talbot's attention while discoursing on his garden's health, and the Captain's gnomic aside that 'he who gardens at sea must accustom himself to loss'. This is a reiteration of Banks' cheerier reported throwaway that, since plants cannot be grown from seeds aboard ship, the seeds should be cast aside. It is the reader, not Talbot, however, who intuits that buried in this colloquy is a sly allusion to *Matthew* 13.3. The parable of the sower whose seeds, having fallen by the wayside, are destined to die in stony places and thorny patches, describes how – despite his losses – the sower would come to reap abundant rewards. For some seeds 'fell into good ground, and brought forth fruit, some hundred-fold, some forty-fold, some thirty-fold'.

Glancing as the *Matthew* allusion here may be in its gesturing towards a consolatory reality, it can be united to those other riddling references embedded in this scene. The purpose to which (in my reading) they are directed is a proffering – both elusive and allusive – of various explanatory myths for complexities and the human effort.[41] Linked to the promissory fable of the sower would be the mythos of the Christian crucifixion as well as the longed-for prelapsarian state of Edenic innocence, Eve garlanded and Adam unexpelled, each of these three myths having been forged in the smithy of the human creature's ancient condition of 'disease', Golding's consistent metaphor for human nature. What then of Anderson's learned allusion to ancient Greeks crowning themselves for feasts, their wreaths made from the very same garlands as those *he* has grown from seed? And if garlanded Dionysian worshipers are insinuated here, does this partial disclosure connect in any way to the repeated emphasis on the 'omniscient, ubiquitous Wheeler' (p. 184) with his '*sanctified* smile' (p. 248), his 'sense of *holy* understanding' (p. 177, my italics), and his uncanny ability to *see* 'round and through' (p. 18, my italics) Edmund Talbot and all the other voyagers on this ship of state? And why, indeed, should so minor a character carry the thematic weight implied by, for example, the following – portentous – depiction, Talbot's description of Wheeler whose 'white puffs of hair, his bald pate and *lighted* face – I can find no other description for his expression of understanding all the ways and woes of the world – gave him an air of positive saintliness' (p. 176, Golding's italics)?

Certainly it is left to the reader, not Talbot, to draw connections: in particular that between the plant struggling to survive in the vessel's noisome cellarage and Captain Anderson's well-watered and blossoming flowers. This connection, once drawn, can be linked to the fact, which has not gone unremarked by Talbot, that the ship is timber, indeed made from English oak. Colley's letter, comprising the second perspective on the story, likens 'this strange construction of English oak' (p. 223) – with its 'complications of ropes and tackles and chains and booms and sails' (p. 219) – to a massive English oak tree. Billy Rogers (the preternaturally toothsome sailor strutting the bowsprit) is fancifully compared to a 'king crowned with curls', balancing in the branches of one of His Majesty's *traveling trees*' (p. 218, italics Golding's).

These oblique references to growing plants, wavering green weeds, 'under the water from our wooden sides' (p. 247), and the stinking cellar of the ship – which Talbot, in jest, calls 'a graveyard' (p. 5) – gradually produce narrative pressure as well as acquire symbolic meaning. For quite apart from its dramatic function in the plot, oak has a rich range of implications. Among the ancients it was considered sacred (worshipped by Dionysus) and, so Graves and Frazer explain, it was associated with sacrificial killings in many primitive religions. Talbot may (once more, in jest) compare the lurching ship to revelling dryads and hamadryads, who 'refused to leave their ancient dwelling' of oak 'from which our floating box is composed' (p. 19). But his conjecture that these inferior deities (closely allied to Dionysus) might have 'come to sea with us' could well be read as ominous rather than arch. Again, it is the reader, however – not Talbot or Colley – who must discover that these plants, like the oak hulk, represent the strange unmanageable tangled undergrowth of human impulses in this 'wooden world'.[42]

Other seemingly impenetrable strands are woven throughout Talbot's journal. We learn of an 'equatorial entertainment' (p. 85) – an oblique piece of information, glancingly presented, since Talbot's journal at this juncture is much preoccupied with its author's sexual encounter with Zenobia Brocklebank, the ship's doxy. At the crucial moment of Talbot's delirium, with perfect slapstick timing, a blunderbuss goes off on the quarterdeck. What, we wonder, has happened? Earlier the notorious free thinker, Prettiman, had threatened to shoot an albatross to prove his freedom from superstition. And yet it was not he who fired the shot. The explanation is bound up in the puzzle of the equatorial entertainment but for a full account we must consult Parson Colley's journal, which will soon come shuddering into view.

V

In our country [...] For all her greatness there is one thing she cannot do and that is translate a person wholly out of one class into another. Perfect translation from one language into another is impossible. Class is the British language (p. 125).

We move from Talbot's complacent narrative to Colley's exclamatory, tortured letter to his sister. Having long empathized with Talbot, we are hard put to shift our sympathies from him, even registering his limitations as now we do, towards Colley. A character in the long line of Golding's unworldly grotesques, Colley, despite his morbidity and grating sentimentality, is no longer Talbot's caricatured social misfit but emerges as a man of deep sensitivity. Inhabiting his being through his letter, we understand his essential unworldliness and sheer ignorance. There is also the fervid spirituality: an excess conveyed, for example, in his record of awe before a sea storm:

What has remained with me apart from a lively memory of my apprehensions is not only a sense of HIS AWFULNESS and a sense of the majesty of HIS creation. It is a sense of the splendour of our vessel rather than her triviality and minuteness! It is as if I think of her as a separate world, a universe in little in which we must pass our lives and receive our reward or punishment [...] I remained motionless by the rail [...] While I was yet there, the last disturbance left by the breeze passed away so that the glitter, that image of the starry heavens, gave place to a flatness and blackness, a nothing! All was mystery. It terrified me [...] (pp. 191–92)

Colley's experience runs parallel to Talbot's. Indeed, the two could well be read as irregular doubles.[43] Both men are dependent upon patronage, both ingratiate themselves with their patrons, both (by neglecting to read the Orders of the Ship's Captain) subvert naval authority and thus enrage the class-embittered Anderson. Talbot can always arrogantly pull rank on the captain, while Colley – who possesses even less worldly cunning than Sterne's Parson Yorick – is both socially and emotionally ill-equipped to grapple with the man's tyranny:

> I am deeply suspicious that the surliness of the captain towards me is not to be explained...readily. Is it perhaps sectarianism? ... Or if it is not sectarianism but a social contempt, the situation is serious – nay *almost* as serious! I am a clergyman bound for an honourable if humble station at the Antipodes. The captain has no more business to look big on me – and indeed less business – than the canons of the Close...(p. 199).

As the voyage progresses, Colley finds himself increasingly excluded from the social world of the quarterdeck. He is quite at a loss to comprehend why 'a humble servant of the Church of England – which spreads its arms so wide in the charitable embrace of sinners,' (p. 199) should be ostracized by the ship's 'gentry' (p. 188). 'The ladies and gentlemen at this end of the ship do not respond with any cheerful alacrity to my greetings,' he writes, puzzling over their 'indefinable *indifference*' (p. 193).

Colley is of course the perfect social victim. Woefully unschooled in the systematic snobberies of stratified society, he is appallingly ignorant of the ingrained contempt for persons of inferior rank which the likes of Talbot exhibit and therefore implicitly sanction in the ship world: 'the shape of the little society in which we must live together for I know not how many months' (p. 188). Indeed, Colley is so ingenuous that he sees Talbot as a true gentleman: 'He is a member of the aristocracy with all the consideration and nobility of bearing that such birth implies' (p. 194).

The final effect of Colley's unworldly innocence – once we inhabit his journal and can compare it to Talbot's – is to make us aware of the latter's worldliness and indeed more ashamed of Talbot's moral blindness than he himself is. Colley's account of the voyage and the strange and gruesome rites into which he is initiated is, expectably, far different from Talbot's, although once again we must decode oblique clues in order to arrive at a complete understanding.

The captain, we discover, hates parsons and his animosity seeps insidiously through the ship.[44] Should the cat-o'-nine tails or grog fail to subdue his volatile men, a suitable object for derisive sport such as a parson could usefully divert. Sailors are a superstitious lot and the captain recognizes that to them 'a parson in a ship' is 'like a woman in a fishing boat – a kind of natural bringer of bad luck' (p. 193).

At this dramatic juncture in the novel the ship lies under a sultry sun in the equatorial belt of calms, the very doldrums to which the Ancient Mariner's vessel was dispatched because of his act of wanton cruelty. In the tumid air, the effluvia of the still ship mix with the stinking pestilence of the surrounding soiled waters. The atmosphere is described vividly enough by Colley – Talbot in his hutch is too intent on playing Mr B. to the ship's rather ironic Pamela: 'Our huge ship was motionless and her sails still hung down. On her right hand the red sun was setting and on her left the full moon was rising, the one directly across from the other. The two vast luminaries seemed to stare at each other and each to modify the other's light' (p. 233), writes Colley, his ecstatic idiom marking his apprehension.

From both Colley and Talbot, we hear more whispers about the badger bag, which in Glascock's *Naval Sketch Book* (1825) is innocuously defined as the 'name given by Sailors to Neptune when playing tricks on travelers on first crossing the line'.[45] The tars prepare for their 'equatorial entertainment' by filling a huge tarpaulin with filthy sea water, dung, and urine – a badger bag to end all badger bags. The poor parson is seized by Cumbershum and Deveral and subjected to a scatological parody of mass and baptism in the bag. And before they inflict on him the mock rite of communion and dunk him in the mock baptismal font, the tars force him to kneel in front of their triton wielding, primitive godhead, Poseidon.

[A]s I opened my mouth to protest, it was at once filled with such nauseous stuff I gag and am like to vomit remembering it. For some time [...] this operation was repeated; and when I would not open my mouth the stuff was smeared over my face [...E]ach question was greeted with a storm of cheering and that terrible British sound

which ever daunted the foe; and then it came to me, was forced in
upon my soul the awful truth – *I was the foe!* (p. 237, Golding's italics)

Poor Colley in extremity has not the means to comprehend that the
'snarling, lustful, storming' (p. 288) sport is no mere equatorial
entertainment. This persecution of a sacrificial scapegoat amounts to a
magico-religious ritual to exorcise fears about the seaworthiness of the
becalmed ship. Covertly handled as the incident is, it recalls the ritual
murders of *Lord of the Flies*, *The Inheritors*, and *The Spire*, where the
scapegoats – Simon, Liku, and Pangall respectively – are all sacrificed to
ensure the terrified group's solidarity. It is only Summers' firing of the
blunderbuss which stops the pack from committing more than a
ritualized persecution. For these pagan sailors venerate, as the ancients
did, the oak of their wooden ship, and might well have killed Colley
out of a generalized feeling that he would make a good guardian of the
bilge. In mythic terms, his murder might very easily have represented
the death of sterility and signalled the release of generative power. That
the ritual release of winds should occur during a Dionysian orgy of
rum is another indication of the myth-enhancing power of *Rites of
Passage*. Dionysus, whose original name, 'Tree-youth', links him to
Colley's crowned king of the traveling tree, once made a ship seaworthy
by causing a vine to grow from the deck and enfold the mast.[46] The
sailors on his ship – like those of *Rites of Passage* with its creepers
growing from the cellarage – became so intoxicated by wine and sexual
licence that they were metamorphosed in phantom beasts.

Colley participates in another Bacchanalian orgy, although neither his
nor Talbot's journal directly recounts the 'Make and Mend' festival.[47] Its
full implications for Colley's disgrace become clear only after the
(undescribed) catastrophe and must be pieced together by Talbot and
the reader. Having painfully resolved (as a result of the badger bag
humiliation) that 'what a man does defiles him, not what is done by
others – my shame, though it burn, has been inflicted on me' (p. 235),
Colley returns to the fo'castle intent, he believes, on God's mission:

Why – even the captain himself has shown some small signs – and the
power of Grace is infinite [...] I shall go forward and rebuke these unruly
but truly loveable children of OUR MAKER [...] I am consumed by a
great love of all things, the sea, the ship, the sky, the gentlemen and the
people of course OUR REDEEMER above all! Here at last is the

happiest outcome of all my distress and difficulty! ALL THINGS
PRAISE HIM! (p. 247)

Unconscious of his growing infatuation for one of the deckhands,
which he sublimates as a passionate longing to 'bring this young man
to OUR SAVIOUR' (p. 218), Colley acts from confused and tangled
motives. Stupefied with rum, he is driven to mad exuberance, although
the entire episode is concealed from our view; we only see him exit
from the fo'castle where, stripped of his canonical finery, he makes a
spectacle of himself by pissing before an 'audience'[48] assembled on the
quarter-deck. He is lugged back to his hutch from which he will never
again emerge; he lies rigid, his hand clutching a 'ringbolt' (p. 127) –
rigid until he dies. When an inquiry into his death is held, with Talbot
in attendance, the captain acts upon an informer's hint and interrogates
a deckhand, Billy Rogers. The captain brusquely raises the issue of
buggery, a delayed disclosure about Colley's unseen actions which is
later confirmed when Rogers laughs to another tar about 'getting a
chew off a parson' (p. 273). We readers are meant to realize that Colley
in drunken forgetfulness of self has committed fellatio on the deckhand
and to conclude, therefore, that he *literally* dies from shame at his
defilement of himself.

VI

You will observe that I have recovered somewhat from the effect of
reading Colley's letter […] You will already have noted some particularly
impenetrable specimens as, for instance, mention of a *badger bag* – does
not Servius (I believe it was he) declare there are half a dozen cruxes in
the *Aeneid* which will never be solved, either by emendation or
inspiration or any method attempted by scholarship? (p. 259).

Colley, then, is to be likened to Euripides' Pentheus, who was driven mad
and torn to pieces by the Bacchae when he resisted the introduction of
Dionysian worship into his kingdom; Colley, having been denied the
quarterdeck, calls the fo'castle his 'little kingdom' (p. 209). But other
conundrums are not so easily solved. Why does Talbot's servant,
'omniscient, ubiquitous' (p. 184) Wheeler, mysteriously disappear? Talbot
assumes that he fell overboard. Can we not assume, however, by way of

Talbot's allusion to Palinurus, who is flung from Aeneas' ship, that Wheeler may have been the captain's informant, having known too much about the 'Make and Mend' chewing, not to mention the dishonest dealings of the shadowy purser, who is yet another 'impenetrable crux' (p. 259) in *Rites of Passage*? For that matter, what is the unnamed ship's title with 'her monstrous figurehead, emblem of her name and which our people [...] have turned colloquially into an obscenity' (p. 34)? *Britannia* , one assumes: a supposition prompted by the proximity of the figurehead to the 'heads' where tars squat, doing their business. Would that the name sounded like 'purser-grind', which is nautical slang meaning 'coition bringing the woman no money, but consolation in the size of the member'.[49] *Purser-Grind* or *Britannia*, both give reason enough for Talbot's jeer when Summers tells him that the infant born aboard ship will be named for her.

Riddles remain, and one is major: the state of Colley's soul at its departure. It is not altogether clear whether Golding intends us to believe that Colley dies a self-flagellated sinner or whether, in his last moment, he is mercifully granted release from his guilt. Neither journal records the last moments. According to Talbot, Colley dies in a condition of despair and shame. However, Golding's novels never conclude with one unequivocal meaning: they insist upon the intermingling of the visible and the invisible, the physical and the spiritual, the world of the burning candle and the burning bush, the cellarage and the spire.

Rites of Passage hints that Colley might have been granted release from the cellarage of his deep sense of self-degradation. Recall, first, that Colley – during his spiritual crisis – invokes Saint Augustine and the comfort of that sinner's theological dictum on the immediate efficacy of grace. Colley also has in his library a copy of Baxter's *Saints Everlasting Rest*, devotional meditations on sudden death. Furthermore, Colley fears 'the Justice of GOD, unmitigated by his Mercy!' (p. 234); he believes – like Augustine before him – that 'the power of Grace is infinite' (p. 247); he believes that the 'happiest outcome' of all his 'distress and difficulty' is OUR REDEEMER' (p. 247). Indeed, these are the last words of his testament.

Turning to Talbot's description of Colley's posture in dying, where one hand is barnacled to 'what both Falconer and Summers agreed was a ringbolt' (p. 131), one may surmise by way of the nagging, reiterative (almost unexplained) reference to the ringbolt that Golding intends us to inspect it as a symbolic shorthand, like the verbal paradox of Jocelin's 'upward waterfall'. Falconer may explain that a ringbolt 'has several uses [...] but particularly hooks the tackles by which the cannons of a ship are secured'.[50] Readers may (if so spiritually inclined) imagine another 'use' and interpret the ringbolt as that bolt from the blue – God's grace – which hooks the penitent believer into the ring of God's everlasting Mercy. Golding, once again, positions his readers to follow such innuendoes, another of which, 'the low fever' – by which Colley's death is officially diagnosed as having been caused – similarly surfaces and resurfaces (pp. 177, 178, 179, 183, 184), yet remains enigmatic. Possibly intended as another 'impenetrable crux', it is my sense that the repeated phrase rewards by being allusively linked both to 'life's fitful fever' that *Macbeth*'s dead Duncan can now evade and to *East Coker*'s vision of a just, yet merciful agency, which T.S. Eliot figures as a surgeon who:

> plies the steel
> That questions the distempered part;
> Beneath the bleeding hands we feel
> The sharp compassion of the healer's art
> Resolving the enigma of the fever's chart.

'What the *devil* is a *low fever*' (p. 178, my italics), shouts an exasperated Talbot while the drunken Brocklebank mutters on about '*spirits* and *low fever*' (p. 178, Golding's italics). 'A low fever is the opposite of a high fever' (p. 179) is Brocklebank's stupefied reply, one which readers are also positioned to tackle in ways beyond the understanding of boozy Brocklebank or impatient Edmund, a tackling that leads to the notion that Colley may well have been granted everlasting rest. To borrow the words of Sir Thomas Browne's meditation:

> The world, I count is not an inn, but an hospital; and a place not to live, but to die in. The world that I regard is myself; it is in the microcosm of my own frame that I cast mine eye on... There is surely a piece of divinity in us... Thus it is observed that men sometimes upon the hour of their departure do speak and reason above themselves.

In *Rites of Passage* Golding once again provided plunder enough for a whole shipload of critics. Once again, he constructed a religious mythopoeia, the spur of a spiritual dimension – at least in the imaginative realm – in which the reader participates. For *Rites of Passage* is, among many other things, about last rites. The novel's structure – with its partial concealments, oblique clues, delayed disclosure – forces us to bring into focus Colley's final and appalling disgrace. We discover that it was Talbot who catalyzed the whole sordid sequence of humiliations, ending in the parson's death. Had Talbot not flaunted his rank, thus undermining the captain's sense of his own authority, the captain, in turn, might not have countenanced Colley's persecution. The final effect of *Rites of Passage* is to implicate the reader in the responsibility for the loss of innocence: Talbot's belated sense of shame becomes our shame, our guilt. We rest at one with him in the final entry he makes in his journal: 'With lack of sleep and too much understanding I grow a little crazy, I think, like all men at sea who live too close to each other and too close thereby to all that is monstrous under the sun and moon' (p. 278).

Endnotes

1 Most explicit about this intentional – and primary – intertextual allusion, Golding was to remark to a radio interviewer: 'Rites of passage […] does not refer to […] a sea voyage [solely]; [it's] an anthropological term marking a man's stages through life.' *Bookmark*, British Broadcasting Corporation, London (January 17, 1984).

2 Long engaged by, and informed about, accounts of the Napoleonic Wars and the emergence under Nelson of the Royal Navy's unchallenged maritime supremacy during the Regency period and afterwards, Golding would have registered Nelson's atypical position and innovative contribution to matters of social rank. In a service long dominated by patronage, Nelson set new standards for a new class of naval officer, establishing for the first time the middle-class, professional naval officer. As the biographer Tom Pocock summarizes, Nelson 'owed no allegiance to any social class, as his family background showed: his brother and sisters had worked as shop assistants even though his cousins were landowners. Indeed he was cold-shouldered by the court and courtly society and his friends ashore were

unfashionable.' (Tom Pocock, *Horatio Nelson*, New York, Alfred Knopf, 1988, p. 308).

3   A Golding intertextual joke rests here. Capturing his nation's imagination with intensities of attention, Nelson became a national hero in his lifetime. On his death, 'every newspaper and periodical printed ballads, orations and hymns in Nelson's praise. There was, announced one orator, "a noble emulation among journalists, poets, historians and artists to enumerate the virtues of his mind, exhibit the heroic deeds of his life and render his memory the admiration of all succeeding generations"' (Pocock, ibid., p. 335). Wonderful that *Rites of Passage*'s inebriate Brocklebank should so situate himself, being so situated by the smiling author, Golding.

4   Especially revealing in this context is Talbot's sentimental library of Richardson, *Moll Flanders*, *Gil Blas*, and the then very popular *Meditations Among the Tombs* of the pious Hervey, all of which will come toppling down when he ravages the ship's doxy.

5   Sharing with Austen's Emma Woodhouse 'a disposition to think a little too well' of himself, Talbot – like Emma – plots and manages and manipulates and performs before attentive observers, himself his best audience.

6   Ian Gregor and Mark Kinkead-Weekes, *William Golding: A Critical Study*, London, Faber and Faber 1984, p. 270.

7   Golding to James R. Baker in 'An Interview with William Golding' *Twentieth Century Literature* 28 (1982), p. 163.

8   Frank Kermode, *Essays on Fiction: 1971–1982*, London, Routledge & Kegan Paul, 1983, p. 132.

9   Neil McEwan, *Perspectives in British Historical Fiction Today*, Wolfboro, New Hampshire, Longwood Academic Press, p. 174.

10 Talbot's journal is 'an encyclopaedia of literary method', declares one critic, including 'simile, personification, metaphor, classical allusion, rhetorical questions, quotation, analogy, slang, metonymy, periphrasis

[and] cliché', Kevin McCarron, *The Coincidence of Opposites: William Golding's Later Fiction*, Sheffield, Sheffield Academic Press, 1995, p. 86.

11 See here Bernard F. Dick, *William Golding* (revised edition), Boston, Twayne Publishers, 1987, p. 114; Peter O. Stummer, 'Man's Beastliness to Man: The Novels of William Golding' in *Essays on the Contemporary British Novel*, Hedwig Bock and Albert Wertheim (eds), Munich, Hueber, 1986, p. 93; and McEwan pp. 170–76.

12 See J.H. Stape, '"Fiction in the Wild, Modern Manner": Metanarrative Gesture in William Golding's *To the End of the Earth* Trilogy', *Twentieth Century Literature* 38 (1992), p. 227. Stape sees the novel as 'a travelogue à la Smollett or Sterne [...] counterpoint[ing] Austenian social comedy or the meditative mode of Mary Shelley's *Frankenstein*'.

13 Robert Towers, 'The Good Ship *Britannia*', *New York Review of Books* (December 18, 1980) p. 6. Indeed, reviewers from the United States were a good deal less sympathetic, even exasperated, demonstrating perhaps their historic antipathy to a literary tradition that celebrated British sea power. *Newsweek* considered the novel one which replicated *Lord of the Flies*, with drunken sailors replacing schoolboys. 'This journey into another heart of darkness has the feel of a rerun' (Jean Strouse, 'All at Sea', *Newsweek*, October 27, 1986, p. 104).

14 Stummer, op. cit., p. 94.

15 Elsewhere, elucidating the question of the reader's production of textual meaning, Lodge has underscored Bakhtin's insight that all language is essentially dialogic: 'Every utterance we make is directed towards some real or hypothetical other who will receive it' (David Lodge, *The Practice of Writing*, London and New York, Allen Lane, The Penguin Press, 1996, p. 196). In *Reading for the Plot*, Peter Brooks offers another critique of narrative and the reader's 'performance': 'Plot [...] is [...] a structuring operation elicited in the reader [...] Plot [...] belongs to the reader's [...] "performance" – the reading of narrative – it animates the sense making process' (Peter Brooks, *Reading for Plot, Design and Intention in Narrative*, New York, Alfred Knopf, 1984, p. 37).

16   William Golding, 'Belief and Creativity' *A Moving Target*, New York, Farrar, Straus & Giroux, 1982, p. 194. In this lecture, as well as during interviews, Golding has insisted upon the active nature of the reader's absorption. See also Golding to John Haffenden, 'William Golding', *Novelists in Interview*, London and New York, Methuen, 1985, p. 107.

17   Golding, 'Belief and Creativity', op. cit. p. 197.

18   Strictly speaking, a distinction must be drawn between an author and the 'implied author' of a particular work. The latter is (according to Chapman) '"implied", that is, reconstructed by the reader from the narrative. He [or she] is not the narrator, but rather the principle that invented the narrator, along with everything else in the narrative [...] We can grasp the notion of implied author most clearly by comparing different narratives written by the same real author but presupposing different implied authors [...] There is always an implied author, though there might not be a single real author in the ordinary sense: the narrative may have been composed by committee [Hollywood films] and etc' (Seymour Chapman, *Story and Discourse: Narrative Structure in Fiction and Film*, Ithaca and London, Cornell University Press, 1979, pp. 188–90). Similarly, there is an 'implied reader', the audience reading the book, although not the creature of flesh and blood who turns the pages. Studies of the 'narratee', as Chapman notes, are not so comprehensive as those devoted to the narrator. Defined by Gerald Prince as 'the character receiver', he or she 'may be a listener [...] a reader [...] he may himself play an important part in the events narrated to him [...] or [...] no part at all.' (Gerald Prince, 'On Readers and Listeners in Narrative', *Neophilgus* 55, 1971, pp. 117–22). Chapman also asks the provocative question 'Are both narrator and narratee unreliable? Or is the narrator reliable despite our misgivings about his narratee?'(Chapman , p. 259)

19   Linda Hutcheon, *A Theory of Parody*, New York, Methuen, 1985, p. 11.

20   Stape, op. cit., p 227. See as well James Gindin, *William Golding*, New York, St Martin's Press, 1988, p. 74, who defines the 'recording journal' as 'a form of reportage'.

21 Jem Poster, 'Beyond Definition: William Golding's Sea Trilogy' *Critical Survey* 5 (1993), p. 92.

22 McCarron, op. cit., p. 81. In his view, Golding's preoccupations with the *acts* of reading and writing amount to a 'postmodernist [...] insistence upon the importance of both production and reception', p. 9.

23 Ian Gregor and Mark Kinkead-Weekes, 'The Later Golding' *Twentieth Century Literature* 28 (1982), p 117.

24 John S. Whitley, '"*Furor Scribendi*" Writing about Writing in the Later Novels of William Golding' in James R. Baker (ed.), *Critical Essays on William Golding*, Boston, G.K. Hall, 1988, p. 190. See also Stape, op. cit., p. 227.

25 David Lodge, *After Bakhtin: Essays on Fiction and Criticism*, London, Routledge, 1990, p. 19.

26 I borrow here from Robert Alter's definition of the self-conscious novel, one 'that systematically flaunts its own condition of artifice and that by so doing probes into the problematic relationship between real-seeming artifice and reality' (Robert Alter, *Partial Magic: The Novel as Self Conscious Genre*, Berkeley, University of California Press, 1975, p. 248).

27 Chapman, op. cit., p. 248.

28 Hutcheon, op. cit., p. 11.

29 Brooks, op. cit., p. 37.

30 Golding to Haffenden,op. cit., p. 104.

31 Golding explained (in an interview with the *Literary Review*, in October of 1981) that the genesis of *Rites of Passage* came from Elizabeth Longford's *Life of Wellington*, in which she describes an episode where 'after three days at sea the unfortunate clergyman got "abominably" drunk and rushed out of his cabin stark naked

among the soldiers and sailors "talking all sorts of bawdy and ribaldry and singing scraps of the most blackguard and indecent songs". Such was his shame […] that he shut himself up and refused to eat or speak […] In ten days he forced himself to die of contrition.' *The Years of the Sword*, vol. I, p. 51.

32   'When you read nineteenth-century life and literature it seems quite remarkable how many people subsequently died: Arthur Hallam, for instance, lay down on a couch and just died.' (Golding to Haffenden, op. cit., p. 100).

33   See S.H. Boyd, *The Novels of William Golding*, New York, St Martin's Press, 1988, p. 160; Donald W. Crompton, *A View From the Spire: William Golding's Later Novels*, edited and completed by Julia Briggs, Oxford, Blackwell, 1985, p 134; Lawrence S. Friedman, *William Golding*, New York, Continuum, 1993, p. 146.

34   James Gindin, 'The Historical Imagination in William Golding's Later Fiction' in James Acheson (ed.), *The British and Irish Novel Since 1960*, New York, St Martin's Press, 1991, p. 118. Golding, however, insisted that his 'Billy had absolutely nothing in common with the other Billy. He is diametrically opposite. He is corrupt. He is the opposite of innocence.' A little later, he admitted he 'had that contrast in mind' (Golding to Baker in 'An Interview', pp. 162–63).

35   Gregor and Kinkead-Weekes, op. cit., p. 276. 'Dejection, An Ode' is present by absence, where the 'joy' of Coleridge's poem represents 'the power to make the universe anew' and whose fouling remakes the universe into its monstrous double.

36   *Humphrey Clinker*, 'an epistolary novel in which the same event is told through letters from different points of view', seems to Dick to be 'one of Golding's many influences' (Dick, op. cit., p. 115), a surmise with which Friedman agrees (Lawrence S. Friedman, *William Golding*, New York, Continuum, 1993, p. 146). The autobiography of an eighteenth-century British sea captain, *August Hervey's Journal: Being the intimate Account of the Life of a Captain in the Royal Navy Ashore and Afloat 1746–1759* is seen as another source. Not only did Golding comment upon the Journal

in 'Intimate Relations', from *A Moving Target*, but he 'modeled Talbot partly on Augustus Hervey' (William Stephenson, 'William Golding's *To The Ends of the Earth, A Sea Trilogy* and Queer Autobiography', *a/b:; Auto/Biography Studies*, Summer 2000, p. 8).

37   William Golding to Frank Kermode, 'The Meaning of It All' *Books and Bookmen* (August 1959) p. 9.

38   The Napoleonic Wars with England's naval power bringing wealth and pre-eminence to the nation occurred in a period when there were considerable social, political, and parliamentary assaults on the established order. These included the American and French Revolutions; the Gordon Riots of 1780; the Irish Rebellion of 1798; the abolitionist movement against the slave trade, with Thomas Clarkson's influential *History of the Rise, Progress, and Accomplishment of the Abolition of the African Slave Trade, by the British Parliament* being published in 1808; the radical Jacobins and their arguments for liberty and the improvement of woman's estate. It is unlikely Talbot would have registered each of these threats to his body politic, but they form the historic background to *Rites of Passage* as surely as does Lord Nelson's absent presence in the novel's world.

39   Stape, op. cit., p. 229.

40   Just as the hiccupping, lurching Brocklebank is depicted as having known Coleridge and drawn a lithograph of Nelson's death, so is Captain Anderson – such is Golding's antic historic energy here – presented as having been counseled by the historical figure Sir Joseph Banks (1774–1826). An eminent explorer, Banks studied the flora of Newfoundland, accompanied James Cook in the *Endeavour*'s voyage – about which Banks wrote in his narrative of the voyage – and brought his valuable New World specimens to London's Museum of Natural History. Scholars are still studying the significance of this collection, which one may also view to this day.

41   Although their interpretation differs from mine, Gregor and Kinkead-Weekes' analysis of the dinner episode, particularly its structural position in the narrative – marking a place between the

two journals and thus delaying the reader's enlightenment – is subtle. The 'reader is made to wait, because before he can turn to Colley's letter, there is Talbot's dinner engagement with the Captain. And it is this scene which is to bring *a different modulation* into the narrative and *alter expectations*' (Ian Gregor and Mark Kinkead-Weekes, 'The Later Golding', *Twentieth Century Literature* 28, 1982, p. 115, my italics).

42 The metaphor recalls *The Spire*, where images of burgeoning plants and a growing mast-like spire symbolize the complexity of human effort.

43 Talbot's observations and 'comments upon half-truths' make him 'the mirror image of his fellow diarist', Colley, who is '[a]n even more naive recorder and interpreter' (Stape, op. cit., p. 229).

44 In the coda to *Rites of Passage*, it is revealed that Anderson is himself the recipient of patronage, having been elevated in the service by way of the influence of his natural father, a Lord L——, who pawned his illegitimate son and the mother off on a parson. 'So that is why a certain captain so detests a parson! It would surely be more reasonable in him to detest a lord! Yet there is no doubt about it. Anderson has been wronged by a lord – or by a parson – or by life' (p. 268), observes Talbot.

45 William Nugent Glascock, *Naval Sketch Book; or the service afloat and ashore: with characteristic reminiscences, fragments, and opinions*, 3rd. ed., 1826; reprinted London, Whittaker & Co., 1843, I, p 42.

46 Robert Graves, *The Greek Myths*, revised edition, reprinted Harmondsworth, Middlesex, Penguin, 1966, I, (27.2), p. 106. And Frazer explains: 'While the vine with its cluster was the most characteristic manifestation of Dionysus, he was also a god of trees in general. Thus we are told that almost all Greeks sacrificed to Dionysus of the tree. In Boetia one of his titles was Dionysus in the tree'; *The Golden Bough*, abridged edition, 1922; reprinted. New York, Macmillan, 1960, p. 449.

47 The Make and Mend festivity has also an innocuous enough

definition; it is 'the naval half-holiday on Thursday, nominally for attending to one's clothes'. Eric Partridge, *A Dictionary of Slang and Unconventional English*, 5th ed., 1961; reprinted London, Routledge & Kegan Paul, 1970, I, p. 506.

48   One reference alone does not adequately demonstrate how persistently theatrical images and metaphors are pursued in the novel. Talbot's first discussion of farce and tragedy – 'Does not tragedy depend on the dignity of the protagonist [...] A farce, then, for the man [Colley] appears a sort of Punchinello' (p. 104) – ironically foreshadows the real nature of Colley's drama while, at the same time, it indicates the narrative mode of *Rites of Passage* which is 'by turns' (as Talbot later says of Colley) 'farcical, gross and tragic' (p. 276).

49   Partridge, op. cit., p. 670.

50   William Falconer, *A Universal Dictionary of the Marine or, a copious explanation of the technical terms and phrases, employed in the construction, equipment, furniture, machinery, movements and military operations of a ship*, 1769; reprinted New York, Augustus M. Kelley, 1970, p. 245.

Close Quarters *and* Fire Down Below

I

The present volume [*To the Ends of the Earth: A Sea Trilogy*] began as three separate books [...] But the truth is I did not foresee volumes two and three when I sat down to write volume one. Only after volume one was published did I come to realize that I had left Edmund Talbot, a ship and a whole ship's company, to say nothing of myself, lolloping about the Atlantic with their voyage no more than half completed. I got them some way on with a second volume and home and dry with a third.

Golding, Foreword

Close Quarters (1987) and *Fire Down Below* (1989), like their informing predecessor *Rites of Passage* (1980), came to us salted through with the languages of Tarpaulin and social rank, the two volumes amplifying Edmund Talbot's moral and sentimental education aboard that wooden world, bound for the Antipodes. What has shifted is Talbot's aim in writing the journal that constitutes *Close Quarters'* narrative, an aim that goes a first step towards unveiling the title and *its* associations with the familiar, the confined, the stifling, the intimate. As he announces at its opening, Talbot is to begin a new year with a new venture, a new vocation and new candor. 'I signalized my birthday by giving myself a present [...] I bought it, of course, from Mr Jones, the purser. As I emerged on deck [...] I met Charles Summers, my friend [...] He laughed when he saw the manuscript book in my hand' (p. 3). This time the narratee will not be his influential godfather, but Edmund Talbot himself. Focused in this way on the self and quoting a fragment from Lord Byron's *Childe Harold's Pilgrimage*, the narrator adjures himself: 'Be a writer!' (p. 5)

As readers of *Rites of Passage* will remember, literary allusions are not so much the warp and woof as the tar and oakum of Golding's narrative strategy. *Close Quarters* is no exception where we are quickly alerted to the changing literary, social, and political epoch,[1] for the imaginative revival heralded by Byron and other romantic poets insisted upon freedom of choice in subject and diction, restoring to poetry the sense of wonder and to representation a mode of realism unafraid of even violent passion. So it is fitting that the rational eighteenth-century gentleman, Edmund FitzHenry Talbot, should, having suffered a *coup de foudre*, fall instantaneously in love, become besotted by poetry, and sustain three great blows to his head. 'My head was singing and opening and shutting' (p. 65), he laments, giving truth to Shakespeare's adage that the lover shares with the lunatic and the poet a seething brain, one that apprehends, as *A Midsummer Night's Dream* puts it, 'more than cool reason ever comprehends'. For as the ship pitches and hogs and sags and rolls and lumbers from an old country to a newer one, she is also moving 'temporally from one era of literary and social history to the next'.[2] Political transformations, of course, have occurred; the year is 1814, and the Battle of the Nations at Leipzig has ended the war, sending Napoleon to Elba, and restoring the Bourbon monarchical authority in France. His head seething from the several blows, Talbot tries to register 'a turning point in history, one of the world's great occasions' (p. 54). What he feels is 'universal fright at the prospect of peace,' since, being a young man of the old dispensation, the implications for him of his compatriots no longer having to fight for king and country could well be dissent, even active resistance to restraint and authority. Then at stake could be the rotten boroughs his patrician godfather controls, which ambitious Talbot intends will secure his future election to Parliament. 'A civilized community,' he expounds with equal pomposity and conviction, 'will always find ways of [...] limiting the electorate to a body of highly born, highly educated, sophisticated professional and hereditary electors who come from a level of society which was born to govern, expect to govern, and will always do so!' (p. 11).[3]

Thus, if Talbot admits readily and repeatedly to Lieutenant Summers – now his friend and confident – that he finds himself 'a little abroad in my wits' (p. 109), such a concussive confusion is the novel's way of marking historical change. 'The transition from one epoch to another becomes the major thematic and formal intent of *Close Quarters*.'[4] For Talbot's friendship and increasingly easier familiarity with Summers – an officer who 'performed the naval operation known as "coming aft through the hawsehole"' (*RP* p. 51), having (in spite of his modest common seaman circumstances) been promoted to First Lieutenant – already map a seismic shock to both public and private notions of rank and hierarchy. Indeed, that friendship is the personal equivalent of the novel's many other markings of the period's fretful changes, changes no more to be stopped – as the spirited object of Talbot's bewitchment, Miss

Chumley, declares – than the fate of 'young persons'. Like ships at sea and continents in change, such attendant young 'do not decide their fate nor their destination' (p. 118). One reverberant scene has two crusty captains discussing the dismal world now that the Napoleonic venture is past along with its prizes: their gold braided epaulets glinting, both muezzins against the advent of other changes. Over wine and port, there is discussion about the world to come, one which Captain Anderson fears may have His Majesty's Royal Navy humiliated by a worrisome innovation: the steamship. 'They will be the ruin of real seamanship' (p. 99), he warns, his opinion being at one with that of the period's naval architects who – convinced as they were of the superiority of sailing ships – delayed the use of the steamboat on the open seas.[5] Anderson's subsequent admonishment about steamships – 'There is too much fire below' (p. 99) – amounts to more than a forewarning since it represents *Close Quarters'* links to the third volume of the trilogy, *Fire Down Below*, as well as an embedded clue to Golding's design in the second novel. As *Close Quarters* gains momentum, one watches develop a greater chain of causes than simply the testing of soon to be outmoded patrician codes. Talbot's education, like that of historical Oxford graduates of the period, with its 'emphases on Greek and Roman authors, ancient history, and the constant diet of stories of war, empire, courage, and sacrifice'[6] has shaped his patriotic attitudes to the British nation, for many other contests are 'under *weigh*' (p. 135, my italics): nothing less than the opposition of two ideological directions: one to submit in terror to the forces of nature and history, the other to incite irreverence and invention. This opposition is orchestrated at several significant textual levels. In particular, it is played out in the persons of two ship's officers, the level-headed, equable Summers and the newly arrived Lieutenant Benét (poet, lover, and seaman *extraordinaire*), as each tries to control a vessel so endangered by weather, rot, weed, and human fallibility that a 'quiet destruction moving inexorably' (p. 171) upon the sinking ship is predicted.

II

To build such a ship in the mind, place it exactly in history, man it with gunners who talk like gunners…with sailors…who are as far from the understanding of the laity as a priesthood – that is one thing. To give this huge and obsolete creation its own mortality, its own evil…that is another.

Frank Kermode[7]

Nothing in Golding's earlier fiction can prepare one for a novel so weighty of plot, where events, episodes and incidents carry such a hefty ballast of narrative excitement. Reviewers of the novel celebrated Golding's ability to fashion such an historical novel: 'this is the stuff of first-rate historical novel [yielding] an admirably documented picture of life at sea in the early 19th century.'[8] Reviewers remarked upon Golding's commanding hand in his imaginative construction of a ship with its seams and planks, its warping capstan, its three chronometers in their beds, and 'all the nautical operations that [would have been] put to hand'[9] to steer and steady such a foundering behemoth. 'One fancies that Golding could have been a shipbuilder if he hadn't become a novelist, and would have become a master in that craft as he has in his chosen one.'[10] If several reviewers seemed all but unqualified in their approval,[11] others dismissed the novel as one becalmed, like the ship itself.[12] 'In *Close Quarters* [Golding's] powers, like his characters, are cramped. He is attempting two difficult acts of narrative, in writing a sequel to *Rites of Passage* and continuing an experimental semi-pastiche of early 19th-century English.'[13] Others argued, as I would, that the novel showed 'a brooding, restless intensity',[14] an eruptive sense of the uncanny that ruptures the narrative's ludic surface. Even so trivial an episode as that in which Talbot tells Miss Granham how *his* governess made him read Richardson's *Sir Charles Grandison* carries metaphysical metaphor, alerting one to the fact that *Close Quarters* is as much concerned with the School of Sentimentality as being schooled by sentimentality.

At sea the ship, in this volume, encounters storms so severe that the deck swings only momentarily to the horizontal as she pitches from leeward to starboard, leeward to starboard. Caught later in what Summers explains is 'the null point', a term used to describe a place where 'two tides meet and so produce motionless water where a current might be expected' (p. 171), she can only be driven downhill, all the way to the Antipodes. With decks spewing oakum, most of the crew, and Oldmeadow's soldiers as well, must pump the water sluicing from one side of the ship's belly to the other. Defectively built, like so many warships (where profits were made by *not* having, for example, full copper through-bolts), she may well be unsound in her main frame. And unlike 'up-to-date nineteenth century vessels' (p. 14) with their copper bottoms, weeds of green locks can and have taken hold, arresting her movement:

> Although her bows were pointed up towards the wind she had next to no forward movement. The waves passed under her – or sometimes, it seemed, over her – but did hardly more than heave up, then slide down into the same trough in the same place (pp. 145–46).

But it is human failure and not tempestuous waters to which the chain of dangerous events is tethered. Subordination, the first and most important branch of naval discipline, has been breached by a drunken Lieutenant Deveral, who disobeys the standing order against leaving midshipmen on watch at sea. Swilling liquor below deck while the witless Willis watches above, neither marks a sudden change of winds. Almost immediately the ship appears to capsize, sails bulge the wrong way while the ship's wheel spins uncontrollably, and ropes become mere spider traces as spluttering and tearing sounds announce the splintering of the ship's topmasts. The vessel is irrevocably crippled, being pulled back to the arena of the doldrums where, were a French warrior to appear, the two ships would certainly be drawn together by the 'mutual attraction of heavy objects' (p. 35), this being the way in becalmed waters.

Again the narrative explodes into robust inventiveness. Fearful of a ship approaching in the chalk-torpor fog of the climate, *Britannia* (one infers this is the name although it is not mentioned) prepares for a possible French assault. Oldmeadow's armed troops line the upper deck while, below on the gundeck, six cannons with their muzzles pointing towards the larboard ports have been loaded and primed, ready for assorted emigrants and gentry to haul ropes, thus positioning the guns for firing. Mindful of his reputation, Talbot joins this group, but far too tall for the gundeck – had it 'been designed for a company of dwarfs, miners perhaps?' (p. 41) – strikes his already thumped and aching head against the beams. He then does so again, having leapt to his feet on hearing a roar from Mr Askew, the gunner. When the bulk of the foreign vessel comes into view, however, it is no alarming French 120-gunner, but 'His Majesty's frigate *Alcyone*…twenty-seven days out of Plymouth' (p. 50) en route to India with precious cargo: Captain Sir

Henry Somerset's wife's orphaned protégé, the bewitching Miss Marion Chumley.[15]

At this point, the Marryat-like naval yarn dissolves into luculent Austen as the two ships tie together, and a seamen's entertainment and a festive ball are organized, the latter featuring cotillions, quadrilles, allemandes, valses. 'In the midst of this watery void Golding introduces a parodic vignette of English social life, with its visiting cards, ball-gowns and minor snobberies.'[16] Lanterns illuminate the glitter of uniforms and the glimmer of taffeta-swathed ladies as the tropical nowhere – 'the minute speck in the midst of infinite extents' (p. 111) – becomes transformed into magical metropolis. The scene's conjury is all the merrier for its depiction of the sailors' entertainment on the fo'castle and their parodic – if licenced – play at the expense of its lambasted audience. Characteristically, 'Lord' (p. 114) Talbot himself does not recognize in the imitative dance by a stocky man, a ship boy on his shoulders the two together reaching 'to a considerable height [while] the rest of the company deferred to them ridiculously' (p. 125) a skilled satiric portrait of his own person.

But then how could he? For Talbot has been all but overwhelmed by emotive incoherence. Dazed by lack of sleep and a thrice-struck skull, in enthralling love, weeping for a simple song sung by the simplest of emigrant women aboard the ship, invaded by confusing 'new palaces of feeling' (p. 116), he finds that restraint, control, even sanity, have been cast aside. Repeatedly, the text underscores Talbot's loss of reason, rationality, decorum, and control, giving truth to the fact that:

> *Close Quarters* [...] is about altered states of consciousness. Its claustrophobic atmosphere [...] its array of accidents and injuries, its frenzy and its hauntings and its violence all contribute to perceptual error, confusion, emotional distress, impaired judgement [...][17]

Thus does the novel mark the move from Classicism to Romanticism, from head to heart, from control to abandonment. As with his epoch so with Talbot, the transformation has been both sudden and too extreme. Talbot seems to go momentarily mad; indeed, following *Alcyone*'s departure taking with it the protégée/prodigy[18] Miss Chumley, he seems to be, doppleganger-like, re-enacting Parson Colley's state of emotional infatuation.

III

[…] without Colley's natural abilities in the art of description there is no way in which I can convey the confusion of what happened […] I had become delirious! […] in the grips of a real, physical fever induced by triple blows […] I became temporarily disordered in my wits […] I was in Colley's bunk […] singing for joy […] (pp. 133–34)

In Golding's later fictions the figure of the doppleganger presides, informing not just *Darkness Visible* and *The Paper Men* but the first two volumes of the sea trilogy. Unquestionably *Close Quarters* restates a preoccupation with, and manipulation of, fictive doubling. Talbot and Colley become similar, yet opposed, counterparts where the mirroring double (as in Dostoyevsky's *The Double*, Robert Louis Stevenson's *The Strange Case of Dr Jekyll and Mr Hyde* or Wilde's *The Picture of Dorian Gray*) embodies those instinctive, impulsive, less rational and suppressed features of the psyche. For the presence of the absent Colley, shade side to Conrad's Leggatt in *The Secret Sharer* or the eponymous narrator of Poe's 'William Wilson', accompanies Talbot from the first page of his new journal. As *Close Quarters* proceeds, its hero seems haunted by the ghost of Colley. 'Indeed, Colley's presiding spirit is repeatedly re-invoked at those moments when Talbot confronts himself as he had first learnt to do in *Rites of Passage*'.[19] It is clear from recurrent references to Colley in the novel (by my count some twenty-four explicit and eight implicit) that through an unconscious identification with the double Talbot's own impulse to escape his prescribed social scripts is enacted. In the opposition between 'Talbot's late Augustan idiom of Taste and Enlightened Good Sense [and] Colley's Romantic idiom of the Man of Feeling'[20] can be seen the psychic split between the man who controls and the man who submits. One symptom of the dissolution of personality, as Talbot wanders progressively into the deepest recesses of his own psyche, seems to be expressed in Talbot's deranged behavior where he acts *as* Colley did. Beside the poor parson's 'low fever' – the cause, so the formal enquiry had concluded, of his death – should be set Talbot's 'real *physical fever*' (my italics), an explicit cause for the temporary demise of his rationality. Indeed, an all but 'satirised version of the swooning heroine of Romantic fiction',[21] Talbot, in a tempest of tears, will come to find himself 'carried like a corpse and laid in Colley's bunk' (p. 135). At the narrative level alone, evidence for this deliberate doubling is persistent and persuasive. 'The calculating careerist is transformed, by concussion and [...] Miss Chumley, into a lovesick fool [...] a figure who recalls the unfortunate Colley.'[22] Just as Colley's shame destroyed his work as God's servant and would have disgraced his family (had the duplicitous letter to his sister not been sent) so Talbot's maniacal plan to board *Alcyone* bound for India shows him prepared to abandon an ambitious future and bring dishonor to his family, godfather and mother alike. An equally lunatic plan is the transfer of Miss Chumley to *Britannia*, towards which end he vacates his cabin and moves into the hutch where Colley had willed himself to death. 'It was a mirror image of the one I had just vacated' (p. 108), he is made to observe. An even more compelling coupling of the two characters occurs after *Alcyone*'s departure with Talbot's delirious emergence on deck after he has fallen from Colley's bunk. Below the mast's ropes stands:

> [A] haggard young man, shaggy as to the hair, and bearded [...] his thin body plainly to be discerned beneath the nightshirt [...] He crawls up the shrouds [...] staring forward at the empty horizon and screaming at it! 'Come back! Come back!' (p. 135)

This exhibition, 'a parodic reenaction of Colley's humiliation',[23] re-orchestrates the clergyman's mad exuberance before the quarterdeck: stripped, stupefied, and shouting: 'Joy! Joy! Joy!' Hauntings, hallucinations, and disorientation are the modes of consciousness commingling in a nightmare where the dream self *becomes* Colley as Talbot's unconscious figures himself unclothed and conjoined illicitly with Miss Granham before the derisive populations of both *Alcyone* and *Britannia*. Such are the anarchic, subversive, and sexual threats to this once self-confident youth, one 'who had come aboard, serenely determined to learn everything and control everything' (p. 188). The Man of Reason, in being mastered, has been unmasted. A *bildungsroman* to end all *bildungsromane*.

From *Wilhelm Meister* to *The Buddha of Suburbia*, the rites of passage towards adulthood of any *bildungsroman* hero involve moral, social, and sexual tests as he prepares to develop a philosophy of life. Talbot shares with earlier protagonists the need – and aptitude – for regressing in order to go forward. With the 'extreme rationality of [his] mind and coolness of [his] temperament' (p. 215) somewhat suborned, he now begins to show the sort of flexibility that permits wider social allegiances. He talks without condescension to Jones the purser, the ship's carpenter Gibbs, the gunner Mr Askew, the sailing master Smiles, the clerk Boyles, and the typesetter Mr Pike. Remarkably, he even enters into a pact with his servant Wheeler, quite quixotically returned – as it were – from the dead. Pushed or fallen overboard, Wheeler – unlike Palinurus – ascends from the Underworld, having been picked up by the *Alcyone* three days after his drowning: 'The life was too strong in me' (p. 52), he cryptically explains. As Talbot comes to apprehend that things can no more be comprehended than controlled, he sees how partial and incomplete is his account of experience's complexity when compared to that integrative sensibility he now judges to have been the defining mark of the Reverend James Colley's perception of the world. 'I need Colley's pen' (p. 156), he ruminates, admiring what he believes he cannot imitate: the imaginative force that comes from 'innocence […] suffering […] and [the] need for a friend' (p. 69).

IV

'Drops deeper than did ever plummet sound'

The Tempest, V. 1

Prospero abjures his rough magic and drowns his book, a moment and phrase Talbot invokes in *Rites of Passage* as Colley's corpse is cast into the sea's depths, depths whose fearful measure the clergyman has always registered. The not unperplexing question of why Colley should inhabit *Close Quarters* so can be connected both to this *Tempest* allusion and to the alternative perspective his absent presence provides. Such a presence manifests itself partly because 'this scapegoat, unlike Matty in *Darkness Visible*, leaves a perspective that becomes articulate through others.'[24] More substantively, I would argue that Golding intends that each of his protagonists' seemingly extemporaneous references to Colley are planted there to provoke *the reader* into imagining how Colley would have responded, thus supplying Colley's point of view on the events. However much Talbot may advertise his account's descriptive inferiority to Colley's invocations of sea and sky, foam and depth, the reader should not conclude that Talbot is the 'sole channel of information and…sensation'.[25] For just as *Rites of Passage* offered two competing views on the same situation so *Close Quarters* provides an alternative way of seeing beside that of Talbot's viewpoint. Thus the strategy of the doppleganger is linked to the habit of ideographic structure. Colley is Talbot's opposed double. Twin-like and oppositional, his perspective – albeit provided by the initiated reader who becomes complicit in the construction of meaning – subverts the order and control that Talbot once relied upon and is increasingly forced not so much to surrender as to have modified by other modes of consciousness.

There are many moments in *Close Quarters* where the limited viewpoint, together with the implied presence of Colley's viewpoint, require the reader to reconstruct their significance in the light of what Talbot cannot imaginatively grasp. One such occurs when Talbot considers how much the passengers and crew have metamorphosed.[26] Menaced by the endless movement and the ship's perilous state, a communal madness starts seeping through the crippled ship, for it is not only Talbot – driven to 'acts of sheer folly' and now composing Latin verses to his phantom angel, Miss Chumley – but others who are greatly altered. The once irreproachably stern Miss Granham laughs hysterically; boozer Brocklebank, his beaver now lashed by a lady's stocking and his fat cheeks pendulous, discourses with dignity on foundering ships, ones that sink unrecorded and 'enter a *mystery*' (p. 240, my italics). Indeed, it is he who has become the ship's philosopher while his daughter, Talbot's onetime inamorata, Zenobia hides in her hutch: 'an old lady…her grey hair matted with sweat, her mouth open, her eyes in their sunken and discolored sockets staring…with terror' (p. 202). Mr Pike now cascades with feminine tears over the likely fate of his children, while Gibbs the carpenter (knowing in his limbs why the vessel's planks crawl) steeps his spirit in rum and brandy, and Jones the parsimonious purser 'continues to calculate profit and loss',[27] his demented plan for survival, should the ship sink, being to secure the one lifeboat. The ship, thinks Talbot, was 'not so much breaking up but decomposing…[her] men, Charles Summers, Wheeler, Mr Gibbs, seeming to change as if something of the same was operating in them' (p. 234). Equable Summers now 'sulks' with a kind of 'feminine weakness' (p. 244), jealous of Benét, who has replaced him as favorite in the once aloof Captain Anderson's now exclamatory indulgence.

And Wheeler? His transformation is the ship's most extreme. Haunting Talbot in hell, although providentially alive, and adamantly refusing to drown a second time, he hovers over *Close Quarters*' narrative as enigmatically and insistently as does the ghost of *his* double, Colley. [28] From the novel's second page, where the two names are first coupled, much is suggested. Teasingly, little is explained about their ambiguous link, however, and nothing at all about the natural or supernatural return of Wheeler. It is left to the reader to connect Talbot's comment to Mr Gibbs while they discuss how unseasoned wood in ships at sea can grow –'There was a [mythic] ship once […] put out so much greenery you could hardly see it for leaves […] There was a vine grew out of the mast and it made everybody drunk' (p. 152) – with Talbot's later conjecture that 'perhaps it was the unappeased "larva" of Colley creeping about the ship like a filthy smell which was the "motus" of our idiotic decline in phantasy!' (p. 220). If larvae are the immature forms of creatures that undergo metamorphosis, what then would be the appeased final transformation of Colley's spirit? How, in turn, might it be bound to Talbot's recollection? My surmise is that Oxford-educated Edmund Talbot is referring to *The Library of Apollodorus*, the ancient Greek handbook of mythology which, aside from the Homeric *Hymn 7, to Dionysus* and Euripides' *The Bacchae*, gives the most extended single account of Dionysus' adventures. In all three accounts, Dionysus' divinity, as he spread joy *and* terror though the Aegean islands, was acknowledged by all of Boetia. Finding one ship unseaworthy, he made his emblematic vine grow from its deck, enfold the mast, while tenacious ivy twined about the rigging. 'He turned the mast and the oars into snakes and filled the ship with ivy and the sound of flutes,' as described in Book 3 of *The Library of Apollodorus*. [29] That vessel, of course, became filled with phantom beasts, mythic counterparts to the disoriented, even lunatic men and women aboard *Britannia*. In addition, both Colley and Wheeler – mutually resonant as they are – can be associated with Dionysus. Liquidity is the natural element most closely associated with the god, and many stories depict Dionysus returning to water as well as describing his journey to the land of the dead at the end of his career on earth. [30] And if Colley's metamorphosis from larva to recipient of God's grace should make him, as I argue in my chapter on *Rites of Passage*, ultimately the symbolic agent of joy, then Wheeler in *Close Quarters* is possibly the symbolic agent of terror. Thus his return from the watery land of the dead can be linked to the recurring themes in Dionysiac myth: departure and return, death and resurrection. Asked by a meditative, if self-involved, Brocklebank to describe how a man drowns when he knows death is descending, for Wheeler is 'about the only man alive who had what must have been a deuced unpleasant experience' (p. 241), Wheeler shaking convulsively takes an unambiguous leave. It should come as no surprise that Talbot, facing mortal peril in the sinking ship, is so terrorized by Wheeler's fear of drowning that he finds himself suffering a sudden syncope.

> The truth is Wheeler had frightened me into a cold perspiration. Whether it was my recent foray into the realms of poetry or his strong gaze at something which existed for him alone – but it might not be his alone. I might conceivably share it with him! (p. 242).

Like Sophy's fainting when, brooding upon the black ink spot, she momentarily loses her carefully hoarded personality, Talbot's momentary loss of consciousness re-orchestrates the eschatology of *Darkness Visible* just as Wheeler's emphatic statement, 'I can't drown, sir. Not again, I can't', (p. 233) re-orchestrates that of *Pincher Martin*. Yet to compare *Close Quarters* with these two earlier novels is to register just how far Golding's fabular imagination – where nothing merely *is* but can be interpreted in broad, spiritual terms – has come, embracing spectral horrors but not, as before, at the expense of the worldly, the genial, the generously comic.

IV

> Roll on, thou deep and dark blue Ocean – roll!
> Ten thousand fleets sweep over thee in vain;
> Man marks the earth with ruin – his control
> Stops with the shore.
> > Byron, *Childe Harold's Pilgrimage* Canto 4, st. 179

It is telling that, in the several enthralled recitations of *Childe Harold's Pilgrimage* by various Byron-besotted characters in *Close Quarters*, only the first line of Canto Four's one hundred and seventy-ninth stanza should be intoned. The absence of the cautionary lines that follow helps locate the deeper significance of the embedded maritime quotation, for *Close Quarters* is, among other things, a trenchant critique of the inadequacy of human control and knowledge; and nowhere is this more readily apparent than in the novel's confrontation scene. Idle for so long in the doldrums, green weed has taken so much hold of the lamèd ship that her speed becomes even more dangerously impeded. Add to the loss of her topmasts the fact that she is spewing hemp in her main frame and Talbot, alone among the passengers, is made to understand how perilous is her future: a long voyage and the not improbable possibility that she may sink. Such is the urgency of the situation that the brilliant Benét has persuaded Captain Anderson to authorize the most daringly inventive of exercises: the bottom is to be careened by a dragrope, a procedure normally undertaken in harbor rather than in mid-Atlantic. Protesting vehemently, Lieutenant Summers opposes what he judges to be a more than irresponsible action. Soon rumor, like a lean whippet, runs through the ship's world. 'What had the carpenter said all those weeks ago,' ponders Talbot:

> They didn't think they'd careen her what with one thing and another so they took what weed they could off her bottom with the dragrope – and Mr Askew, the gunner – If they took the weed off her they might take the bottom with it (p. 245).

So does Golding prepare for the novel's most horrific of narrative moments: a scene reverberant with the rhythm of nightmare and, therefore, as rationally inexplicable as it is terrifying. A formless thing is made to emerge slowly, terrifying in its ungraspable 'thereness'. As in other confrontation scenes, the conjunction of several worlds is dramatized, by means of which the protagonist is forced to undergo an erasure of conscious control, conscious understanding, and conscious balance. Midway through the process of scraping away the streaming weeds, the dragrope catches on something. As the crewmen are sent spinning over one another to flee from their effort – as though it were 'unlawful' – and with the ship in confusion from one end to the other, Talbot witnesses a shape rising from the waterline: 'something like the crown of a head pushing up through the weed':

> The thing rose, a waggonload of weed festooned round and over it. It was a head or a fist or the forearm of something vast as Leviathan. It rolled in the weed with the ship, lifted, sank, lifted again (p. 257).

Traditionally the male hero makes a sea journey to the center of earth, the belly of the whale, the underworld; having crossed the malodorous River Styx, he slays or is slain. *Close Quarters'* mimetic modulation of this archetypal psychic voyage permits no such defeats or heroics. Neither vanquished nor victorious, Talbot registers – like Golding characters before him – how many realities there are in his one reality.[31] Confounded, he registers one matter alone: the birthed Leviathan rising and then sliding sideways to disappear is one with those monsters from 'unknown regions'. As the awful aquatic parturition erases 'the *insecure "facts"* of the deep sea' (p. 257, my italics), Talbot confronts a cosmos that is unassimilable: phallic birth wedded to uterine death. Like Colley before him and Wheeler soon afterwards, Talbot encounters here 'the ever-unknown alien in nature [and] the fundamentally unknowable in the self '.[32] And what is it that has been torn from the ship's bottom and now sinks? Flotsam? Rotten timber? Or the bilge keel, upon whose frame the whole vessel rests?

V

> Now would I give a thousand furlongs of
> sea for an acre of barren ground; long
> heath, brown furze, anything. The wills
> above be done! but I would fain die a
> dry death.
>
> *The Tempest,* I.1

Ungraspable as this experience is – one that would henceforth return in nightmares throughout the course of Talbot's life – it is rapidly followed by an act that is itself unfathomable and unforgettable. However enigmatically figured Wheeler may have been up to this point, the astonishing fact of his self-inflicted death is much more inexplicable in narrative terms, or rational terms for that matter.[33] Borrowing Brocklebank's hidden blunderbuss, Wheeler blows his brains out, an act witnessed by Talbot on his return to his cabin, the very cabin where Colley willed his own death and one which (we are intended to recollect here) was commandeered by Talbot. Are Wheeler's actions credible in narrative terms? To try to decode riddles is one thing: to be convinced that the strategy permits both a rational and perhaps even a supernatural explanation is quite another.[34] That the reader has been positioned to forge an interpretative link between the three men and thus the symbolic splicing of Talbot to the two pained creatures, Wheeler and Colley, rests on the clues peppering the account of Wheeler's death. Despite the excoriating drama of the ship's state with its bilge keel still plummeting downward, Talbot, walking towards his hutch, indulges in frequent memories of the late Reverend James Colley. Arriving and witnessing the act of suicide, he then tries:

> [T]o report what happened next as accurately as I can. That grim baulk of waterlogged timber was still, I suppose, sinking towards the ooze where Colley stood on his cannon balls when I approached my hutch – his hutch. I see it still and try to change what happened but cannot. I saw that Wheeler was inside… Then his head exploded and disappeared after or with or before, for all I know, a flash of light (pp. 261–62).

The forged interpretative link, of course, turns on Golding's practice of having readers make connections the texts' surfaces themselves shade, indeed conceal. Golding's narrative practice of inversion in *Close Quarters* is once again teasingly informative, a strategy plotted by Hamlet: 'by indirections to find directions out'. Although associated with Dionysian sacrifice, the all-knowing Wheeler is no Tiresias or Palinurus; nor is he Odysseus, and never Aeneas. Having returned from the land of the dead once, Wheeler has determined not to undergo that watery underworld voyage again. Since he – along with the others – judges the ship will soon sink, he determines to save himself from Hades, the hellish state he described himself inhabiting to Talbot when he hung about his master's hutch. And what does Talbot in his gibbering fear understand?

So close are life's quarters that any notion of detached distance from spiritual regions – whether Wheeler's hell or Colley's heaven – has to be washed as clean away as the ship's white line, demarcating class distinctions will soon be. 'I was to find this more than a simple fact – it was indeed a metaphor of our condition' (p. 277), as Talbot is made to observe about the dissolved line in his journal's '*Postscriptum*'. For a coda ending concludes *Close Quarters* in which we learn that Talbot has survived the journey. Much time has separated the journal's composition and the writing of its *postscriptum* and a third retrospective narrative describing the remainder of the voyage will come to follow, all three volumes to constitute what Talbot here titles: *Talbot's Voyage* or *The Ends of the Earth* (p. 281). The coda is in fact 'both postscript and preface, explicitly foreshadowing the succeeding volume even as it unreliably purports to be rounding off the current one'.[35] A brilliant stroke, this addendum, and all the more so since it moves the reader away from the perspective of the youthful Talbot – his volatile point of view having shaped the journal – to plunge abruptly into the phlegmatic perspective of the older man he is to become. If the 'Talbot who repeatedly and unabashedly dissolves into tears in *Close Quarters* […] is a far cry from the aloof distant Lord Talbot'[36] of *Rites of Passage*, then the Talbot of the second novel's coda is a man substantially steadier and certainly more compromised than his romantic, unpredictable and younger self. Once again the reader of another quintessential Golding text is required to conjoin and combine. Nor would *Close Quarters'* coda be vintage Golding if we, the readers, were not to comprehend that, reviewing the preceding narrative events, we have been positioned to build what *Free Fall* called 'a bridge', supplying our own perspective, perhaps to pierce the veneer of outside things as narrated, and to inspect some of the multiple meanings carried by such a title as Talbot plans: 'the ends of the earth'.

VI

There are, in fact, three mysterious characters in *Rites of Passage* who are not explained. Summers comes the nearest to being explained, but in a sense I think he needs another book to be explained.

Golding to Haffenden[37]

Although a case can be made for Wheeler and Colley as two of the three characters to whom Golding was alluding when he discussed *Rites of Passage* with interviewers on its 1980 publication, the third 'mysterious' character, Charles Summers, needed not only 'another book to be explained', but yet a third volume in 1989. This time it was almost too conspicuously titled *Fire Down Below*. It is a title carrying many suggestive meanings, not least of which is the repressed fire in this novel's most realized character: Lieutenant Charles Summers. Despite his name's promisory seasonal bounty and good cheer, despite his outward demeanor of equanimity, the officer himself is shown to hold below fires of neediness, burning ambition, class resentment, and even repressed homosexual longings.[38] Husband to his partnered ship, caressing the vessel's wood as a man 'might stroke the side of his onetime bridal bed' (p. 272), he patiently husbands his own resources so as to attend to ship affairs. These include the middle watch; the navigation by means of the wheel, the ascertaining of longitude by means of the chronometer then latitude by means of the sextant; the security of the lashings; and the securing, should they be needed in heavy weather, first of anchors on deck then bags of oil to spread on troubled waters. Add to this his administration of petty officers – sailmakers, caulkers, the purser, the carpenter, the blacksmith – and his supervision of all the common seamen, plus the fact that Summers must (as he sardonically puts it) 'be seen about the ship and detect such awful crimes as a hammock left slung or a rope uncheesed' (p. 11) [39] and one appreciates how multifarious, although unspecific, are the responsibilities of this first lieutenant. Yet the Admiralty's *Regulations and Instruction Relating to His Majesty's Service at Sea* states that a lieutenant:

> When appointed to one of His Majesty's ships is to be constantly attentive to his duty and is diligently and punctually to execute all orders for his Majesty's service which he may receive from the captain or any senior lieutenant of the ship. [40]

Attached to these rather sonorously defined duties was a code of conduct scripted by the then English way of officering, with its 'cult of class superiority and its conception that a naval officer should possess the innate gallantry and honorable nobility of an English gentleman'. [41] Summers consequently inhabits a world where social rank, ambition, and patronage both fuel and foil his desires. Promoted from the lower deck, along with only three per cent of the whole officer corps in that historical period, Summers would have reached commissioned rank, having been warranted by the Board of the Admiralty after entry as a common seaman. As naval encyclopedists like Golding have been aware, in the early nineteenth century midshipmen came from a wide social background. Several were from the highest ranks of the aristocracy, although the landed gentry provided a much higher proportion – some twenty-seven per cent – while the largest group – close to fifty per cent – were the sons of professional men. A mere ten per cent, like Charles Summers, came from the commercial or working class.

Provided with a denser texture of historical references than its predecessor, *Fire Down Below* broadens the trilogy's critique of social snobbery, this final novel linking its thematic analysis to the personal tempests and burning naval ambitions of first lieutenant Summers, Talbot's now fast friend. If Talbot, in donning 'slops', the practical garments of a common seaman, has put aside pride of caste – 'Indeed [from that moment] I date my own escape from a certain unnatural stiffness and even *hauteur*' (p. 28), he observes – his friend Summers, by contrast, is revealed to wear armour, beneath which resentments burn. And with some reason, given the pyramidal and stratified structure of subordination in the British navy. First, he secured the atypical promotion from common seaman to midshipman solely by (comedic) accident, an imagined incident that allowed Golding to insert one of *Fire Down Below*'s several inside jokes. Ever the firm Methodist, a much younger Summers was evidently caught reading while on anchor watch; just as he was being rebuked by his divisional officer, Admiral Gambier made a surprise appearance. 'Dismal Jimmy', as Admiral Lord Gambier was historically known for having taken aboard and disseminated to the fleet his Evangelical faith, asked to see the offending book and, seeing it was the Good Book, forthwith had lowly seaman Summers advanced to midshipman.

Patronage and interest counted at every stage in a naval career, however. Having successfully passed the greatest ordeal in an officer's career, the examination for lieutenant, and secured a commission, albeit on the superannuated *Britannia*, Summers' only way of rising above his thousands of companions would be to attract the attention of higher authority. Numerically alone the competition would have been very stiff; according to Burney's 1815 *Universal Dictionary of the Marine* there were 3,104 lieutenants and 777 captains in 1812. With no formal method of assessing whether an officer was fit for promotion, there were several ways for officers to attract attention, the foremost being to have political influence in the Admiralty. It comes as no surprise that the sons of the peerage commanded automatic influence while, in the electoral politics of the period, commoners whose family had influence in the election of Members of Parliament for counties and boroughs could often gain an advantage.

It is within this historical context that Golding firmly places Summers' expectation that he will benefit from gaining the patronage of Talbot, who is himself ambitiously planning to run for Parliament in one of his godfather's rotten boroughs. Summers requires Talbot's championship, since the officer has neither familial nor political connections to attract the notice of the Admiralty. And, of course, the other avenue for advancement – distinguishing oneself in action – is as closed to Summers as to the extravagantly capable Benét, the war having unfortunately ended. For all these reasons, the rivalry between the two lieutenants as depicted in *Close Quarters* is intensified in *Fire Down Below*, as is Summers' disgruntled sense that he is the more deserving.

Then again, while commissioned officers would historically have always been concerned with their status, Summers is made to be particularly preoccupied. Commenting on the character's evolution after his first appearance in *Rites of Passage*, Golding observed:

> He started by being much more saintly [...] I therefore reduced him to someone who could be insulted and who could find that his social standing was a thing of great personal moment to him.[42]

This character trait is developed more fully in *Close Quarters* and palpably so on the occasion when Summers takes Talbot to Deverel's former bunk in the wardroom where other officers, Cumbershum and Benét, reside. Bitterly, Summers describes the space as one designed for 'a mere lieutenant, some poor man with no prospects, no hope; designed perhaps for a man thrust out of his legitimate place' (*CQ* p. 267). Of course, he is referring to himself, convinced then that Talbot has withdrawn his esteem, preferring the rival Benét. The nitroglycerine of envy is mightily mixed with an ammonium nitrate of jealousy as Summers' self-portrait shows, including as it does the provocative insinuation about his sexual temperament, an inclination from which he himself would seem to have been dissociated:

> I have no family, Mr Talbot, and I do not believe myself inclined to marriage. Yet my attachments are deep and strong. Men, like cables, have their breaking strain. To lose my place in your regard, to see a younger man, one with all the advantages which were denied me, achieve on every level what I could never hope for... (*CQ* p. 269).

By the end of the conversation, their squall has blown over. But with an eye to the ironic as well as the inferential, Golding has Talbot's journal entry, marking the restoration of their amity, describe its renewal thusly: 'Hesitantly I held out my hand; and like the generous-hearted Englishman that he is, Charles seized it with both his own in a *thrilling* and *manly* grip' (*CQ* p. 270, my italics). Thus is the stage set for the concluding volume: *Fire Down Below*. Lieutenant Charles Summers would fain be *Persuasion*'s Captain Frederick Wentworth, only he doesn't fancy the Musgrove sisters or even Miss Anne Elliot. Nor will there be any Napoleonic high glory, or prize money, or possibility of promotion to a captain's rank. On to such a stage do gender, sexuality, class, and invention walk forward to declaim themselves aboard *Fire Down Below*'s foundering ship as it still makes its way to the Antipodes.

VII

[T]he conflict which Benét and Summers personify is that which exists between flair and caution, excitement and worthiness, passion and prudence. The two officers exemplify the eternal battle between the new and the old [...]

Kevin McCarron[43]

Reviewers of *Fire Down Below* were intrigued by the contrasting modes of seamanship 'personified by [intrepid] Benét and dutiful first lieutenant Summers'.[44] Some observed that the contrast informed not only the novel's theme but also its design. Talbot, the narrator, stands between the two men: 'self-effacing, thoughtful, carefully kind, the Good (and Christian) Friend [and] his intolerably resourceful rival [...] Handsome Devil, son of French emigrés, lover of Older Women, a Poet who versifies everywhere, even in the fighting top and the teeth of the tempest'.[45] Emblematic as these two officers are of alternative ways of envisaging and inhabiting the world, so too is Tallbot's position emblematic: situated, like his epoch, halfway between the Augustan and the Romantic, the conventional and the innovative, the religious and the scientific.

That these binary oppositions inform not just the two fictional characters but also the plot and pace of the novel as a whole was not lost on one reviewer. Extolling the work as 'Sir William Golding's most genial, most various and most harmoniously structured novel,' the *Times Literary Supplement* stressed the skilled 'alternation of passages of excitement with passages of rest',[46] an observation I shall later amplify when my discussion turns to two linked episodes midpoint in the novel. About the novel's geniality there was considerable agreement among critics. 'Like the trilogy it completes, [*Fire Down Below*] increasingly explores and rejoices in the resources of the comic, not as a refutation but as a kind of final extension of the Euripidean irony that has informed all his work.'[47] In this 'wonderfully comic novel', the characteristic coda ends up being uncharacteristically unsad:

> Mr Golding says, probably with tongue in cheek, that the happy ending was a gift to his readers. The gift is an affirmation on a grand scale, which only an artist with much of the 'fire up there', in his heart and mind can bring off.[48]

Strong accolades such as this by no means persuaded other reviewers from assessing the novel negatively. While once again American responses were less frequently positive than they were negative,[49] British reviewers tested the degree to which *Fire Down Below* could be read independently from its two older brothers and found the young Jacob lean.[50] And, as always in the culture of reviewing where the *soi disant* literary monument is considered the suitable object for toppling, there were those commentators who obliged in the ritual of ridiculing: 'The book is neither conceived nor written along 19th century lines: it is not the simulation of a 19th century novel, but a modern novel encumbered by the fancy-dress of a Victorian vocabulary'.[51]

I take particular issue with the judgement that 'the events of the novel are narrated with no particular intensity and are not really involving'.[52] When Golding writes in *Fire Down Below* about the infinitely tricky details of a star-studded, luminously mooned southern night sky or describes the face of a grave wave, we recognize that we are in the presence of a mesmerizing imagination, a creative intelligence at the height of its power. He similarly delineates a ravishing icescape full of chaotic shapes, growler contours, hummady silhouettes and the extremes of light and shadow on an advancing iceberg. At the same time he reveals obliquely the subtlety of the shipboard relations so that Talbot is made to portray, 'without ever properly understanding [...] the co-operation of Captain Anderson's authority, Lieutenant Benét's brilliant technical intelligence and Lieutenant Summers' religiously inspired duty [...] in the management of the vessel'.[53] He further involves the reader in the engineering details of Benét's plan to repair the wooden foremast 'by securing the split shoe with bars of hot iron which contracting as they cool will draw the wood together with great force'.[54] One of the glories of Golding's storytelling in *Fire Down Below* is its passionate precision; whether in its moments of dramatic intensity or its moments of rapturous calm, the novel involves its readers in the details of things. We feel in our fingers and at the bottom of our belly the characters and creatures and elements his imagination inhabits.

And what we most experience is the perilous journey: hour to hour, bell to bell, watch to watch, while sails thunder, black clouds emit cold, hiss rain, and the ship thumps and groans as loudly as any dark Satanic mill. To 'the cranky hull, the jury rig, the distance, the terrible weather towards which we are making our clumsy way and which we need because it is the only force which will get us to land and shelter before the fresh water and even the food run out' (p. 24) has been added Benét's hazardous strategy. Fire is to be used in the ship's cellarage whereby the red–hot metal bored through the mast's base will force the split shoe together, thus full sails can again be set and speed will increase. Like the dragrope execution, this is a brilliant but dangerous gamble. 'Any mistake and the foot of the mast may slip and go through the ship's bottom' (p. 22), joining Colley's corpse and *Britannia*'s bilge keel on the vast seabed. And she's wooden, this cranky hull, a fire down below and she could well go up in smoke. Summers persists in taking a realistic view of her plight, but is no match for the enthusiasms of the exuberant Benét, whom Captain Anderson supports. 'I had a sudden awareness of the two of them, Benét and Charles, the one brilliantly putting us at risk, the other soberly and constantly taking *care*! (p. 56) observes Talbot, having come to dislike Benét, thinking him too clever by half. Although he has taken a firm and intelligently grounded stand against his subordinate's position, the First Lieutenant is rebuked by his superior Anderson: commanded indeed to cease his 'obstruction'. Of course, the reprimand amounts to a door slammed shut on any chance of advancement. And in addition to his battle with jealousy and spite, there is searing humiliation. 'It was such a humbling, such a shaming rebuke! It was so unjust' (p. 118) cries Summers, his sense of shame recalling Colley's mortification. Transformed as he has been by having acknowledged his responsibility in the Colley affair, Talbot can now reiterate that lesson, promising his friend that he will see to it that justice and fair play triumph. 'The first ship that returns from Sydney Cove shall carry not just my journal in which you are described with such admiration but a letter to my godfather giving reasons and declaring that you deserve to be made "post" [captain] on the spot!' pledges a more engaged Talbot.

VII

> I have not been so moved by a man's kindness – it is exactly like the story of Glaucus and Diomede in Homer. You know they exchange armour – gold armour on the one side for bronze armour on the other – my dear fellow – I have promised you the bronze armour of my godfather's patronage – and you have given me gold! (p. 29)

Self-reflexive literary allusions are much diminished in *Fire Down Below*, although Talbot cannot help but perfume his prose with such worthies as Euripides, Homer, Pindar, Swift, Voltaire, and Shakespeare (*Hamlet*, *The Merchant of Venice*, and, of course, *The Tempest*). Yet threaded through his account are references (some ten in number) to a minor episode from the *Iliad* where Glaucus and his enemy, Diomede, meet on the field of battle. Recognizing they are connected by ties of ancient family friendship, they not only refrain from fighting each other but exchange gifts of arms in token of amity. Since Lycian armour was of gold and that of the Greeks bronze, the exchange – a 'Glaucus swap' a 'Diomedian exchange' – comes down to us to mean that all the benefit is on one side, a coding well known to the classics-crazed Talbot. The gold armour this Diomede receives is the costume of the midshipman, for Summers (more constant ship husband than battling warrior) provides dry and comfortable clothing: 'Item: a vest, apparently made of string. Item: a rough shirt such as a petty officer might wear. Item: a woolen overgarment of jersey worsted about an inch thick. Item: a pair of seaman's trowsers […] Finally a leathern belt' (p. 27).

While the specter of 'Lord Talbot' so garmented in common slops is hugely comic, the sartorial transformation marks just how far he has travelled from the young man who first came aboard, his assumed social privileges swilling round his beaver hat 'like a cloud of pinchbeck glory' (p. 151). Then there is his commitment to and 'awareness of the ship's mechanical and social life,'[55] which express themselves not by archly imitating the language of Tarpaulin, but rather by mastering its meaning in the performance of the duties of a sailor in sea service. For in the 'profound allegory of friendship' (p. 120), as encoded in the Glaucus and Diomede story, Summers invites Talbot to stand the middle watch (from midnight until four o'clock in the morning) as his 'doggy'. Walk forward on deck Mr Midshipman Talbot, reporting for duty.

As is so often the case in Golding's fiction, there are deliberate narratorial gaps, the burden of bridging them being the reader's responsibility. *Fire Down Below* reintroduces this strategy by way of the arcane reference. The frequency with which the Glaucus/Diomede allusion appears alerts us to the probability that information, withheld from the narrator, is there to be excavated and that excavation will require us to see with eyes wider open than those of the narrator. Talbot may take their alliance to be as friendly as that of Glaucus and Diomede. We may see, however, what Talbot does not by remembering – unlike Talbot – the *Iliad*'s nodal affiliation: the attachment of Achilles and Patroclus, with Patroclus wearing Achilles' armour in battle so as to guarantee his lover's honor.

Clues to Summers' motivation in orchestrating their shared watch can be discovered in a moon-drenched scene, radiant in its beauty and liquid calm: 'The ship was a ghost, a spirit of silver and ivory […] The sails were unbearable, their whiteness seeming to invade the very apple of the eyes' (p. 83). Music from the sailors singing the duty watch drifts towards the two men, gentle as the wind and magical as the moonlight. With the sea glittering and the celestial stars glistening, the night's poetry enters the two men's souls. Quoting from *Psalm* 8, 'For I will consider thy heavens, even the works of thy fingers: the moon and the stars, which thou has ordained,' Summers seems on the brink of an intimate confession when, with typically exclamatory lack of restraint, Talbot blurts out: 'Oh, Charles, Charles, I am so deeply, so desperately, so deeply, deeply in love!' (p. 91).

That Summers too is deeply in love is clearly detectable. Talbot may construe the contrivance of the shared watch as Summers' way of sparing him the dark hours of the haunted hutch, with Colley's ring bolt at the bunk's side and its wounded ceiling bearing still some splinters of Wheeler's skull. What he describes as the 'warm and *manly* thoughtfulness' (p. 96, my italics) of a friend we construe as something very different. The object of Talbot's ardor is Miss Chumley, not Summers. Yet given the evening's rare communion, the enamored Summers might well be cherishing the hope that he is the treasured beloved, only to have the hope cruelly dashed. Such is his narcissistic myopia that Talbot neither registers Summers' pain or the desire which provoked it. So the trilogy's mapping of Talbot's slow maturation, as this lengthy *bildungsroman* draws to a close, charts some areas still needing to be conquered. In Talbot's remarks immediately following his declaration – 'You say nothing. Charles. Have I annoyed you?'; 'Why so brusque?' – the reader is positioned to intuit Summers' state and then observe – as Talbot does not – the self-restraint as he silently struggles to acquire composure. Unlike *his* double Colley, a creature who found himself undone by his desires, Summers restrains and so sustains himself: desirous he may be, but his actions will be amicable.

The homosexual sounds a minor chord throughout Golding's fiction; several characters, although initially presented from the limited – sometimes biased – perspective of the novels' various unreliable narrators, nevertheless function as agents of enlightenment, frequently articulating otherwise concealed implications in the palimpsest of the text.[56] However, nowhere else is homosexuality as subtly and as sympathetically represented as in *Fire Down Below*, a novel linking together several fires. The title has several resonances. First there is Benét's process of mending the mast, literally involving fire and the constant threat that the burning metal could incinerate the ship. Then Summers' emotional and sexual conundrums can best be represented by fire; a man of strong faith, his ideas have been 'tested in the fire of his religion' (p. 210). To the literal, sexual, and religious applications of the title should be added the social since the ship society burns with class animosities as well as a transformative utopian vision. For Prettiman's ideas have been tested in the fire of 'cruelties and torments of social condemnation, derision, dislike' (p. 210).

The notorious freethinker whom Talbot dismisses in the earlier journals as an *opera buffa* anarchist, Aloysius Prettiman, is – Talbot now understands, having become engaged in passionate conversation with him about Pindar's Fortunate Isles and Voltaire's Eldorado – a man of substance and courage. His intention is to lead a group of convicts, reformed criminals, and settlers into the Australian interior and there found the Ideal City, a plan in which the governess Miss Granham will participate. For if Prettiman is to be the William Godwin of Australia, Letitia Granham Prettiman will be its Mary Wollstonecraft. 'She is all that the ages have looked forward to' (p. 171), chants Benét, the heady representative of dynamic change. Like her husband – for the two have been married, Captain Anderson officiating[57] – Mrs Prettiman seems much transformed to Talbot's immature eyes. 'As the voyage lengthened towards a year, her own years had become less and less obvious to the casual beholder' (p. 190). Intimidated though he may be by the lady, Talbot notices how her abundant hair has a habit of escaping to 'catch the eye irritatingly'. But he is too much the conventional priggish young man to imagine that a female *d'un certain âge* could possibly be a woman.

'Conventional' is not an adjective one can apply to Letitia Prettiman. Dean's daughter though she may be, she nevertheless despises the social inequities Talbot personifies and does not hesitate to ridicule his pretentions. Avatars of their changing era, both Prettimans are skeptical of all authority, abjuring any deference to rank or position, whether in secular or religious spheres. That Golding should depict Prettiman as having chosen Australia as the country where the communal experiment should occur demonstrates again *Fire Down Below*'s attention to historical authenticity. Australia has a rich history of utopian experimentation, being a country that took in marginals, rebels of all kinds, convicts, Chartists, Irish exiles, German Moravians, and Italian socialists. Furthermore, Prettiman's utopian anarchism and belief in the innate perfectibility of mankind had a long pedigree in Australia. His is an eclectic blend of humanitarian enlightenment, its ideals of equality, fraternity and sorority,[58] liberty, and tolerance conjoined to a vision of salvation through love and reason: 'I tell you, Edmund, there is not a poor depraved criminal in the land towards which we are moving who could not, by lifting his head, gaze straight into the fire of that love' (p. 219). So Prettiman predicts, his visionary faith invoking the novel's title once again. The full metaphysical implications of *Fire Down Below*'s title become symphonically blazoned, the imagery given to Prettiman invoking his aspirations: his attraction to mystery, his pull towards social justice and illumination, his search for knowledge, and his quest for love.

> Imagine our caravan, we, a fire down below here – sparks of the Absolute – matching the fire up there – out there! Moving by cool night through the deserts of this new land towards Eldorado with nothing between our eyes and the Absolute, our ears and that music (p. 219).

As vision, this passage is one of the more resonant representations of the paradoxes of belief interrogated by so much of Golding's fiction. Like Boehme, Swedenborg, Newton (who practically abandoned mathematics for mysticism after he was thirty) and other rationalists, deists, and communitarians before him, Prettiman is made to believe in miracles. In this case it is the miracle of possible social transformation and the return of humanity from a state of alienation to a state of innocence, even grace.

VIII

So this, then, was the beginning of what for me was the strangest adventure of our long voyage. Still battered [...] we sped eastward towards our goal and life was *irradiated* by the nature of them both [...] I threw off my upbringing as a man might let armour drop around him and stand naked, defenceless, but free! (p. 209)

Armour comes to be restored, for Talbot's conversion to the Prettimans' progressive dream is only partial. He finds himself, however, testing its philosophical ideals, so threatening to the established order – egalitarian ideas about the illegitimacy of hereditary honors, the abuses of intolerance and superstition in dogmatic religions, the 'divine fire up there and down here' (p. 226) – against Summers' absolute integrity. During their night watches, Talbot comes to understand how inflexible the practical naval man is in his resistance to change: equality, fraternity, and liberty are the blood-soaked banners of the guillotine, not a call to parity. Prettiman is an infamous Jacobin with whom a future civil servant should not consort. His intensity is the sort that provoked Spithead and the Nore, two celebrated mutinies where crews sent officers ashore and ran the ships themselves until grievances were addressed. Resenting the triumphant Benét, whose innovative solution has so far proven successful since the ship is making steady progress, he is suspicious about Talbot's intellectual liaison. Now sharing the watch, Talbot considers his friend's limitations. Although he possesses complete knowledge of the economy of a ship, were he to be promoted to post captain on Talbot's recommendation would Summers prove to have the innate authority to command a warship in the Admiralty? And should he demonstrate his inadequacy would this reflect ill upon Talbot's political fortunes? Thus broods Talbot, knowing (with some small degree of self-recrimination) 'that the only human quality to the depths of which there could be no limit was my personal meanness' (p. 212).

The broodings are interrupted by another political and navigational warp in this ship-society: the question of longitude. As we remember from the uncanny and edifying rite of shooting the sun in *Rites of Passage*, latitude could be ascertained with relative ease at the meridian hour of noon with the use of a sextant, the instrument for measuring angular distances and the altitudes of celestial bodies in navigation. The taking of the noon sight was an important event aboard ship, vibrantly demonstrated in that scene where a purely computational operation was given the force of 'the solemnest moment of a religious service' (*RP* p. 38), with the congregation of passengers, ship's people, and immigrants observing in silent raptness. Golding unquestionably wanted attentive readers to combine what would appear to be contradictory ways of understanding this marine activity, accepting the legitimacy of both the scientific and the spiritual. To observe daily the *celestial* body of the sun so as to ascertain something as essential to nautics as latitude is to depend on a universe so ordered that what Prettiman later calls the good, the Absolute, the music of the fiery spheres might be implied. 'What could be better than ascending from the trivial matter of our exact position on this globe to a contemplation of the universe into which we have been born,' the visionary Prettiman of *Fire Down Below* is made to summarize.

Although longitude is far more difficult to ascertain, the problem was solved technically in the 1790s with the Board of Longitude giving its prize to John Harrison, who invented the chronometer, an accurate clock ingeniously able to make compensatory measurements for temperature, a ship's movement, dampness and dust. So successful was the device that thenceforth any naval ship going on a foreign voyage was entitled to have a chronometer. However, *Britannia*'s chronometers can no longer be trusted, after the great length of the voyage and the many storms and soakings. With no accurate knowledge of longitude *Britannia* could well strike land before sighting it. Given such a perilous predicament, another reasonably accurate method of finding longitude could be adopted, Benét tells Talbot, one that the great Captain Cook used in all his voyages: celestial navigation. Observing the heavenly bodies, the fixed stars and the moving bodies of the sun, moon, and planets, the navigator could measure the angles between the celestial body, the horizon, and the pale, thus solving what was called the 'celestial triangle'. A 'cobweb of measurements' (p. 186) sneers the mathematically untutored Summers, himself preferring the more pragmatic method of 'assisted dead reckoning' based upon ascertained latitude and analyses of competing chronometers, faulty as they are. The dragrope, the masthead with its burning metal: Benét once more is fired to ingenuity. And so begins Benét's contest of wit with the universe, teasing out angles between winks of light in the skies to challenge by sheer mathematical genius the cherished theory that celestial navigation is less accurate than determining latitude with reference to chronometers. 'We shall present it to their lordships,' crows a triumphant Benét, his eye on advancement: 'the Anderson–Benét method' (p. 214).

IX

'You can see it clearly, Charles, what is the matter with you? It is no ghost – look there and there […]'
He was silent for a moment while the grip of his right hand tightened on my arm.
'Heaven help us all!'
'Why, what is the matter?'
'It is ice!' (p. 226)

Thus has *Fire Down Below* prepared for an episode Wagnerian in the immensity of its blast. Calm as the two men's discussions have been, they take place on the brink of what will be, literally and metaphorically, a predatory confrontation with nature. Currents have carried the vessel to cliffs of ice, an iceberg some two hundred feet high. 'Foam whiter than the ice climbed the cliff…part of the cliff…collapsed into a climbing billow. Two huge pieces…sprang upwards like leaping salmon! They were, I swear, ship-size fragments and falling again as the fog swept all from our sight' (p. 231). As in the incandescent creation of the forest of flame at the ghastly conclusion to *Lord of the Flies*, Golding pulls his descriptive powers to full throttle here. *Fire Down Below* bears a narrative intensity so adamant that it forges fresh anxieties as currents push the ship – like a child's toy – at great speed closer and closer to the indifferent icy wall. In Talbot there is created the need for a whole new etiquette of fear.

How to explain the disorganized fury of the sea, the towers, pinnacles […] Columns of green water and spray climbed the ice cliff and fell back from it. Wind against wind, wave against wave, fury feeding on itself […] I was a present panic, an animal in the article of death (p. 242).

Anguished yells, tarpaulin shouts, passengers crowding forward, sheets groaning, pumps grinding and – over riggings – men 'swarming like bees at an unwonted season' (p. 228), flying spray, roaring winds, thunderous explosions of ice, deliriums of seas pocked with pancake ice, cataclysmic falls of cliffs: this confrontation scene rivals all others in the fiction's repertoire in its symphonic orchestration of helplessness before an Antagonist Other. 'My brain went. I saw a *melange* of visions in the ice which swept past me […] A cave opened […] the end of everything' (p. 244).

Like Sammy Mountjoy in his cell, and just as mysteriously, Talbot escapes erasure. The ship does not sink. In this culminating ordeal, from which rationally no one could have been expected to survive, there is survival. All but two of the wooden world's inhabitants are saved, for as in *Rites of Passage* and *Fire Down Below*, death makes an appearance, purser Jones and seaman Tommy Taylor being swept into the swelling waters. Nevertheless, unknowable forces inexplicably reverse its southerly course to drive the frigate forward: northwards towards Australia. How to account for this titanic change in fortune? Are we to give credence to Talbot's conclusion, just nanoseconds before the ship turns north, that they all would be undoubtedly smashed 'unless there is a miracle' (p. 232)?

Adopting the characteristic strategy of 'narratorial lacuna',[59] the text glances aside, a perspective other than Talbot's being superimposed. Interleaved at just this narrative ellipsis is a letter – one written long after the incident – from a member of Talbot's former Oxford college, a learned hydrologist/geographer who claims to be able to 'lend an objective mind to the problems of terrestrial behavior' (p. 245). As doubly ironic as this invested last phrase is, the letter's impartiality is clearly subverted, its judgement smacking less of pedagogy than of pedantry. In substance, the hydrologist dismisses Talbot's account as 'fiction in the wild, modern manner!' (p. 245). A cliff of such size, so argues the man of science, would be a 'a floating continent [and not] a patch of ice' (p. 246). The existence of such a reef would imply a vast continent round the South Pole, which is '*geographically impossible*' (p. 246, Goldings italics), fulminates the hydrologist, one who has perfected (he reminds reader–Talbot) a proof as to its unfeasibility.

As in *The Paper Men*, Golding sets up huge enjoyments (for himself, too) at the expense of hidebound 'ologists'. Without once introducing the word 'Antarctica', *Fire Down Below* means its readers – rather than its unreliable narrator – to intuit that the sea whipped by cold, violent winds and clogged with tongues of berg into which *Britannia* has drifted is the sea sweeping round what would later be known as the Antarctic continent. A continent completely unknown until modern times (and still imperfectly known), its coast has always been protected from intruders by belts of packed ice, thousands of miles wide. For centuries, tradition held it that another land lay south of the known world, although attempts to find it were regularly defeated by the inhospitable sea and drifting ice packs. Navigators – notably Captain Cook as early as 1774 – voyaged into Antarctic waters, but it was not until 1819 (four years after Talbot's putative journey) that the British mariner William Smith discovered South Shetland. Thus the mountainous floe that threatened Talbot and the *Britannia* crew was one single chip made from Antarctica's glaciers and ice shelves. And thus too the abiding irony. Momentously present, Talbot would always be momentously absent, never knowing what the reader is positioned to discover: they had been in the veritable jaws of the fabled land. In turn, one explanation then for the ship's fortuitous change of direction from south to north could have been the effect of the circumpolar current, circling the continent of the South Pole.

X

Out of whose womb came the ice?
And the hoary frost of heaven

Job

Ice and fire provide some of the earliest of tropes for representing opposing states. As reverberant metaphors, each is a controlling force in *Fire Down Below*'s design; coupled, they best illustrate the novel's exploration of rivalling antitheses. Is the agency for the ship's survival, for example, scientific causation or miraculous intervention? When *Britannia* does burn, shortly after her permanent mooring in the harbor of Sidney Cove, is the ignition caused by sparks from a firework display then in progress? Or is the conflagration a consequence of the slow combustion in the ship's shoe, the fire down below to which the title refers? In the novel's two astronomer/poets,

Benét and Prettiman, do two seemingly antithetical ways of operating in the world converge? For the officer navigates mathematically by means of the celestial constellations while the philosopher pilots his voyage towards the dream of social meliorism by way of the stars, linking those substantial fires up there to the spiritual fires down here. As to the matter of longitude and the best method for its calculation, the two approaches are inconclusive. By relying on two chronometers and dividing by half, Charles achieves the same result (by a mile or two) as Benét :

> The Benét-Anderson method, therefore, might be good or bad. Nothing was proved or disproved […] Luck must be considered to have favoured both parties. The land was where they said it was. So everyone and no one was satisfied (p. 260).

So an intended riddle remains; having set up the thematic opposition between the forces of cautious pragmatism and those of flexible innovation, *Fire Down Below* does not endorse one approach as more valuable than the other.

Equivocal too – and hugely so – is the question of whether Benét's contrivance of heated iron in the mast's shoe was 'the principal agent [of the ship's] preservation' (p. 196), thus saving the lives of all on board, or whether it was the principal cause of Summers' death. *Fire Down Below* neither affirms nor denies. Nevertheless, shortly after having received the Glaucus gift of golden armour, Talbot having used his influence to have his friend promoted to captain of the permanently moored ship,[60] Summers dies in the burning vessel's cellarage.

> The frapping burst, went flying in the air, and at once, there were two explosions, one after the other. I saw the deck split open […] The whole ship opened and sent up a tower of bright flame in the midst of which what was left of the mainmast fell thunderously (p. 281).

While the mast's symbolically valent final fall presents little ambiguity, more elliptical is an earlier brief glimpse of a much altered Zenobia Brocklebank, aged and inert in Talbot's former cabin. Nothing further is made of this, a narrative crux that is matched by the equally unexplained reference at the novel's end to Zenobia's death in Australia and her message to Talbot that she is 'crossing the bridge' (p. 295). Talbot may explode, 'Devil take it, there were no bridges anywhere near Sydney in those days,' interpreting the farewell literally, but is the text nudging one back to an early scene in *Rites of Passage*? Having glanced at the woman whom he then judged to be a manipulating Magdalene, Talbot suddenly came to be startled by Zenobia's countenance. The 'directed stillness of the orbs and eyelids' suggested 'a different and watchful person' (*RP* p. 61), one possessing a spirit Talbot could never have fathomed at the conclusion of *Fire Down Below*, not being able to perceive the bridge linking the body and its soul.[61] If such a fleeting nudge is intended, then in Talbot's self-serving use of Zenobia the trilogy can be seen to re-orchestrate Golding's abiding obsession with, and presentation of, male violence with its concomitant violation of females: Sammy Mountjoy's desecration of Beatrice Ifor, Christopher Martin's of Mary Lovell, Oliver's of Evie Babbacombe, Wilf Barclay's of Mary Lou Tucker.

Were one to continue to speculate on such embedded references to the other works, one would still be confronted by other puzzles in *Fire Down Below*, many of which remain undecoded. In the perishing of the purser, given a nasty send off, the lifeboat which selfishly he alone had commandeered being shredded by a block of the berg, should one detect a recasting in minor key of Pincher Martin's rapacious – and supremely mistaken – hoarding of self against oblivion? Or merely recall in the episode an ironic inversion of an historical event, a 1799 sloop named *Weazel* sinking in Barnstaple Bay leaving but one survivor: the purser? As always in Golding's fiction the indeterminacy of meaning leads to an increase of meaning. What then to make of the other echoes over which one is made to puzzle? For *Fire Down Below*'s closing chapters depict a Talbot adjusting to life as a civil servant in an islanded colony where the pyramidal structure of stratified British society has reasserted itself, here at the farthest reaches of Great Britain's empire.

Talbot not only grieves for the loss of his Diomede, Captain Summers, he also misses what was, although in class terms a motley group, nevertheless a family of now vanished friends: 'Those friends, I now saw, were the people with whom I had passed the best part of a year and whom I knew as well if not better than I knew my own family!' (p. 274) – the young military lieutenant Oldmeadow, the lithographer Brocklebank, the immigrant Mrs East, the fellow passengers Mrs Pike and her typesetter husband, the blacksmith Bowles, the sailing master Smiles, the common seaman Tommy Taylor, and the Prettimans, who have disappeared into the interior, dream-inspired:

I grieved for my friends the Prettimans, not really knowing which of the two meant the more to me – I grieve anew for Miss Chumley, that bright and unattainable *star* in the distant north (p. 276, my italics).

Then there is the revoking of Edmund FitzHenry Talbot's great expectations; his godfather has died, and his future has fallen in ruins round his feet. 'Like Summers in the earlier years I should now have to *work my passage*' (p. 277), he broods, conscious that the nautical metaphor has very real meaning. No longer fate's favored child, the desired star all the more unattainable from his abject status as a junior secretary with little hope of preferment to help him rise to fame or fortune, sunk in a depression, the once supremely confident Talbot knows: 'The future was hard and full. Nevertheless I girded myself and walked towards it. But I firmly believed that whatever might happen to me in the future, this was the unhappiest period of my life' (p. 282).

Should *Fire Down Below* conclude here it would offer one more typically unhappy ending to a Golding narrative of *sturm und drang*. And characteristically too what seems to be the posited ending is immediately undercut, the next chapter shunting readers abruptly from dolorous realms into regions of 'phantasy, of "faerie", of ridiculous happiness' (p. 283). So is the characteristic subversion of narrative closure given an uncharacteristic – even gleeful – twist, subverting what readers expect from a Golding text: 'grief, sheer grief, grief, grief, grief '.[62] Instead there is a happy ending, the tried and true formulaic conventions for narrative closure, inheritance, and marriage, practically bringing Talbot's story to a fortunate end. In cheerful succession, *Alcyone* arrives, her precious cargo Marion Chumley waving from the deck; Lady Somerset permits the couple a carriage ride, Miss Chumley's fan busy flicking aside flies as the two ardently commune. And among *Alcyone*'s other cargo lies a heavy bag of letters from England, in one of which rests the heady news that, without one single sycophantic blandishment or the finesse of honeyed flattery, Talbot has, *in absentia*, been promoted to Parliament:

> By agreement one of the incumbents of my godfather's rotten boroughs had asked for the Chiltern Hundreds and I, Edmund FitzHenry Talbot, had been elected! Beat that, Goldsmith! Emulate me, Miss Austen, if you are able! (p. 307)

In even more jovial succession, a ship bound by way of India for Britain is boarded, matrimony is formally proposed and the ceremony expeditiously performed by the Bishop of Calcutta. And in the retrospective reminiscence that brings the story all but to the ends of its metaphoric earth, we learn that back in England an elderly Talbot has become something of a sclerotic official personality. Elevated to the Foreign Office and on whisky-drinking terms with the Prime Minister ("'Talbot, you're becoming a deuced bore about that voyage of yours'" (p. 294)), now it is *his* patronage which is sought. In one letter from the long ago acquaintance Oldmeadow requesting preferment for his grandson, Talbot learns of the Prettimans. En route to the interior, she leading in trousers, he riding astern and behind a miscellany of immigrants, freed convicts and aborigines, they push forward on their mission. 'As he said in his letter, not a hair nor hide of any of them has been seen since' (p. 295).

XI

They that go down to the sea in ships: and occupy their business in great waters. These men see the work of the Lord; and his wonders in the deep.

Psalm 107

As well as being his last completed work, *Fire Down Below* is the zenith of Golding's oeuvre. 'It is his *Hamlet*, his *Ulysses*, his *A la recherche du temps perdu*, his *Seven Pillars of Wisdom*, his *Life and Opinions of Tristram Shandy*, his *White Album*. It is a *vade mecum* of his themes and concerns and characters and obsessions and techniques,' to borrow the inspired accolade given another writer and another text.[63] Earlier in this chapter I wrote that sounding through *Fire Down Below* were echoes from the other novels, and I would here add other whispers – personal, if not autobiographical – that become audible when one turns a trained ear, the novel functioning rather curiously as a venue for Golding's own self-discovery. That the themes and techniques and strategies of the earlier fiction become both reiterated and transformed need not be argued. Talbot's distant view, for example, of the disintegrating ship and his friend's fiery incineration, employing the technique of objective reportage, is as menacing in its production of pain as was the distanced perspective on Lok's death in *The Inheritors* or the scrupulously focused depiction of Matty's fire-swirled end in *Darkness Visible*. The technique of concealed, impacted clues is also much present, the naming of the *Alcyone* being one case in point. Unscrambled, the ship's performing signature becomes 'halcyon', the bird fabled by Golding's beloved ancients to breed in floating nests on sea at winter solstice and to charm wind and wave into calm. Another pelagic association from the ancient world concerning Alcyone/Halcyon is that, along with the other Pleiades (seven nymphs transformed into seven constellations), Alcyone's rising in the middle of May and setting in October marked the start and finish of the sailing season. Then too the halcyon (referring back to the Greek *alkyon*) when translated from the Greek is 'kingfisher', the creature invoked in *The Spire* as a bluebird/over/panicshot darkness and imaging that novel's vision of the intermingling of physical and spiritual antimonies.[64]

As stellar text, *Fire Down Below*, like a magnet, pulls to itself many of the incidental fibers of other Golding engagements. Included among these are his sympathy for homosexuality; his abiding infatuation with Homer; his scathing distaste for the class system; his knowledge of all things navigational; the powerful influence of accounts of voyages by early explorers [65]; and his merry amusement with all things comedic, a humor much in evidence here down to the waggish application of his own once plastered grin to Captain Anderson's mug.[66]

And while, in my judgement, caution should be practiced by those who would describe *The Paper Men* and *Rites of Passage* as novels primarily about the writing of novels, *Fire Down Below* exhibits some rather elegant self-referencing and reflexivity. Its happy ending, for example, seems intended to thumb noses at positioned critiques branding him forever as an incurable pessimist in high-dudgeoned pursuit of original sin. Consider in this context the exchange between Mrs Prettiman and the land-bound Talbot as he reminisces about the voyage. In her stern response one can hear the dissent of the much dissected, paradigmed, and allegorized author of *Lord of the Flies*: 'Do not refine upon its nature. As I told you, it was not an Odyssey. It is no type, emblem, metaphor of the human condition. It is, or rather it *was*, what it was. A series of events' (p. 275). Having Miss Chumley frequently flick her fan to clear away flies – 'the eternal and infernal flies' (p. 305), expostulates Talbot/Golding – is thus a sly aside indeed.

Personal, if not autobiographical, whispers are audible too. *Fire*

Down Below is, in one sense, Golding's recasting of his own *Free Fall*, a work immersed, like *Fire Down Below*, in both the physics and the metaphysics of existence. This earlier work – a *bildungsroman* like the later sea story [67] – had been much strained by the then recent death (at eighty-one) of his father, Alex Golding, whose portrait came to be drawn in *Free Fall*'s Nick Shales, the benevolent science master with a polymathic passion for knowledge so insistent that he inspired – and received – devotion. Having reached at seventy-eight an age close to that of his father at his death, Golding summons forth another tribute in the figure of Aloysius Prettiman, thereby putting to final rest the ghost of his father and burying, perhaps, his own now ancient quarrels.

'Golding's accounts of his early life prompt the suspicion that the Prettimans may be seen as fictional representations of Golding's parents,' argues Golding scholar John Carey, who sees in the reverie that ends *Fire Down Below* 'a son's dream of his dead parents: alive, radiant, and together in an unintelligible paradise'.[68] In characteristic fashion, a coda brings this – Golding's final novel – to closure, one that characteristically calls into question all that has preceeded, thus offering another, bittersweet, perspective that undermines and makes unexpectedly provisional the tenure of security which the adult Talbot had acquired.

In respectable old age – close, in fact, to Golding's own seventy-eight years, to judge from the novel's inferential clues – Talbot casts his memory back to that voyage, his recollections provoking 'a kind of dream':

> I hope it was a dream, for dreams, in any event, are mysterious enough. I do not mean their content but the very fact of them. I do not wish it to have been more than a dream: because if it was, then I have to start all over again in a universe quite unlike the one which is my sanity and security (p. 312).

Were it vision rather than dream, Talbot would be compelled to abandon his carefully sustained commonsensical world view and embark on a new excursion into the unknown. Dream or vision, he imagines the Prettimans on their journey, remembering that those many years ago he had refused the invitation to join them in their founding of a Celestial City. Indeed, he apparently never even countenanced such an adventure. In his dream, Talbot is appropriately earthbound, 'as if he were a child looking up at adults'[69]: he is buried up to all but his (judicious) head while the Prettimans ride forward, laughter, excitement, and happiness irradiating their expedition:

> You would have thought from the excitement and the honey light, from the crowd that followed them, from the laughter and, yes, the singing, you would have thought they were going to some great festival of joy [...](p. 312).

Paradise achieved and a dream deferred: 'the world must be served, must it not?' (p. 313), a rueful Talbot is made to concede, *Fire Down Below* concluding with an open-ended, deceptively simple sentence: 'Still, there it is'.

If *To the Ends of the Earth: A Sea Trilogy* maps the making of Edmund Talbot's soul and his education by a magisterial and unforgiving metaphoric sea, the trilogy's final volume is a testimonial to the grit, stubbornness, intelligence, devotion, saving sense of humor, and that inextricable combination of passion and desperation that drives the writer to cling to and steer his ancient craft. Sir William Golding's 'firkin', *Fire Down Below* should also be understood as a fable about his own life – the saga of a lifetime's acquittal and loss. In Talbot's dream deferred there is perhaps a fictionalized gesture towards those intervening twelve years between *The Pyramid* and *Darkness Visible* when the most capable of writers wrote only in the most private of modes: the unpublished personal journal. Two cruces in *Fire Down Below* needing emendation provoke such a surmise. Tucked away in the elderly Talbot's retrospective reminiscence is a veiled allusion:

> None of these volumes is able to be published until we are all forgotten. In any case, *journals* tell so little. I leafed through these and found myself able to do no more than sample here and there. I shall not reread them. (p. 294, my italics)

It is a remark quite contradicting the intention Talbot was given in the *Postscriptum* to *Close Quarters* where the journal writer determines he will publish the three volumes under the title *Talbot's Voyage or The Ends of the Earth*. Could it not be the case that the author has embedded himself in the persona of his narrator, thus devising a cunning self-reference? If so, this ambiguous erasure of intent should be linked to Talbot's (otherwise narratorially inexplicable) imaginative leap six generations into the future when, in *Fire Down Below*'s near final sentence, Talbot describes his rapturous meeting with his – here unnamed – affianced. 'I swept off my hat – and she broke into a run – and your great-great-great, great, great-grandmother fairly sprang into my arms' (p. 311). By my calculation the year into which the text has leapt here is 1942, the year of the birth of William Golding's daughter, Judith. And *Fire Down Below* – with its animated tribute to his own parents, its ironic referencing of his own writing, and its disguised portrait of the artist as a young and elderly man – also contains in this veiled dedication a loving, luminous gift to his daughter: the odyssey of his life.

Endnotes

1   Observing that two ghosts haunt the novel, one being the shade of Parson Colley, a *TLS* reviewer adds that the other is 'the ghost of literature itself [...] throughout the novel muffled resonances from [...] innumerable other sea-faring yarns and mysteries turn this ship into a floating echo-chamber' (David Nokes, 'Metaphysical Voyagers', *Times Literary Supplement*, June 19, 1987, p. 653). My sense is that Golding's plan for his protagonist's new project (and *his* new project) did not include a *Close Quarters* echo-chamber but rather an ocean-dangerous testing. Talbot, for one, is turned inside out: the text demonstrating this shift by having Byron – not Pope, not Coleridge – interleaved.

2   Gindin, James, 'The Historical Imagination in Willaim Golding's Later Fiction', in James Acheson (ed.), *The British and Irish Novel Since 1960*, New York, St Martin's Press, 1991, p. 116.

3   In the period, a common path to election to the House of Commons was marriage to the daughters of peers: a path Talbot intends to take. The British governing elite (as Cobbett and others repeatedly complained) influenced the election of members of the Lower House as well as packing their own Upper House. Talbot's speech, then, is no historical aberration. 'In 1807 at least 234 of the MPs representing constituencies in England, Wales and Scotland

owed their seat in some way to aristocratic intervention' (Linda Colley, *Britons: Forging the Nation 1707–1837*, New Haven and London, Yale University Press, 1992, p. 155).

4   J. H Stape, '"Fiction in the Wild, Modern Manner": Metanarrative Gesture in William Golding's *To the End of the Earth* Trilogy', *Twentieth Century Literature* 39 (1993), p. 231.

5   As *Close Quarters* recreates political and literary history, so too does it recreate navigational history. Almost before Watts' steam engine was on the market there were attempts to power ships by steam. Fulton was experimenting with steam power in Paris in 1807, and the Forth–Clyde canal had steamships in 1812. Thus the fictional Sir Henry Somerset's description of his ship, the *Alcyone*, being taken out of Plymouth Sound with a steam tug bears historical accuracy. Furthermore, 'the Board of the Admiralty found it "their bounden duty to discourage, to the best of their ability, the employment of steam vessels as they considered that the introduction of steam was calculated to strike a fatal blow at the naval supremacy of the Empire".' J. F. C. *The Conduct of War* (London, 1961) as quoted in Woodward Llewellyn, *The Age of Reform: 1815–1870*, 2nd ed., Oxford: Oxford University Press, 1992, p. 42.

6   Colley, op. cit., p. 154.

7   Frank Kermode, 'Taken Aback', *London Review of Books* (June 25, 1987), p. 9.

8   Ian Stewart, 'Ripping Fiction', *Illustrated London News* (September 1987), p. 88.

9   Francis King, 'Still in Peril on the Sea', *Spectator* (June 3, 1987), p. 41.

10   John Bayley, 'Log of a Master Seaman', *Observer* (June 7, 1987), p. 25.

11   'The final chapters dealing with the cutting away of weed and coral to free the ship are as good and strange as Conrad at his finest' (Ronald Blythe, 'Lord of the Tides' *Guardian Weekly*, July 5, 1987,

p. 22). 'Golding has produced his finest, funniest, most humane work' (Christopher Hirst, 'Rites of Passion', *Books*, June 1987, p. 14).

12   See Robert M. Adams, 'Close Quarters', *New York Times Book Review* (May 31, 1987), p. 44; Rosemary Ashton, 'Becalmed', *Listener* (June 11, 1987), p. 25; and Richard Hough, 'Close Quarters', *Los Angeles Times Book Review* (June 7, 1987), p. 3.

13   Barbara Hardy, 'Narrative Teasing' *Times Educational Supplement,* (June 19, 1987), p. 23.

14   Nokes, op. cit., p. 653.

15   As one knows, not only do the British have a certain genius for names, they say those names in ways that frequently bear little re-semblance to their spelling. Thus, if in real life London's Beauchamps Place is pronounced Beecham Place so *Close Quarters*' characters pronounce 'Miss Cholmondeley' (p. 211) as 'Miss Chumley' (p. 66).

16   Nokes, op. cit., p. 653

17   Robert E. Knolan, 'Golding's Sea Novel Sails into Dangerous Waters', *Chicago Tribune* (June 14, 1987), p. 6.

18   Brocklebank's malapropism, describing Miss Chumley as a prodigy of the captain's wife and not her protégée, allows Golding to have Talbot ascribe to the young women the divinity so habitually associated with the beloved female in Golding's idealized depiction of womanhood. A prodigy is, of course, a person endowed with surprising qualities, 'a marvelous thing, out of the course of nature'.

19   Lawrence S. Friedman, *William Golding*, New York: Continuum, 1993, p 150.

20   Ian Gregor and Mark Kinkead-Weekes, 'The Later Golding' *Twentieth Century Literature* 28 (1982), p. 113.

21   Michèle Roberts, 'Young Mariner', *New Statesman* (June 12, 1987), p. 28. In addition, Golding intends a parody of the period's literary

stock persona, the Man of Feeling. 'Talbot's rebellion against his previous self [...] sees his near complete transformation into [...] the "Man of Feeling", a version of MacKenzie's lachrymose title-hero or of Goethe's Werther' (Stape, op. cit., p. 232).

22   S.H. Boyd, *The Novels of William Golding*, New York, St Martin's Press, 1988, p. 179.

23   Kevin McCarron, *The Coincidence of Opposites: William Golding's Later Fiction*, Sheffield: Sheffield Academic Press, 1995, p 110.

24   Gindin, op. cit., p 122

25   Rosemary Ashton, 'Becalmed', *Listener* (June 11, 1987), p. 25.

26   In the interests of what he calls its 'metamorphic theme', Friedman argues that the novel's war plot and love plot – each of which is subverted on being introduced – are both deliberately 'drained of their narrative potential' (Friedman, op. cit., p. 151).

27   Kermode, op. cit., p. 9.

28   Wheeler appears some twenty-seven times by my count, and references to him balance nicely with the twenty-four allusions to Colley in the text. None of the other characters has so symbolically dominant a place in *Close Quarters* as do these two ghosts.

29   In a footnote to this account in the *Apollodorus Library*, the translator Michael Simpson writes: 'Dionysus and the pirates are the subject of the Homeric *Hymn 7, to Dionysus*. In this version, sweet wine streams through the ship and a heavenly fragrance fills it. Sail, mast and oarlocks are covered with vines, ivy, flowers, and garlands. Dionysus changes himself into a lion and springs upon the captain, so frightening the sailors that they jump into the sea from fear and are changed into dolphins' (Michael Simpson, *Gods and Heroes of the Greeks: The Library of Apollodorus*, Amherst, University of Massachusetts Press, 1976, p. 155).

30   'Dionysus was not solely, or even mainly, the god of wine... [he

embodied] the liquid fire in the grape, the sap thrusting in a young tree, the blood pounding in the veins of a young animal, all the mysterious and uncontrollable tides that ebb and flow in the life of nature' (E.R. Dodds, *Euripides: Bacchae*, Oxford, Oxford University Press, 1960, pp. xi, xii).

31   In the context of what I have defined as the characteristic strategy of the confrontation episode is the observation that in *Close Quarters* '[t]he ocean's rising waters definitely figure the Leviathan that was first recognized in *Lord of the Flies*' (Nadia D'Amelio, 'Golding's Trilogy as a *Bildungsroman*', in Frédéric Regard (ed.), *Fingering Netsukes*, Saint-Etienne, Publications de L'Université de Saint Etienne in association with Faber and Faber, 1995, p. 188.

32   Stape, op. cit., p. 233.

33   'So [...] isolated from common humanity by his [...] reserve [is Talbot] that he fails to see another tragedy ripening aboard the ship [...] His servant Wheeler, whose appeals for sympathy and understanding Talbot has loftily ignored, eventually reaches the end of his tether.' (John Carey, 'Lost (and Found) at Sea', *The World and I* 4, March 1989, p. 367) As to the unexplained mystery surrounding Wheeler, commentators have not been too loquacious: 'Wheeler [...] commits suicide; no one knows why' (Gindin, op. cit., p. 120); his 'only ever partly decoded suicide [...is] an act that eludes and intentionally defies Talbot's [...] habitual modes of apprehension' (Stape, op. cit., p.233); the character 'functions [...] as an embodiment of that incomprehensible and irrational element of life which Talbot never knew existed until he read Colley's journal' (McCarron, op. cit., p. 118).

34   Golding's project engages deliberately with what is not entirely explicable, as readers have come to know. Of interest here in this context is his observation: 'If a novelist makes an entirely explicable character, then his story drops dead; he's done away with the possible human attribute of free will' (Golding to John Haffenden, 'William Golding', *Novelists in Interview*, London and New York, Methuen, 1985, p. 103).

35   Jem Poster, 'Beyond Definition: William Golding's *Sea Trilogy*' *Critical Survey* 5 (1993), p. 95.

36   Friedman, op. cit., p. 150.

37   Golding to Haffenden, op. cit., p. 102.

38   Among the many reviewers, only two inferred this significant feature of Summers' character: Peter Kemp, 'A Bonfire of Vanities' *The Sunday Times* (March 19, 1989), PG1a and Carey, whose engrossing discussion appeared in his review essay in *The World and I* (368–9). As he happily added: 'it is appropriate (though also a bit corny) that the narrative, like that of Golding's earlier novel *The Spire*, should be dominated by a huge phallic symbol [the shattered foremast].' Another discussion of Summers' sexuality appeared in William Stephenson, 'William Golding's *To The Ends of the Earth, A Sea Trilogy* and Queer Autobiography', *a/b:; Auto/Biography Studies* (Summer 2000), pp. 15–16.

39   '...*that* is a properly cheesed rope, for your information,' Summers unhelpfully explains to Talbot. A mark of the slowly maturing Talbot here in *Fire Down Below* is the degree to which he has absorbed – rather than colonized –Tarpaulin talk. Not that the language of the sea is absent from *Fire Down Below*, where appear such linguistic sweets as: all standing; baggynet; bitts; boltropes; bowse; chasing the wind; doggy; end for end; handsomely; lubber's hole; shake out a reef; slops; Stockholm tar; wheel's whipstaff.

40   Admiralty, *Regulations and Instructions Relating to His Majesty's Service at Sea*, 1808, p. 17.

41   Jonathan Raban, 'Journey to the End of the Night', *New York Review of Books* (June 6, 1999), p. 15.

42   Golding to Haffenden, op. cit., p. 102.

43   McCarron, op. cit., p. 128.

44   Victoria Glendinning, 'Fire Down Below', The Times (March 23, 1989), p. 21a.

45   Galen Strawson, 'All Hands on Deck', Observer (March 19, 1989), p. 48.

46   Stephen Medcalf, 'Into the Southern Seas', Times Literary Supplement (March 17, 1989), p. 267–68.

47   Frank McConnell, 'William Golding's Sea-Fever' Book World/ Washington Post (March 12, 1989), p. 3.

48   'Water and Fire', Economist (April 1, 1989), p. 82. See also John Bayley, 'Seadogs and Englishman', Guardian Weekly (April 2, 1989), p. 29; Paul Gray, 'Long Haul', Time (March 30, 1999), pp. 81–83; Robert E. Kuehn, 'Golding's Novel of the Sea Ends a Memorable Trilogy', Chicago Tribune (February 19, 1989), p. 5; and Paul Stuewe, 'Fire Down Below', Quill & Quire 55 (July 1989), p. 47.

49   See Deidre Bair, 'At Sea in Volume Three', New York Times Book Review (April 12, 1989), p. 37; Rose Marie Beston, 'Fire Down Below' America (May 6, 1989), pp. 434–35; Duncan Spencer, 'Boredom and Sogginess Plague Voyage Far Too Long in the Making', Washington Times (March 6, 1989), p. 8.

50   See David R. Smith, 'Rite of Passage on a Square-Rigger', Los Angeles Times Book Review (March 19, 1989), p. 13; and W. L. Webb, 'Sea Pictures', New Statesman and Society (April 14, 1989), p. 34.

51   Philip Glazebrook, 'Sicklied o'er with the pale cast of thought', Spectator (March 25, 1989), p. 34. While it was the case that some reviewers found the novel's mannered style annoying (Bair, op. cit., p. 370), Glazebrook alone displaced 'Talbot's style – that of a priggishly literary young gentleman in 1815' (Bayley, op. cit., p. 29) some twenty-five years forward to Queen Victoria's reign and all things Victorian.

52   Beston, op. cit., p. 435.

53   Medcalf, op. cit., p. 267.

54   Patrick O'Brien, *'Fire Down Below'*, *London Review of Books* (April 20, 1989), p. 11.

55   Stape, op. cit., p. 228.

56   These include an unlubricious experiment by Christopher Martin in *Pincher Martin*; Father Watts Watt in *Free Fall*; Evelyn de Tracey in *The Pyramid*; the polymorphous Leopard Men in 'Clonk Clonk'; Sebastian Pedigree in *Darkness Visible*; the Reverend James Colley in *Rites of Passage*; Johnny St John John in *The Paper Men*; Ionides Peisistratides in *The Double Tongue*.

57   The marriage scene is merry indeed, Golding revelling in the comic possibilities at hand: a bedridden groom, a bride bearing a bouquet of real flowers from Captain Anderson's private paradise, Benét having induced the sacrifice – and a captain delivering from his raised prayer book the lines 'Man that is born of woman,' the first words in the burial service. After shrieks and giggles from the attending immigrants, Anderson begins again: 'Dearly beloved – '. And who should catch the bouquet? Edmund FitzHenry Talbot.

58   That *Fire Down Below* should find a role for a bluestocking in its projected Ideal City underscores again the novel's historical authenticity. The Protestant Anglo Saxon millenarian tradition in the eighteenth and nineteenth centuries gave prominence to women, witness 'Mother' Ann Lee and her Shakers.

59   Stape, op. cit., p. 236

60   Talbot is astonished to hear from the governor's deputy that Captain Anderson and Lieutenant Benét had both pressed the claims of First Lieutenant Summers for the position, but readers should not be. Once more and deftly, yet another Golding text shifts beyond the limitations of an unreliable narrator, letting the reader intuit that neither naval man was Summers' perfidious enemy – as Talbot would have the reader believe – but instead respected the considerable maritime experience that their colleague possessed.

61   That Golding intends the reader to view Zenobia Brocklebank from

eyes other than Talbot's is underscored in another passage where, during Colley's Sabbath service, 'the candles of the saloon *irradiated* her face, took from it the damaging years, while what had been paint now appeared a magical youth and beauty' (*RP* p. 66, my italics). 'Irradiated' is, of course, the word associated with the Prettimans of *Fire Down Below*, thus is it associated with spirit, as should Miss Brocklebank be..

62   William Golding, 'A Moving Target', *A Moving Target*, New York, Farrar, Straus & Giroux, 1982, p. 163.

63   So writes the biographer W. Stephen Gilbert of his subject Dennis Potter and the playwright's brilliant achievement in the television series *The Singing Detective* (*The Life and Work of Dennis Potter*, Woodstock & New York, The Overlook Press, 1998, p. 263).

64   The 'crowned kingfisher' (p. 284) Talbot first imagines the approaching, yet still distant, *Alcyone* to be the Australian tufted bird. For Friedman the creature is 'an emblem of redemption' (Friedman, p. 157). He also makes the happy point that *Alcyone*'s unexpected appearance amounts to a 'deus ex machina worthy of Golding's admired Greek drama' (Friedman, op. cit., p. 157).

65   Such as George Vancouver, James Cook, William Barents, Bristol's Thomas James, and David Crantz, the mariner who charted the inhospitable Arctic Sea with its lands of mist, snow and ice.

66   During his active duty at sea as lieutenant on a rocket-launching craft during World War II, Golding's terror took the shape of a fixed grin, his crew believing that he relished the razor edge of mortality and weaponry!

67   In the context of the two *bildungsromane*, the following observation is informative: *Fire Down Below* 'solved a problem which has baffled [Golding] before. Previously he has found it difficult to write a novel in the first person' (Medcalf, op. cit., p. 267).

68   Carey, op. cit., p. 372.

69   Carey, op. cit., p. 372.

The Double Tongue

I

The lord to whom the Oracle at Delphi belongs neither tells nor
conceals, but indicates.

Plutarch Moralia 404d

istarum visionum et divinat ionum causas et modos vestigare si quis
potest certoque comprehendere, cum magis audire vellem quam deme
exspectari ut impse dissererem.

Augustine de Genesi ad litteram xii.18

A primeval waterfall in *The Inheritors*, medieval England in *The Spire*,
Imperial Rome in 'Envoy Extraordinary', aboard a stinking ship during
the waning years of the Napoleonic wars in *To the Ends of the Earth*, an
early Pharaonic dynasty at the Nile's edge in *The Scorpion God*. In what
would be his last novel, *The Double Tongue*, an aged prophetess at
Delphi, Apollo's ancient shrine in Aetolia early in the first century BCE,
reviews her life. It represents some sixty years of mantic utterances
amid the dismantling of both Delphi's fortune and influence in an
Hellenic age being overcome by Roman imperial triumph. Thus did
Golding's final novel witness a lifelong narrative conviction that the
'past is not another country, it's joined directly to us'.[1] Like the earlier
fictions with their remote settings and distant epochs, *The Double Tongue*
derived its provenance from a culture quite distant from the late
twentieth-century world and perhaps one most innately hospitable to
the workings of Golding's imagination. For, like classical Greek legends
and myths or the Homeric epics, the Hellenistic age, even in the
declining years invoked here, shared a sense of oneness. Divine
revelations emanated from omens, signs, dreams, visions, the
pronouncements of seers, and the promise that the gods spoke directly
to – as well as through – mortals. In a narrative thriving on paradox,
riddle, contradiction, and the warring claims of skepticism and belief,
that Euripides' *Ion* should be one of *The Double Tongue*'s interleaved
sources is informative in several ways, principally by way of that drama's
iconoclasm. Euripides' most irreverent and unconventional treatment

of mythology depicted the god Apollo as shifty, devious, and, indeed, bungling in his rape of Creusa. From that bruising violation was the infant Ion conceived, the son whom Creusa abandoned at birth and who, through the agency of Hermes and the Pythian prophetess, would become the sanctuary of Delphi's high priest. Only an appearance by Pallas Athene as *deus ex machina*, mouthing patriotic officialese at the end of the play, could defend against charges of irreligiosity in the representation of the mighty god Apollo. Indeed, Euripides was the Greek dramatist with whom Golding said he had felt the greatest kinship, and his *Ion* in particular stood most as touchstone to the rewards of the Euripidean double-edged technique, where two perspectives are offered on one event, the very strategy Golding had successfully adapted – as I have argued – in novel after novel. Responding to questions regarding the influence of Greek tragedians upon his own method, Golding specifically cited Euripides' *Ion* and the effectiveness of its deliberate indeterminacy:

> A girl has been raped by Apollo [...] you can take it either that she's been raped by a completely irresponsible force or that Apollo must have a priest for his temple, a priest who must be born of a woman.[2]

And while 'Ancient Greece...is frequently central to Golding's imagination,'[3] as Gindin remarked long before the book's posthumous publication in 1995, *The Double Tongue* showed (even in its fragmentary state) in joyous immediacy Golding's respect for and love affair with the life-proclaiming, life-enhancing mysteries of that long-ago world: all the more bracing in this our interrogative contemporary world.

I write of the book's 'joyous immediacy' mindful that such a phrase might well seem to ring with uncritical over-confidence. For *The Double Tongue* is an unfinished work, one that Faber and Faber assembled from journal references, working notes and the two drafts Golding had written – and typed – by the time of his sudden death early on a Sunday morning in June 1993.[4] As the 1995 'Publishers' Note' at the volume's beginning informs, 'the draft which we publish here had more or less the form of the novel he planned to send [...] in the autumn of the year. It would almost certainly have been longer, as the other, more unfinished draft was.' Thus the editor John Bodley, who assembled the published text, stood in relation to *The Double Tongue* as John F. Callahan did to Ralph Ellison's unfinished

Juneteenth, or Toni Morrison to Toni Cade Bambara's *Those Bones are Not My Child*, and a decade earlier Tom Maschler, the chairman of Jonathan Cape, to Hemingway's *A Moveable Feast*. All four posthumously published works represent constructions where, to greater or lesser degrees, informed judgements had to be based on educated guesses about the informing movement of – in the end – narrative fragments. So the reader's contract with the published text is a skeptical one. In Golding's case, it might appear to be an almost Aeschylean irony that what turned out to be the novelist's last (written) words were to be published as a fragment and not as the shaped and solidly constructed whole, so much a characteristic mark of his narrative project. I would argue a contrary position, however, remembering how the author had always revered the fragment, seeing a late twentieth-century Western preoccupation with the remnant as one engaged by the allusive and the elusive. The notion is plausible: that truths in our time can only be grasped fleetingly and then through that which is incomplete, yet suggestive. Ancient Egypt's Unfinished Colossus, for example, had been one fragment Golding had mentioned. To this I would add the suggestibility of the Pharaoh's bed on the island of Philae, Michelangelo's sculptures of the shackled giants, Schubert's *Unfinished Symphony*, Mozart's *Requiem* or Puccini's *Turandot*. As *An Egyptian Journal* put it, inhabitants of a skeptical age such as we seldom grasp with confidence: 'in fact, if we saw in any way it was the Mosaic way, seeing not the face of Truth but his or rather her back parts from our cleft in the rock and covered by her hand'.⁵ The observation, although made in the late twentieth century, happily suits the spirit of another cultural landscape, namely that of Heraclitus' early fifth century BCE dictum upon the Pythian revelations at Delphi: 'The lord to whom the Oracle at Delphi belongs neither *tells* nor *conceals* but *indicates*.' As quoted at the opening of this chapter, this passage was taken from Plutarch, himself a Delphi priest, as recorded in his first century CE *Moralia*. The italics here are mine. I would argue that, in turning to the ancient shrine at Delphi with all its riddles, Golding had tackled another arena of indeterminacy in which his own preoccupations with the possible eruption of the numinous might be given a narrative shape that would match – as it were – the Heraclitian: neither to conceal nor to tell, but rather to indicate.

II

> Ideas lose their forms when they decay, yet do not necessarily lose their
> place in the mentality of the age. They turn to imaginative compost.
>
> Francis Spufford, *I May Be Some Time*

I quote this passage as it directly addresses not only the riddles of Delphi but also the syncretic nature of belief systems, a figuring forth of which I will argue was one of *The Double Tongue's* intentions. Hindsight instructs that one of the more habitable regions for Golding's imagination to cultivate another fictional, and once again distinctly different, world might have been watered as richly as that of the Delphic Oracle. Historical fact and legend, the surfeit of allusions to the place in classical hymns, ancient oracle collections, idylls, histories, tragedy, and ode, saturated the site. So did pictorial representations on pottery and vases, like the Codrus Painter Vulci Cup depiction showing King Aegeus in consultation with the Pythia Themis, who sits quite calmly on her tripod.[6] Consider too how the confluence of various myths of origin have percolated, since Hellenic religious belief, like all religions, was a cumulation of various worships. Over the years, some scholars have argued – on the basis of archaeological excavations in the region of small clay statues of the Earth Mother – that the most primitive Greek religion was one worshipping the Great Mother. Gaia (Ge/Earth) and her daughter Themis spoke oracles at Pytho in the world's early day, long before the male Apollo was recounted as having taken possession of the worship.[7] Whether or not Apollo did wrest the patronage of the sanctuary from Gaia's original rule, the persuasive Delphic mythology of the sixth century BCE held that Apollo had slaughtered the great serpent Pytho. The serpent's meandrous body inhabited the cave at the foot of Mount Parnassus in the very omphalos of the world, Zeus having sent two eagles from both east and west, according to myth, with their meeting point determining the earth's centre: Delphi.

Legend and myth aside, it is an historic fact that from the sixth century BCE onwards the Delphic Oracle did draw patrons, clients, tourists from all Hellenic Greece and beyond. The period of Delphi's greatest prestige when powerful and wealthy clients – cities as well as individuals – came to consult its oracle through the Pythia lasted (according to Joseph Fontenrose, H. W. Parke and D. E. Wormell) from approximately 580 to 320 BCE. Fontenrose and Parke also place the

Delphic Oracle's real decline in prestige after Alexander the Great's death, continuing through the 300-odd years of the Hellenistic period into that of the early Roman. Thus *The Double Tongue's* historical positioning in Hellenic Greece in early first century BCE authentically renders an impoverished, politically suspect Delphic Oracle and an exhausted Greek *polis*, enervated by a puissant Rome with its then progressively steady policy of intervention and systematic seizure of the eastern Mediterranean. In its fictional representation here, as in fact, Delphi and Athens have lost their supremacy, a point the narrative underscores slantingly in having both a young Julius Caesar and another man, named Cimber, come to consult the Oracle over who will achieve political dominance.[8] 'Any oracle consulted both by Alexander the Great and Socrates must be taken seriously,' Golding once mused in his 1963 essay 'Delphi'.[9] Indeed, for over a thousand years – and one is astonished by this mysterious fact – the Delphic Oracle's incumbent Pythia, attended by male priests, ascended the tripod to speak (sometimes in hexameter verse) the kind of oracles that were reported by Aeschylus, Euripides, Herodotus, and Plutarch, all of whom having had acquaintance with Delphi. It may have been Cicero who contributed most substantially to Delphi's considerable reputation as a major force in promoting colonial settlements and city-founding in the period of Greek colonization from 750 to around 500 BCE[10]; however, another and loamy body of legendary tales reveal by their pseudo-historical stories how firmly the Aetolians and others believed in the Pythia's divinations and the power they assigned to her as the god Apollo's spokesperson. As Golding would undoubtedly have recalled while considering the subject of *The Double Tongue*, one can go so far back as to Homer's bard Demodokos, who sings in the *Odyssey's* Telemachia about the beginning of the Trojan war when Agamemnon journeyed to consult Apollo at Pytho over his future success. Think too of Creon journeying on Oedipus' command from Thebes to Delphi to seek some remedy for his city's devastating plague in *Oedipus Rex*. Also present in Sophocles are mythographic accounts of Apollo's agency, as in many of Euripides' dramas, including the *Ion*, *The Phoenician Women*, and *The Suppliants*, as well as in Aeschylus' *Orestia*. Orestes' revenge of his father's death in the murder of his mother, Clytemnestra, had divine sanction from Apollo, secured after a consultation in Delphi. Why Delphi? And why does *The Eumenides* have him argue before the Court of Areopagus that his act of matricide should be exonerated, since

Apollo's authority superseded the Eryines' right to avenge the killing of blood-kin? The Homeric Hymn to Apollo, Hesiod's *Works and Days*, Pindar's *Pythian* – the Delphic Oracle legend has long been interleaved through many literary works. Some of these Golding could well have known, but none so resonantly as the oracle the Pythia was said to have announced to the richest man in the world, King Croesus of Lydia. We all enjoy this story, Aesop-like in its regulation of ruin. In Herodotus' account, Croesus wanted immortal assurance that he would succeed in battle against the vast empire of Persia and so decided to test three oracles. On discovering the Delphic Oracle to be the most reliable, he lavished the sanctuary with fabulous gifts of gold and silver, necklaces for the Pythia, huge sculptured lions and statues in gold of a rather large figure for that time: a woman standing four and a half feet. Then King Croesus, according to Herodotus' account, proceeded to ask the crucial question: should he invade Persia? The Delphic response was characteristically astute. And characteristically ambiguous, for the Pythia's pronounced: 'If you make war on the Persians, you will destroy a great realm'.[11] Almost immediately, Croesus attacked Persia and promptly found his own kingdom to be destroyed. Croesus' next message to Apollo was, in Golding's rueful gloss on the Herodotus narrative, 'reproachful':

> But the priests of the oracle waved it aside, saying: '*The god said you would overthrow an empire and so you did. You overthrew your own.*' [12]

Recent critics of Herodutus' material have insisted that this is a quasi-historical transmission. Still the best know of all Delphic oracular predictions, however, it has impressed upon its countless hearers a notion that over time has turned to imaginative compost. Not only did the Pythian First Lady, in her mantic rapture, utter what to citizens' ears were unintelligible sounds, these babblings were subsequently interpreted, adjusted, slanted, modified, organized, and interpolated by the male Delphic priesthood. Thus was Delphi's pan-Hellenic clientele kept satisfied.[13] It is useful to quote here a passage from *The Cults of the Greek States*, the pre-eminent scholar L. R. Farnell's 1907 description of the Pythia in light of the cult view of the prophetess, which became so influential:

> [The Pythia] ascended into the tripod, and, filled with the divine afflatus which at least the later ages believed to ascend in vapor from a fissure in

the ground, burst forth into wild utterance, which was probably some kind of articulate speech, and which the 'holy ones' [priests], who with the prophet [Pythia] sat around the tripod, knew well how to interpret [...] What was essential to Delphic divination, then, was the frenzy of the [Pythia] and the sounds which she uttered in this state which were interpreted by the 'holy ones' [...] according to some convental code of their own.[14]

Farnell's description of an oracular session summarizes a cult view of rites and ways concerning Delphi's First Lady. Vapors from a chasm induce mantic ecstasy under which she speaks Apollo's oracles; laurel leaves are burnt before the tripod and incoherent utterances made, while priests give the response in adjusted – if ambiguously shaped – form to the enquirer. It is likely that Plutarch's often cited record in *Moralia*[15] providing the stereotypical notion of the consultation – with a frenzied Pythia raising unintelligible bayings then falling unconscious – has most often been used to endorse, over a remarkable length of time, this cult view. Geologists among others have questioned the reports of rapt ravings, suggesting they resulted not from vapors, which are non-existent at the site, but rather from chewed laurel leaves which can induce in both humans and animals a mild cyanide poisoning. There is a further deconstruction: recent scholarship having discredited the entire long-held cult notion that the male god Apollo invaded a female prophet's body so she would, under raped submission, emit the words he had chosen her to utter. As far as the historical evidence shows, the Pythia 'was not seized with a frenzy; she spoke coherently, and it was she, not the priests, who gave the response'.[16]

These are inductive theories which, to the sensibility of the sort possessed by someone like Golding, would not have explained away the implicit mystery posed by almost one thousand years of Pythian divination. One might today variously term the mental state extra-sensory perception, telepathy, clairvoyance, precognitive hallucination, mediumistic trance, thought-transference and still be left staring straight at the mysterious. Yet it is an historical fact that successive Pythian priestesses prescribed or prohibited on matters as weighty as cult foundations, religious laws and customs; rulership, civic legislation, city and colony founding; warfare, alliances, and truces. In the domestic realm they pronounced on marriage and sexual relations; death and burial; vocations; penalties and punishments and rewards;

trials; acquittals. There were also predictions regarding the birth of children; recall that, although the *Ion* attacked Delphi with Apollo emerging as a barbaric god, Euripides brought the long-married but childless Creusa and Xuthus to consult Apollo about the chances of having children. So those questions that continue to nag rest not only with, as Golding put it in his Delphi essay, the historical and the philosophical, but pre-eminently with the religious. Which brings me to one of *The Double Tongue's* central explorations, that any examination of intuitive divination will discover not so much 'a theory but a religious belief-pattern – or rather, one belief-pattern super-imposed upon the remains of another'.[17] The canvas was thus ready for an imagination like Golding's to 'draw parallels in silence', marking as it had in *The Spire*, *To the Ends of the Earth*, and *The Inheritors* the fretful, guilty, pained, dark, and miraculous connection between our species' past and its present.

III

Creusa: Apollo! Then and now unjust to her,
The absent woman whose complaints are here.
You did not save the child you should have saved.
A prophet, you have no answer for its mother.

Euripides Ion 384–89

Ion: I must confront
Apollo with his wrongs. To force a girl
Against her will and afterward betray!

Euripides Ion 436–38

Ion: But, mother, does Apollo tell the truth,
Or is the oracle false? With some good reason
That question troubles me.

Euripides Ion 1537–39

That the *Ion* was the moving center from which the thematic spokes of Golding's *The Double Tongue* emanated would seem, in my judgement, to be transparently obvious. The passages cited above articulate for the classical world such late twentieth-century issues as how arbitrarily power is wielded, how shot through with skepticism belief is, and how always and often women are 'instruments to be played on by gods or men' (p. 68). In Creusa's impassioned denunciation of Apollo, the god who raped her in girlhood; in Ion's appalled rejection of the god whom, since youth, he has served in cloistered belief; in Ion's pained question to his mother – are oracles false? Does Apollo lie? – one confronts in Euripides what *The Double Tongue* knows: the numbing erosion of faith soldered to the savage, incommunicable conviction that the gods live. As *The Double Tongue's* narrator Arieka is made to put the matter, re-inscribing herself at fifteen years of age: 'There is a void when the gods have been there, then turned their backs and [were] gone. Before this void as before an altar there is nothing but grief contemplating the void' (p. 23).

Arieka, the first-person narrator, is the daughter of Anticrates, an Aetolian provincial aristocrat of the first century BCE, whose expansive Phocian estate on the north of the Gulf of Corinth lies under the shadow of Parnassus, a half day's walk from the Apollo sanctuary at Delphi. Although mostly only tourists visit the shrine in Arieka's report on her childhood, back in 'the year in which the God Alexander was born' (p. 8) (*viz.* 356 BCE) her grandfather Anticrates, son of Anticrates had been told (when he was a small boy) by *his* grandfather Anticrates, son of Anticrates that the then incalculably rich Delphi must be protected against mercenaries, lest its treasures be 'wasted in impious ways' (p. 7). Thus does the naïve narrator render the prolonged military mess of the Peloponnesian wars and the three centuries following Alexander the Great's death that issued in the tide of Roman triumph, including Sulla's campaigns with their looting, atrocities, blood-dimmed slaughter, and the ultimate plunder of Delphi in 83 BCE.[18] In fact, the Romans replaced the Aeotolians as protectors of Delphi in 189 BCE. One hundred years later, an insolvent Athens had lost both its political prestige and its political privileges, an historical background implied rather than dramatized in the incomplete draft of *The Double Tongue*.

Naïve this unreliable first-person narrator may be in her retrospective reminiscence, for she is depicted as writing her memoir (on tablets, of course!) in great old age. Nevertheless, Arieka is brutally honest about her sixty or so years of divination at Delphi and especially the warped condition of her childhood, circumscribed by the prevailing gender restrictions. Like the female narrator of another reminiscence, Jane Eyre, who admitted to an unmarriageable plainness, Arieka describes her unattractive body as at best scrawny and her face as being 'uneven […] the one side not properly balanced by the other' (p. 11). Although, unlike Eyre, Arieka wins no Rochester, the meaning of her name – 'little barbarian' – like the double nature of her face promotes her adult destiny: to become a Pythian prophetess and speak with the double tongue, 'the tongue Apollo [...] inherited from a huge snake he killed at Delphi' (p. 8).

With no beauty to barter, she is too stubborn to acquiesce to her father's purchase of a husband; a dowry of two thousand silver pieces nearly ensnares a callow, poorer neighbor, but an accident results in the disgrace of a raised skirt revealing her parts and he bolts. Closely touched, following some odd events in her childhood, by what the superstitious believed to be magic, the adolescent Arieka is unmarriageable, unlovable, solitary, and defensive. The very conditions of these privations, again paradoxically, promote her adult destiny: girls so blighted acquire what the author has his narrator call 'a furtive power':

> They wish: and if they wish in the right way – wrong way? –sometimes, if the balance is ever so slightly on their side, then [...] they get what they want or somebody does. The world is riddled with coincidences and the girl sees this [...] As I said it is furtive [...] knows how to hide, how to claim, how to disguise, avoid, speak double like the snake or not at all (pp. 15–16).

Her face unbalanced, the moment's balance slightly tilted in her favor, speaking double, like the unloved and double-faced Matty before her, Arieka develops special capacities to see the coincidence in things. And if in all Golding's fiction Arieka represents only the second female protagonist through whose focalization readers apprehend narrative events, the novelist has his character direct her furtive 'weirdness' (p. 16) in ways diametrically opposite to those of her dark doppleganger, *Darkness Visible*'s Sophy. That is, not towards feelings of everything running down – Sophy's gospel of entropic coincidence – but rather the blazing operations of consolation and healing.

III

> The quality I was concerned with [in writing *The Spire*] was how a mystery presented itself to me and raised the question of how far a novelist knows what he is writing...
>
> Golding, *A Moving Target*

Just as, by way of its defiance of easy analysis, the spire of Salisbury Cathedral had appealed so directly to Golding's enquiring imagination thirty years earlier, so 'god-haunted Delphi with its bright air' (p. 68) and its hanging cliffs, the Phaedriades or Shining Rocks, posed an insoluble riddle. It seemed as though the door to the earth was locked shut at this ancient sanctuary. If a key were to be found for 'this locked door into the earth',[19] it would perhaps be by way of telling a story, Golding's long-held conviction having been that story-tellers are discoverers, not inventors, of truth. The fact that the journal notes show four working titles – The Double Tongue, The God Business, A Three-Legged Stool and The First Lady – suggests he must have still been weighing the balance between A, the human agency of the Pythian prophetess, and B, the cosmic agency of indescribable deities. Perhaps the titles The First Lady [20] and A Three-Legged Stool, the tripod upon which she sat during consolation, invoked (for me, at least) equation A, while the second set of titles The God Business and The Double Tongue, Apollo's riddling forked tongue, invoked equation B. Are there realms of spirit, the unfinished fragment that is The Double Tongue seems to be asking, beyond (or beneath) human consciousness that speak through human words? The double nature of this enquiry would seem to have been seeking a formal mirror in the double nature of the narrative. Arieka's dark meditation upon the enigmas surrounding her adult life as the Pythia, Delphi's First Lady, is also a guileless memoir showing her fond memories of her younger self and her abiding affection for Ionides Peisistratides, the Delphi sanctuary's High Priest of Apollo.

Guileless Ionides Peisistratides is not. His recruitment of the wide-eyed adolescent for Delphi is an impresario's act towards two enterprising ends. Firstly it is to secure the unmarriageable Arieka's considerable dowry for the emptying coffers of the shrine and, secondly, to become in exchange Arieka's guardian, tutoring her in hexameter verse, opening the doors of the 'bookroom', the sanctuary's library that contains the even then canonically great works of Greek literature. A wry Golding has his donnish priest explain that 'now of course, it's the custom for every author to send a copy to the Foundation' (p. 45). Ionides' plan is to teach his ward the 'duties and methods of the position which […] one day you will hold' (p. 39), the confused girl hears her mentor exclaiming, fortissimo. For this contriver's grand scheme is to forestall the glory that could be Rome's and restore the grandeur that was Greece. 'You can help to rescue Hellas. Rescue Athens and bring back Delphi' (p. 40), he thunders, rolling the great names: Socrates, Euripides, Aeschylus, Herodotus; the lyricists Pindar, Simonides, and Bacchylides; Homer's *Iliad*; the poet Theocritus – especially his double-visioned *Second Idyll* with the deserted Simaitha alternating between hatred of her lover and the hope that black magic will make Delphis return: 'Magic wheel, draw the man to my house.'

Besides the Hellenic literatures he so rotundly celebrates, Ionides is also in possession of data more pragmatically expedient to the shrine's other, more immediate, goals. The Delphi priesthood historically accumulated, by way of an intelligence network, relevant information to ensure its oracles suited the political needs of suppliants. That intelligence network, in Golding's invention, was none other than pigeons, all bound for Delphi, flying from other oracles: Dodona, Tegyra, Delos, Patarae, Branchidae, Claros and Siwa in Africa, as well as Smyrna, Ptolemaic Egypt, Cyprus, and Rome. Ionides has other avenues to useful information as well, intuiting – as he observes to and about the adolescent Arieka – that: 'there may be qualities lying dormant – I mean asleep –in you which are – dare I say? Unusual…' (p. 28).

Then there is what will be especially useful for reinstating Delphi and rescuing Athens. As a girl, Arieka is, by convention, uneducated.[21] Ignorance such as yours, the mercurial Ionides remarks, 'makes you look like a seer' (p. 39). To which he adds, ominously: 'You are a virgin. That disarms any god' (p. 77).

One must take Ionides' remark as an oblique reference to that convulsive act: a virgin's rape by a distant god, which propels the plot engine of Euripides' *Ion*. There are, by my count, some nine references – explicit as well as implicit – to the *Ion*. These include Ionides showing Arieka a tattered roll and explaining – one can imagine the merriment of the scribbling Golding here! – that it was the prompt copy Euripides had allowed the bookroom to keep: 'it's a rather cruel story and I think that perhaps you wouldn't like it' (p. 46), Ionides warns his female charge. But *The Double Tongue*'s Ionides – Ion, for short, as he quips to Arieka – is not the baleful and ingenuous Ion of corseted virtue whom we encounter in Euripides, but rather a yeasty brew of Athenian wordiness, easy homosexuality, cynicism, skepticism, and even atheism. He does not so much believe as wish that the new Pythia will actually speak Apollo's will. In the meantime, he's anxious to persuade fee-

paying visitors – even those Romans he so despises – to visit the
sanctuary. Explaining the realities of power to the bewildered young
Arieka, he remarks about the imminent consultation of a Julius Caesar,
'a Roman, officially a private citizen':

> Our power is spiritual. Rome's power is quite another matter. So though
> he pretends to be private we'd better be ready with something about the
> sucklings of the she-wolf. You've no idea how credulous the Romans are.
> [His] question could be worth millions of those gold coins of which we
> have so few (p. 82).

Ionides' surname, Peisistratides, speaks closer to his managerial
and manipulative character, for the text hints towards the reader
locating his ancestry through *the* Athenian tyrant Peisistratides, back
in the fifth century. A politician *par excellence* and a genius on the
political persuasiveness of culture, Peisistratides the Tyrant not only
solidified Attic hegemony in the ever-warring Dardenelles but, in his
quest for power, built monuments to his prestige: fountains and
temples. An inestimable legacy of the man's enterprise was the
scribing of the official text of Homer, about which Golding
wickedly has his fictional scholar, Ionides Peisistratides, declaim: 'you
see that little note written at the side? That's what we call a scholiast'
(p. 46). The diminished branch of that once mighty ancestral tree,
Ionides Peisistratides, can only labour in the rather restricted realms
of making the new Pythia chant again in hexameters or in visiting
Athens and Corinth to raise the daunting sums of money needed to
repair the shrine's decaying roofs. However, skeptic and cynic as he
is first depicted, later in the narrative Ionides gains a grudging belief
in the oracle.[22] And yet madder than the Delphian Pythia herself,
Ionides will try to organize a conspiracy in the hopes of provoking
mainland Greece into ridding itself of Roman rule. Of course, the
plot is both foolish and futile and so fails miserably. Ionides
Peisistratides, Apollo's High Priest, suffers such humiliation upon
being arrested by a Roman soldier – 'the officer in charge wasn't
even a colonel' (p. 159) – and then ignominiously released that he
can never again regain his former dignity. 'There was oblivion and
presently his body died' (p. 164), the eighty-year-old wise woman,
Arieka, ruefully remembers. And with Ion's death comes the death
of the oracle.

IV

[A]t first sight the damage was terrible. Fortunately, however, we discovered that it was almost all confined to that part of the bookroom which contained the Latin books [...] The scrolls and codexes [...] had been removed and stacked at the other end [...] out of danger. I believe both Ion and I – particularly Ion, I should say – was secretly a little pleased that Apollo should have spared the Greek books but made a real mess of the barbarian Latin ones (p. 154).

Like *Rites of Passage*, *The Double Tongue* depicts a time of historical transition as the foundering ship that was once the Hellenistic epoch becomes submerged under Roman rule. And like its predecessor, *The Double Tongue* relishes the time it is invoking. Its surface is furnished by historical period pieces, from writing tablets in the 'tablinum' or estate office to the increase in crime along the Macedonian border with brigands in the mountains menacing Phocians, and grain meal made on a rotary 'guern' turned by an obviously daft donkey, coyly named Pittacus after one of Greece's seven sages.[23] On the fragment's occasional error or anachronism a couple of reviewers were to comment. Sappho is made to throw herself from 'the non-existent cliff of Leuctra not Leukas' while 'Corinth [the place where Arieka and Ionides are feted by a wealthy businessman who has promised to provide the needed roof repair monies] was a heap of ruins after its 146 destruction', and intelligence gathering by secret pigeons never happened.[24] That the 'characters in the novel react in a curiously modern way to the issue of the oracle's authenticity' was one criticism.[25] However, the judgement of both these reviewers that the choice of a non-Greek name for the heroine was erroneous misses the mark, in my view. My guess, although I have yet to assemble the puzzle, is that there is an intended allusion, as so many of the Greek and Roman namings in the text carry deliberate reflexive meanings.

A more striking similarity between *Rites of Passage* and *The Double Tongue* than the pleasures taken in summoning the historical quotidian is the mixing of narrative modes and moods with the ruminative and contemplative being jostled by the antic and comedic. For the work's narrative tension – to the degree this has been realized in the fragment we call *The Double Tongue* – comes, in part, from the contrasting temperaments of Arieka and Ionides, their double natures offering another link to the title. In addition, we see events through the memory of only one focalizing character, Arieka, yet incidents themselves are described, each with their distinctive emphasis and idiom, from two (different) emotional perspectives. There are those that humorously record encounters with men and women, their manners and surroundings: the atmosphere, for example, of an Athens, which is now nothing more than a university town with the Field of Mars looking 'like a stonemason's yard. All these gesticulating heroes and clean, bare altars' (p. 137). And there are those narrative memories that try to see round the edges of what were her Pythian moments, her experience of a force that she herself did not so much possess as was in her, possessing her. To best demonstrate the alternation between what might be termed the mundane and the miraculous in *The Double Tongue*, two episodes can be isolated. The first gives an (exuberant) account of the observed social life of the times while the second operates on an entirely different – even, preternatural – level, reminiscent of the eerie atmosphere created in *Fire Down Below*'s encounter with the iceberg.

The exuberant account portrays a sumptuous feast laid on for the Pythia Arieka and the High Priest Ionides Peisistratides on their return, via Corinth, from Athens by a wealthy Phoenician businessman, whom Ionides has been courting. Fat and indolent, prosperous enough to have his marbled halls run round with ostentatious statues of the Olympians, this non-Greek – and therefore in Hellenic eyes barbarian – is nevertheless a 'genuinely religious man who believed in the oracles' (p. 141). When a slave arrives bearing upon a cushion a crown with 'delicate gold thin branches with nodding leaves and flowers', a near inebriated Arieka bursts out in spontaneous hexameter 'a poem in the extravagant modern manner', singing 'how before smoking Ilium, Menelaus stood calling for his false wife Helen with his sword in his hand, and how she came from the smoke wearing this crown and the sword fell from his hand' (p. 142).

Lights flutter and sputter, dancers fling themselves through sinuous somersaults, shawms bray with brazen throats, guests fondle and nuzzle, a boy of epicene beauty whispers into Ionides' ear. And when the Propraetor of southern Greece, Lucius Galba, arrives unexpectedly (indeed, inauspiciously, given the traitorous plottings of the High Priest) the Roman is made to be diverted by a ravishing boughten slave, dressed in the filigreed crown and a robe of cloth of gold. 'It is

Macedonian work,' the curatorial-minded host explains, congratulating himself – as have businessmen through time – on the acquisition of the rarest of works of art. 'It is said to have belonged to the royal family, even before the time of the God Alexander the Great' (p. 143). Despite its brevity, this episode presents, in exemplary ways, a cornucopia of vivid and witty details, just the sort of reportorial strategy that makes readers feel what it must have been like to be present at such a party, at such a time.

V

> I had believed in the Olympians, all twelve of them. How much did I believe now, after years of hearing Ionides inventing speeches for me? How much after years of inventing them myself? (p. 136)

It is not just the daily life of a world far removed from the late twentieth century in which *The Double Tongue* immerses readers, as this second episode reveals. Equally distant from our time is the narrative's shaping of (albeit, imagined) habits of perception – belief and doubt and awe and disbelief. And equally compelling is its depiction of those states of confused ardor, 'muddle' being the aged Arieka's reiterative word for her own inability to decide whether or not a life-time's mouthing of Apollonian oracles was god-inspired or merely man-made: Ionides' inventions or her own. Hers is a query that has, of course, considerable historical precedent, and the episode in *The Double Tongue* to which I turn here reveals not only the other side of Arieka's doubled perspective as a memoirist, but also the novel's imaginative deconstruction of the traditional view that '[a]ccording to the canons of the heroic age, the act of rape, if committed by a god, was a favor conferred on the woman.'[26] The episode to which I refer re-orchestrates a common strategy in Golding's fiction, what I have earlier described as the confrontation scene wherein a character is depicted as suffering a species of syncope. In *The Double Tongue* that annihilation of self begins when the dutiful Arieka, a credulous girl of fifteen years and utterly inexperienced in the ways of the world, finds herself compelled to participate in what will be an oracular session: her first.

Lugging heavy dread like stones on her shoulders, she follows her guardian's instructions. After being purified by drinking from the icy fountain of Castalia, she descends the sanctuary's steps to enter its dimly lit adytum. This is the innermost sanctum and site of the tripod: the brazier with its burning laurel leaves and the gap, at once appalling and awesome, into the earth's belly where legend held it that:

> the air of oracular utterance was breathed forth to become the breath of the Pythia on her tripod as she writhed and cried out when the god had her in his hands (pp. 68–69).

Forced into becoming the god's obedient servant, as she knows herself to have been, such a silenced and unknowledgeable creature could never have imagined that she might also have to become his slave, an instrument to be bloodied and torn by a force – a will? – outside or beyond her own conscious mind. As she gropes in the adytum's darkness with its menacing back-curtain depicting – in crude weaving – the Pytho's slaying by Apollo, convulsions suddenly overwhelm Arieka's slender young body. Spasms shudder through her, turn her sideways and back, thrust her downward as she feels flesh tear. Then from her violated mouth spews forth uncontrollable 'rolling, rollicking laughter that went on and on, louder and louder'. And then follow two cryptic cries: 'Evooee!' and then 'Evooee-ee, Bacche!' (p. 87).

What has happened? Certainly, a Pythia has been ravished by the gods, but in the seizure there is nothing assuring or pious. Nor is any sentimental religiosity enacted in the seizure. The barking laughter that the god seems to be pushing through her torn throat appears to be some kind of sport: a game played at the expense of mere mortals. In this confrontation scene to end all other confrontation scenes, Golding has apparently thrown into reverse all the anticipated conventions, in this case those rituals so closely associated with the Pythia of legend. By a process of 'defamiliarization' – to borrow Victor Shklovsky's concept – the state of mumbling conventionally ascribed to the prophetess has been made so 'unfamiliar' as to impart the sensation of things as they might have been experienced, not as they have been recorded and analyzed by male chroniclers, tragedians, poets. In *The Double Tongue*'s depiction of the oracular moment, possession is as violent – and repellent – as any act of rape suffered by any woman. Indeed, the possession *is* rape, with the girl's bloody mouth torn wide for the passage of the god's voice. 'It was the god. He had come,' is Arieka's summation, a simple sentence requiring no phallic exegesis. To be so brutally abducted by a god: can such an encounter be construed as consecration, favor, honor? The encounter is awful and, it would seem, the gods remain indifferent to mere mortals, using them – as did Euripides' Apollo in his rape of Creusa – for their own indolent or important ends.

So, like the gods in Euripides, are *The Double Tongue*'s gods irresponsible? Are they – or were they ever – moral powers? Do these gods disappear if individual fate comes no longer through higher dispensation? And if not higher dispensation, then through what? The perverseness of accident: free fall? That such a dilemma – not so much a religious truth as a human one – is given shape one discovers in turning to the confrontational encounter's next movement. Bloody as Arieka's throat may be, she will still be forced to utter words: the confrontation with that which is other has yet to be completed. Crouched on the sanctuary's ground for what she feels as measureless time, soaking with sweat and groaning with exhaustion, the violated girl drags herself to the holy tripod – 'I felt it was the god who helped me then to crawl towards it and lay hands on the thick, cool bronze of its ankles' (p. 88) – where she shouts with her own voice: 'One mouth or the other!' And then the madness in her mind stops, her lungs ease as does her heart, so that later the forever violated Arieka will insist to the cynical High Priest, Ionides, that there are more gods than those dreamed of in his philosophy.

Twice does the ravished Arieka cry out cryptically in (ancient) Greek, for in the imagined encounter she speaks with the Pytho's riddling double tongue. She also speaks the tongues of the doubled gods: Apollo and his symbiotic opposite, Dionysus. After the Apollian 'Evooee' comes her second mantic and Dionysian cry 'Evooee-ee Bacche,' with its explicit reference to the Bacchae and so therefore an implicit reference to the god Dionysus.[27] Of course, Dionysus' link to frenzied god-maddened women in his pre-eminent tie with the Bacchae has long been a mythic conflation. As though to underscore the informing presence of the god, whose semiotics of meaning have always been the fueling of madness, *The Double Tongue* makes a couple of references to Dionysus. On waking from one of her (later) trances, Arieka asks Ion whether it was Dionysus – she does not mention Apollo – who had been present. Less enigmatically, she is described as sitting between the Priest of Dionysus and the Priest of Apollo when she attends a Delphi performance of the *Ion*. Her internal aside that she understood 'better than the poet himself had done' (p. 116) is an unriddling allusion to her own rape by the gods whom the male priesthood represents. But as in fiction so in fact, for Dionysus was historically the other deity worshipped at Delphi when, in winter months, it was imagined that Apollo, the god of light, was absent. In her first seizure, describing the shouts that emanated from her as 'more male than female' (p. 89), Arieka comes to the radical – and dangerous – understanding that the Pythia's place is:

a woman's place [...] They trespassed, that over-male god, those *two male gods* coming in and forcing their cries of worship through my twisted mouth which still tasted blood. (p. 89, my italics)

Thus her puzzling announcement, 'one mouth or the other' (p. 88), follows tradition in having the prophetess utter an obscure and ambiguous pronouncement, one then to be transmitted to the assembled petitioners by the High Priest of Apollo. But Ionides' reply to the group of solicitors is an 'answer which he had not heard and the Pythia had not given' (p. 89), as the then troubled Arieka puts it, alarmed by the sacrilege and fraud practiced by the priest.

But is Arieka's pronouncement so riddling that readers, familiar with Golding's habitual strategy of indirection, are unable to grasp *The Double Tongue*'s intimation here? In the shout 'one mouth or another' a gendered difference is surely voiced, the double tongue being the riddling words of a female prophetess who cannot *but* speak in riddles. In no other way would her utterances (like those of Cassandra) be given credence. Straight talk – like authority, Athenian citizenship and participation in the hallowed Court of Areopagus – belongs, by law and custom, solely to free men. To this, however, must be added the paradox that 'slave of the gods or the idea of the gods' as the Pythian is, she commands – for a mere female – a most atypical respect. This is the paradox implicit in Ionides' insistence that 'when sitting on the tripod', the possessed and god-enslaved priestess is 'the freest being in the world' (p. 139).[28]

VI

[In] Henry James's droll [...] tale, 'The Figure in the Carpet' [...] a writer teases an admirer by dangling before him the idea that there is some hidden clue somewhere in his work – a figure in the carpet – which was always unobtrusively and almost invisibly there; and which, if the reader grasped it, would explain the whole.[29]

Few more astute observations can be found than the suggested relation here between the 'droll' lesson of James' 'The Figure in the Carpet' and the narrative method that is Golding's, but can one grasp one hidden clue in the unfinished fragment which is *The Double Tongue*? For me, the 'figure in the carpet' which began to emerge was an object (maddeningly unexplained) which the slave Perseus was instructed by the goaled Ionides to give to Arieka, an object evidently important enough to have suitably impressed the superstitious Roman Intelligence officers. She, in turn, attached the object to a silver chain to hang round her neck. The object was a silver key. Shaped explicitly at each of its ends as a labrys (the Cretan double axe), although never early on so identified by *The Double Tongue*, the object is described as 'doubly doubled' (p. 160). Its barrel is figured at both extremities so that four axes point, two at top and two at bottom, in two – therefore, doubled – directions: the bottom doubling the top. In Arieka's guileless remark that she 'had no idea what to do with the key, or even if it was *more than* symbolic' (p. 160, my italics), one knew oneself to be before some sort of cryptogram, demanding some kind of deciphering. Not only had the narrative played deliberately with the double – symbol for potency since remotest antiquity – threading through its texture the double tongue, the double voices, the double gods, but the labrys or Cretan double axe itself could be susceptible to several suggestions. Originally, the labrys was the Cretan scepter of Great Mother Earth/Gaia. The Delphic shrine had been founded first – as Graves insisted – by the Cretans, 'who left their sacred music, ritual, dances, and calendar as a legacy to the priestly corporation at Delphi, [the men of the axe or] the Labryade'.[30] As the final member of the soon to be extinct Labryade priesthood of antiquity, Ionides – in Golding's inventive speculation – might easily have had its signifying key, no longer knowing its original signification and how that underscored two of antiquity's historical facts. The original oracular authority of the Earth goddess at Delphi, superseded by the Apollian and Hellenic cultural indebtedness to Cretan civilization, are rankling arrears a man like Ionides Peisistratides would be loathe to honor. In turn, by way of its figured shape, the labrys could also merge into another religious icon, that of the cross-form known as the tau cross, T-cross, or Egyptian cross. In ancient Egypt the ankh or Coptic *onech* – a loop elongated downwards to which a tau was attached – symbolized generative energy, the Coptic Christians adopting the figure as the cross of the Christian community in Egypt.

A powerful cryptogram then this riddling doubly doubled labrys and all the more an informing clue for the uses to which Arieka is made to put it when, at the fragment's conclusion, she enters the sanctuary's adytum. She turns her face towards drawn curtains at the back of the grotto on which, for sixty-odd years, she has always turned her back. Naggingly, in fact, the closed curtains with their crudely woven representation of the struggle between Apollo and the serpent have appeared and reappeared in Arieka's memoirs. Each time it has caused her flesh to shudder with the remembered question: 'Did that [curtain] then hide the fabulous cleft in the rock up which once upon a time vapors had risen from the centre of the earth?' (p. 95). Do those veils, in other and more portentous words, conceal the hidden centre of existence? Or is what they shroud sheer negation, the gods who have, in her reiterative phrase, turned their backs? 'They vanished and there was grief before the void. The Void' (p. 162), she remembers painfully.

Inspecting the archaic weaving braided through the potent closed curtains, she decides it must have been woman's work, perhaps some Pythia instructed by a god to make an image of him and the dark monster he confronted. And so the woven figure resembles that superannuated cart which once transported her from Delphi to Athens on which she had seen an ancient drawing, one repainted hundreds of times over. More closely examined, the drawing revealed again an archaic image of the Pytho in the cave, but no Apollo. In his place rests 'our fat Mother Gaia' (p. 131). Along with the excavated statues of monstrously fat women whom Arieka reads about in the bookroom, the painting amounts to historical evidence – at least for Arieka – for what legend had held: preceding Apollo's reign at Delphi, the divinity first worshipped there was, indeed, female. Gaia, the primeval source of the prophetic vapors, set her son, the serpent Pytho, to guard the vaginal cavity – as I construe the crevice trope – leading to and emerging from the earth's belly. So powerful had Gaia's authority become that the invading Apollo seized her shrine and suppressed her cult. Killing the Pytho, Apollo came into patriarchal possession of the oracle, which henceforth would – like Western culture – be almost always dominated by and directed to male rites and rituals: laws and customs; warfare; colonization; alliances and truces.[31] At Delphi, the Labryade would henceforth intervene between prophetess and votary, translating her utterances. The prophetess would now be linked to the godhead only through the

Dionysian template of madness and otherwise relegated to service as Apollo's servant, indeed slave, suffering perhaps the metaphoric rape imagined in *The Double Tongue*.

My sense is that Golding was engaged in *The Double Tongue* upon interrogating the oppressive historical fact that males have overwhelmingly constricted females. By domination or intimidation, they have seized women's agency simply by the kind of brutal power that is presented in *The Double Tongue*, which results in the grief-stricken male world that the earlier fable *Lord of the Flies* isolates. But the Jamesian figure in the carpet suggests something else, perhaps more valent. That is *The Double Tongue*'s dramatization of the syncretic nature not only of culture but also its ally religion, the amalgamative and adaptive process whereby belief patterns – like civilizations – impose upon, as well as adhere to, the remains of other belief patterns. This particular period of historical transition was therefore chosen as background for the planned novel for a host of reasons. Not only had Greece become a sluggish backwater in the Roman Empire, but Roman hegemony was being ever so slightly stirred by what would become one of those typhoons of change that would ultimately have it buckle and break. The stirring is being initiated among Israelites in Palestine, restive under the Roman rule so corruptly administered by the house of Herod.

The old Olympian gods are dying and will – as had Gaia worship long before them – dissolve into and be transformed by another belief structure: that celebrated by the Roman pantheon. Change is the period's defining feature, a fact to which the reader is additionally alerted by way of a couple of cryptic comments. Twice the aged Arieka is made to allude to the arrival in Greece – and Rome too, had she been so apprised – of the Egyptian god, Serapis: 'a new god...put together out of the remains of three old gods' (p. 125). Serapis is introduced so glancingly that the reader is prodded into unscrambling a characteristically embedded clue. It is one bearing connection, in my view, to the book's theme of amalgamation and adaptation and so to *its* question about what would happen if one were to unlock by a key the closed door to the universe's belly.

Serapis, as Apollodorus, Herodotus, and Pausanias all described, was one of the two principal healing gods in the Greek and Roman pantheon and one then emerging in Egypt from the worship of the double god Apis and Osiris, thus the conflated name, Serapis.[32] In the halcyon time of Ptolemaic Egypt, when Alexandria had become the centre of Hellenistic learning and culture – the great library and museum having been established under the patronage of Ptolemy Soter (*viz.*, savior), with none other than Euclid teaching mathematics there – Ptolemy had introduced the worship of Serapis. He constructed in favored Alexandria the god's most munificent sanctuary, although others existed: in Memphis, for example, and later in Greece at the Delos Temple (200–100 BCE) and in the Roman temples of Miletus and Puteoli. When Serapis worship spread from Egypt to Greece and Rome, the god was reproduced in the Greek style rather like the figure of Zeus/Jupiter, with whom he came to be identified. Like Hades/Pluto in his capacity as god of the lower world, like Asclepias in his capacity as god of healing and like Zeus by way of his pre-eminence, the thrice-empowered Serapis figure represented a widely extended concept. Thus it foreshadowed, through its syncretic nature, the kind of henotheistic belief that would pave the way for what in that region would later be described as Christian monotheism, the godhead figure in its capacity as father, son, and holy ghost, being thrice-empowered.

The Double Tongue remains an incomplete work; its ephemeral reference to the god Serapis may not seem to bear the weight of the detailed exegesis I have provided above. There is, however, Golding's consistent method of veiled subtleties. That Arieka is made twice to comment on the homage being paid to this 'new god, Serapis' carries significant weight, in my calculation, and all the more should one connect it to a another clue, although one considerably more transparent. I refer here to the moments when, grieving over the gods' apparent desertion of her, Arieka frequently describes them as turning their backs. Calling upon the account in *Exodus* in which Moses is presented as being hidden 'in a *crack* in the rock' so that all he was permitted to see of 'his god was the back-parts' (p. 71, my italics), Ionides, the Pythian's constant friend and mentor, consoles her by insisting that she has been no more abandoned than the Hebrew leader was. In the remark immediately following – 'So you saw their back-parts. Perhaps they'll cover you with their hands and put you in the *crack* at the oracle' (p. 72, my italics) – one is surely meant to conflate two ways (in widely divergent belief structures) of figuring forth religious mysteries.

So it is at this moment that one should turn to Arieka's concluding entry and her action with that silver key: the enigmatic and talismanic doubled Cretan double axe that hangs around her neck. Some sixty years of Delphic service weigh as she enters the holy adyton, stares at the curtain – having a 'convulsion of pure fear when I thought that my breath might lend the monster breath and *he/she* start into life and overwhelm me' (p. 161, my italics). She then draws strings to uncover the curtain's veiling of what that ancient, fearful, and ponderous crevice in the rock might possess: the godhead or the void.

> So I put the silver labrys into the silver lock and turned the key. The doors were easy enough to open. There was solid, impenetrable rock of the mountain behind them (p. 165).

Void or godhead, the reader is positioned to decide, remembering that Golding's Pythian has up to this point always kept her *back* to the mysteries of this wall, just as the gods either turned their backs on her or turned only their backs to her. As with *Darkness Visible*, *Pincher Martin* or *The Paper Men,* where textual intentions prompted readers to embrace paradoxes which both are and are not what they seem, readers are similarly challenged in *The Double Tongue*. They must either accept or reject possibilities and, in the case of this final work, consider again the fact that religious belief perseveres through a piecemeal continuity: building and rebuilding itself, dividing and substituting itself, claiming and reclaiming itself.

Then comes the (muted) coda ending, one that for me seems all the more incandescently an assured narrative gesture for its having followed – surely with self-reflexivity – the coda-convention of the earlier novels. In recognition of her long service, Athenian authorities propose erecting 'a stone image' of the 'Pythia of the Apolline oracle'. It will stand on the venerable, although now unvenerated, Field of Mars, thus to reside in a place whose empty altars and 'gesticulating heroes' Arieka had earlier likened to nothing more than 'a stonemason's yard' (p. 137). Rather than stone image – surely an intertextual nod towards the graven image in the Moses exemplum is intended here – Arieka requests a simple altar. And carved upon it a simple inscription, one that provides *The Double Tongue*'s final line: 'TO THE UNKNOWN GOD'.

'Did Golding mean to suggest indirectly that Arieka, in her doubts and concerns, was anticipating the arrival of Christianity?' questioned the *TLS* reviewer, having pointed out that 'St Paul […] mentions such an inscription in his sermon on the Areopagus'.[33] My answer is a confident 'yes'. *Acts* 17.22 documents how, in an effort to establish a congregation in Athens, Paul sought to explain a traditional Judaic apocalyptic scheme to a Hellenistic audience strongly opposed to a ministry whose bedrock was 'not to imagine God in terms of gold or silver or stone, contrived by human art or imagination' (*Acts* 17.22). During a council at the Court of Areopagus in the first century CE, Paul arose, observing that Athenians struck him as being a scrupulously religious people; he then singled out one of their altars 'on which were inscribed the words, "TO GOD THE UNKNOWN"' (*Acts* 17.22). The next verse of *Acts* shows even more closely how *The Double Tongue*'s concluding invocation, 'TO THE UNKNOWN GOD', resembles (thus reassembles) the engraving which Paul had quoted in order to proclaim the majesty of the everlasting Lord, the invisible godhead Athenians had, without knowing, been worshipping: 'To an Unknown God', as *Acts* 17.23 rephrases and recasts the inscription. 'TO THE UNKNOWN GOD'; 'TO GOD THE UNKNOWN'; 'To an Unknown God': the thrice-empowered invocations contradict at the same time as they converge: a matter that readers probably were intended to inspect.

That Golding's imagination would have been seized by the potency of place is certain. The Areopagus – before which Aeschylus' Orestes had been positioned to argue the primacy of Apollo's worship over that of the Eriynes, their tribal justice being replaced by peer judgement in a court of law – being also the site for Christian ministry. It is thus a *genius loci* so filled with the debris of years that it compels. Complex in its potency, the meanings of the Aeropagus – like those of Delphi – seem not so much conflicting as inter-connected. Perhaps more arresting to his imagination would have been the conversion at this very Areopagus council of 'Dionysius a member of the Areopagus' (*Acts* 17.22). Described as 'Dionysius the Areopagite' (*Acts* 18.32), he came to be known as Saint Dionysios the Areopagite, a figure erroneously revered in the Middle Ages as the author of Neoplatonic treatises. One should here recall how Golding borrowed for *Pincher Martin*'s confrontation the thesis propounded by Dionysios Areopagitkos and which I here argue both informed and formed the planned foundation of *The Double Tongue*. 'Dionysios Areopagitkos says that no matter how profound contemplation is, or how perfect the beatific vision is, there remains that secret part of God that can never be known,' as Golding put it to me many years ago and which later he was to describe as 'the Mosaic way' of knowing: 'seeing not the face of Truth but his [...] back parts from our cleft in the rock'.[34]

Arieka confounded by the gods who have turned their backs upon her; Arieka who has turned her back upon the curtain with its inscrutable veilings; Moses in the creviced rock, permitted to see only Jehovah's backside; a Pythia before earth's crevice, seeing only impenetrable rock; Athenians before a script inscribed upon an altar: each is a visualization (or borrow Golding's terminology and call it a 'picture') of that Areopagitkos precept. Steeped as the fragment is in the themes that have appeared, although frequently in chiaroscuro, throughout Golding's entire writing career, *The Double Tongue* insists upon belief, worship, and the continuing perplexity of the unknown. And although, with its scripted historical period, it could not possibly have pulled *On the Morning of Christ's Nativity* to itself, like iron to a magnet, the nineteenth verse of Milton's ode is a fitting conclusion to *The Double Tongue*:

> The oracles are dumb
> No voice or hideous hum
> Runs through the arched roofs in words deserving.
> Apollo from his shrine
> Can no more divine,
> With hollow shriek the steep of Delphos leaving.
> No nightly trance or breathed spell
> Inspires the pale-eyed priest from the prophetic cell.

Endnotes

1   Golding to Alex Hamilton in Hamilton, 'First Lord of the Novel', *Manchester Arts Guardian* (Dec 20, 1971), p. 8.

2   Golding to John Haffenden in Haffenden, 'William Golding', *Novelists in Interview*, London and New York, Methuen, 1985, p. 118.

3   '[Having] studied Greek while in the Navy during the war [...] Greek myths and symbols infuse his novels'. (James Gindin, *William Golding*, New York, St Martin's Press, 1988, p. 11.

4   Indeed, his last journal entry indicated the intention to start a new draft on the Monday following that weekend.

5   William Golding, *An Egyptian Journal*, London, Faber and Faber, 1985, p. 40.

6   The Vulci Cup resides in the Staatliches Museum in Berlin and a photograph of Eduard Gerhard's 1858 reproduction of the Codrus-painter forms the jacket illustration of *The Double Tongue*.

7   A female-centric conjecture that may well not be historical fact, the tradition that the Great Mother was worshipped has been solidified through time by reference after reference appearing in the pronouncements of Aeschylus, Aristonoos, Plutarch, Apollodorus, Pausanias, among others. In his remarkable study *The Delphic Oracle,* Joseph Fontenrose is adamant that nothing but myth supports such a view, the myth having been first fostered after 500 BCE, since the Delphic Oracle was by then the most prestigious of the Greek Oracles. 'In the earliest account that we have of the Delphic Oracle's beginning, the story found in the Homeric *Hymn to Apollo*, there was no oracle before Apollo' (Joseph Fontenrose, *The Delphic Oracle: Its Responses and Operations*, Berkeley, The University of California Press, 1978, p. 1).

8   Although the fact could not possibly have been known to the novel's narrator and so could not have been reported, contemporary readers may enjoy the joke seeded here. The narrator may, in an aside, mention an innocuous Roman visitor by the name of Cimber, but we know that Cimber was no less an historic figure than Metellus Cimber, a warlord who became one of Caesar's assassins.

9   William Golding, 'Delphi', *A Moving Target*, New York, Farrar, Straus & Giroux, 1982, p. 43.

10   H. W. Parke and D. E. W. Wormell, *The Delphic Oracle, The History*, Oxford, Blackwell Press, 1956, pp. 49–51.

11   'Quasi Historical Response #100'.

12   Golding, 'Delphi', p. 38.

13   In this context, Peter Green's point in *Alexander to Actium: The Hellenistic Age* (London, Thames & Hudson, 1991) is informative; he explains that 'Delphi was not normally given to issuing favors, except in return for very tangible benefits' (p. 593).

14   Lewis Richard Farnell, *The Cults of the Greek States* vol. 4, Oxford, Clarendon Press, 1907, p. 189.

15   Plutarch's *Moralia* (438b).

16   Fontenrose, op. cit., p. 202.

17   E.R. Dodds, *Euripides: Bacchae*, Oxford, Oxford University Press, 1960, p. 368.

18   That the dictator Sulla 'epitomized the triumph of everything the Greeks fought to escape: elitism, authoritarianism, the rule of privilege, alien brutality' (Green, op. cit., p. 133) informs, however, the text's other major character, the Delphi priest Ionides Peisistratides, who is active in an underground movement to overthrow *imperium romanum*. As Golding jokes: 'Home Rule for Hellas' (p. 106). There is one reference to Sulla, as a matter of fact; during a visit to Athens Ionides is asked to give his reminiscences of those whom he had met at Delphi, and the character is made to mention Sulla.

19   Golding, 'Delphi', p. 40.

20   *The First Lady* as a title for a novel about Hellenic Greece might not have encouraged sales in the United States. I would not, however, have put it past the author of *The Paper Men* to see in Imperial Rome's domination of Athens – substituting military might for cultural colonization – the United States' supremacy over Britain in the late twentieth century. The Romans 'remained dourly pedestrian [...] who anyway never had more than superstition instead of religion and law instead of philosophy' (William Golding, 'The Funeral Games that Lasted 300 Years', *Guardian*, January 17, 1991, p. 24).

21 In the ancient world, women were illiterate. That Arieka learned to read is by happy chance, since her brother encouraged this skill. The gendered sphere she occupies is quite representative in the nature of its passivity: 'Every decision that affects her fate is taken by a male relative or guardian [or god, should we affirm what she knows about Apollo]' (Mary Lefkowitz, 'A Dish for the Gods', *Times Literary Supplement*, June 23, 1995, p. 25).

22 This transformation is truncated, most probably because the fiction had yet to be completed.

23 A more thorough reading might also include: an emptied 'kylix', into which unmixed dark wine will be poured during a festive banquet in a Corinithian 'exedra' or entertainment hall; gold coins with Alexander the Great's head figured on one side; house slaves born on the estates or foreign-born 'boughten', those individuals plundered in battle and raid; stone fish tanks filled with seawater; 'egg and dart' embroidered dresses; 'brakes' (carriages) and 'wains' (wagons); 'besoms' (sacred brooms) and 'chlamys' (military outer garments); the High Priest's sounding 'shawms' (musical reed instruments); traffic 'herms' or erect directional pillars with the god of travel Hermes' head above and the significant mark of his male sex below; unveiled Athenian women atypically reclining – just like all Hellenic men – on couches during banquets; legionary techniques and tactics of the indomitable Romans with their soft-iron pointed javelins, wide shields and broad short swords; pirates in 'caiques' under sail then whole fleets of 'triremes', sweeping through stretches of the sea; the price of corn and how to keep the Hellespont open to Athenian shipping through increasingly pirate-infested waters; abacus for counting in the new decimal system; an irreligious Athenian architect given the same name as the historic Andocides of Athens, the exiled aristocrat involved in a notorious political scandal where sacred Herms were mutilated so as to reveal secrets about the rites of Demeter.

24 Peter Green, 'Speaking in the Oracular' *Washington Post* (October 1, 1995), p. 5.

25 Lefkowitz, op. cit., p. 25.

26 Philip Vellacott, *Ironic Drama: A Study of Euripides' Methods and Meaning*, Cambridge, Cambridge University Press, 1975, p. 88.

27 The ecstatic cry 'Evoe' does not have a translation, but since 'Bacche' is in the vocative case, the mantic call goes something like 'Yahoo! Bacchus!'

28 Preoccupations with the nature of freedom and the then historical fact of slavery would, in my speculation, have been more tightly (and capaciously) woven through the text had Golding been able to finish the fragment. A minor character, the slave – significantly named Perseus – is in happy liberty as the librarian of the bookroom, just as Arieka is freed to – and by – reading its collection: Erinna; Arctinus; Plato; Herodotus; Histiaeus; Nearchus, 'Alexander's Admiral of the Fleet'; and Sappho, whom Golding (slyly, if anachronistically) has Ionides call 'the little brown nightingale of Lesbos' (p. 47).

29 John Bayley, 'Light and Darkness Visible', *Times Literary Supplement* (September 16, 1994), pp. 13–14.

30 Robert Graves, *The Greek Myths I*, revised edition, reprinted Harmondsworth, Middlesex, Penguin, 1966, p. 181.

31 'The Delphic Oracle,' reports the redoubtable mythographer Graves, 'first belonged to Mother Earth, who appointed Daphnis as her prophetess; and Daphnis, seated on a tripod, drank in the fumes of prophecy, as the Pythian priestess still does. Some say that Mother Earth later […] ceded [her rights] to Apollo […] But others say that Apollo robbed the oracle from Mother Earth' (Graves, op. cit., p. 178). That Golding should have chosen the latter legend for *The Double Tongue*'s scaffolding should come as no surprise.

32 In having Arieka refer to Serapis as being constructed from three Egyptian deities, Golding may have had in mind Osiris and Apis, the latter – in his capacity as God of the Underworld – being an emanation of Ptah and identified as the 'second Ptah'. This remains a supposition only, given the fact that in Hellenistic times cults of Egyptian deities influenced one another, layer upon layer.

33 Lefkowitz,op. cit., p. 25.

34 William Golding, *An Egyptian Journal*, London, Faber and Faber, 1985, p. 140.

Conclusion

> Crypton is inert, they say. But if one teased it sufficiently, a matter of temperature and pressure, a spark gap in sufficiently dense cloud of crypton and another element – One might produce entirely unnatural substances.
>
> *The Pyramid*

Enlarged skulls on wasp-thin bodies, men with huge ganglia being pushed forward by some intensity, some vision. That seemed the persistent image saturating William Golding's early fiction. The preoccupations of *Lord of the Flies*, *The Inheritors*, *Pincher Martin*, *Free Fall*, and *The Spire* seemed widely religious ones where such perennial themes as innocence, guilt, mystery, and malignancy were treated in their antique religious sense. It was possible to argue then, as I once did, that the early effort was to try to construct a mythopoeia relevant to the mid twentieth-century world of the West where mystery was experienced as a dark and threatening void.

Decades later, when literary tastes, the politics of cultures – consciousness itself – had been so hugely altered, it no longer seemed advantageous to provide such neat categorizations. That the later fiction seemed several steps away from the fabular, and mythopoeic strategies adopted by the first five novels made it more – rather than less – difficult to define what might be termed the 'Goldingesque'. Perhaps it was no longer even useful to ponder the author's place 'in the ruined pantheon of the Great Tradition'.[1] During a literary career showing more than one atypical feature – a late start as a publishing author; the extravagant (and sustained) success of a first novel, the rapid appearance of early works, an equally rapid emergence as a major figure in contemporary British literature, the subject of scholarly exegesis amounting to a kind of literary light industry – Golding was to fall silent. Twelve long years were to elapse between *The Pyramid* (1967) and *Darkness Visible* (1979). Then – as though to give the lie to the Second Law of Thermodynamics, that everything runs down – the seventy-year-old writer published four more novels: *Rites of Passage* (1980); *The Paper Men* (1984); *Close Quarters* (1987); *Fire Down Below* (1989). And upon the posthumous publication of *The Double Tongue* in 1995, not only had its author been awarded D. Litts from the

Universities of Sussex, Kent, Warwick, Oxford, and the Sorbonne, an LL.D from the University of Bristol, fellowship in the Royal Society of Literature, the Booker Prize, a CBE, a knighthood[2] but also – 'garlanded in accolades' during his lifetime – laurel of all laurels, the Nobel Prize for literature.[3]

Fictional narrative, like crypton, can be coerced into combustion only when its willing reader participates in the production of what may become an entirely new substance. I borrow this conceit in order to suggest what I take to have been a characteristic of William Golding's fiction: the intention to make the contemporary reader in the West encounter, by the imaginative impact of words, those experiences that words conventionally no longer reached, formulated, or communicated – the primacy of the mysterious, the magical, the terrible, the dangerous, the awesome. To Golding, the contemporary world appeared ill at ease with the ambiguous, the obscurely meaningful, the tentative, the unexorcized – all that threatened the assumptions of the materialist, who builds a world view on collected fact. The individual had to be positioned, somehow, to feel on his or her pulse not as a supposition but an imaginative experience the unseen world: that Egyptian amulet which is 'at once alive and dead', which suggests 'mysteries with no solution', which mixes 'the strange, the gruesome and the beautiful'.[4]

My discussion in the Introduction has made clear the reasons why I view *The Pyramid* as a mid-point novel pointing backward to the earlier fictions and forward to those of the later period. I share the view with other commentators that the body of Golding's work can now be decisively seen in two phases. The second was to begin with *Darkness Visible*, his – for me, incandescent – realization of an intention, first expressed twelve years earlier, to write a novel about England: 'not about Britain, about England', as he then remarked to me. Looking back now from *The Double Tongue*, *Fire Down Below*, *Close Quarters*, *The Paper Men*, *Rites of Passage*, and *Darkness Visible* to *Lord of the Flies*, another book about England, we can see that the latter's stark, fierce, implacable, even luminous denunciation was in a profound sense untrue. For Golding too, the darkness of man's heart came to be modulated into a central opacity, good as well as not-good. 'So everything ended happily and all changes were for the best…though the mountain's eruption overwhelmed the spa that had grown up round the Hot Springs, by that time there were plenty of people in other places, so it was a small matter', as 'Clonk Clonk' so genially and so wisely concludes.

Endnotes

1   W. L. Webb, 'Lord of the Novel', *The Guardian* (June 21, 1993), p. 8.

2   When Golding was awarded the Nobel Prize in 1983, Downing Street (Margaret Thatcher's administration not excelling in literary sophistication) rang around to enquire from the arts world who he was. '"Author of *Lord of the Flies, Pincher Martin, The Spire*," the reply began. To be interrupted by "No, no, that's not what we meant, what we meant was is he *divorced* or anything, or can we send him a congratulatory telegram?"' (Margaret Drabble, *Angus Wilson, A Biography*, New York, St Martins Press, 1995, p. 543).

3   That the 1983 award was attended by controversy should not go unnoticed. When the Novel Committee's decision was announced, the Swedish Academician and novelist Artur Lundkvist made an unprecedented attack on the allegedly biased selection procedure of the Academy, calling Golding 'a little English phenomenon of no special interest'. His own candidate was Claude Simon. (E. C. Bufkin, The Nobel Prize and the Paper Men: The Fixing of William Golding', *Georgia Review*, Spring 1995, p. 57).

4   Golding, 'Egypt from My Inside', p. 54.

Epilogue

What fever is it in our monstrous blood
That brings a crazed serenity of love?
What absurd germ found entry where it could
And fed and bred and multiplied and throve
Till you whose years are shorter than this beard
Fewer in number than these broken teeth
Could share the instant brilliance of the bird
Then rage against my necessary death?
We'll call it living in a world of wars
A world of pointless ambiguity
Of angel-apes, of shit and quasistars
Of bad good luck that flashed your face on me.
Come lovely then with young Medusa's hair
Sweet monster, come – who are already here.

William Golding

Bibliography

Admiralty, *Regulations and Instructions Relating to His Majesty's Service at Sea*, 1808.

Anon., Obituary, *The Times*, London, (June 21, 1993), p. 17.

_____, 'Water and Fire', *Economist* (April 1, 1989), p. 82.

Aaseth, Inger, 'Golding's Journey to Hell: An Examination of Prefigurations and Archetypal Pattern in *Free Fall*', *English Studies* 56 (1975), pp. 3–15.

Adams, Robert M., 'Close Quarters', *New York Times Book Review* (May 31, 1987), p. 44.

Adriaens, Mark, 'Style in W. Golding's *The Inheritors*', *English Studies* 51 (1970), pp. 16–30.

Alter, Robert, *Partial Magic: The Novel as Self Conscious Genre*, Berkeley, University of California Press, 1975.

Ashton, Rosemary, 'Becalmed', *Listener* (June 11, 1987), p. 25.

Axthelm, Peter, *The Modern Confessional Novel*, New Haven, Yale University Press, 1967.

Babb, Howard S., *The Novels of William Golding*, Columbus, Ohio State University Press, 1970.

Bair, Deidre, 'At Sea in Volume Three', *New York Times Book Review* (April 12, 1989), p. 37.

Baker, James R., 'An Interview with William Golding', *Twentieth Century Literature* 28 (1982), pp. 130–70.

_____, (ed.) *Critical Essays on William Golding,* Boston, G.K. Hall, 1988.

_____, 'Golding and Huxley: The Fables of Demonic Possession', *Twentieth Century Literature* 46 (2000), pp. 311–27.

_____, *William Golding: A Critical Study*, New York, St Martin's Press, 1965.

Bakhtin, Mikhail, *The Dialogic Imagination: Four Essays*, Michael Holquist (ed.), Caryl Emerson and Michael Holquist (trans), Austin, University of Texas Press, 1981.

_____, *Rabelais and His World,* Helene Iswolsky (trans). Bloomington, Indiana University Press, 1984.

_____, *Readings in Russian Poetics: Formalist and Structuralist Views*, Ladislav Matejka and Krystyna Pomorska (eds), Cambridge, MIT Press, 1979.

Bayley, John, 'Light and Darkness Visible', *Times Literary Supplement* (September 16, 1994), pp. 13–4.

_____, 'Log of a Master Seaman', *Observer* (June 7, 1987), p. 25.

_____, 'Seadogs and Englishman', *Guardian Weekly* (April 2, 1989), p. 29.

Bergonzi, Bernard & John Whitley, *The English Novel: Questions in Literature,* London, Sussex Books, 1976.

--, Rose Marie, '*Fire Down Below*', *America* (May 6, 1989), pp. 434–5.

Biles, Jack, *Talk: Conversations with William Golding*, New York, Harcourt, Brace & Jovanovich, 1970.

_____ and Robert O. Evans (eds.), *William Golding: Some Critical Considerations*, Kentucky, The University Press of Kentucky, 1975.

Black, Elizabeth, 'Metaphor and Cognition in *The Inheritors*', *Language and Literature* 2 (1993), pp. 37–48.

Blake, Ian '*Pincher Martin*: William Golding and Taffrail', *Notes and Queries* (August 1962), 309–10.

Bloom, Harold, *William Golding's Lord of the Flies Bloom's Notes*, Broomall PA, Chelsea House Publishers, 1996.

Blythe, Ronald, 'Lord of the Tides', *Guardian Weekly* (July 5, 1987), p. 22.

Bodenheimer, Rosemarie, *The Politics of Story in Victorian English Fiction*, Ithaca, Cornell University Press, 1988.

Boyd, S. H., *The Novels of William Golding*, New York, St Martin's Press, 1988.

Broich, Ulrich, 'William Golding and the Religious Function of Literature', *Functions of Literature: Essays Presented to Erwin Wolff on his Sixtieth Birthday*, Ulrich Broich, Theo Stemmler and Gerd Stratmann (eds.), Tubingen, Niemeyer, 1984, pp. 305–26.

Brooks, Peter, *Reading for the Plot, Design and Intention in Narrative*, New York, Alfred A. Knopf, 1984.

Brown, Steven, 'Political Literature and the Response of the Reader', *American Political Science Review* 72 (1977), pp. 567–84.

Bufkin, E. C., 'The Nobel Prize and the Paper Men: The Fixing of William Golding', *Georgia Review* 39 (1985), pp. 55–65.

————, '*The Spire*: The Image of the Book', *William Golding: Some Critical Considerations*, Jack I. Biles and Robert O. Evans (eds.), Lexington, University of Kentucky Press, 1975, pp. 136–50.

Burroway, Janet, 'Resurrected Metaphor in *The Inheritors*', *Critical Quarterly* 23 (1981), pp. 53–70.

Byatt, A.S., '*The Pyramid*', *New Statesman* (June 2, 1967), p. 761.

————, 'William Golding: *Darkness Visible*', *Passions of the Mind*, New York, Turtle Bay Books/Random House, 1992, pp. 169–73.

Cammarota, Richard S., '*The Spire*: A Symbolic Analysis', *William Golding: Some Critical Consideration*, Jack I. Biles and Robert O. Evans (eds.), Lexington, University of Kentucky Press, 1975, pp. 151–75.

Campbell, Arthur, 'William Golding's *Pincher Martin*', *From the Fifties*, Michael Bakewell and Eric Evans (eds), London, British Broadcasting Corporation, 1961, pp. 30–5.

Capey, A.C., 'Questioning the Literary Merit of *Lord of the Flies*', *Readings on Lord of the Flies*, Claire Swisher (ed.), San Diego, CA, Greenhaven Press, 1997, pp. 140–46.

Carey, John, 'Lost (and Found) at Sea', *The World and I* 4 (March 1989), pp. 366–72.

_____, 'William Golding talks to John Carey', *William Golding The Man and his Books: A Tribute on his 75th Birthday*, John Carey (ed.), New York, Farrar, Straus & Giroux, 1986, pp. 171–89.

Carver, Judith, 'Editor's Preface', *Areté* (Spring Summer 2000), pp. 23–24

Cazamian, Louis, *The Social Novel in England 1830–1850*, Martin Fido (trans), London, Routledge and Kegan Paul, 1973.

Chance, M.R.A., 'The Nature and Special Features of the Instinctive Bond of Primates', *The Social Life of Early Man*, S.L. Washburn (ed.), Chicago, University of Chicago Press, 1961, pp. 29–32.

Chapman, Seymour, *Story and Discourse: Narrative Structure in Fiction and Film*, Ithaca and London, Cornell University Press, 1978.

Cleve, Gunnel, 'Some Elements of Mysticism in William Golding's Novel *Darkness Visible*', *Neuphilologische Mitteilungen* 83 (1982), pp. 457–70.

Clews, Hetty, '*Darkness Visible*: William Golding's *Parousia*', *English Studies in Canada* 10 (1984), p. 317–29.

Coates, John, 'Religious Quest in *Darkness Visible*' *Renascence: Essays on Value in Literature* 39 (1986), pp. 272–91.

Colley, Linda, *Britons: Forging the Nation 1707–1837*, New Haven and London, Yale University Press, 1992.

Connor, Steven, 'Rewriting Wrong: On the Ethics of Literary Reversion', *Liminal Postmodernisms: The Post Modern, the (Post) Colonial, and the Post Feminist*, Theo D'haen and Hans Bertens (eds.), Amsterdam–Atlanta, GA, Rodopi B.V., 1994, pp. 79–97.

Cox, C.B., '*Lord of the Flies*', *Critical Quarterly* 2 (1960), pp. 112–7.

Crompton, Donald W., *A View From the Spire: William Golding's Later Novels,* Edited and completed by Julia Briggs, Oxford, Blackwell, 1985.

_____, '*The Spire*', *Critical Quarterly* 9 (1967), pp. 63–79.

D'Amelio, Nadia. 'Golding's Trilogy as a *Bildungsroman*', *Fingering Netsukes*, Frédéric Regard and Norman Page (eds), Saint-Etienne, Publications de Université de Saint Etienne in association with Faber and Faber, 1995, pp. 183–93.

_____, 'No Inheritors in *The Paper Men*', *William Golding: The Sound of Silence,* Jeanne Delbaere (ed.), Liège, English Department University of Liège, 1991, pp. 152–65.

Davis, Douglas M., 'A Conversation with William Golding', *New Republic* (May 4, 1963), pp. 28–30.

Delbaere-Garant, Jeanne. 'The Artist as Clown of God: Golding's *The Paper Men*' *William Golding: The Sound of Silence,* Jeanne Delbaere (ed.), Liège, English Department University of Liège, 1991, pp. 166–75.

_____, 'Describing the Indescribable: The "Things of God" in Golding's Fiction', *Sense and Transcendence: Essays in Honour of Herman Servotte*, Ortwin De Graef *et al.*(eds), Leuven, Leuven, University Press, 1995, pp. 129–40.

_____, 'The Evil Plant in William Golding's *The Spire*', *Revue des Langes Vivantes* 35 (1969), pp. 623–31.

_____, 'Lok – Like – Log: Structure and Imagery in *The Inheritors*',

William Golding: The Sound of Silence, Jeanne Delbaere (ed.), Liège, English Department University of Liège, 1991, pp. 61–73.

_____, 'Time as Structural Device in *Free Fall*', *William Golding: The Sound of Silence*, Jeanne Delbaere (ed.), Liège, English Department University of Liège, 1991, pp. 92–106.

Derrida, Jacques, *The Truth in Painting*, Geoffrey Bennington and Ian McLeod (trans), Chicago, University of Chicago Press, 1978.

Dick, Bernard F., *William Golding* (revised edition), Boston, Twayne Publishers, 1987.

Dickson, L.L., *The Modern Allegories of William Golding*, Gainesville, University of South Florida Press, 1990.

Dodds, E. R., *Euripides: Bacchae*, Oxford, Oxford University Press, 1960.

_____, 'Telepathy and Clairvoyance in Classical Antiquity', *Greek Poetry and Life*, Cyril Bailey *et al.* (eds), Oxford, Clarendon Press, 1936, pp. 364–85.

Drabble, Margaret, *Angus Wilson, A Biography*, New York, St Martins Press, 1995.

Eagleton, Terry, *Literary Theory: An Introduction*, Minneapolis, University of Minnesota Press, 1983.

Eilersen, Gillian Stead, 'A Password for the Darkness: Systems, Coincidences and Visions in William Golding's *Darkness Visible*', *Critique: Studies in Modern Fiction* 28 (1987), pp. 107–18.

Epstein, E.L., 'Notes on *Lord of the Flies*', *Lord of the Flies*, New York, Capricorn Books, 1959, pp. 188–92.

Falconer, William, *A Universal Dictionary of the Marine or, a copious explanation of the technical terms and phrases, employed in the construction, equipment, furniture, machinery, movements and military operations of a ship*, 1769; reprinted, New York, Augustus M. Kelley, 1970.

Farnell, Lewis Richard, *The Cults of the Greek States* vol. 4, Oxford, Clarendon Press, 1907.

Faulks, Sebastian, 'In Pursuit of a Subject', *Books and Bookmen* (February 1984), p. 21.

Figes, Eva, 'All that Glitters', *New Statesman* (February 10, 1984), p. 23.

Fontenrose, Joseph, *The Delphic Oracle: Its Responses and Operations*, Berkeley, University of California Press, 1978.

Forster, E. M., 'Introduction', *Lord of the Flies*, New York, Coward McCann, 1962, pp. ix–xii.

Fowler, R., *Linguistic Criticism*, Oxford, Oxford University Press, 1986.

_____, *Literature as Social Discourse*, London, Batsford, 1981.

Fowles, John, 'Golding and "Golding"', *William Golding The Man and his Books: A Tribute on his 75th Birthday*, John Carey (ed.), New York, Farrar, Straus & Giroux, 1986, pp. 146–56.

François, Pierre, 'The Rule of Oa in *The Inheritors*', William Golding: The Sound of Silence, Jeanne Delbaere (ed.), Liège, English Department of the University of Liège, 1991, pp. 74–83.

Frazer, James, *The Golden Bough*, abridged edition, 1922, reprinted New York, Macmillan, 1960.

Friedman, Lawrence S., *William Golding*, New York, Continuum, 1993.

Gallagher, Catherine, *The Industrial Reformation of English Fiction 1832–1867*, Chicago, University of Chicago Press, 1985.

Gekoski, R.A. & P.A. Grogan, *William Golding: A Bibliography 1934–1993*, London, André Deutsch, 1994.

Gilbert, W. Stephen, *The Life and Work of Dennis Potter*, Woodstock & New York, The Overlook Press, 1998.

Gindin, James, 'Gimmick and Metaphor in the Novels of William Golding' *Modern Fiction Studies* 6 (1960), pp. 145–52.

_____, 'The Historical Imagination in Willaim Golding's Later Fiction', *The British and Irish Novel Since 1960*, James Acheson (ed.) New York, St Martin's Press, 1991, pp. 109–25.

_____, *William Golding*, New York, St Martin's Press, 1988.

Glascock, William Nugent, *Naval Sketch Book; or the service afloat and ashore: with characteristic reminiscences, fragments, and opinions*, third edition, 1826, reprinted London, Whittaker & Co., 1843.

Glazebrook, Philip, 'Sicklied o'er with the pale cast of thought', *Spectator* (March 25, 1989), pp. 34–35.

Glendinning, Victoria, '*Fire Down Below*', *The Times* (March 23, 1989), p. 21.

Goff, Martyn, 'Introduction', *Prize Writing: An Original Collection of Writings by Past Winners to Celebrate 21 Years of the Booker Prize*, London, Hodder & Stoughton, 1989, pp. 1–15.

Golding, William, 'A Moving Target', *A Moving Target*, New York, Farrar, Straus & Giroux, 1982, pp. 154–70.

_____, *A Moving Target*, New York, Farrar, Straus & Giroux, 1982.

_____, 'Advice to a Nervous Visitor', *Holiday* (July 1963), pp. 42–43, 93–97, 125–26.

_____, 'An Affection for Cathedrals', *Holiday* (December 1965), pp. 35–9.

_____, *An Egyptian Journal*, London, Faber and Faber, 1985.

_____, 'All or Nothing', *Spectator* (March 24, 1961), p. 410.

_____, 'All that Unmitigated Wet', *Guardian* (April 26, 1992), p. 27.

_____, 'Belief and Creativity', *A Moving Target*, New York, Farrar, Straus & Giroux, 1982, pp. 185–202.

_____, 'Before the Beginning', *Spectator* (May 26, 1961), p. 768

_____, 'Billy the Kid', *The Hot Gates*, London, Faber and Faber, 1965, pp. 159–65.

_____, 'Bookmark', British Broadcasting Corporation (January 12, 1984), unpublished talk.

_____, *The Brass Butterfly*, London, Faber and Faber, 1958.

_____, 'Caveat Emptor', *Prize Writing*, London, Hodder & Stoughton, 1989, pp. 149–61.

_____, 'Clonk Clonk', *The Scorpion God*, London, Faber and Faber, 1971, pp. 68–115.

_____, *Close Quarters*, New York, Farrar, Straus & Giroux, 1987.

_____, 'Crabbed Youth and Age', *A Moving Target*, New York, Farrar, Straus & Giroux, 1982, pp. 99–103.

_____, *Darkness Visible*, New York, Farrar, Straus & Giroux, 1979.

_____, 'Delphi: The Oracle Revealed', *A Moving Target*, New York, Farrar, Straus & Giroux, 1982, pp. 36–43.

_____, 'Digging for Pictures', *The Hot Gates,* London, Faber and Faber, 1965, pp. 61–70.

_____, *The Double Tongue*, London, Faber and Faber, 1995.

_____, 'Egypt from My Inside', *The Hot Gates*, London, Faber and Faber, 1965, pp. 44–55.

_____, 'Egypt from My Outside', *A Moving Target*, New York, Farrar, Straus & Giroux, 1982, pp. 56–83.

_____, 'Envoy Extraordinary', *The Scorpion God* London, Faber and Faber. 1971, pp. 1–67.

_____,'Fable', *The Hot Gates,* London, Faber and Faber, 1965, pp. 85–101.

_____, *Fire Down Below,* New York, Farrar, Straus & Giroux, 1989.

_____, 'Foreword', *To The Ends of The Earth: A Sea Trilogy*, London, Faber and Faber, 1991, pp. vii–xii.

_____, 'Foreword', *William Golding A Bibliography 1934–1993*, R.A Geboski and P.A. Grogan (eds.), London, André Deutsch, 1994, pp. xi–xiii.

_____, *Free Fall*, London, Faber and Faber, 1959.

_____,'The Funeral Games that Lasted 300 Years', *Guardian* (January 17, 1991), p. 24.

_____, *The Hot Gates*, London, Faber and Faber, 1965.

_____, 'In My Ark', *The Hot Gates*, London, Faber and Faber, 1965, pp. 102–5.

_____, 'In Retreat', *Spectator* (March 25, 1960), pp. 448–9.

_____, *The Inheritors*, London, Faber and Faber, 1955.

_____, 'Into the Labyrinth', *Author! Author!*, Richard Findlater (ed.), London, Faber and Faber, 1984, pp. 283–89.

_____,'Irish Poets and their Poetry', *Holiday* (April 1963), pp. 10; 16–9.

_____.'The Ladder and the Tree', *The Hot Gates*, London, Faber and Faber, 1965, pp. 166–75.

_____, *Lord of the Flies*, London, Faber and Faber, 1954.

_____, 'Miss Pulkinhorn', *Encounter* XV (August 1960), pp. 27–32.

_____, *Miss Pulkinhorn*, British Broadcasting Corporation Third Programme (April 20, 1960), unpublished play.

_____, 'Nobel Lecture, 7 December 1983', Leamington Spa, R.S. Gekoski, The Sixth Chamber Press, 1984.

_____, 'Our Way of Life', British Broadcasting Corporation (December 15, 1956), unpublished essay.

_____, *The Paper Men*, New York, Farrar, Straus & Giroux, 1984.

_____, *Pincher Martin*, London, Faber and Faber, 1956.

_____, *Poems*, London, The Macmillan Co., 1934.

_____, *The Pyramid*, London, Faber and Faber, 1967.

_____, *Rites of Passage*, London, Faber and Faber, 1980.

_____, 'Rough Magic', *A Moving Target*, New York, Farrar, Straus & Giroux, 1982, pp. 125–46.

_____, 'Scenes from a Life', *Areté* 1 (Spring Summer 2000), pp. 23–38.

_____, *The Scorpion God*, London, Faber and Faber, 1972.

_____, *The Spire*, London, Faber and Faber, 1964.

_____, *To The Ends of the Earth: A Sea Trilogy*, London, Faber and Faber, 1991.

_____, 'Utopias and Antiutopias', *A Moving Target*, New York, Farrar, Straus & Giroux, 1982, pp. 170–77.

_____, 'Why Boys Become Vicious' *San Francisco Examiner* (February 28, 1993), pp. B–1;4.

Gordon, Mary, *Joan of Arc*, New York, Lipper/Viking, 2000.

Graves, Robert, *The Greek Myths*, revised edition reprint, Harmondsworth, Middlesex, Penguin, 1966.

Gray, Paul, 'Long Haul', *Time* (March 30, 1999), pp. 81–83.

Green, Peter, *Alexander to Actium: The Hellenistic Age*, London, Thames & Hudson, 1991.

————, 'Speaking in the Oracular', *Washington Post* (October 1, 1995), p. 5.

————, 'The World of William Golding' *Transactions and Proceedings of the Royal Society of Literature* (1963), pp. 37–57.

Gregor, Ian, '"He Wondered": The Religious Imagination of William Golding', *William Golding The Man and his Books: A Tribute on his 75th Birthday* John Carey (ed.), New York, Farrar, Straus & Giroux, 1987, pp. 84–100.

———— and Mark Kinkead-Weekes, 'The Later Golding', *Twentieth Century Literature* 28 (1982), pp.109–29.

————, *William Golding*, London, Faber and Faber, 1967.

————, *William Golding: A Critical Study*, London, Faber and Faber, 1984.

Grumbach, Doris, 'Parables of Darkness', *Books and Art* (December 21, 1979), p. 9.

Guillen, Claudio, *Literature as a System: Essays Towards A Theory of Literature*, Princeton, Princeton University Press, 1971.

Haffenden, John, 'William Golding', *Novelists in Interview*, London and New York, Methuen. 1985, pp. 97–120.

Halliday, M.A.K., 'Linguistic Function and Literary Style: An Inquiry into the Language of William Golding's *The Inheritors*', *Literary Style: A Symposium*, Seymour Chatman (ed.), London, Oxford University Press, 1977, pp. 330–68.

Hallissy, Margaret, '"No Innocent Work":Theology and Psychology in William Golding's *The Spire*' *Christianity and Literature* 47 (1997), pp. 37–56.

Hamilton, Alex, 'First Lord of the Novel', *Manchester Arts Guardian* (December 20, 1971), p. 8.

Hanscombe, Gillian, *William Golding: Lord of the Flies*, Middlesex, Penguin Passports, 1986.

Hardy, Barbara, 'Narrative Teasing', *Times Educational Supplement* (June 19, 1987), p. 23.

Hawlin, Stefan, 'The Savages in the Forest: Decolonizing William Golding' *Critical Survey* 7 (1995), pp. 125–35.

Herndl, George, 'Golding and Salinger, A Clear Choice', *Wiseman Review* (1964–1965), pp. 309–22.

Henry, Avril, '*The Pyramid*' *Southern Review* 3 (1968), pp. 5–31.

_____, 'The Structure of Golding's *Free Fall*', *Southern Review* 8 (1976), pp. 92–124.

Higdon, David, 'William Golding's *Free Fall*', *Time in English Fiction* London, Macmillan, 1977, pp. 51–6.

Hirst, Christopher, 'Rites of Passion', *Books* (June 1987), pp. 14–15.

Hodson, Leighton, *William Golding*, Edinburgh, Oliver and Boyd, 1969.

Hoover, David L., *Language and Style in* The Inheritors, New York, University Press of America, 1999.

Hough, Richard, 'Close Quarters' *Los Angeles Times Book Review* (June 7, 1987), pp. 3–6.

Hutcheon, Linda, *A Theory of Parody*, New York, Methuen, 1985.

Hynes, Samuel, *William Golding, Columbia Essays on Modern Writers* 2nd edition, New York, Columbia University Press, 1968.

Jameson, Frederic, *The Political Unconscious*, Ithaca, Cornell University Press, 1981.

Johnson, B.R., 'Golding's First Argument: Theme and Structure in *Free Fall*', *Critical Essays on William Golding*, James R. Baker (ed.), Boston, G. K. Hall, 1988, pp. 61–72.

_____, 'William Golding's *The Inheritors*: Dualism and Synthesis' *Southern Review* 19 (1986), pp. 173–83.

Johnston, Arnold, *Of Earth and Darkness: The Novels of William Golding*, Columbia & London, University of Missouri Press, 1980.

Jones, D.A.N., 'Shivering Timbers', *Listener* (March 23, 1989), p. 34.

Josipovici, Gabriel, *The World and the Book: A Study of Modern Fiction* Stanford, Stanford University Press, 1971.

Karl, Frederick, 'The Novel as Moral Allegory: The Fiction of William Golding', *A Reader's Guide to the Contemporary English Novel*, New York, Noonday Press, 1962, pp. 236–55.

Kelly, Rebecca, 'The Tragicomic Mode: William Golding's *The Pyramid*' *Perspectives on Contemporary Literature* 7 (1981), pp. 110–16.

Kemp, Peter, 'A Bonfire of Vanities' *The Sunday Times* (March 19, 1989), p. G1a.

Kermode, Frank, 'Adam's Image', *Spectator* (October 23, 1959), p. 564.

_____, 'The Case for William Golding', *New York Review of Books* (April 30, 1964), pp. 3–4.

_____, *Essays on Fiction: 1971–1982*, London, Routledge & Kegan Paul, 1983.

_____, 'The Meaning of It All', *Books and Bookmen* (August 1959), pp. 10–16.

_____, 'The Novels of William Golding', *International Library Annual*, III (1961), pp. 20–31.

_____, *Puzzles and Epiphanies*, London, Routledge & Kegan Paul, 1962.

_____, 'Superplot', *London Review of Books* (March 1,1984), p. 15.

_____, 'Taken Aback', *London Review of Books* (June 25, 1987), p. 9.

Kettle, Arnold, 'The Early Victorian Social Problem Novel', *From Dickens to Hardy*, Boris Ford (ed.), London, Pelican, 1958, pp. 167–87.

King, Francis, 'Still in Peril on the Sea', *Spectator* (June 3, 1987), pp. 40–1.

Knolan, Robert E., 'Golding's Sea Novel Sails into Dangerous Waters', *Chicago Tribune* (June 14, 1987), p. 6.

Kuehn, Robert E., 'Golding's Novel of the Sea Ends a Memorable Trilogy', *Chicago Tribune* (February 19, 1989), p. 5.

Lakshmi, Vijay, 'Entering the Whirlpool: The Movement towards Self-Awareness in William Golding's *Pincher Martin*', *The Literary Criterion* 17 (1982), pp. 25–36.

Lasdun, James, 'Bridges and Gods', *Encounter* (May 15, 1984), p. 65.

Leclaire, Jacques, 'William Golding: *The Pyramid* as a Study in Mediocrity', *De William Shakespeare à William Golding* Publications de L'Université de Rouen, 1984, pp. 143–54.

Lee, D., '*The Inheritors* and transformational generative grammar', *Language and Style* 9 (1976), pp. 77–92.

Leech G. and M. Short, *Style in Fiction: A Linguistic Introduction to English Fictional Prose*, London, Longmans, 1981.

Lefkowitz, Mary, 'A Dish for the Gods', *Times Literary Supplement* (June 23, 1995), p. 25.

Lerner, Laurence, 'Jocelin's folly; or, Down with the Spire', *Critical Quarterly* 24 (1982), pp. 3–15.

Lessing, Doris, 'Introduction', *The Golden Notebook*, New York, Simon and Schuster, 1962, pp. xi–xxiii.

Llewellyn, Woodward, *The Age of Reform: 1815–1870*, 2nd edition, Oxford, Oxford University Press, 1992.

Lodge, David, *After Bakhtin: Essays on Fiction and Criticism*, London, Routledge, 1990.

_____, *The Language of Fiction*, New York, Columbia University Press, 1966.

_____, 'Life Between Covers', *The New Republic* (August 16, 1984), pp. 32–5.

_____, *The Practice of Writing*, London and New York, Allen Lane, The Penguin Press, 1996.

_____, 'William Golding', *Spectator* (April 19, 1964), pp. 489–90.

Maufort, Marc, 'Golding's Stilbourne: Symbolic Space in *The Pyramid*', *William Golding: The Sound of Silence*, Jeanne Delbaere (ed.), Liège, English Department of the University of Liège, 1991, pp. 125–32.

May, Derwent, 'A Spate of Sneers', *Listener* (February 9, 1984), p. 23.

McCarron, Kevin, 'Alcoholism as metaphor in William Golding's *The Paper Men*', *Beyond the Pleasure Dome: Writing and Addiction from the Romantics*, Sue Vice *et al* (eds.), Sheffield, Sheffield Academic Press. 1994, pp. 275–82.

_____, *The Coincidence of Opposites: William Golding's Later Fiction*, Sheffield, Sheffield Academic Press, 1995.

_____, '"In Contemplation of my Deliverance": *Robinson Crusoe* and *Pincher Martin*', *Robinson Crusoe: Myths and Metamorphoses*, Lieve Spaas and Brian Stimpton (eds.), New York, MacMillan Press, 1996, pp. 285–93.

McConnell, Frank, 'William Golding's Sea-Fever', *Book World/ Washington Post* (March 12, 1989), pp. 3, 9.

McCullen, Maurice, '*Lord of the Flies*: The Critical Quest', *William Golding*: Some Critical Considerations, Jack Biles and Robert O. Evans (eds), Kentucky, The University Press of Kentucky, 1975, pp. 203–36.

McEwan, Ian, 'Schoolboys', *William Golding The Man and His Books: A Tribute on his 75th Birthday*, John Carey (ed.), New York, Farrar, Straus & Giroux, 1986, pp. 157–60.

McEwan, Neil, *Perspective in British Historical Fiction Today*, Wolfboro, New Hampshire, Longwood Academic Press, 1987.

_____, 'Golding's *Lord of the Flies*, Ballantyne's *Coral Island* and the Critics', *The Survival of the Novel: British Fiction in the Later Twentieth Century*, London, Macmillan Press, 1981, pp. 147–62.

McKeating, H., 'The Significance of William Golding', T*he Expository Times* 79 (1968), pp. 329–33.

Medcalf, Stephen, 'Bill and Mr Golding's Daimon', *William Golding The Man and his Books: A Tribute on his 75th Birthday*, John Carey (ed.), New York, Farrar, Straus & Giroux, 1987, pp. 30–44.

_____, 'Into the Southern Seas', *Times Literary Supplement* (March 17, 1989), pp. 267–68.

_____. 'William Golding', *Independent* (June 21, 1993), p. 14.

Melada, Ivan, *The Captain of Industry in English Fiction, 1821-1871*, Albuquerque, University of New Mexico Press, 1970.

Merivale, Patricia, '"One Endless Round": *Something Happened* and the Purgatorial Novel' *English Studies in Canada* 11 (1985), pp. 438–49.

Monteith, Charles, 'Strangers from Within', *William Golding The Man and his Books: A Tribute on his 75th Birthday*, John Carey (ed.), New York, Farrar, Straus & Giroux, 1986, pp. 57–63.

Morrison, Blake, 'In Death as in the Life' *Times Literary Supplement* (March 2, 1984), p. 215.

Moss, Peter, 'Alec Albert Golding, 1876–1957', *William Golding The Man and His Books: A Tribute on his 75th Birthday*, John Carey (ed.), New York, Farrar, Straus & Giroux, 1986, pp. 15–26.

Nelson, Marie, 'Two Narrative Modes, Two Modes of Perception: The Use of the Instrumental in Golding's *The Inheritors*' *Neophilologus* 70 (1986), pp. 307–15.

Niemeyer, Carl, '*The Coral Island* Revisited', *College English* (1961), pp. 241–45.

Nokes, David, 'Metaphysical Voyagers', *Times Literary Supplement* (June 19, 1987), p. 653.

Oates, Joyce Carol, '*Darkness Visible*', *The New Republic* (December 8, 1979), pp. 32–34.

O'Brien, Patrick, '*Fire Down Below*', *London Review of Books* (April 20, 1989), p. 11.

Oldsey, Bernard S. and Stanley Weintraub, *The Art of William Golding*, New York, Harcourt, Brace and World, 1965.

Owens, Brad, 'Golding's New Morality Tale: Hard to Believe', *Christian Science Monitor* (November 28, 1979), p. 24.

Parke, H. W. and Wormell, D.E.W, *The Delphic Oracle: The History*, Oxford, Blackwell Press, 1956.

Partridge, Eric, *A Dictionary of Slang and Unconventional English* 5th edition, 1931, reprinted Routledge & Kegan Paul, 1970.

Pemberton, Clive, *William Golding*, London, Longmans Green & Co., 1969.

Peter, John, 'The Fables of William Golding', *Kenyon Review* 19 (1957), pp. 577–92.

_____, 'The Fables of William Golding: Postcript', *William Golding's Lord of the Flies: A Source Book*, William Nelson (ed.), New York, Odyssey, 1963, pp. 21–34.

Pocock, Tom, *Horatio Nelson*, New York, Alfred A. Knopf, 1988.

Poster, Jem, 'Beyond Definition: William Golding's Sea Trilogy', *Critical Survey* 5 (1993), pp. 92–96.

Prince, Gerald, 'Notes Toward a Categorization of Fictional Narratees' *Genre* (March 1971), pp. 100–6.

_____, 'On Readers and Listeners in Narrative', *Neophilgus* 55 (1971), pp.117–22.

Prickett, Stephen, 'Inheriting Paper: Words and William Golding', *Journal of Literature & Theology* 6 (1992), pp. 145–52.

Pringle, David, *Modern Fantasy: The Hundred Best Novels*, New York, Bedrick, 1989.

Pritchett, V. S., *The Living Novel and Later Approaches*, New York, Vintage Books, 1967.

Quinn-Lang, Caitlin, 'Jets, Ships and Atom Bombs in Golding's *Lord of the Flies*', *Images of Technology in Literature, the Media and Society*, Will Wright and Steven Kaplan (eds), Pueblo, Colorado, University of Southern Colorado Society for Interdisciplinary Study of Social Imagination, 1994, pp. 78–83.

Raban, Jonathan, 'Journey to the End of the Night', *New York Review of Books* (June 6, 1999), p. 15.

Rahman, Khandkar Rezaur, *The Moral Vision of William Golding*, Dhaka, University of Dhaka Press, 1990.

Redpath, Philip, *William Golding: A Structural Reading of his Fiction*, London, Vision Press Limited, 1986.

Regard, Frédéric, 'The Obscenity of Writing a Reappraisal of Golding's First Novel', *Fingering Netsukes*, Frédéric Regard and Norman Page, Publications de l'Université de Saint-Etienne in association with Faber and Faber, 1995, pp. 31–47.

Reilly, Patrick, *Lord of the Flies: Fathers and Sons*, New York, Twayne Publishers, 1992.

Roberts, Michèle, 'Young Mariner', *New Statesman* (June 12, 1987), pp. 27–28.

Rosso, Henry David, 'Interview with William Golding', *Ann Arbor News* (December 1985), p. 5.

Russell, Kenneth, 'The *Free Fall* of William Golding's *Pincher Martin*', *Studies in Religion, Sciences Religieuses* 5 (1975/6), pp. 267–74.

_____, 'The Vestibule of Hell', *Revue de l'Université D'Ottawa* 46 (1976), pp. 452–59.

Schreurs, Willy, 'Darkness Visible: The Choice between Good and Evil', *William Golding: The Sound of Silence*, Jeanne Delbaere (ed.), Liège, English Department University of Liège, 1991, pp. 133–45.

Simon, Irene, 'Vision or Dream? The Supernatural Design in William Golding's *The Paper Men*', *William Golding: The Sound of Silence*, Jeanne Delbaere (ed.), Liège, English Department University of Liège, 1991, pp. 176–185.

Simpson, Michael, *Gods and Heroes of the Greeks: The Library of Apollodorus*, Amherst, University of Massachusetts Press, 1976.

Sinfield, Alan, *Literature, Politics and Culture in Postwar Britain*, Oxford, Blackwell, 1989.

Skilton, David, 'Golding's *The Spire*' *Studies in the Literary Imagination* 2 (1969), pp. 45–65.

Smith, David R., 'Rite of Passage on a Square-Rigger' *Los Angeles Times Book Review* (March 19, 1989), p. 13.

Southall, Raymond, 'Reviews and Reestiminations: *Lord of the Flies*', *Marxism Today* 18 (1974), pp. 51–54.

Spencer, Duncan, 'Boredom and Sogginess Plague Voyage Far Too Long in the Making', *Washington Times* (March 6, 1989), p. 8.

Spring, Brian, *Lord of the Flies: Helicon Study Guide*, Dublin, Helicon, 1976.

Spufford, Francis, *I May be Some Time: Ice and the English Imagination*, New York, Picador, 1997.

Stape, J. H., ' "Fiction in the Wild Modern Manner": Metanarrative Gesture in William Golding's *To the End of the Earth* Trilogy' *Twentieth Century Literature* 38 (1992), pp. 226–239.

Steiner, George, *Language and Silence*, New York, Atheneum, 1967, pp. 288–94.

Stephenson, William, 'William Golding's *To The Ends of the Earth, A Sea Trilogy* and Queer Autobiography' *a/b:; Auto/Biography Studies* (Summer 2000)

Stewart, Ian, 'Ripping Fiction', *Illustrated London News* (September 1987), p. 88.

Strawson, Galen, 'All Hands on Deck', *Observer* (March 19, 1989), p. 48.

Strouse, Jean, 'All at Sea', *Newsweek* (October 27, 1980), p. 104.

Stuewe, Paul, '*Fire Down Below*', *Quill & Quire* 55 (July 1989), p. 47.

Stummer, Peter O., 'Man's Beastliness to Man: The Novels of William Golding', *Essays on the Contemporary British Novel*, Hedwig Bock and Albert Wertheim (eds), Munich, Hueber, 1986, pp. 79–100.

Subbarao, V. V., *William Golding: A Study*, New York, Envoy Press, 1987.

Sullivan, Walter, 'The Fables and the Art', *Sewanee Review* (1963), pp. 660–64.

———, 'The Long Chronicle of Guilt: William Golding's *The Spire*' *Hollins Critic* 1 (1964), pp. 1–12.

Surette, Leon, 'A Matter of Belief: *Pincher Martin*'s Afterlife' *Twentieth Century Literature* 40 (1994), pp. 205–25.

Swanson, Roy Arthur, 'Versions of Double Think in *Gravity's Rainbow, Darkness Visible, Riddley Walker* and *Travels to the Enu*' *World Literature Today* 58 (1984), pp. 203–8.

Swisher, Claire, *Readings on* Lord of the Flies, San Diego, CA, Greenhaven Press, 1997.

Tanzman, Lea, 'Poe's "A Tale of Ragged Mountains" as a Source for Golding's Post Mortem Consciousness Technique in *Pincher Martin*', *Notes on Contemporary Literature* 25 (1995), pp. 6–7.

Tebbutt, Glorie, 'Reading and Righting: Metafiction and Metaphysics in William Golding's *Darkness Visible*', *Twentieth Century Literature* 39 (1993), pp. 47–58.

Thomas, Sue, 'Some Religious Icons and Biblical Allusions in William Golding's *The Spire*', *Journal of the Australasian Universities Mode* 64 (1985), pp. 190–7.

Tiger, Virginia, '*Darkness Visible*: Naming, Numbering and Narrative Strategies', *Style* 24 (1990), pp. 284–301.

———, *William Golding: The Dark Fields of Discovery,* London, Calder & Boyars, 1974.

———, 'William Golding's Wooden World: Religious Rites in *Rites of Passage*' Reprint *Critical Essays on William Golding* James R. Baker (ed.), Boston, G.K. Hall, 1988, pp. 135–49.

Tillotson, Kathleen, *Novels of the Eighteen-Forties*, London, Oxford University Press, London, 1954.

Timmons, Daniel, 'Sub–Creation in William Golding's *The Inheritors*', *English Studies in Canada* 22 (1996), pp. 399–412.

Towers, Robert, 'The Good Ship *Britannia*', *New York Review of Books* (December 18, 1980), pp. 4, 6, 8.

Vellacott, Philip, *Ironic Drama: A Study of Euripides' Methods and Meaning*, Cambridge, Cambridge University Press, 1975.

Vichy, Thérèse, 'Tragic Experience and Poetic Innocence in *Darkness Visible*', *Fingering Netsukes*, Frédéric Regard and Norman Page (eds), Saint-Etienne, Publications de l'Université de Saint-Etienne in association with Faber and Faber, 1995, pp. 129–36.

Walters, Margaret, 'Two Fabulists: Golding and Camus', *Melbourne Critical Review* 4 (1961), pp. 18–29.

Waugh, Auberon, 'Wrap Up *The Paper Men* and Freeze It', *Daily Mail* (February 9, 1984), p. 7.

Waugh, Patricia, *Metafiction*, London, Methuen, 1984.

Webb, W L., 'Interview with William Golding', *Guardian* (October 11, 1980) p. 12.

_____, 'Lord of the Novel', *Guardian* (June 21, 1993), p. 8.

_____, 'Sea Pictures', *New Statesman and Society* (April 14, 1989), p. 34.

Webster, Owen, 'Living with Chaos', *Books and Art* (March 1958), pp. 15–16.

Whitehead, Lee M., 'The Moment Out of Time: Golding's *Pincher Martin*', *Critical Essays on William Golding*, J.R. Baker (ed.), Boston, G.K. Hall, 1988, pp. 41–60.

Whitley, John S., '"*Furor Scribendi*" Writing about Writing in the Later Novels of William Golding', *Critical Essays on William Golding*, James R. Baker (ed.), Boston, G.K. Hall, 1988, pp. 176–93.

_____, *Golding: Lord of the Flies*, London, Edward Arnold, 1970.

Wikborg, Eleanor, 'The Control of Sympathy in William Golding's *Pincher Martin*', *Studies in English, Philology, Linguistics and Literature Presented to Alarik Rynell*, Mats Ryden and Lennart A. Bjork (eds), 7 (1978), pp. 179–87.

Williams, Nigel, 'Programme Commentary', *Pilot Theatre Company Production of* Lord of the Flies, Lyric Theatre, Hammersmith, London (July 1998), p. 4.

Williams, Raymond, *Culture and Society 1780–1950*, New York, 1958.

Wilson, Raymond, *MacMillan Master Guides:* Lord of the Flies *by William Golding*, London, MacMillan, 1986.

Wohrer, Franz, '"Face to face with the indescribable, the inexplicable, the isness": Intimate Relationships with the Divine in *The Paper Men*', *Fingering Netsukes*, Frédéric Regard and Norman Page (eds), Saint-Etienne, Publications de L'Université de Saint-Etienne in association with Faber and Faber, 1995, pp. 151–82.

Woodward, Kathleen, 'On Aggression: William Golding's *Lord of the Flies*', *No Place Else: Explorations in Utopian and Dystopian Fiction*, Martin H. Greenberg and Joseph D. Olander (eds), Southern Illinois University Press, 1983, pp. 199–224.

Index